William Claiborne:
Jeffersonian Centurion in the American Southwest

William C. C. Claiborne

WILLIAM CLAIBORNE:
JEFFERSONIAN CENTURION IN THE AMERICAN SOUTHWEST

JOSEPH T. HATFIELD

University of Louisiana at Lafayette Press

Library of Congress Catalog Number: 76-19654
ISBN Number: 978-1-935754-61-9
Copyright 1976

University of Louisiana at Lafayette Press
P.O. Box 40831
Lafayette, LA 70504-0831
http://ulpress.org

*To Ruby and the Hatfield Three--
Steven Randolph, Pamela Kay, and Myra Jo*

CONTENTS

Preface   xiii

Chapter I
Road to Preferment   1

Chapter II
Republican Congressman   19

Chapter III
Mississippi:
Politics, Indians, and Frontier Justice   41

Chapter IV
Mississippi:
Problems on Both Sides of the River   67

Chapter V
Louisiana:
Acquisition, Appointment,
and an American Introduction   96

Chapter VI
Orleans Territory:
The Dynamics of Politics   136

Chapter VII
Orleans Territory:
Militiamen, Indians, and Slaves   163

Chapter VIII
Orleans Territory:
The Routine of Administration   189

Chapter IX
The Sabine Frontier
and The Burr Conspiracy   211

Chapter X
The West Florida Controversy
and Statehood   237

Chapter XI
Louisiana:
Politics, Redmen, and The Baratarians   259

Chapter XII
Louisiana:
The War of *1812* and Its Aftermath   277

Chapter XIII
Louisiana:
Anticlimax and Epilogue   309

Notes   327

Bibliographical Essay   374

Index   381

ILLUSTRATIONS

The Lower Mississippi Valley	inside front cover
William C.C. Claiborne	frontispiece
Old American Southwest	facing p. 42
Mississippi Territory	facing p. 43
Louisiana Purchase Transfer Ceremonies	facing p. 96
Juan Morales	facing p. 97
Julien Poydras	facing p. 136
Jean-Noel Destrehan	facing p. 137
Sabine Frontier	facing p. 212
Aaron Burr	facing p. 213
West Florida	facing p. 238
General James Wilkinson	facing p. 239
Battle of New Orleans	facing p. 278
General Andrew Jackson	facing p. 279

William Claiborne:
Jeffersonian Centurion in the American Southwest

PREFACE

Born in colonial Virginia during the opening skirmishes of the American Revolutionary War, William C. C. Claiborne (1775-1817) devoted well over half of his life to public service. He served as a congressional enrolling clerk, lawyer in frontier Tennessee, state supreme court justice, member of the national House of Representatives, governor of the Mississippi and Orleans territories, and as Louisiana's first elective governor. Ineligible to serve a second gubernatorial term, Claiborne was elected to the United States Senate in early 1817, but he died before taking the oath of office.

The career of William Claiborne is more than a mere chronicle of a regional leader. It is a study of emerging federalism and evolving governmental relationships. It focuses on the ascendency of Jeffersonian republicanism and the dynamic development of the nation. It follows the westward trek of ambitious men who conquered and transformed the primitive and often explosive "Old Southwest." It is a narrative of western settlement and refinement, the acquisition of the vast and undefined Louisiana Territory, Spanish-American boundary tensions, the Burr conspiracy, the West Florida controversy, the struggle for statehood, and the War of 1812. It is throughout a narrative of the personal rivalries of assertive frontier leaders. Finally, it is the story of conflict and recrimination between bumptious American newcomers and refined "old world" society in Gallic New Orleans and the gradual cohesion of these disparate cultures under the patient leadership of Governor Claiborne.

The Claiborne study originated as a doctoral dissertation at Emory University, but further research resulted in major revisions and refinements. The author received research, editorial, and advisory assistance from many institutional staffs and individuals, for which he feels a deep sense of gratitude. These include the directors and staffs of the Emory University Library, Louisiana State University Library, Tulane University Library, Central Missouri State University Library, Library of Congress, National Archives, Tennessee State Library and Archives, Mississippi Department of Archives and History, Louisiana State Museum and Library, New Orleans Municipal Library and Archives, and the Kemper Foundation's Historic New Orleans Collection. Of the several persons identified with the above, the writer expresses his special appreciation to Mr. Buford Rowland of the National Archives, Mrs. Gertrude M. Parsley of the Tennessee State Library and Archives, Mrs. Patti Black of the Mississippi Department of Archives and History, Mrs. Connie Griffith, formerly of Tulane University Library's Special Collections, and to Dr. F. Mark McKiernan, formerly of the Historic New Orleans Collection.

The author wishes to acknowledge and express his abiding appreciation to Professor Walter B. Posey who provided invaluable service as his dissertation advisor and subsequently encouraged him to prepare the study for publication. Professors William E. Foley of the History Department and David D. Daniels of the Geography Department at Central Missouri State University respectively provided editorial assistance and maps to accompany the text. Professor Glenn R. Conrad, Director of the Center for Louisiana Studies at the University of Southwestern Louisiana, served as editor of the Claiborne manuscript and made many helpful suggestions. Professor James B. Shrewsbury of Concord College, a close personal friend, contributed significantly to the study by reviewing earlier drafts, serving as critic, and offering steadfast encouragement. Finally, Ruby Rutherford Hatfield, my wife, offered constant understanding and support, spurred me on to greater effort, and displayed an inexhaustible patience throughout, for which I am especially grateful.

Joseph T. Hatfield, Dean
School of Arts and Sciences
Central Missouri State University
Warrensburg, Missouri

I

ROAD TO PREFERMENT

Horace Greeley's highly publicized admonition to America's youth to go west was clearly *ex post facto*. Seasoned veterans of the Revolutionary War who witnessed the birth of the American nation had done precisely that. Some bore the scars of combat to prove it; others had indelible impressions and romantic memories. No longer restrained by proclamation lines or the appeals of colonial officialdom, they returned to vaguely conceived plans to carve out niches and places of distinction for themselves in the lands to the west. They rushed into the wilderness and transformed it. In turn, it transformed them. Maybe this was essential to their survival. It was a grim, unrelenting, bareknuckle fight in the best buckskin tradition. They confronted the harsh elements and dread diseases. They challenged the lurking dangers of the dense forests, mountain valleys, and surging streams. They often fought among themselves when greater threats to their persons were more relaxed, even if momentarily. Status and prestige gravitated toward those whose skill in the use of the flimsy flintlock was unmatched. It went to those who could fell the mighty oak in record time, and who could persevere for unlimited periods in the largely uncharted and lonely wilderness. It went to those whose physical prowess and accommodating dispositions invited challenge from friend and foe alike. It went to those who sired numerous progeny and thereby increased the odds of family survival. And the men of education, culture, and refinement who joined them were obliged to "conceal their vintage-marks and pare down their cultural standards" to a level acceptable to the sturdy and resourceful frontiersmen.[1] Many of those who spurned the settled seaboard refinements and crossed the mountains to face uncertain futures were ambitious men "on the make" whose dialects were markedly alien to Back Bay Boston. Some chose the mutable dominion of the Old Southwest as their particular field of challenge and opportunity.

In this primitive setting a complex of competing interests quickly manifested themselves. Indian tribes fought among themselves and against alien intrusions in an unrelenting and losing battle for survival. Individual greed was but a microcosm of national greed as nations plotted, maneuvered, and made their bids for dominance. America's sparsely populated lands became an object of dark intrigue in Washington and London, Paris and Madrid. The uncertainties engendered by these competing nations were heightened further by the ambitions of designing and unprincipled men. These included such personalities as Aaron Burr whose fortunes in the American political arena were snuffed out at Weehawken; and James Wilkinson, ranking general of the United States Army, whose services were always up for bid and whose loyalty never extended beyond the last bribe.

Among those who helped to shape and mold the new land and to attach it more firmly to Washington were such powerful and commanding frontier leaders as John Adair, William Blount, Andrew Jackson, James Robertson, and John Sevier. Of gentler nature but equally ardent in his love of country and republicanism was William Charles Cole Claiborne, a youthful Virginian who competed with these restless centurions for leadership and prominence. Later denigrated by the haughty and aristocratic Creoles of New Orleans as awkward and slovenly,[2] the rather enigmatic Virginian was gentle, patient, and unobtrusive by comparison with his more flamboyant associates and competitors. But he sedulously cultivated relationships with men who could advance his own considerable, if less apparent, ambitions. He was often able to command favors and political support from major political rivals—an indication of Claiborne's substantial political skills. He won appointments coveted by more prominent individuals. Some viewed him as one who subordinated all other considerations to his own notions of dignity and personal integrity, as one who was obnoxiously vain and pompous, and as one who was mesmerized by his own inflated sense of self-importance.[3] Although ambitious, his ambition was tempered by charm, friendliness, sincerity, and warmth.[4] Moreover, he never allowed personal ambitions to influence his judgments unduly or to compromise his integrity. Like the Jacksons, Blounts, and Seviers, he was sensitive to criticism and challenges to honor, and like them he committed himself relentlessly to assigned tasks with little fear of failure. William Charles Cole Claiborne was an arch-republican, patriot, war hawk, and advocate of manifest destiny.

The Claiborne family had migrated to Virginia even earlier than the illustrious Lees. William Claiborne, younger son of a middle-class merchant family in Westmoreland County, England, established the Claiborne family in Virginia in 1621. He came to Jamestown as a company surveyor and shortly built up a successful fur trade with the Indians. Within four years he became secretary of state for Virginia and a member of the ruling council.[5] A clever, resourceful and powerful leader, Claiborne emerged as an advocate of personal liberty and a champion of colonial rights.[6]

A century and a half later, William Charles Cole Claiborne, a descendant of the original Claiborne settlers, was born in Sussex County, Virginia. The second son of Colonel William and Mary Leigh Claiborne, his birth, in 1775, came in the midst of turbulence, violence, and a mutual testing of intentions and capabilities touched off by the Boston Tea Party two years earlier. The emotionally charged encounters at Lexington, Concord, and Breed's Hill and the ill-fated colonial invasion of Canada in 1775 lent belated credence to Samuel Adams' incendiary activities and dark allusions to an atmosphere of stress and peril. This untenable situation impelled the colonies, after much lengthy debate and cautious hesitation, to issue a proclamation of independence. Although probably less than half of the colonial population was committed to the cause of independence, the patriots quickly transformed Good King George into the Royal Brute. Among the active adherents of independence was Colonel Claiborne whose service in the continental army kept him away from his home and family during much of the war. During this period of crisis and warfare Colonel Claiborne offered his children graphic impressions of the horrors of British prison ships and the beastly conduct of the hated British "lobsterbacks." He reserved much of his ire and indignation for the neutralists, estimated by John Adams to embrace fully a third of the colonial populace and humorously described by one writer as the "do-nothings," the "armful of sulking slackers who cowered on the side-lines and cheered whichever team seemed to be winning" and who "worked both sides of the street."[7] The patriotic colonel roundly denounced these elements, as well as those who would dare to "raise a parricidal hand to destroy the fair fabric of American liberty." But dedication and commitment commanded an exorbitant fee. Colonel Claiborne apparently had never been very successful financially, and the war aggravated the family's financial plight. The parents were therefore hard-pressed to maintain their sons Ferdinand and William in Richmond Academy.[8]

The republican zeal and commitment stressed by Colonel Claiborne were also imparted to young William by his mentor at Richmond Academy. Nathaniel Herbert, William's younger brother, remarked that Eldridge Harris, chancellor of the institution, had few equals and no superiors as a teacher. Under the tutelage of Harris, William progressed rapidly in his classical studies and acquired some proficiency in Greek and Latin. When only eight years old he supposedly wrote in Latin: "Dear my country, dearer liberty—where liberty is, there is my country." Chancellor Harris made a few corrections but, apparently reacting both to the emotionalism of the time and the content of his student's Latin composition, utilized the occasion to deliver a protracted polemic on the virtues of republican government. He hoped that his students, when assuming responsible roles in society, would prize that "invaluable boon" and be willing to make whatever sacrifices were necessary in defense of liberty.[9] Claiborne's subsequent public conduct and his numerous utterances as a public servant indicated that he had been receptive to the basic message of both family and school.

William's formal educational training was restricted to his years at Richmond Academy with one brief exception. He and his older brother, Ferdinand Leigh, matriculated at William and Mary

College, but William had an unpleasant encounter with an usher who treated him "amiss." Having become attached to Richmond Academy, where he knew both faculty and students, William used the unidentified "offense" as a pretext to return to more familiar surroundings. Meanwhile, financial need finally forced the parents to withdraw their children from the institution. When the elder Claiborne painfully informed his fifteen-year-old son, William responded that he was aware of his father's financial plight and expressed gratitude for the parental support he had received. In fact, he indicated that he had already formulated tentative plans, subject to his father's approval. William announced that he hoped to secure employment in the office of John Beckley, a fellow-Virginian then serving as a clerk of the United States House of Representatives. If possible, he wanted a supplement to his wardrobe and passage to the federal capital in New York. He added that his fortune would be made if he succeeded; if not, his education would recommend him elsewhere because there were numerous commercial possibilities in the city. Since Congress would be moving shortly to Philadelphia, Claiborne hoped to arrive in New York before the transfer was effected.[10] The elder Claiborne must have been startled and emotionally touched, both by his son's mature response and by the knowledge that young William would emerge shortly from the protective family fold to seek his own way in life.

When William announced that he was leaving Richmond Academy, he was invited to deliver a valedictory address. He prepared his speech and submitted it to an unidentified judge for possible corrections and suggestions. The judge returned the draft the following day with "one or two immaterial alterations," and an admonition to lead a moral and industrious life. If he did so, the judge predicted, Claiborne would be acclaimed and his "path with the blessing of God would be strewed with roses and lighted by the sun of true glory."[11] William's willingness to ask the judge to review his draft and his apparent confidence that John Beckley would offer him a position indicated that the Claiborne family continued to enjoy social and political prominence despite its financial difficulties.

Even though he bade farewell to Chancellor Harris and Richmond Academy, William did not leave immediately for New York. According to his brother, who long afterward reminisced and, in retrospect, fondly attributed to William sterling qualities and virtues reflecting brotherly love and loyalty rather than objective evaluation, the youth spent the next several months studying the New Testament. Nathaniel described William on the eve of his departure from the Old Dominion, saying that his brother's intellect was embellished with a profound knowledge of Greek and Roman literature, strongly fortified by his religious education. His form was erect and manly, his manners urbane. His face was so "exquisitely beautiful," Nathaniel exclaimed effusively, "that it might have been mistaken for the emblem of spring." Not yet sixteen years old and with about fifty dollars in his pocket, William set sail for New York without visible doubts about the uncertain future that loomed before him.[12] In fact, Claiborne's self-confidence and quiet certitude became a trademark in the years ahead when new and unfamiliar leadership responsibilities were suddenly thrust upon him.

The first real test of the youngster's mettle came quickly after leaving the security of the Claiborne home. Almost immediately after boarding the sloop he was stricken by a severe case of measles. The ship's captain lavishly administered "sudorifics" to his seriously ill patient. Although the crisis passed by the time the ship docked in New York harbor, the weak and shaken young man remained aboard ship another two days before going in quest of a job.[13]

True to William's expectation, John Beckley did give "Billy" employment immediately as an enrolling clerk assigned to copy bills and resolutions. As he gained experience, the lawmakers sometimes called upon him to draw up original bills for themselves or their committees. This, too, provided invaluable experience in the years ahead. When not engaged in his work as an enrolling clerk, William spent much of his time listening to congressional debates, reading "political works of merit," and learning French. Evenings were set aside for the ladies, "to whose conversation and company through life he was most passionately devoted."[14] Claiborne would have done himself an infinitely greater service had he devoted less attention to his social life and more time to the study of French. Years later his lack of proficiency hampered his efforts to establish a smooth relationship with the aristocratic elements of the Creole society following his appointment as governor of the Orleans Territory.

When Congress moved from New York to Philadelphia in 1790 "Billy" went along with John Beckley. While continuing his work in the new capital he met many prominent national and regional figures including Vice-President John Adams, Secretary of State Thomas Jefferson, and Congressman John Sevier, who was then representing the Southwest Territory. Jefferson, whose partisan and unswerving disciple he became, sometimes invited him to dinner and gave him access to his personal library in Philadelphia.[15] Impelled by ambition and determined to rise above his modest beginnings, the youthful Virginian displayed an obvious talent for making himself known to the right people and for being in the right place at the right time.

While in the City of Brotherly Love, Claiborne, already determined to seek a career in public service, sought to prepare himself as fully as possible. He became active in a polemic society where he often engaged in animated discussions of public affairs. This was a golden age for masters of oratorical imagery, hyperbole, and metaphor who were always eager to display their talents extemporaneously. His participation in the society was attended by some considerable éclat and enthusiasm. Impressed by William's debating prowess, an "enlightened" congressman, unidentified but probably John Sevier, exclaimed after observing the young Virginian in action that Claiborne "shivered to atoms the arguments of his opponents and bore off the uncontested prize of superior eloquence." Sevier, representing the "Territory South of the Ohio River," recommended to the youthful enrolling clerk that he study law and then pursue a career in the territory. Conceivably Sevier viewed the young man as a potentially valuable political supporter who could assist him in his ongoing political rivalry with William Blount. Alert and receptive to recommendations that might advance his interests, Claiborne quickly notified John Beckley that he would be leaving as soon as a replacement could be found.[16]

William left Philadelphia shortly afterward and returned to Virginia. He remained in Richmond for about three months where, according to his brother, he was again caught up in the social whirl. He did, however, spend part of his time continuing the study of law, which he apparently had begun prior to his departure from Philadelphia under the tutelage of the prominent Philadelphia lawyer and land speculator Alexander J. Dallas.[17] According to the aspiring youth, he read only the revised legal code and a chapter or two in the first volume of Sir William Blackstone's *Commentaries on the Laws of England.* This was the extent of his "dispreparation," as he humorously expressed it, but it enabled him to pass the bar examination a few weeks afterward and he was admitted to the legal profession. The ease with which he won admittance to the bar he attributed mainly to participation in the polemic society in Philadelphia, remarking that it was one of the "best law schools in the Union." The adulatory Nathaniel agreed, observing that William had acquired a sound knowledge of "natural, national and municipal law" at minimal expense and effort and which years of study could hardly have afforded. Passage of the bar examination entitled William to practice law immediately and to forego the probationary period in other states and territories normally required of those not admitted to the legal profession.[18] Having paused in Richmond long enough to accomplish his most immediate objective, the twenty-year-old William was ready to make the next move, one that would advance his career and provide scope for his restless ambition.

With a copy of the revised statutes and Blackstone's *Commentaries,* Claiborne hastened westward to frontier Tennessee as "Nolachucky Jack" Sevier had advised. According to territorial records, Claiborne was licensed to practice as an "Attorney in the several Courts of Law and Courts of Equity in the Territory" on May 22, 1794.[19] Within a short time he hung out his shingle in Sullivan County in northeastern Tennessee. In making his move Claiborne followed in the footsteps of an interesting and colorful assortment of personalities who had hurried before him into the Southwest to launch or advance their legal, political, and business careers. These "fire and steel" centurions of the frontier included a number of Watauga and Franklin veterans, as well as others intent on making names for themselves: the aristocratic William Blount, "ever lynx-eyed where his personal interests were involved" and the "prince of the western speculators"[20] who seized every possible opportunity to advance his personal fortunes, and was governor of the Southwest Territory for several years; James Robertson, Scotch-Irish founder of the transmontane Watauga settlement, North Carolina assemblyman, Indian agent to the Cherokees, militia brigadier, and land agent and confidante of William Blount; John Sevier, Blount's political rival and ex-governor of Franklin, ruthless Indian fighter who did not hesitate to take advantage of a flag of truce to wipe out some Indian leaders,[21] and later territorial delegate to Congress and governor of Tennessee; and Andrew Jackson, the "swagger sandy-haired youth who saw clearly where his chances lay and strutted so confidently on his own through frontier society" and who moved steadily westward from his "native Waxhaw settlement" until he rode into Nashville in the fall of 1788 to launch a career that would take him to Washington as congressman and senator less than a decade later, and ultimately to the White House many years afterward.[22] This was indeed fast company for the young Virginian who would soon work closely with them to advance the Southwest Territory to statehood. Claiborne first concentrated upon establishing his law practice in order to acquire a reputation and to enhance his financial position.

William was eminently successful in his brief period of active legal practice. Nathaniel asserted that his brother had by now forsaken amusements for serious study and was working hard to acquire an outstanding legal reputation. Yet he admitted that his brother was constitutionally lazy but ambition and necessity forced him onward. In Nathaniel's opinion, William was among the ablest lawyers in the profession, for he said that "as an advocate in a criminal case, I hazard nothing by saying that he stood unrivaled." Within some two years after Claiborne became an attorney, another admirer suggested that he "had gained the distinction of standing without a rival as an advocate at the criminal bar." Jurors supposedly wept copiously at his graphic descriptions of human woes and "enlightened tribunals of justice wept under the influence of his touching eloquence." Persons close to Claiborne obviously exaggerated his talent, but discounting their adulatory comments, it appears that Claiborne did attain speedy recognition as a lawyer and was able to command attractive fees for his services. He had taken advantage of his four years as an enrolling clerk to study the techniques of the nation's lawmakers and as a member of the polemic society to master the basic techniques of oratory and histrionics. In one instance, he traveled to Virginia to defend a man accused of murder, for which he received compensation for his expenses and a fee of $500. In another case involving a vast amount of property, Claiborne traveled some two hundred miles to serve as legal counsel. He won the case and refused an undisclosed but reputedly exorbitant fee. He did, however, accept as remuneration for his services an "elegant horse estimated at two hundred and fifty dollars, in lieu thereof." [23]

Although he had been in the Southwest Territory for only slightly over a year, Claiborne displayed considerable insight into the territory's problems and prospects in a letter he wrote during the summer of 1795 to an unidentified friend in Richmond, Virginia. At the time incursions by Creek warriors against both white settlers and the Chickasaw tribe threatened to erupt into a full-scale war. Nonetheless, Claiborne was cautiously optimistic about improved relations, observing that "the savages on our frontiers have felt too severely the calamities of war, to be desirous of disturbing the friendship which at present exists between us." He pointed out that the Chickasaws were the friends of the Americans and that they served as a barrier between "the settlement of Cumberland and the hostile Indian tribes." Highly critical of the failure of the American Congress to provide the settlers with protection—frontier settlers usually were critical of what they regarded as the government's inattention to their security needs—Claiborne added that the defeat of the Chickasaws would enable hostile Indian forces to overrun the Cumberland settlement as well. Although periods of uneasiness and tension continued, Claiborne's assessment of the situation proved generally correct. [24]

The young attorney also recognized the territory's opportunities for growth and development. We are, he said, "possessed of every advantage which nature could give us; some of our lands are equal in point of fertility to any in the world...." But he was also very much aware of the vital necessity of western access to the Mississippi, declaring: "The citizens enjoy now plentifully, all the necessaries of life, and when that great privilege of the Western country, the free navigation of the Mississippi is obtained, we shall find a market for the surplus of our produce, and we will then become a numerous and wealthy people." Moreover, since popular agitation in the Southwest Territory for admission to statehood was becoming too voluble to ignore much longer, Claiborne assumed that statehood would be forthcoming shortly, But, beyond this, he predicted that "to complete our felicity, we shall shortly possess a government founded on the rights of man."[25] Most of these predictions were realized shortly afterward.

Although viewed as a "real comer" in rural northeastern Tennessee and enthusiastic about the territory's future, William toyed with the idea of returning to Richmond. His family was delighted and encouraged him to return to practice law in the more sophisticated and refined atmosphere of the state capital. He had continued to harbor a nostalgia for Virginia after going to the Southwest Territory;[26] however, the contemplated return home did not occur. Instead, he was called upon to represent Sullivan County in the Tennessee statehood convention of 1796.

Popular sentiment in the Southwest Territory for admission to statehood had been mounting steadily. As early as 1791 the territory had a sufficient population according to the terms of the Northwest Ordinance to establish a territorial legislature. However, the governor had to initiate action, and Governor William Blount did not wish to share his authority with a legislature and thus delayed the election of territorial legislature until 1794. Once chosen, the newly elected house of representatives submitted to President George Washington a list of ten nominees for the legislative council, and in accordance with the Northwest Ordinance the chief executive named five. John Sevier and four other long-time associates and business partners were selected to the upper house. "If the Southwest had been combed, no other five with an equal interest in exploiting the land could have been found."[27] But this second phase of territorial government lasted only a short time. The conclusion of Pinckney's

(San Lorenzo) Treaty between the United States and Spain in 1795, which established the northern boundary of Spanish-owned Florida at the thirty-first parallel and opened up the Mississippi River to the Americans, produced an influx of settlers into the Southwest Territory. Moreover, Governor Blount, having earlier impeded efforts to make the territorial government more representative, now changed course and led the move for statehood. By 1795 the territorial population was estimated to be in excess of 75,000 persons, 15,000 more than the Northwest Ordinance required for admission to statehood. Consequently, the clamor for admittance into the Union became increasingly vociferous. Governor Blount called for the election of delegates to a constitutional convention by manhood suffrage, and following their selection the convention convened at Knoxville on January 11, 1796.[28]

The list of delegates to the statehood convention included several prominent frontier personalities, particularly the Watauga and Franklin veterans. Davidson County, which included Nashville and was the center of activities in the central part of the territory, had among its representatives James Robertson and Andrew Jackson. Both men assumed active roles in the convention. John Adair and William Blount were influential delegates from Knox County, located in the eastern part of the Southwest Territory and the site of the territorial capital, Knoxville. Sullivan County had five representatives including the youthful William Claiborne. Undaunted by the presence of such powerful leaders, Claiborne took an active part in the convention from the first days of its proceedings. The convention unanimously chose Governor Blount as its president.[29]

Claiborne served on a four-man committee to formulate rules for the transaction of the convention's business. Not wishing to delay the proceedings, the committee drew up and presented a set of rules on the day following its selection. No member was permitted to speak more than twice upon the same subject unless authorized by the house, or unless it was in a committee of the whole. If a delegate inadvertently digressed from his subject when he had the floor, the convention authorized the president to call him to order.[30] Having helped formulate rules governing the convention's proceedings, Claiborne strongly advocated the Jeffersonian principle of "oeconomy." Economy, he declared, was "an amiable trait in any government." Therefore, the "situation and resources of the country should be attended to" in determining the salaries of the delegates. After these preliminary remarks, he moved that the members of the convention be given a dollar for every thirty miles of travel in coming to and returning from the convention site in Knoxville, and that they be paid ten shillings and six pence per day, in Virginia currency, for their services. Finally, he proposed that convention members should pledge themselves not to draw a greater amount of money from the public treasury. John Rhea, a fellow delegate from Sullivan County, moved to amend the motion to provide for a per diem allowance of a straight dollar and a half. An effort was made to postpone the consideration of the amended motion, but the attempt failed and the delegates unanimously approved the Claiborne motion.[31]

On the same day, James Robertson moved the appointment of a committee composed of two persons from each county to draft a constitution. The delegates approved and the committee was formed. Included among its members were Jackson and Blount, as well as Claiborne. The delegates approved a motion to prefix a bill of rights to the constitution. Claiborne moved that the bill of rights be drawn up as expeditiously as possible by the committee and presented to the plenary body. The motion was seconded, voted upon, and approved.[32] In taking this action the delegates displayed a deep republican concern for the preservation of human liberties by means of written guarantees. Moreover, they probably had been influenced by the earlier republican insistence that a bill of rights be attached to the federal constitution so that there would be no possible question about the sanctity of individual rights.

When the committee presented its proposed constitution to the convention, it called for a bicameral legislature. Earlier, there had been extended discussions about the composition of the legislative body. Claiborne, who brought with him to the transmontane a typical republican fear of the senate as a citadel of the privileged classes, was very active in the debates. Although he favored a bicameral legislature, he would have allowed the upper house, or senate, only a qualified negative. According to Claiborne's motion, a bill could become law, provided two-thirds of the house of representatives concurred, notwithstanding the dissent of the senate. The motion was defeated. The members of the committee also considered the feasibility of creating a single legislative chamber which could legislate only with the approval of two-thirds of the members present. It, too, failed of passage. As finally drawn up and presented on January 30, the constitution provided for a general assembly composed of two houses. For the first sixteen years, the senate would be composed of one member from each county and the house of representatives would have two members from each county. In the interim, provision would be made for the permanent composition of the state legislature.[33]

A provision of the constitutional draft called for the election of legislative members by ballot. Joseph Anderson of Jefferson County moved to amend it to allow for voting *viva voce*. But if voting by *viva voce* proved "less conducive to the satisfaction of the citizens," he added, he would be agreeable to the use of ballots. Anderson felt, however, that such change should be effected only by a majority vote of those delegates present in both houses. The convention defeated his amendment by a vote of 20-33, with Claiborne voting negatively.[34] Although there is no record of the actual debates, Claiborne apparently recognized the potential abuses inherent in Anderson's proposed system of voting and favored one offering greater assurances of free choice.

The drafting committee also included provisions in the constituion restricting dual officeholding. It stipulated that no judge of any court of law or equity, attorney general, secretary of state, or clerk of any court of record would be eligible to serve in the legislature. Moreover, no state officer would be permitted to hold more than one lucrative office at a given time. However, appointments in the militia and service as justice of the peace were not to be regarded as lucrative offices. When Joel Lewis of Davidson County offered an amendment extending those restrictions to include offices under the authority of the United States, Claiborne hastened to second the motion. The convention then approved the amended motion.[35]

The eligibility of both clergymen and nonbelievers to hold civil or military office under the state was also discussed at some length by the delegates. Claiborne's effort to prevent the imposition of civil and military officeholding restrictions on clergymen was quickly defeated by a vote of 24-31. On the same day, a motion was approved which barred them only from service in the general assembly.[36] Discussions later focused on a resolution offered by George Doherty of Jefferson County which declared that any person denying God or disbelieving in future rewards and punishments would be ineligible to hold civil office. As the convention was drawing to a close, a vote was taken on the measure and it was approved by a vote of 28-26, with Jackson and Claiborne voting affirmatively.[37]

The delegates also debated the status of those state citizens whose religious beliefs forbade the bearing of arms or service in the militia. John Shelby, Jr., one of Claiborne's colleagues from Sullivan County, moved to exempt such persons from the payment of fines for refusing to serve in the state militia, provided the religious sect or denomination to which they belonged opposed the bearing of arms. The Shelby motion was handily defeated by a vote of 16-39, with such persons as Blount, Claiborne, and Jackson joining forces to strike out the exemption from the militia service on religious grounds.[38]

Although the American right to the use of the Mississippi River had been confirmed the previous year, a recognition of this waterway's vital importance to the future of the West—as well as the knowledge that eastern leaders and commercial interests had been willing to forego the American right of navigation on the lower Mississippi in return for a favorable trade treaty with Spain as a feature of the Jay-Gardoqui negotiations in 1785—invited a declaration from the delegates assembled at Knoxville. Initially the drafting committee stated that the citizens of Tennessee possessed an inherent right to use the Mississippi River and that this right could not be surrendered. John Sevier demanded a more cogent and emphatic statement, shouting out to Claiborne, who formulated the provision: "D--n me, Major Claiborne, that ain't enough, give us some of your Coke upon Littleton." As a result of the truculent Sevier's stringent prompting and lively encouragement from Governor Blount, Claiborne struck a more uncompromising posture. The inherent right of the Tennesseeans to the Mississippi River could not be surrendered, according to the amended statement, to "any prince, potentate, power, person or persons whatsoever."[39]

Having taken such an unequivocal stand on this matter, the Knoxville delegates proceeded to act on behalf of those settlers living in the more exposed regions of the Southwest Territory lying south of the Big Pigeon and Tennessee, the French Broad and Holston rivers. Although they had not acquired land titles a number of people had moved into the region between the end of the Revolutionary War and 1790. The convention delegates provided preemption rights for them, and decreed that such persons were eligible to serve in all capacities where a freehold was a constitutional qualification. This provision would remain in force until a land office had been opened and the settlers could legally acquire land titles. [40]

Having met for twenty-seven days, the delegates acted quickly to complete their work. They devoted most of their last session to providing for payment of expenses and to approving expressions of appreciation to individuals who had provided assistance. The delegates then departed. Although no records were kept of the convention debates, its proceedings seem to have been characterized by harmony and a sense of common purpose. The constitution that emerged from the proceedings contained some principles that benefitted vested interests and impeded democracy. These included a provision that all acreage was to be taxed at the same rate regardless of value, which no doubt was a source of comfort to landed proprietors, including Blount and his longtime associates. Also, the Tennessee frame of government provided that the general assembly would elect justices of the peace for life. These influential and important figures in the frontier settlements in turn chose most of the other county officials. On the other hand, other features of the constitution advanced the cause of democracy and provided for more representative government. The people rather than the general assembly elected the governor. Moreover, the document eliminated any property qualification for voting. Representation was apportioned "according to taxable population instead of by territorial units," as other constitutions sometimes provided.[41] Withal, it was a document that compared favorably with many state constitutions. Thomas Jefferson appears to have been singularly impressed, remarking that the Tennessee constitution was "the least imperfect and the most republican" of the several state constitutions then in existence.[42]

William Claiborne's contribution to the formulation of the constitution had been more than incidental; despite his youth and inexperience, he had taken an active role in the convention proceedings. He displayed at this early date an abiding concern for basic human liberties, and for the republican virtue of economic stringency. He sought preemption rights for those settlers living in the exposed regions beyond established settlements, and, like most westerners, he insisted that access to the Mississippi River was a right. Moreover, he attempted to broaden the franchise, and expressed a preference for voting by ballot to insure a freer exercise of this privilege. His brother Nathaniel asserted that William's political career actually began at the Knoxville convention, adding that his imposing contribution had been made possible by his education, reading, and the political circles in which he mingled. Governor Blount was impressed with the young man, asserting that, making allowances for his youth, Claiborne was the most extraordinary man he had met. If Claiborne lived to the age of fifty, he predicted, nothing but narrow, local prejudices would prevent him from emerging as one of the most distinguished political leaders in the United States.[43] But allowing for Blount's adulation and praise in this rural setting and at a time when pride in handiwork was in order, it was abundantly clear that the young Virginian's star was on the rise.

Governor Blount had ordered a census of the territorial inhabitants and convoked the Knoxville convention without consulting with the United States Congress. Following the Knoxville convention the governor selected a representative to present the constitution to the national lawmakers and to request admission to statehood. Some Federalist senators, attempting to impede the development of the west, recommended that admission be delayed until "the state should be laid out and the census taken under congressional authority." Despite the absence of congressional authority or even a popular referendum, the convention ordered that elections be held under the new instrument of government, including the election of two persons to the United States House of Representatives and two persons to the United States Senate. Congress ultimately sanctioned these measures, but it allowed Tennessee only one representative. Tennessee thus entered the Union as the sixteenth state on June 1, 1796.[44]

Although Claiborne had made a substantial contribution to the proceedings in Knoxville and was singled out for praise by Governor Blount following the convention, he was neither appointed nor elected initially to public office. The delegates had given the convention president permission to issue writs for the election of the new legislature, governor, and sheriffs. On the day the convention adjourned Governor Blount issued the writs for the election. Blount subsequently relinquished the governorship for a seat in the United States Senate. The newly elected members of the general assembly convened on March 28, 1796, two months before Tennessee was formally admitted to statehood. Three of

Claiborne's Sullivan County colleagues who had served in the convention—David Looney, John Rhea, and George Rutledge—were among the state's new lawmakers. Moreover, the general assembly ignored Claiborne in its initial appointments. Only after others had refused appointments to the superior court of law and equity, the state supreme court, was Claiborne considered. Those initially selected while Claiborne marked time and hoped that he would not continue to be ignored or forgotten were Willie Blount, John McNairy, and Archibald Roane. Willie Blount was Governor William Blount's half-brother; John McNairy and Archibald Roane were longtime friends and associates of the powerful Blount. The three appointees to the judiciary were also older state residents, probably the most plausible reason why the anxious Claiborne was not singled out immediately. McNairy declined and Howell Tatum was selected. When Willie Blount declined the judgeship, Claiborne was tendered the post. [45] Although Claiborne was urged to decline the position by some friends for political and professional reasons, he starchily rejected their advice, saying: "My motto is honor and not money; Governor Sevier is my friend, and if I can, I am bound to aid his administration." At the time of his appointment by Governor Sevier, Tennessee's first elective chief executive, Claiborne was not yet twenty-two years old. [46]

Even though the youthful Claiborne felt honored to serve on Tennessee's highest legal tribunal, he remained a member of the supreme court only until the autumn of 1797. In accepting the post, Claiborne made a financial sacrifice because of the more lucrative income he would have realized as a practicing attorney. Moreover, the judgeship was a rather inactive one since few cases attained that level of adjudication in sparsely settled Tennessee. Although a committed political personality, he seemingly blotted out his political aspirations by removing himself from the immediate swirl of partisan politics. Having donned the judicial robe and far removed from the intoxicating influence of the national capital he had known as an idealistic young enrolling clerk, he obviously had no real intimation that the position he would assume within a short time would have a profound national impact. Moreover, the political principles and ideals which had been assuming shape and direction in his mind as student, enrolling clerk, attorney, constitutional delegate, and as judge would attain maturity and crystallize. Within weeks of his resignation as a state justice, Claiborne would travel from Knoxville to Washington where he would serve two terms as a member of the United States House of Representatives.

II

REPUBLICAN CONGRESSMAN

The Blount conspiracy provided Claiborne with the opportunity for which he had been waiting. When Tennessee was admitted to statehood, the legislature chose William Blount and William Cocke to serve in the United States Senate. While preparations were being made in the Southwest Territory for statehood and officers were being chosen to head up the new government, developments in Europe, then engulfed in war, unexpectedly affected the future of the western frontier. Spain, hitherto a British ally, withdrew from the war against France during the summer of 1795. The next year Spain joined France against England. This produced some speculation on both sides of the Atlantic that Spain would cede Florida and possibly Louisiana to France and that westerners would again be denied navigation rights on the Mississippi River. Blount, the western land baron who was at the time confronted by serious financial difficulties caused by declining land prices and overextension, immediately recognized the implications, both for the West generally and for his landed interests particularly. Consequently, Blount, who at an earlier time had been pro-English in the Federalist tradition, and other interested parties formulated some general plans to use the frontiersmen and Indians to cooperate with the British in a filibustering expedition against the Floridas. On April 21, 1797, Blount wrote a letter to James Carey, an interpreter in the Cherokee nation, discussing the plan and indicating that, if the plan received approval in London, he "would probably be at the head of the business on the part of the British."

Although he instructed Carey to read the dispatch three times and then destroy it, Carey turned it over to his employer who then hastened to Philadelphia where he turned over the incriminating letter to Secretary of War James McHenry and Secretary of State Timothy Pickering. Upon disclosure of the plot, Blount's Senate colleagues accused him of high misdemeanor and abuse of public trust. On July 8, by a vote of 25-1, Blount acquired the dubious distinction of becoming the first United States senator expelled from that body.[1]

At the time Blount had been chosen to be one of Tennessee's two senators, Andrew Jackson had been selected as the state's lone member to the House of Representatives. Disappointed, disinterested, and beset with serious financial problems, Jackson attended only the first session of Congress. During that time, he displayed interest only in securing compensation for a Tennessee militia unit which had engaged in an Indian expedition in 1793 without state or federal authorization. Failing to attend the second session altogether, he seriously considered retirement, but when Blount was unexpectedly expelled from the Senate, the state legislature chose Jackson to fill the vacancy. After serving in the Senate for only a few months he submitted his resignation; his Senate record equalled that of his days in the House of Representatives.[2]

When Jackson's seat in the House of Representatives became vacant, Judge William Claiborne relinquished his seat on the bench and made a bid for it. John Rhea, a fellow politician from Sullivan County who had served with Claiborne in the constitutional convention and was a man of "fine talents, of great wealth, and extensive connexions," opposed Claiborne. But despite certain political handicaps, such as being a newcomer to the state and his youth, Claiborne in fact had displayed some dazzling political footwork during the short time had had been in Tennessee. Although John Sevier, who dominated politics in eastern Tennessee, and William Blount, who held political sway in middle Tennessee, were powerful and antagonistic rivals, both supported Claiborne. This enabled him to circulate freely in the two rival camps. He had been appointed brigade major under General John Sevier in late 1795,[3] and after Tennessee achieved statehood Governor Sevier gave him a position on the bench. When Jackson resigned his seat in the House, Senator Blount wrote to Governor Sevier and recommended that Claiborne be elected to fill the vacant seat.[4] In the subsequent election Claiborne defeated Rhea by an impressive majority.[5]

Having made his decision to become a lawmaker, rather than continue as an interpreter of the law, Claiborne recognized that his triumph opened up new political vistas. As he savored sweet success and pondered the political avenue recently opened to him, the young representative—Claiborne was then only twenty-two years old, three years under the constitutional minimum—could be particularly thankful for the four years he had spent in New York and Philadelphia as an enrolling clerk. His victory would again enable him to hover close to the vitals of national politics. But as a voting member of Congress, he would experience the power and prestige that came with admittance to such select ranks. Such thoughts may well have hastened his preparations to abandon the primitive environment he had embraced three years earlier in favor of the excitement, stimulation, and greater refinement of the national capital. Despite the self-confidence and self-assurance that he normally exuded as he faced new challenges and responsibilities, the young solon-elect would have blanched at the faintest hint that he would be thrust unexpectedly into the role of national kingmaker during the course of his two congressional terms.

The House of Representatives began the second session of its fifth term on November 13, 1797, and the Tennesseean answered the roll call for the first time ten days later. As a political neophyte on the national scene, William did not initially take an active part in the legislative deliberations, but within a short time he began to express his views freely on a wide range of issues. As a member of the important Ways and Means Committee, he served with Albert Gallatin, Robert Goodloe Harper, Abraham Baldwin, and James Bayard. He also served as chairman of the Committee on Indian Relations.[6] The latter appointment was a "natural" in terms of the constituency he represented, and it proved helpful in his later territorial service.

Although he later displayed a broad range of national interests, the Tennesseean seems to have been preoccupied initially with the interests of his constituency, much as Andrew Jackson had been during his brief and sterile congressional service. While he voted on a number of measures, he nevertheless concentrated on securing legislation to settle disputed Tennessee land titles, a matter Claiborne and his fellow delegates at the Knoxville constitutional convention had taken up earlier. The Tennessee legislature had presented a petition and remonstrance to Congress following the conclusion of the Treaty of Holston in 1791, negotiated principally by William Blount. The treaty provoked a boundary dispute between the Cherokee Indians and the citizens of Tennessee. When the boundary line was fixed, a number of white settlements were declared an integral part of the Indian territory. According to the Tennessee petitioners, many citizens had been compelled to abandon their homesteads and were encamped in nearby forests. The petitioners requested that Congress appropriate monies to extinguish claims to the disputed lands and afford temporary relief to those settlers who had been driven from their homes. When the petition was laid before Congress, Claiborne remarked that the president's extension of the Indian boundary line to include a number of white settlements was common knowledge. If it were true that citizens of Tennessee were being forced to relinquish possessions obtained under the government of North Carolina when these now disputed western lands were claimed by that state, then any measure intended to insure adequate and immediate relief was certainly warranted.[7]

About two months after Claiborne had taken his seat in Congress, a bill was offered to permit financial aid to those Tennesseeans who held land claims under the agreement between the United States and North Carolina but had become victims of deprivation because of the boundary changes. Claiborne moved to amend the measure by calling for the appropriation of an unstipulated amount of money for the purpose of extinguishing Indian land claims within Tennessee, and for the relief of the affected persons. Congressman Chauncey Goodrich of Connecticut objected on the ground that the proposal was too general, and added that it would be wiser to wait until a report had been submitted by the boundary commission appointed by President John Adams to formulate a treaty with the Indians. Obviously not desiring to defer action where his constituency was concerned, Claiborne replied pointedly that further delay was hardly in order since action on the proposition had been pending for several weeks. The delay was causing major hardships to Tennesseeans who had been driven from their homes in the disputed area by armed American troops. Many of those people, he lamented, were attempting to find shelter in the woods during the most inclement season of the year. Where was humanity, he cried out to his colleagues, if the House elected to "procrastinate a decision?" Despite his impassioned appeal, Claiborne's amendment was declared out of order on the ground that it constituted a substitute motion.[8] Claiborne attempted several times in the ensuing weeks to bring the matter of the state petition before the House for action but to no avail.

Finally, on February 21, 1798, Representative Abraham B. Venable of Virginia reported from the committee which had been considering the president's request for the appropriation to finance negotiations with the Indians regarding the contested land titles of North Carolina and Tennessee. A colleague moved to amend the measure by omitting the names of the two states. Instead, he proposed that the president be permitted merely to conclude a treaty, or treaties, with the Indians. By deleting the names of the two states, the federal government therefore would not specifically assume responsibility to extinguish Indian land claims within the United States for either a state or an individual citizen. As expected, Claiborne and some of his colleagues responded quickly to the challenge. They contended that it would penalize persons with legitimate claims against the federal government, and might even induce Tennesseeans who had been driven from their homes to migrate to Spanish territory, or simply to hold their property in defiance of the Treaty of Holston. Nonetheless, the House merely voted an appropriation of $25,880 which was to be used to conclude a treaty with the Indians.[9] Young Claiborne had just been dealt his first personal defeat in the national legislative arena. If he suspected that either regional or political differences had influenced the course of the debates and contributed to his defeat, he carefully refrained from making such charges.

Some time afterward a property tax bill providing for the evaluation and taxing of houses, along with an enumeration of slaves within the United States, was proposed in the House of Representatives. Acutely aware that the particular interests of his western constituency were involved, Claiborne trumpeted his opposition to the imposition of direct taxes on houses having an estimated value of $200 or less. Such edifices were "abodes of poverty." He could scarcely visualize a system in which tax collectors would be sent "to the door of the humble cottager to ask half a dollar for the privilege of his shelter from the inclemency of the seasons." His own constituents had essentially the same economic status as the people of neighboring Kentucky. That is, most of them enjoyed the bare necessities of life, but few experienced the "conveniences which flow from wealth." He pointed out that his constituents were encountering difficulty in the disposal of their agricultural goods and thus had little capital. In making this statement, Claiborne was alluding to the commercial disruption resulting from the European wars and the subsequent inability of the westerners to sell their agricultural surpluses. He was convinced that the tax would impose a grievous burden upon the people of Tennessee. The bill would lay the foundation for a land tax, Claiborne charged, and the people of his state simply would be without the means to pay it. Nonetheless, the House approved the measure by a vote of 69-19.[10]

Although he was quick to speak out in behalf of his Tennessee constituents, Congressman Claiborne emerged within a short time as a regional representative and spokesman. He expressed concern about the limited knowledge of the masses, particularly of the South and West, regarding the federal Constitution. Even as some of his closest associates were expressing disagreement with the Constitution while advocating states' rights, Claiborne was making an effort to insure that the masses developed a greater knowledge and understanding of the document. About a year after he entered Congress, he moved that an unstipulated number of copies of the Constitution and its amendments be printed and distributed among the people. His motion was laid on the table, but he succeeded in having it called up the next day for consideration. Perhaps the people of the eastern and middle states were well informed, he suggested, but the people of the more rural South and West knew very little about the document. Claiborne then lashed out savagely at Congressman George Thacher of Massachusetts who had remarked that the westerners were not uninformed about the Constitution and were not in need of political information. Rather, they needed, according to Thacher, "moral information, fixed principles, and correct habits." Such language need only be despised, shouted the irate Tennesseean. When the Speaker declared his remarks out of order, Claiborne retorted that the public had learned of Thacher's brutal criticism of the Westerners and he fully intended to brand it as calumny. He moved that 50,000 copies of the Constitution be printed, estimating the cost would be less than $1,000. Thacher suggested that the state legislatures assume the responsibility, but Claiborne insisted that it would be more fitting and proper for Congress to disseminate such information. A motion was made to refer the proposal to a select committee and it passed by a vote of 38-33. But even as his motion went down to defeat, Claiborne declared that the committee should be instructed to investigate the extent to which the promulgation of the laws of the United States had been carried out and to determine if further provisions would be in order.[11]

Even though his initial efforts as a national lawmaker had chiefly centered around the interests of his state and region constituency, Claiborne was drawn inexorably into the national political struggle then approaching its climax. Having been largely preoccupied with political, constitutional, and judicial affairs in remote Tennessee, he simply was unaware of the extent to which partisan politics had come to characterize the national political environment. Similarly, he had no way of knowing the extent to which his own role as a national lawmaker would be colored and influenced by the charged political climate. Party divisions, increasingly manifested over the issue of the Constitution, had been widening for some time. Unhappy Republican leaders had resigned their cabinet posts during President Washington's second administration. The Federalists succeeded in eking out a victory in the elections of 1796, but Thomas Jefferson emerged as vice president, partly because of internecine conflict and plotting within Federalist ranks. Over the succeeding four-year period, covering Claiborne's two congressional terms, party lines crystallized much more and the burgeoning Republican party exploited Federalist mistakes and rivalries.

As the Federalist party architect and colossus, Alexander Hamilton had fashioned policies and programs intended to appeal to "gentlemen of principle and property." Furthermore, Hamilton's capitalistic measures strongly favored northeastern interests which fostered resentment in the South and West. By contrast, Jefferson and the Republican leadership drew much of their support from the less privileged, more rural classes. They harbored strong state loyalties and challenged Federalist endeavors to strengthen and expand the powers and prerogatives of the central government. As might have been expected, therefore, Federalist and Republican leaders clashed with increasing bitterness and ferocity over national and international policies. When the young Tennesseean arrived in Philadelphia, Federalist hegemony had entered the twilight years of its political dominance. When Claiborne left the new national capital four years later, the Federalist decade had come to a jarring, acrimonious end and the "Revolution of 1800" had ushered in the era of Jeffersonian democracy. Although too youthful, unknown, and inexperienced to exert a decisive influence, even within the Republican party, Claiborne nonetheless became increasingly involved in the political ferment and contributed in no small measure to the profound changes that accompanied the transfer of power to the Republicans.

The infamous Griswold-Lyon confrontation on February 15, 1798, witnessed by the incredulous young Claiborne, less than three months after his arrival in Philadelphia, sprang in part from the incendiary personalities involved. However, in the larger sense, it pointed up the extent to which Federalist-Republican acrimony and bitterness had developed. Some two weeks before the bizarre encounter, Republican Matthew Lyon of Vermont had responded to some offensive and embarrassing remarks made by Federalist Congressman Roger Griswold of Connecticut by expectorating in Griswold's face. As the Speaker prepared to call the House to order on February 15, Griswold suddenly advanced on his fellow New Englander and attacked him with a heavy stick. Lyon seized a pair of firetongs and sought to repulse his charging adversary. Calm was restored and the sullen combatants composed themselves only when the Speaker's call for order finally prevailed. The House subsequently attempted to determine an appropriate penalty for the affront to its dignity. The Republicans appeared willing to dismiss both congressmen for their violent and reprehensible behavior, but the Federalists chose to defend Griswold. In the course of the trial for the dismissal of the two offenders, Claiborne testified that the usual prayer had been offered but the House had not been called to order. The Tennesseean asserted that he was standing near a letter box when he heard the cry to "part them." Griswold, he said, had proceeded to the attack and was vigorously swinging a stick. He saw Lyon holding up his hands to ward off the attack and to protect himself, but he was without a weapon at this stage of the battle. The antagonists fell to the floor near a stove, and Claiborne helped to separate them. As they were being separated, Claiborne saw a fellow congressman take a pair of firetongs from Lyon. The lawmakers finally agreed to censure the two men for engaging in riotous and disorderly behavior, an action which Claiborne supported.[12]

If Claiborne's stand on the Griswold-Lyon incident was largely lacking in partisan *esprit de corps*, he nonetheless moved inexorably into the Republican fold. As expressed by his brother

Nathaniel, William emerged early as "an acquisition to the republican party, and in that light was universally received."[13] The republican concepts, principles, and ideals which had been planted in his mind during his formative years at Richmond Academy and later as a congressional enrolling clerk had germinated and come to assume definite form. Although courteous and circumspect toward the opposition, Claiborne was stubborn and steadfast in his enunciation and support of Republican policy issues and positions. In short, his political philosophy developed and matured during his two terms in the House of Representatives. From that time, his commitment to Thomas Jefferson and the Republican party was firm and irrevocable. His years in the House and his later career in the Southwest merely confirmed this obvious fact.

The Jeffersonian Republicans regarded economic restraint by governmental leaders as a paramount virtue, and Congressman Claiborne proved to be one of his party's most vociferous and committed adherents. The Republicans bitterly opposed the controversial Judiciary Act of 1801, mainly because they knew that most of the appointments in an expanded judiciary would be conferred upon Federalists before the Adams administration came to an end. Although the Federalists had been soundly trounced at the polls and were in disarray, these appointments would enable them to perpetuate their ideology and influence for a number of years, hopefully until they could rehabilitate and reestablish themselves politically. However, Claiborne's principal concern centered chiefly around the salaries the judges would be paid. The salaries proposed would be regarded as immoderate in Tennessee, he declared. Although the motion calling for a more convenient organization of the federal courts was approved by a vote of 51-43, Claiborne prevented a "shameful profusion of money" by reducing the salaries of the three judges who would preside over the three circuit courts in Kentucky and Tennessee.[14]

Later during discussion about the feasibility of maintaining an enlarged army because of tensions with France, Claiborne vigorously opposed the measure, in part because of the exorbitant expenses it would entail. "Nothing has a greater tendency to tame the spirits of a free people," he proclaimed in good republican form, "and sooner to prepare their minds for political servitude, than an immense national debt and heavy taxation." The man who was burdened with debt and guarded by creditors often sank into despair and lost his firmness of character, and the same application might be made to a national state. England was an excellent case in point, he asserted, and that was why the English people were tolerating their corrupt government. In Claiborne's view, one of the best ways to economize and contain the national debt was to reduce the size of the armed forces.[15]

Despite his usual propensity for "oeconomy," there were a few instances in which the young congressman relented slightly. He had done so when he sought reimbursement for those Tennesseeans who had been dislocated because of the Treaty of Holston. He did so again when Congress was considering a proposed mausoleum for George Washington. When Congressman John Smilie of Pennsylvania complained that it would be an unnecessary expense, Claiborne disagreed with him while proposing an equestrian statue as being more justifiable "upon the principles of economy." Suggesting that the subject of the mausoleum had been introduced to create dissension in the House, the implication being that it would cause the Federalists to close ranks behind the measure and the Republicans to oppose it, Claiborne urged his colleagues to unite "in the last act of attention which we propose to show this venerable character." The subject was discussed intermittently over the succeeding months, with Claiborne continuing to insist that an equestrian statue would evoke "more lively emotions than a mass of stones formed into a pyramid." Finally losing his argument to those who advocated the latter, Claiborne called unsuccessfully for an appropriation to deposit Washington's remains "within these very walls, in such a manner as would not disgrace them." The lawmakers finally appropriated $200,000 for the Washington memorial, with Claiborne voting affirmatively.[16] Nonetheless, the frugal Tennesseean did not view his support of the measure as a substantive departure from his usual commitment to economic conservatism.

Although Claiborne was a strong supporter of the Constitution, he, like most Republicans, sometimes expressed a fear of the power and influence of the chief executive and the Senate, particularly when the Republicans were the minority party. Indeed, in the Tennessee constitutional convention of 1796, he had sought to give the lower house greater powers than the upper house. Then in the course of a debate about America's delicate diplomatic relations with France, Claiborne asserted that if our government were threatened internally, it would come from the president and Senate uniting in opposition to the House. If a bold, intriguing, and ambitious person should become chief executive, and two-thirds of the Senate supported him, he would be in the position to overthrow the government by his treaty-making powers and deprive American citizens of their liberties. Claiborne and his Republican colleagues observed a tendency during times of stress and peril to grant the president powers that were intended for Congress. The history of Europe proved, they insisted, that the expansion of the executive's powers enabled that authority to enslave the people.[17] In short, the Republicans viewed the House of Representatives as a counterpoise to the presidency and Senate at the time, and as the most fundamental guardian of popular rights and liberties.

At the same time, Claiborne agreed with Jefferson, his mentor, and other Republicans that that government is best which governs least. Theirs was, in large measure, a laissez-faire approach to government. This commitment, buttressed by their propensity for economy, meant that they opposed measures which would broaden and expand government responsibilities at increasing costs to the American taxpayers. These generally became the trademarks of both Thomas Jefferson when he later emerged as president and of Congressman Claiborne when Jefferson appointed him governor of the Mississippi Territory and then as governor of the Territory of Orleans.

Two other issues which came increasingly to divide the Federalists and Republicans revolved around relations between the state and national governments and interpretations of the Constitution. Jefferson and his Republican followers were more inclined to place greater emphasis upon the rights and responsibilities of the state governments, or at least to insist upon a more balanced state-national relationship than Alexander Hamilton and his Federalist colleagues were inclined to concede. Likewise, the Republicans were prone to emphasize strict interpretations of the national Constitution. Their positions regarding both state-national relations and the Constitution were influenced in part by the very fact that they were the minority party, and therefore were attempting to limit the powers and prerogatives of their political opponents. Nonetheless, their positions on both issues were still determined in large measure by their philosophical commitments and ideology. The Tennesseean easily fit into the Republican mold on both issues. Although there is no evidence to suggest that he was committed either to state rights or to strict constructionist principles to the extent that some Jeffersonians were, his policy positions clearly reflected a commitment in principle, and his stand on issues involving them was easily predictable.

Again in the emerging tradition of the Republican party, young Claiborne expressed isolationist sentiments and questioned American ties with Europe. The isolationist theme had been expressed earlier by President Washington, of course, but the Republicans inclined to this advice more than the Federalists, particularly as the European war continued and Franco-American relations deteriorated to the point of imminent clash. Claiborne's opportunity to express his isolationist views came when Congressman Robert Goodloe Harper of South Carolina proposed an appropriation of $40,000 to provide salaries for the American ministers in London and Paris. Further, he sought to reduce the rank of the American ministers plenipotentiary in Berlin, Lisbon, and Madrid to that of resident ministers. Responding to the proposal on January 24, 1798, some two months after he had answered his first roll call, the young Claiborne contended that the House could rightfully restrict diplomatic appointments through its appropriations. This was one of the first specific instances under the new government in which members of Congress discussed the possible application of the old adage that the powers of the executive authority could be limited through legislative control of the purse strings. Claiborne saw no reason why the United States should have any association with the politics of Europe since this country was so far removed from the transatlantic world. He asserted flatly that the United States should have no interest whatsoever in European wars resulting from the efforts of the European leaders to establish or preserve a political balance of power. America's responsibilities were to preserve harmony among nations; to protect our country's "unoffending commerce," insofar as it was possible; and to follow "the peaceful pursuits of agriculture." The United States should most emphatically remain aloof and isolated from "the intrigues and designs of European Princes, as well as Republics."[8]

As members of the House continued to discuss American representation in leading European capitals, Claiborne stubbornly pressed his case. Our "foreign political connexions" had been attended by evil. To increase our diplomatic relations with Europe would introduce foreign politics into the United States, influence American sentiments and views, and possibly become a bane to liberty. If Europe was "convulsed to its centre," and ignored the laws of nations, and if its people were largely devoid of morality and virtue, would it not be better to reduce our presence in Europe, he inquired. A congressman from Delaware suggested that the United States employ "spies" abroad to acquire information about European conspiracies having as their purpose the enslavement of America. Claiborne scoffed at the idea, saying that such a proposition might have some merit if this country were a Swiss canton, but the United States was separated from Europe by an immense ocean. Although he opposed an expansion of diplomatic ties, Claiborne finally agreed with his associates that it would be in the national interest to retain American diplomatic representation in London, Paris, Madrid, Berlin, and Lisbon at their prevailing levels.[19]

During congressional discussion about the feasibility of raising a provisional army in the event of war, the Republicans and Federalists clashed repeatedly over the relative merits of the militia and regular military forces, with Claiborne frequently serving as spokesman for his party. Scoffing at the opposition's contention that disciplined army troops were superior to militia, he proclaimed that "when an army of these disciplined troops, who fight *only for pay*, are opposed by a body of citizens who contend for everything dear to man, victory never fails to crown the cause of freemen." Xerxes had fallen back before advancing militiamen; Hannibal had been driven from the Italian peninsula by the Roman militia; and, most recently, Napoleon had marched from victory to victory at the head of a militia force. American colonial militiamen had plucked "from the British Crown the brightest gem which had ever ornamented it," and had then guaranteed the security of the fledgling nation. Regular troops were "organs of oppression," and a "bane to liberty." He reminded his colleagues that regular troops had driven Tennesseeans from their homes after the conclusion of the Treaty of Holston. Despite Claiborne's impassioned arguments, the House approved the army bill by a vote of 51-40.[20] The Senate and president concurred and the bill became a law in July 1798. Nevertheless, this did not deter Claiborne in subsequent debates from arguing in support of the militia as a desirable alternative to regular forces.

Although the Federalists and Republicans were poles apart philosophically and clashed repeatedly on a wide range of issues, one of their most acute sources of antagonism revolved around American policies toward France and Great Britain. The issue of war or peace and preference for France or Great Britain deeply divided the Hamiltonians and Jeffersonians and led to the closing of party ranks between these antagonistic and irreconcilable forces at a time when the American government could do little to influence the course of European diplomacy and politics. While asserting stoutly that he was unafraid of the "*Power* of France, or *even of all Europe* combined,"[21] Claiborne steadfastly opposed measures directed against France and insisted that French leaders did not harbor ulterior designs toward the United States. On May 22, 1798, Representative Samuel Sitgreaves of Pennsylvania offered a proposal which would permit American naval commanders to take or destroy French cruisers that attacked them on the high seas for purposes of search and seizure. The measure would have also permitted American commanders to retake American vessels seized earlier by French ships and to destroy or capture armed cruisers of the French navy that were found prowling off the American coast. Claiborne protested that such action could lead to war. When a colleague insisted that all efforts to restore normal relations between the two countries had been explored and exhausted, Claiborne reminded him that there was yet hope because American commissioners had been dispatched to Paris to resolve outstanding differences. This was an allusion to the Pinckney, Gerry, and Marshall mission, of course, which culminated in the infamous XYZ Affair and led to the recall of the American representatives. Although Claiborne was tolerant of French excesses, he argued against the Sitgreaves' proposal on the grounds of American military unpreparedness, which at this early date was beginning to emerge as an American tradition. He estimated that the country needed forty times as many ships as it then had, but to enact legislation to strengthen the navy could frustrate the efforts of the American commissioners and offend the unsavory French Directory. After further discussion, the Sitgreaves' proposal was referred to the Committee for the Protection and Defense of the Country.[22]

Other possible punitive measures against France were discussed during the succeeding weeks, with Claiborne generally insisting that the proposals were "replete with impolicy."[23] If the United States could avoid war while maintaining its honor, it certainly should do so. Probably startling colleagues traditionally inclined to think in terms of the more obvious and immediate implications, Claiborne suggested that popular repugnance to war did not derive so much from the loss of human life itself. Instead, it was from the consequences of war. "Those who lose their lives in war, lose less than those who suffer the burdens which it lays, not upon the present, but upon future generations." The greatest burdens came in the form of higher taxes and burgeoning national debts. Even though a majority of the congressmen appeared to favor war, according to the Tennesseean's conclusion at the time, he was convinced that the American people opposed it.[24]

The question of American obligations under the Franco-American agreements of 1778 became inescapable as the threat of war persisted. Representatives from the two countries had concluded two pacts in that year, a Treaty of Amity and Commerce and a Treaty of Alliance. In May and July 1798 Congress responded to public pressure by authorizing the seizure of armed French ships, but not commercial vessels. In the interim, Congress debated a measure to suspend commercial intercourse between the United States and France, including French possessions. During the House debates, Claiborne came out in strong support of the measure. First, American merchantmen were being preyed upon simply because the United States could not provide protection. Second, Claiborne reasoned that American revenue actually would increase because American trade with the neutral European countries would increase, including the transport of American goods by European merchantmen to markets in the West Indies. A vote was taken shortly afterward and the measure passed overwhelmingly. Commercial intercourse with France was suspended officially on June 13, 1798. Some three weeks later the House approved by a vote of 47-37 a senate-sponsored bill to declare the two treaties of 1778 with France null and void on the ground that the French government had violated them with impunity.[25] Although most of his colleagues were incensed toward France at the time, Claiborne apparently was not convinced that France's aggressive conduct justified the renunciation of American obligations under the treaties, as reflected by his negative vote. Nonetheless, Claiborne and his fellow Republicans were not at all averse to the principle of regulating American commerce and trade as a means of achieving political and diplomatic leverage over both France and its European foes, much as Jefferson did later as president.

As Congress debated the possibility of a Franco-American war and grudgingly moved toward military preparedness while suspending commercial intercourse with France and authorizing the capture of armed French ships, it also made a bid to deal with suspected security risks in the United States. On May 21, 1798, Congress took up the question of naturalization, with Federalist Congressman Samuel Sewall spearheading a drive to change the naturalization law of 1795. He moved that a declaration of intention be submitted five years before an application for naturalization could be made. When the motion carried, Sewall moved that the residence requirement be extended from five to fourteen years. That motion also carried. He next proposed the insertion of a clause prohibiting any alien from a nation engaged in war with the United States from being admitted to citizenship as long as the war was in progress. Congressman Albert Gallatin of Pennsylvania, who had been born in Switzerland and who later would become President Jefferson's secretary of the treasury, amended the measure to provide that any alien who was a resident of the United States and under its jurisdiction before January 29, 1795, or any alien who arrived after that date and declared an intent to become an American citizen, could be admitted to citizenship. In essence, Gallatin was seeking to strike out the retroactive feature of the Sewall proposal since it included both resident aliens and newcomers, thereby still making it possible for those who arrived after that date and had declared their intent to become American citizens. During the ensuing debates, Congressman Claiborne announced support of the measure, but only if it included the Gallatin amendment. The Sewall motion, if allowed to stand without amendment, would be grossly unfair to the people he represented and would deny to them their legal rights. He spoke of their "peculiar" geographic location, and of his state's having been given representation in the House only a short time earlier. Many persons had failed to take advantage of the naturalization laws of 1790 and 1795 only because they were uninformed of their provisions, owing in large measure to the absence of newspapers and lack of roads. Many loyal Tennesseeans had fought and sacrificed for the United States, and were as much "wedded to the Government of the United States as any men born on American soil." The Gallatin amendment was voted upon and rejected. A proposal to permit aliens who were residents of the United States before 1795 up to two years to become residents was then considered and was defeated by a vote of 39-32. The House agreed to permit such persons to become citizens, provided they declared their intent within one year after the passage of the act. The main motion to extend the residence requirement to fourteen years was passed on the following day.[26] When the bill reached the Senate, the Republicans made a strong bid to reduce the residence requirement to seven years, but they were unable to muster enough support.

Congressman Sewall of Massachusetts, a leading figure in the passage of the Alien Act which originated in the Senate, launched a drive on May 22, 1798, to give the president extraordinary powers over objectionable aliens. Two days later the House agreed to recommit the bill by a vote of 46-44, an action which Claiborne and most Republicans supported. However, the bill was again brought before the House a few weeks later and approved after some debate.[27] When the bill was enacted, it included an Alien Friends Act and an Alien Enemy Act, which gave the president authority to order persons whom he regarded as dangerous aliens to leave the country; if they refused or returned after having departed, the president could have them imprisoned.

The Senate-sponsored Sedition Act followed closely on the heels of the Alien Act. During the House discussions on the measure, Claiborne expressed the belief that the number of libel cases would increase if the bill were enacted. To substantiate his position, he cited legal developments in Great Britain. In libel cases in that country, juries had earlier judged the fact of libel while the courts had determined the law, but more recently the juries had come to judge the law as well as the fact. Claiborne then proposed an amendment that in all cases arising under the Sedition Act, that "the jury who shall try the cause, shall be judges of the law as well as the fact." When Congressman Harper suggested that the amendment was unnecessary because Claiborne's proposal was already in effect, Claiborne responded that it would prevent misunderstandings. Gallatin offered a slight modification of Claiborne's amendment and it was approved by a vote of 67-16. On July 10 the House voted on the main bill and it passed by the narrow vote of 44-41,[28] with most opposition coming from the Republicans.

In mid-December Congressman Harper offered a bill providing for the printing and distribution without cost of 20,000 copies of the Alien and Sedition Acts. Claiborne supported the motion, saying that the information needed dissemination, especially among the people of the West. Often the Westerners received only fragmented and belated accounts of it all, of developments in the nation's capital because of their geographic isolation. With some judges expressing the conviction that the legislation was unconstitutional, Claiborne pointed out that the publication of the Alien and Sedition Acts would convince Americans that Congress had erred in the enactment of such odious legislation. Nevertheless, the Harper motion was defeated.[29]

A few days later Claiborne engaged in a heated exchange with Representative James A. Bayard of Delaware over the Alien and Sedition Acts when the latter severely castigated the Republicans for their opposition to the measures. The aroused Claiborne lashed back at Bayard for his "continued tissue of invective." Because he and other Republicans disapproved of the odious legislation did not imply that they were friends of the French or firebrands who were endeavoring to promote discontent. The laws were simply reprehensible and served as a source of popular discord. He had been an active opponent of the laws' passage, and he would most certainly support any drive to repeal them.[30]

The conduct of a Quaker pacifist, George Logan, caused Congress to extend its legislation for the punishment of certain crimes against the United States. Carrying a private letter from Vice President Jefferson, Logan went on a personal mission to France in 1798. Returning to this country following consultations with members of the French Directory, Logan called on George Washington at Mount Vernon to assure him of France's peaceful intentions. In December Congress acted to block similar efforts by self-appointed diplomats through appropriate legislation. In the course of the debate, Claiborne acknowledged that foreign relations were the responsibility of the executive department; nevertheless, he did not believe that he could sanction punitive measures against private citizens who attempted to use their influence to compose differences between the United States and foreign governments. Congressman Josiah Parker of Virginia later offered an amendment to the proscriptive motion which would allow a private citizen to exercise his individual rights to redress a personal injury sustained from a foreign country. The Parker amendment was approved by a vote of 69-27, with Claiborne voting affirmatively.[31] In its final form the Logan Act of 1799 declared such missions as the one made by Logan a misdemeanor, punishable by a maximum fine of $5,000 and imprisonment up to three years.

Of the several measures emerging during the excitement in anticipation of war with France, the Sedition Act possessed the greatest political overtones. It became, in fact, an ingenious device by which the Federalists were able to embarrass their Republican opponents politically. Matthew Lyon was among those Republicans who experienced Federalist wrath. In February 1799 the Federalists engineered a move to expel Lyon from the House, charging that he was a "malicious, seditious person, and of a depraved mind, and wicked and diabolical disposition." Moreover, he was accused of "wickedly, deceitfully, and maliciously contriving to defame the Government of the United States, and John Adams, . . . and to bring the said Government and President into contempt and disrepute." The vote on Lyon's expulsion was 49-45, with Claiborne and his colleagues constituting the minority who fought to retain him.[32] Lyon, nevertheless, continued to serve in the House since expulsion requires a two-thirds vote of the membership. The accused clearly had been singled out for punishment by the Federalists because he was one of their most outspoken critics. Moreover, he had been a special target of Federalist anger and vitriol from the time of the highly publicized Griswold-Lyon exchange on the House floor.

After Napoleon's dramatic overthrow of the Directory on November 9-10, 1799, Franco-American relations improved appreciably. As the prospect of war receded, Congress began a more objective review of the legislation enacted during the height of the crisis. Thus, on January 28, 1800, a bill was introduced in the House to abolish the second section of the Sedition Act, which prescribed penalties for false and malicious writings against the federal government, president, and Congress. It passsed by a vote of 50-48.[33] This action amounted to an important Republican victory, but some Federalists joined them in the repeal effort.

About a year later, the House brought the Sedition Act under scrutiny. A committee, established to study the feasibility of continuing the act, recommended its retention. As was to be expected, Claiborne argued strongly for repeal, insisting that national sentiment opposed the measure. He argued that the pact posed a threat to the freedom and happiness of the people and was an outrage upon American rights. Moreover, he predicted that popular tranquility would never be restored as long as it remained in force. Following two days of discussion, the lawmakers resolved on January 23, 1801, that the Committee of Revisal and Unfinished Business be directed to draw up a resolution to retain the Sedition Act. The final vote stood at 48-48. The Speaker then cast his vote, breaking the tie and giving his support to the proposal.[34]

How did the country at large react to the Naturalization, Alien and Sedition Acts? Although the extent to which the Federalist-sponsored legislation aroused the American electorate has been exaggerated considerably, it nonetheless encountered a substantial amount of popular opposition. The Kentucky and Virginia Resolutions, drafted by Madison and Jefferson respectively and intended basically to provide a platform for the latter in his presidential bid in 1800, were circulated widely. Segments of the American public briefly looked upon James C. Callender, Thomas Cooper, William Duane, and Matthew Lyon, all victims of the Sedition Act, as popular heroes. The Republican leadership worked assiduously to fan public discontent with the legislation, but with only limited success at best. Jefferson was infinitely more interested in achieving political success in the presidential election than he was in the right or power of the individual states to declare such "palpable and alarming infractions of the constitution" void and of no force.

By the time the presidential campaign began, Franco-American relations had taken a turn for the better after about three years of undeclared warfare. This development, together with the adverse publicity given the Naturalization, Alien and Sedition Acts, boosted the cause of the Republicans, but their position remained precarious. Either a hostile gesture from France or a lively case of sedition would seriously damage the political groundwork laid by the Republicans. Fortunately for them, nothing of the kind occurred, but the election still proved to be especially interesting and exciting. Congressman William Claiborne, reelected to the House of Representatives, was a prominent participant in the political drama. Having earlier carried a modest part of the burden for the Republican party in House debates, the frequently assertive young congressman was yet to perform his single greatest service to his party and country.

The opportunity came with the famous Jefferson-Burr presidential imbroglio—an episode which transcended strict party lines, invited an intraparty split of disastrous proportions, and threatened to engulf the nation in civil war. As the national election of 1800 neared, the Republicans selected Thomas Jefferson and Aaron Burr as their standard bearers. The Federalists ran incumbent President John Adams and Charles C. Pinckney, a former U. S. minister to France whom the French government had stubbornly refused to receive following James

Monroe's recall by President Washington and who was involved in the XYZ Affair. At the time, the Constitution provided merely that the presidential electors should vote for two persons, with no designation of whom they desired for either the presidency or vice presidency. The candidate getting the greatest number of votes, provided that it was a majority, was to be president. Unhappy over President Adams' refusal to call for war against France, the Hamiltonian faction of the Federalist party shrewdly plotted an intraparty coup d'etat. The plan was to have an elector throw away a vote that normally would have been cast for Adams. This would have allowed Pinckney to forge ahead of his running mate and emerge as president. But the election took an unexpected twist. Adams received sixty-five electoral votes, one more than Pinckney. Jefferson and Burr ran ahead of the Federalist candidates, but the two Republicans were tied with seventy-three votes each. The responsibility for selecting between Jefferson and Burr then shifted from the Electoral College to the Federalist-dominated House of Representatives.

Claiborne, like many of his colleagues, was cultivated by the Federalists, who sought to play upon his personal vanity and consequently influence his vote. In effect, if their strategy worked, the Federalists would be able to name the next president. In their blatant bid to influence Claiborne's vote, the Federalist intriguers "insinuated that nature had designed him [Claiborne] for the army; to what command had he not a right to aspire?" As the voting was about to begin, Alexander Hamilton offered the "speculative opinion" that Tennessee would fall in line behind Burr,[35] but Hamilton was wrong. Vote after vote was taken. The atmosphere crackled with tension, and excitement attained a feverish pitch. A number of congressmen, fearful that violence would intrude and shatter the dignity of the legislative chamber, armed themselves with knives and revolvers. But tempers were held under control, and the voting proceeded methodically. Finally, on February 17, 1801, the tie was broken on the thirty-sixth ballot and Jefferson emerged as victor.[36]

The Tennesseean's role was critical to the ultimate outcome of the electoral marathon, of course, because the competing forces had achieved a delicate political balance and were stalemated. As Vincent O. Nolte, a European writer who traveled extensively in the United States, observed, ". . . the vote of . . . William Cole Claiborne . . . turned the scale of the election, and secured

Jefferson's success."[37] At no time during the tense and uncertain months had Claiborne displayed even the faintest hint of indecision and uncertainty. Why this unwavering loyalty? Jefferson, the politician, was fully capable of holding out high promises and concluding a political deal; but there is absolutely no evidence to indicate that Claiborne was approached by Jefferson himself or by Jeffersonian emissaries serving as political pawnbrokers. One factor strongly influencing Claiborne's preference was his commitment to the ideals and principles of the Republican party, as enunciated by Thomas Jefferson as its founding father.

Moreover, it was a personal commitment to the Virginia statesman and politician, strengthened and cemented by Claiborne's years in Congress but probably having its genesis in his earlier contacts with Jefferson while working as an enrolling clerk.

Claiborne's political philosophy had matured and crystallized during his two congressional terms. His attitude and stand on national issues and foreign policy matters, especially as they focused on the American southwest, would be heavily influenced in the years ahead by his Jeffersonian philosophy. He had been among the earliest figures to expound the ideals and principles of the Republican party, and he never tired of his role as party exponent and exemplar, whether in Washington or in the remote and isolated Southwest. Indeed, he had helped to press the offensive which enabled the Republican party to sweep the Federalist opposition from the field of political contention and usher in the long era of Republican supremacy.

Claiborne had managed to maintain only limited and tenuous links with his Tennessee electorate during his years in Philadelphia and Washington because of limited transportation and communications facilities. During one of his infrequent visits to Tennessee, he married Elizabeth ("Eliza") W. Lewis, the daughter of William Terrell Lewis, a prominent Nashville leader. His young bride returned with him, but the two hardly had time to settle into their new life together in the nation's capital. Although they had no inkling of what lay in store for them, a presidential appointment loomed ahead which would necessitate another move. In his new position, he would be able to make practical applications of his political philosophy while emerging as a dominant regional leader.

III

MISSISSIPPI: POLITICS, INDIANS, AND FRONTIER JUSTICE

If Thomas Jefferson's election to the presidency was due in part to the constancy of Congressman William Claiborne, how was he to express his gratitude to the Tennesseean, if at all? Jefferson's record of appointments as president certainly bore out the charges of his critics that he was an ardent practitioner of the fine art of patronage. In this respect he was hardly different from other American presidents of the period; the art merely attained new heights and was practiced with less discrimination several years afterward by Andrew Jackson. Thus young Claiborne might reasonably anticipate some presidential reward for his unwavering support in the face of intense political pressures from maneuvering factions in both major parties. The Federalists, in particular, sensed certain personal weaknesses and attempted to exploit them in Burr's behalf. Claiborne's conduct and demeanor in Congress had reflected considerable personal vanity. Consequently, the Federalists played upon that weakness by holding out the oblique prospect of a military command with its appealing implications of martial splendor and heroism. But Claiborne held fast, his candidate carried the day, and the prospect of political advancement loomed large in the Tennesseean's mind.

Political forces long at work in the remote southwest made it easy for Jefferson to discharge his indebtedness to Claiborne. The Spaniards, having agreed to Pinckney's Treaty in 1795, came to abide by its provisions only very grudgingly. Hence, they did not evacuate Natchez, they did not withdraw south of the thirty-first parallel, nor did they agree to a boundary survey until March 28, 1798. A few days after the Spaniards evacuated Natchez, Congress passed an act to establish the Territory of Mississippi out of the land ceded by Spain under Pinckney's treaty. The newly created territory, claimed both by Georgia and the federal government, included those lands lying between the Chattahoochee and Mississippi rivers from the thirty-first parallel northward to Tennessee. The only significant pockets of settlement in the territory at the time were around Natchez on the Mississippi River and St. Stephens on the Tombigbee River. The act also authorized the president to establish a government for the Mississippi Territory, and to appoint three boundary commissioners to negotiate a settlement of the disputed land claims with Georgia.[1]

According to the terms of the Northwest Ordinance, the administration of the territory in its first stage of government was to consist of a governor, secretary, and three judges. The Adams administration appointed Winthrop Sargent, former secretary of the Northwest Territory (who hoped to return there as governor), chief executive of the Mississippi Territory. A native of Massachusetts and stanch Federalist whose appointment had been confirmed by a vote of 11-10, Sargent did not fit easily or comfortably into the frontier environment. Even his friends were disturbed by his "phlegmatic and austere disposition." His problems were compounded further by his haughty pretensions and ongoing criticisms of local standards of morality which grated on his puritanical conscience. Moreover, Governor Sargent's task was made more difficult by his fellow appointees. John Steele of Virginia was chosen as secretary, but he was unable to assist the governor because of delicate health and mediocre ability. Peter B. Bruin of the Mississippi Territory, William McGuire of Virginia, and Daniel Tilton of New Hampshire were appointed to the judgeships. Of the three, only Bruin was familiar with the people and their problems, but he lacked legal training and experience. Judges McGuire and Tilton did not put in their appearances in the territory until the following year. This forced Sargent, whose health was poor at the time of his own tardy arrival, to rule for some time by executive decree. Virtually all of the appointed officials were subjected increasingly to strong vocal criticisms. Local frictions further compounded the tasks of the Sargent administration.[2]

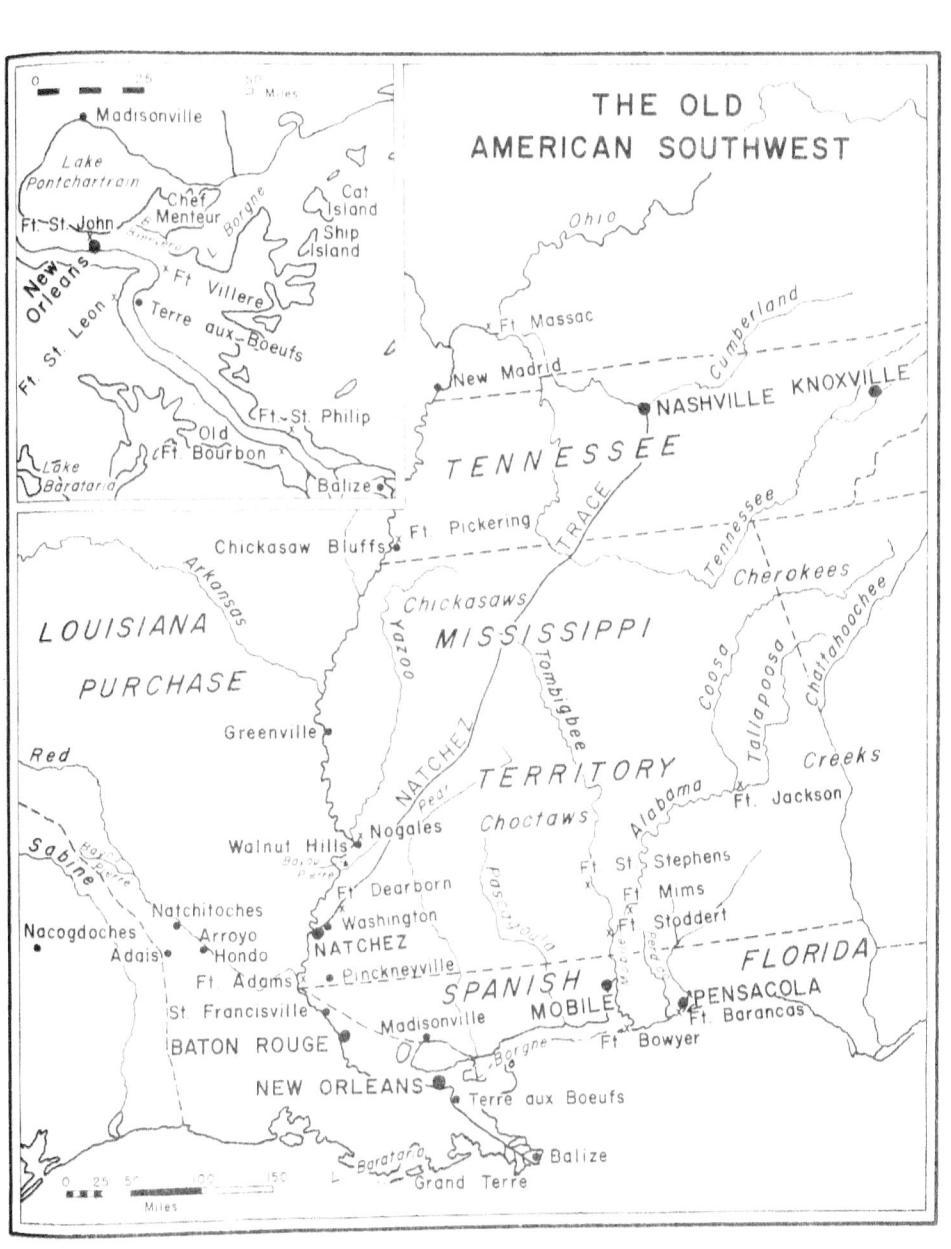

The Old American Southwest

The Mississippi Territory

Within a short time factionalism achieved new levels over the question of Mississippi's advancement to the second stage of government. Under the terms of the Northwest Ordinance, when a territory had a minimum of 5,000 free male inhabitants, the freeholders could choose a representative assembly. Upon meeting, the assembly would then nominate ten persons, from whom the president would select five to serve on a legislative council or upper house. This bicameral body could then enact whatever legislation it chose, subject to veto by the governor. Moreover, the territory would be allowed to send a nonvoting delegate to Congress who could participate in congressional debates and introduce measures. Supported by Governor Sargent, the "richer and better informed" elements, who feared that increased taxes would result, had vigorously opposed this move. Andrew Ellicott, the American commissioner charged with determining the boundary between the Mississippi Territory and Spanish Florida, supported this group and identified himself as Sargent's friend. The partisan Ellicott declared that the opposition faction was, with few exceptions, "composed of the most abandoned, and profligate part of the community, and consists of british [sic] subjects, discontented americans [sic], and fugitives from justice." Jefferson and the Republicans of course refused to accept this Federalist description of the anti-Sargent forces. In Jefferson's view they constituted the "body of the people," and he supported them.[3] Under these circumstances the Republican victory of 1800 made it increasingly clear that Winthrop Sargent's days in the Mississippi Territory were numbered.

As these developments unfolded, Congressman Claiborne was drawn inexorably into the territorial controversy. His interests at this particular moment were those of the typical Republican who gleefully welcomed the opportunity to turn the Federalist rascals out. Moreover, as chairman of the congressional committee on the Mississippi Territory, he became aware of the growing antagonism between Governor Sargent and his supporters and a determined opposition led by Cato West, the son-in-law of Thomas M. Green who shared Pickering County's political leadership with West. At first Claiborne was skeptical of the "committee" of the "West junto" which had selected Narsworthy Hunter as its agent or lobbyist to influence members of Congress against Sargent. In late January 1800 Claiborne pointedly asked Hunter about the composition of the opposition "committee," how it had been chosen, the source of its authority, and the purpose it was intended to serve. Hunter responded that it had been chosen by the "principal inhabitants" of Mississippi at a special meeting in early July of the preceding year for the purpose of seeking a solution to their "unhappy situation." The committee, presumably acting on instructions from its constituents, had first petitioned Governor Sargent for a redress of alleged grievances. Finally, on October 2 the disgruntled committee members sent a petition to Congress in which they requested that Mississippi be advanced to the second stage of government. At the same time the petitioners included a bill of personal, political, and legal accusations against the governor and territorial judges.[4] The petition was laid before the House by Congressman Claiborne, who apparently had decided that the committee was legitimate after having discussed the matter with Hunter. With this, the national lawmakers began displaying a livelier interest in the territorial imbroglio. Party affiliation largely determined whether Governor Sargent was supported or attacked. During the course of an attack on Sargent, Representative Thomas T. Davis of Kentucky moved quickly to the heart of the controversy by exclaiming: "The sun of Federalism is nearly set—not three months, and it sets forever." Following a motion to present the petition to the president, with papers, documents, and witnesses to confirm the charges alleged, Claiborne tried unsuccessfully to delete that part of the motion calling for supporting evidence. He argued that such incriminating evidence had already been provided and therefore nothing more was needed. Although he did not wish to punish an innocent person, he said, testimony "forbids the indulgence of such a fear." Claiborne concluded dramatically, to the applause of partisans in the gallery: "Let gentlemen who hesitate on this subject, recollect that a delay of justice is often equal to a denial of it." The motion to present the petition to the president was approved, and a committee, of which Claiborne was a member, was appointed to investigate Governor Sargent's conduct. The committee later reported that Sargent was guilty of some irregular practices but it found no evidence of criminal intent. Shortly afterward the House rejected, by a vote of 38-40, a resolution that it decline to consider further complaints of maladministration by the Sargent administration. Although the succeeding vote was close, the scales were tipped against Sargent. Moreover, Congress approved the advancement of the Mississippi Territory to the second stage of government on May 10, 1800, although some questioned whether the territory had the requisite 5,000 free male inhabitants.[5]

Although aware of the continuing erosion of his position locally and nationally, Governor Sargent nonetheless held on grimly a few months longer. He stubbornly insisted that the majority of the territorial population did not approve the petitions. In a letter to President John Adams on June 20, 1800, the governor spoke of the calumny to which he had been subjected by the West-Green faction, adding that a "federal governour" was "to *them* a most obnoxious Character." He related that Claiborne had passed through Natchez on his return to the national capital for the next congressional session, and that he had detected "no Abatement of his [Claiborne's] Enmity to the general Government." On April 3, 1801, he told Secretary of State James Madison that he did not wish to attribute improper or impure motives to Claiborne and Davis; however, " if *they* have not been very grossly deceived they have most certainly been *so* imposed upon." While recognizing the futility of his position but not wishing to appear to capitulate to his enemies, Sargent informed Madison of his plans to take a leave of absence. He justified the indulgence on the grounds of almost constant duty since the Revolutionary War, improved Franco-American relations, and poor health. Having made the necessary preparations, Sargent left the Mississippi Territory on the same day and the acting territorial secretary, John Steele, temporarily assumed the duties of acting governor.[6] For Sargent the battle had ended; he would not return to Natchez and Bellemont Plantation in an official capacity. The Republican victory at the polls in 1800 had determined his political fate. In fact, Jefferson had informed him by letter before he took the leave of absence that expediency dictated a leadership change. The president added that his decision was the consequence of varied and delicate considerations but the basic reason for the change was a lack of harmony between the Sargent administration and the territorial inhabitants.[7]

Congressman William Claiborne's selection as the Republican replacement for Federalist Winthrop Sargent was common knowledge in the territory several months before the official appointment in May 1801. Indeed, the territorial legislature expressed its approval of Claiborne's selection in a resolution sent to Jefferson about five months earlier. Jefferson responded that the task of judging those in office was always painful, but in the case of Sargent, the "grounds of judgment . . . were such as to leave no room to doubt the line of duty which I had to pursue." Claiborne, he added, would avail himself of every opportunity to promote the happiness, prosperity, safety, and welfare of the people of Mississippi. [8]

Why was Claiborne given the appointment and why did he accept it? Jefferson's desire to discharge his political indebtedness for Claiborne's steady support during the uneasy and nervous days of the Jefferson-Burr marathon probably was a factor but not an overriding one. Claiborne was a fellow Republican, virtually a prerequisite to appointment, and Jefferson clearly intended to appoint a member of his own party to the post. The appointment of Claiborne was made easier because Jefferson, who had known Claiborne from the latter's early days as a congressional enrollment clerk, was impressed by the young congressman's leadership potential and ability to adequately and conscientiously discharge the responsibilities with which he was charged. While making every possible effort to serve the Mississippians to the very best of his ability, Claiborne at the same time would remain steadfast in his political commitment and would do his utmost to establish the supremacy of the Republican party in the territory. In a sense, this was but a part of Jefferson's greater plan to make his party preeminent nationally while carrying out the aims and objectives of the "Revolution of 1800." Furthermore, Jefferson was influenced by the knowledge that Claiborne himself was a product of the frontier. Claiborne had established himself politically as a frontier leader, and he knew and understood the surging frontier peoples and the problems confronting them.

Finally, if Claiborne's political and administrative horizons were not unlimited, neither were the challenges and responsibilities of the remote and isolated post at the time. That is, if Claiborne's talents were not sufficient to merit appointment to a senior post at the national level, his abilities were still substantial enough to enable him to serve with some distinction at a lesser level.

Claiborne's reasons for accepting the appointment are less discernible. There is certainly nothing to indicate that his political support in Tennessee had eroded significantly or that his political future seemed in doubt. Service to the Republican party might well have appealed to him since, as governor, he would be able to implement his party's principles and objectives. Moreover, having launched his political career on the frontier, he probably viewed the appointment as an opportunity to advance his political aspirations in a region of the country which would become increasingly important politically with the passsage of time. In a sense, Claiborne also typified the itinerant politician who roamed widely in an often never-ending search for the proper political niche. The developing areas of the frontier were favorite hunting grounds for these peripatetic aspirants. In any event, Claiborne once more demonstrated that he knew the right people and was in the right place at the right time to advance his political aspirations.

While Claiborne was still in Congress, Governor Sargent had come increasingly to regard him as an adversary who was in league with the anti-Sargent forces in Mississippi. He also hinted without elaboration that Claiborne opposed him for selfish and impure reasons. Although Claiborne laid the petitions of the dissident West faction before Congress, he did not wage a personal campaign among his congressional colleagues to discredit Sargent. Rather, Claiborne's motives were preponderantly the more impersonal motives of the partisan Republican, jubilant that the political millenium was dawning at last and that Federalist heads were about to roll.

Claiborne's commission—a recess appointment—was dated May 25, 1801, but he did not receive official notification from Secretary of State Madison until July 10. Six months elapsed before he actually arrived in Natchez to assume his new duties. In his letter of acceptance on August 2, he expressed modest feelings of inadequacy and promised to exercise "all possible dispatch" in getting to his new assignment. However, he indicated that he probably would be unable to leave until late September or early October. In mid-September he wrote to Madison from Knoxville that he would leave for his assignment within a few days, and flattered himself that the "public service has not as yet sustained injury by my absence." Continuing westward to Nashville, the Claibornes visited with Elizabeth's family and made additional preparations for the journey to Natchez. The Claiborne party, consisting of Claiborne, the lovely "Eliza" who was described as a "tall graceful and handsome lady of some education and talent," one of Elizabeth's sisters, and several domestic servants, finally left Nashville by boat on October 8. Unfavorable weather conditions and apprehension about what lay in store for them in an isolated land surrounded by Spanish territories and by hostile Indian tribes produced an understandable sense of trepidation. The Cumberland, Ohio, and Mississippi rivers were lower than usual, and high winds added to the dangers of the trip. Claiborne observed that much of the land along the Mississippi River was very fertile and well suited to agriculture; he also noted that there were few signs of human life on either side of the river. Only three settlements dotted the western, or Spanish, side of the Mississippi between the mouth of the Ohio and Natchez, a distance he estimated at about eight hundred miles. Claiborne halted briefly at New Madrid, the largest of the three settlements, where the Spanish commandant cordially received him. The party then resumed its lonely journey.[9] The eastern, or American, side of the Mississippi was even more desolate. The first settlement south of the Ohio was Fort Pickering, located at Chickasaw Bluffs. The only other "improvement" was at Walnut Hills, then known as Fort Nogales and later as Fort McHenry. Caliborne casually made these observations, whiling away the hours as the boat slowly proceeded southward. Finally, on November 23, after forty-six weary days of travel, the new governor arrived in Natchez and immediately took charge from the acting governor.[10]

Congress had established the Mississippi Territory three years earlier, after Spain finally agreed to a boundary survey. When Georgia ceded its western land claims to the federal government in 1802, the eastern boundary was extended northward to Tennessee and the territory embraced the present states of Alabama and Mississippi. The territory was sparsely populated and most of the inhabitants lived in the Natchez district near the Mississippi River and along the lower Tombigbee River north of Spanish-occupied Mobile. Settlers were initially reluctant to migrate to the newly established territory. Cheap lands were still readily available in Georgia and Tennessee, and direct communications with the settled areas in the Mississippi Territory were largely limited to rivers and a few primitive trails. Moreover, the presence of the powerful Cherokee and Creek tribes, in particular, and the threat posed by the Spaniards to the south discouraged settlement. However, the cotton gin had been introduced into the lower Mississippi six years before Claiborne's arrival, and the consequent increase in demand for cotton and cotton-producing lands would lead shortly to substantial population increases. At the time of Claiborne's arrival in Natchez, the territory was occupied mainly by American royalists driven there from Georgia and the Carolinas during the American Revolution, American newcomers, and by a limited number of Spaniards who remained when the Spanish government agreed in 1798 to relinquish claim to the lands north of the thirty-first parallel.

The isolated and remote Mississippi Territory figured to some extent in Federalist-Republican atmospherics and in American policies toward Spain, especially as they concerned the Southwest and the navigation of the Mississippi River. Although conveying a surface appearance of self-effacing modesty and aloofness from partisan politics, the ambitious young governor did not hesitate to advance Republican interests at Federalist expense, or to exploit Spanish weaknesses and uncertainties that would work to the advantage of the United States. Claiborne was also aware of lingering separatist sentiments and popular doubts in the region about the national government's commitment to western issues and concerns. As territorial governor, he endeavored to remove the doubts and uncertainties and to reassure his constituency of the newly established Jefferson administration's interest.

Administrative and governmental affairs had ground to a virtual halt by the time Claiborne arrived in Natchez. John Steele had been almost totally ineffective as acting governor and had declined to sign a number of territorial measures. The judiciary still was not functioning effectively, due mainly to continuing absenteeism among the territorial judges who tardily assumed their duties, and were "loath to remain on the job, and eager to leave." The territorial lawmakers displayed little inclination to cooperate closely with the new governor. Moreover, Claiborne was new and he badly needed a "honeymoon period" in which to familiarize himself with the political climate and crosscurrents, but local political forces were not disposed to be so generous. Claiborne was further handicapped by his failure to recognize that "the revolution of 1800 in Mississippi was as much an attack upon the office of the governor as it was a revolt against the personality of Sargent."[11] Consequently, when it became clear that Caliborne fully intended to provide assertive leadership as governor, local leaders attempted to frustrate his efforts.

The twenty-six-year-old governor stepped suddenly into a local political struggle which he had not anticipated. In early September he had written to Madison from Knoxville that political rancor was dissipating in Mississippi.[12] In view of his earlier political experience and personal involvement in the territorial dispute that culminated in Governor Winthrop Sargent's removal, this opinion constituted an unconscionable optimism or naivete. Moreover, he had aligned himself loosely with Cato West and the dissident elements in their sustained drive to have Sargent removed from office. Consequently, when Claiborne arrived in Natchez, he had to contend with "ready-made enemies and with friends hungry for patronage,"[13] as well as a refractory constituency.

In his maiden address before the general assembly, nine days after his arrival, the governor appealed for political harmony. But within two months he conceded that his fond hope of political unanimity had diminished considerably. He then sought consolation in the knowledge that the opposing parties had formed prior to his appointment. Maybe, he speculated, he would be able to act independently of them or possibly win them over by providing firm and impartial administration.[14]

Elections to the territorial legislature afforded Claiborne an improved political perspective and brought into sharper focus the territory's emerging but still somewhat murky political alignments. As the campaign gained momentum, the seemingly startled governor told Madison that the political flames were quite evident. Although he had informed Madison earlier that there were a "few domestic factions," he now exclaimed that party spirit was more rancorous than anything he had witnessed in the states, and added that "This Tempest of popular Passions" would persist until the elections were concluded.[15] The so-called Winthrop Sargent-John Steele faction, representing a heterogeneous collection of people, opposed the territorial administration of the new governor. Steele proved to be a great source of opposition and irritation by virtue of his position as territorial secretary. Indeed, Steele, himself a Federalist, had the temerity to use his office as an opposition headquarters, much to Claiborne's frustration and annoyance. When Steele's term as secretary ended in May 1802, President Jefferson refused to reappoint him. Many Federalists were in the Sargent-Steele camp, of course, along with the usual number of disappointed officeseekers. Moreover, Claiborne's transfer of the territorial capital from Natchez, a Federalist bastion, to Washington, a little village located about six miles north of Natchez, understandably affronted the business community. Segments of the legal profession became incensed over the policies and codes of the judiciary and certain personalities associated with it. Much of this controversy swirled around Seth Lewis of Massachusetts and Tennessee who had replaced William McGuire as chief justice in May 1800. Lewis was regarded as an able justice, but he had been appointed by

President Adams and elements of the legislature harassed the Federalist judge mercilessly in an effort to force his resignation. The judicial controversy, in fact, had prompted Sargent to return briefly to the territory and fan the flames of partisan controversy. In addition, upon learning of Claiborne's preference for the militia, retired and disbanded professional soldiers gravitated to the enemy camp. On the other side of the political coin, Claiborne enjoyed the support of the Republicans generally and the West-Green element more specifically. However, Claiborne's moderation in the dispensation of political patronage caused him to lose the support of much of the West-Green group, although West continued to serve as territorial secretary in the Claiborne administration following his appointment to replace John Steele in the spring of 1802. Further support derived from the "governor's placemen" and "reformed Federalists," whose support Claiborne cultivated, as well as the "back country gentry." [16]

As Claiborne had predicted on the eve of the election, the opposition registered impressive gains at the polls. A sufficient number of their candidates were swept into office to enable them to seize control of the house of representatives. The appointive legislative council remained pro-administration. Any faint hope that Claiborne had of erasing political differences and being universally accepted thereby flickered out with the election returns of July 1802.[17] Just as Sargent had been obliged to fight an unceasing, unrelenting battle against his resourceful and determined political adversaries, Claiborne's first few months in Mississippi clearly indicated that his administration would function under the same handicap.

While Claiborne had been caught up in the "Tempest of popular Passions" produced by the election, he could not allow election issues to monopolize his time and detract from his broader political responsibilities. The problems of a surging frontier Mississippi obviously would not permit a holiday. The task of maintaining stable relations with the Indians demanded patience, understanding, and tact on the part of the governor who also occupied the post of superintendent of Indian affairs. A few days after his arrival in Natchez, a perplexed Claiborne queried Madison about his duties within that realm while pointing out that the question had been a source of embarrassment to his predecessor. Secretary of War Henry Dearborn, whose jurisdiction included Indian affairs, responded. President

Jefferson was interested in the welfare of the Indians, he indicated, adding that the Indians should be encouraged to engage in husbandry and domestic manufactures. Four days later Dearborn authorized Claiborne to appoint agents to assist him in the administration of Indian affairs.[18] Aside from this, Dearborn apparently assumed that Claiborne was cognizant of the basic, if implicit, responsibilities of the post.

Maintaining peace between the Mississippi settlers and Indians was Claiborne's primary responsibility as superintendent of Indian affairs. It was in itself a formidable task. That animosities should develop with the Indians was accepted as an almost natural accompaniment to the white man's westward progression. Usually, after displaying initially a spirit of friendliness and desire to cooperate, the Indians came to harbor a smouldering resentment toward the constantly increasing encroachments of the white settlers. To the whites, the philosophy that "the only good Indian is a dead Indian" developed rapidly and won almost universal acceptance. Moreover, this philosophy afforded the whites a convenient rationalization for indignities and injustices heaped upon the Indians. Placed between these opposing and formidable forces was a young and inexperienced governor with only a very limited acquaintance with the frontier.

The white man's insatiable desire to possess Indian lands was the root cause of tension and conflict, but Indian indebtedness also conveniently lent itself to white designs. Moreover, Governor Claiborne quickly became a party to the white man's conspiracies without feeling any real sense of guilt. In June 1802 Dearborn wrote to Claiborne that he had learned through John McKee, the Choctaw agent, that Panton, Leslie and Company of Pensacola was negotiating with the Choctaws for a tract of land to erase the tribe's indebtedness to the company. McKee apparently supported the plan, which obviously irked Dearborn, who remarked that McKee should have known that governmental authorization would be necessary. Furthermore, Dearborn stated that McKee should "have been aware of the extreme impropriety of permitting foreigners," meaning the Scottish-owned Panton, Leslie and Company which continued its trading activities under Spanish auspices following the British transfer of Florida to Spain in 1783, "to possess a large tract of country among any of our Indian nations." Dearborn instructed Claiborne to inquire from Silas Dinsmoor, who succeeded McKee as Choctaw agent, about the extent of the indebtedness, the quality of the land, and the proposed settlement. Further, he wished to know if a tract of land could be obtained along the navigable waters of the Alabama and Tombigbee rivers. If so, Dearborn pointed out, Congress might conceivably authorize the president to "accept it in behalf of the United States" and pay off the Choctaw debt to the mercantile company. In short, the federal government was proposing to outflank Panton, Leslie and Company. Claiborne then notified Dinsmoor of the government's interest, saying that the president would "probably" buy the land if the Choctaws offered it on modest terms. Keenly aware of Choctaw sensitivity to the proposal, Claiborne advised Dinsmoor to approach them "with delicacy and caution lest the jealousy of the Choctaws might be aroused, and the opinion received that the United States coveted their lands."[19]

Three days later, Claiborne wrote to Dearborn that the company had made an unreasonable proposal to the Choctaws. As far as the governor was concerned, the United States had "sufficiently indulged" Panton, Leslie and Company by allowing it to trade within the limits of this country and, therefore, the "indulgence" should be withdrawn. Claiborne's impatience with the mercantile company derived from the interests of the national government, as reflected in Dearborn's directives, as well as a fear that the company would be in competition with a factory, or trading post, that he was establishing in the Choctaw country.[20] Although the Choctaws and other Indian tribes ultimately gave way to the unremitting pressures, competition among the white land-grabbers, whether Panton, Leslie and Company, the American land companies, or the federal government temporarily buttressed their staying power.

The ingenious tactical approach employed by the mercantile company was not lost on the young and aggressive governor. Stimulated by the Choctaw experience, he sounded out the Chickasaw tribe through Samuel Mitchell, the Chickasaw agent. If the Chickasaw government would assume the debts of its individual citizens, it might then pay off the indebtedness through the sale of some Chickasaw land holdings. Knowing that the Chickasaws were just as sensitive as the Choctaws about the land aspirations of the whites, the governor hurriedly informed Mitchell that he personally opposed the plan. Yet the prospects were so appealing that Claiborne only momentarily concealed his eagerness. In mid-summer 1802 he wrote to Mitchell that the president might be "willing" to accept land in payment of the Chickasaw indebtedness to the United States. More specifically, Claiborne was interested in lands lying adjacent to or in close proximity to the Mississippi River, adding that "a cession of the Chickasaw Claim to certain Lands adjacent to the big River would best answer both parties." In another instance, Claiborne alluded to some land located in the Duck River country of central Tennessee whose ownership was being contested between the Cherokees and Chickasaws. Declaring that the latter's claims were of "long and good standing"—both tribes had signed treaties with the United States but relations between the Chickasaws and the American settlers were particularly friendly—Claiborne instructed Mitchell to make an inquiry into the quality of the land, and to determine the Chickasaw conditions for sale.[21]

Claiborne was in Mississippi for only a short time, and his administration consummated no great land transactions, but it was obvious that Claiborne learned quickly. His attitude typified the frontier approach to Indian lands. If it were possible to seize upon Indian ignorance or helplessness to deprive the tribes of their lands, the governor did so with alacrity. Whether the lands belonged to the Chickasaws, Choctaws, Creeks, or to other tribes, friendly or otherwise, was of no consequence. It was not a matter of conscience or morality. Indeed, to profit at Indian expense was to the frontiersman a source of personal pride, just as it was for the Yankee trader who put in at the port of Canton to "take" the unwary "heathen" Chinese.

Another proverbial source of contention and misunderstanding emanated from the sale of whisky to the Indians. When Claiborne inquired about his duties as superintendent of Indian affairs, he spoke of the Choctaws committing depredations upon the property of white settlers. According to Claiborne, the Indians imbibed freely and then became "abusive and viciously inclined." But the governor was not the only one to express concern. Some of the chiefs of the Indian nations appealed to President Jefferson to suppress the sale of "ardent spirits" to their people. Congress subsequently authorized the president to comply with the request. Shortly afterward, the secretary of war instructed Claiborne to restrict any trader who sold whisky to the Indians, although he neglected to tell him how it might be done.[22] Yet the task of preventing the whites from selling whisky to the Indians, or of preventing the Indians from buying it, was a formidable one, to say the least. In January 1803 Samuel Mitchell, the Chickasaw agent, informed Dearborn that he had tried for five years to get the Indian leaders to prevent their people from buying "firewater," but the chiefs had repeatedly responded that the task was beyond them. They admitted candidly that they had lost control of their braves. And often the Indian agents were themselves powerless. The Indians sometimes bought whisky from boats plying the Mississippi, and the Indian agents were not empowered to interrupt the sales. Moreover, some whites and Indians maintained taverns along the highway between Natchez and Nashville. While the taverners were ordered to sell whisky only to the whites, enforcement was virtually a physical impossibility. Even if the governor denied offenders the privilege of buying liquor supplies, taverners could still acquire them from boats on the Mississippi and at the Spanish settlements on the western side of that river.[23] Claiborne tried conscientiously to prevent the whites from selling liquor to the Indians, but he confessed to Silas Dinsmoor a few months before he left Mississippi that he had been unable to prevent "bad men" from engaging in the illicit traffic. Recognizing his failure, he asked Dinsmoor to confer with the Choctaw chiefs and request that they prevent their people from coming to the white settlements in great numbers.[24] By controlling Indian visitations, he might, at least, prevent the eruption of a major incident.

The "frequent and oppressive" visits of the Choctaws to Natchez, together with improper conduct by some red visitors had produced feelings of resentment and uneasiness among white settlers. The Choctaws continued to pour into Natchez in increasing numbers so that some two hundred to three hundred Choctaw men, women, and children were encamped in white neighborhoods around Natchez by the spring of 1802. The unwanted visitors then sustained themselves mainly by theft and plunder. Complaints of stolen horses, cattle, corn, and vegetables flooded the governor's desk. In an effort to head off a serious clash, the exasperated Claiborne had some lingering Choctaw stragglers, whom he charged with being pests and vagabonds, brought to Government House, where he addressed them. He began his talk on a lofty and general plane, frequently using loquacious expressions intended to appeal to the Indian mind. The young governor expressed hope that the existing friendship between the United States and the Choctaw nation would endure as long as the mountains stood and the rivers flowed. Thus dispensing with the preliminaries, Claiborne shifted into the role of the benevolent parent who feels the necessity of lecturing wayward children. The errant Choctaws had not been sent by their chieftains, he scolded, but had come to imbibe and spend their time in idleness. Meanwhile, the white community was complaining loudly of stolen property and, if anything was stolen, he vowed that he would conduct a systematic search of their camps. If stolen properties were found among the stragglers, the guilty parties would be punished according to the white man's law. Therefore, he advised them to cease drinking because it would transform them into "Fools and Old Women." Instead, they should return to their homes and earn bread for their families. After all, the farming season had arrived and they should be planting their crops. Finally, if they accepted his advice, he would give them provisions for their return, but if they remained, they would get nothing.[25]

The governor's success in dealing with the Choctaw stragglers was more apparent than real. In early June 1802 Claiborne wrote to John McKee that the problem had been resolved and that the people of Natchez were not as "embarrassed" by the Indian visits as before. A now more tolerant and expansive Claiborne even hinted that the people of Natchez were partially responsible for what had happened. But by autumn the problem was again before Claiborne. Daniel Grafton reported that several Choctaws had set up camp near one of his cornfields and were slaughtering his cattle. The governor asked David Berry, his interpreter, to go among the Indians and ask them to appear before him. If they refused, Berry was not to allow them to be abused. When the Indians refused the invitation, as Claiborne apparently anticipated, the governor sent them a message. They were informed that he did not allow his people to "treat the red man amiss," and he certainly would not permit the reverse. To forgive and forget would be possible, but only if the Choctaws returned to their homes and committed no further mischief.[26] By June of the following year, Claiborne was back where he had started about a year earlier. Livestock was being killed and fields were being plundered. In a letter to Dinsmoor, Claiborne acknowledged that part of the trouble emanated from "bad men" selling whisky to the Indians, but he directed Dinsmoor to solicit a plan from the Choctaw chiefs for controlling the visits of their people to the white settlements. While he did not wish to forbid Indian visits to Natchez, he suggested that only a chief or warrior of integrity who was a friend of the United States should come. When a qualified Choctaw wished to visit Natchez, he should inform Dinsmoor, who, in turn, would notify Claiborne.[27]

Even though the governor and his Indian agents remained alert and watchful, isolated instances of violence occasionally erupted. When they did, Claiborne attempted to resolve them at once. In dealing with individual cases, however, Claiborne's approach was similar to that of other frontier leaders, except that he seems to have shown more concern and appreciation of the Indian's position than some of his contemporaries. He was prone to offer token material rewards and compensations for losses or injustices to the Indians, which they came to expect. That is, Indian injuries and deaths were frequently translated into compensatory dollars. For example, a Choctaw chief called Hooshee Hoomah, or Red Bird, reported that the family of a Choctaw warrior killed earlier in Kentucky was contemplating revenge. The chief recommended presents to the family to erase "this debt of blood," to which Claiborne agreed. After consulting with his agent, Dinsmoor, and later with Secretary of War Dearborn, the latter authorized gifts amounting to some $200, which satisfied the relatives.[28]

Governor Claiborne seized upon the case of the murdered Choctaw warrior in an effort to head off a problem that was rapidly attaining serious proportions. He suggested that Dinsmoor use the incident to protest to the Choctaw leaders about the outrages their people were committing along the Wilderness Road, or Natchez Trace. The agent complied, but the chiefs complained that they did not have the power to take punitive action against offenders. Dinsmoor's offer to assist the chiefs in enforcing their authority excited some alarm among the Choctaw leaders, who hastily declined. Nonetheless, Claiborne believed that the offer had the desired effect and that it would restrain potential offenders. But if more violence erupted along the Wilderness Road, the governor warned that "an example ought and must be made."[29]

Another means by which the governor sought to curb violence along the highway between Nashville and Natchez was to appeal for assistance from the more pacific Chickasaws. In a letter to Samuel Mitchell, the Chickasaw agent, Claiborne cited several acts of violence committed on the Wilderness Road, including the death of an Indian at Natchez Landing, and instructed Mitchell to solicit the assistance of the Chickasaws in curbing the more precipitate Choctaws. The Chickasaws were reminded that "the path of the Cumberland" had been a peaceful one, and that the governor grieved when blood was spilled. Claiborne then invoked Chickasaw support to protect "the weary and defenseless traveller." About two months later, Claiborne told Mitchell that he was pleased to learn that the Chickasaws disapproved of the conduct of the more volatile Creeks and Choctaws. It was a source of consolation, he declared, to know that travelers were finding safety and protection among the friendlier Chickasaws. Claiborne reported to Dearborn in June 1803 that the depredations committed along the Wilderness Road had been exaggerated and that travelers could use the highway with some sense of security.[30]

As Claiborne sought to prevent Indian outrages, he also offered support to Indians who became victims of white outrages. In mid-1803 the governor suggested to Dinsmoor that compensation should be provided for some Indian property stolen by whites. However, he pointed out that the federal government would assume obligation only if the offender were unable to offer compensation himself and provided satisfaction or revenge had not been sought through force by the Indians. Claiborne instructed Dinsmoor to make the necessary compensations as quickly as possible since time often became a critical factor. At the same time, Dinsmoor should utilize the occasion, Claiborne shrewdly proposed, to remind the chiefs of properties taken from whites traveling along the Wilderness Road, and to inform them that they would be held responsible for depredations committed upon white travelers.[31]

Governor Claiborne tried to provide travel accommodations, as well as safety, for travelers on the Wilderness Road. He directed Dinsmoor to visit the Choctaws and persuade them to permit the whites to provide accommodations every twenty-five miles along the highway. Each white person participating in such enterprise should be allowed to lease several hundred acres of land from the Indians, and to form a partnership with an Indian selected by his tribe. If the Choctaws agreed, the federal government would provide financial support to construct a small house and stable at each place. The Choctaws would benefit from the profits realized, Claiborne added hopefully, in addition to learning more about agriculture and the household arts.[32]

Governor Claiborne made the same overture to the Chickasaws in a written "talk" on October 5, 1803. He apologized for his inability to personally confer with them but stated that his busy schedule in Natchez at the time precluded it. As a preliminary, he assured them lamely and condescendingly that he would not give them advice, "but such as a father would give his Children." Having inquired concerning the reasons that the Chickasaws had not been settling in greater numbers along the highway leading to Nashville, he then offered his proposal. Hurriedly denying that the whites coveted Chickasaw land holdings, he added weakly that they wished to lease a part of the Indian lands to benefit the Chickasaws and to provide accommodations for travelers. The Chickasaws indicated a willingness to build taverns, as Claiborne desired, but they declined any partnership with the whites. The disappointed governor wrote to them in October, saying that provisions would be inadequate and "accommodations indifferent" if they alone built the stations. Never one to give up easily, Claiborne asked Mitchell to use his influence among the Chickasaws. Between his "talk" and the agent's influence, he still hoped to win Indian approval for the project.[33] However, another assignment prevented Claiborne from implementing his plans.

While Governor Claiborne was encouraging the Indians to cooperate in the construction and operation of taverns along the Wilderness Road, he also actively promoted the establishment of government-operated factories, or trading posts, which when well-run were popular among the Indians. Shortly after his arrival in Mississippi, he corresponded with the secretary of war about the best location for a factory for the Choctaws. He finally chose a site on the Tombigbee River, near the mouth of the Alabama. In support of his decision to locate it there, he pointed out that it would discourage trade with Mobile and Pensacola, "which interferes considerably with the arrangements of our Government, to introduce the benefits of civilization among the Choctaws." Yet Claiborne questioned whether the Spaniards would permit the Americans to use the Mobile River to supply the post, but the governor regarded it as a calculated "risque." After much debate and the arrival of a consignment of goods for the factory, the governor ordered Joseph Chambers, the factor, to go to the site of the proposed factory at Fort St. Stephens on the Tombigbee River. General James Wilkinson had been instructed to repair the buildings there and to provide a guard of about a dozen men. Claiborne admonished Chambers to extend every courtesy and civility to the Indians when they visited the factory.

In June 1803 Claiborne reported to Dearborn that the factory was open and doing business. Although Chambers was concerned about possible competition from Panton, Leslie and Company, the confident Claiborne lightly brushed aside his agent's concern.[34]

Thomas Peterkin operated a trading post for the Chickasaws which had been erected earlier at Chickasaw Bluffs. The tribe came to view the factory with suspicion and subsequently inaugurated a partial boycott. Claiborne wrote to the regular agent, Mitchell, and directed him to explain to the Chickasaws that the factory had been established primarily for their benefit. Possibly feeling the competition which was being provided by private traders, the governor told Mitchell to apprise the Indians that better terms could be had from the trading post. In fact, he said, some items, such as iron tools, were being offered to the Chickasaws at about their original cost to the federal government. Sensitive to Chickasaw criticism of the factory and of their obvious reluctance to patronize the trading post, Claiborne asserted that they should at least try out the factory before condemning it. To encourage trade, Claiborne asked Mitchell to tell the Chickasaws of the many advantages that had accrued to the Cherokees from their trading post at Tellico, located about forty-five miles southwest of Knoxville.[35]

Governor Claiborne carefully supervised the trading posts and protected them from competition. Looking upon private traders with disfavor, Claiborne usually declined to grant licenses to them until their applications had first been approved by the factory supervisors.[36] Private traders were very difficult to supervise and often sold proscribed goods, but the chief reason for Claiborne's resentment of them seems to have emanated from the fact that they were in competition with Chambers and Peterkin, the and Chickasaw factory supervisors. Thus, Claiborne used his position to protect the factories and to expand their trade with the Indians. But in doing this, he also afforded the Indians some protection from unscrupulous traders and thereby reduced the possibility of a major clash or misunderstanding between the whites and Indians.

The establishment of factories at Fort St. Stephens and Chickasaw Bluffs was only a part of Claiborne's greater plan to improve white-red relations and to help the Indians to help themselves. In early 1803 he instructed Dinsmoor to introduce husbandry and domestic manufactures among the Indians.

Weavers should be employed to teach them to weave, and wheelwrights should teach the young males how to make wheels. Agricultural implements should be provided and medical supplies should be secured for them. The governor, who was actually implementing President Jefferson's benevolent Indian policies, hoped that Dinsmoor would be the principal agent in "removing the dormant faculties of the Choctaws and in reclaiming his poor and humble people from a State of Savage Ignorance." Mitchell hopefully would serve in the same capacity among the kindred Chickasaws. While teaching the Indians various skills, Claiborne's agents sometimes distributed goods among them, recognizing that it would be some time, at best, before the Indians would be able to enjoy any real degree of economic independence. But in dispensing goods to the Indian tribes, the whites traditionally had given the Indian chiefs preferential treatment. Claiborne renounced this politically expedient practice; instead, he directed his agents to be "most liberal to the old and helpless." [37] To Claiborne, humanitarianism transcended petty politics.

Although he sometimes warned his agents and factors about Indian fickleness, Governor Claiborne foresaw the strengthening of bonds between the several Indian tribes and the federal government. He predicted the transfer of Louisiana to the United States would insure a closer association because it would force the Indians to "court the friendship of that power, which has no longer any rivals within their reach." The Indians would benefit from the American system, he declared, and even the Choctaws would have nothing to fear if they conducted themselves with friendship and sincerity. The Indians would soon enjoy incorruptible justice and legal equality, he promised, "which affords equal protection to the humblest Indian Stranger that traverses our pathless woods, and the proudest Captain in our Country."[38]

While Governor Claiborne tried to improve the lot of the Indians and to create greater understanding between Indians and whites, he also attempted to provide both with greater security through the establishment of law and order. But the country was sparsely settled, and law enforcement was difficult. The number of law enforcement officers was never sufficient, and their salaries were often too low to attract competent personnel. Few courts existed, and they were usually convened at irregular intervals. Jails were usually flimsy structures and few in number. The sheriff of Adams County wrote to Claiborne, for example, to complain and make him aware of the handicaps under which the sheriff's office was functioning. The jail badly needed repairs, he said, but repairs were too expensive. One prisoner had escaped and other inmates could have just as easily. Prisoners who declined to take advantage of the insecure jail sometimes suffered from the "inclemency of the season." Heat was needed, and some prisoners were indisposed. Only limited funds were available, the sheriff lamented, and many of the prisoners were unable to pay for their maintenance. Such handicaps were the rule, rather than the exception. Because of these difficulties, Governor Claiborne sought funds to improve and expand penal facilities and often granted pardons and remitted fines for lesser offenders.[39] As a practical matter, he utilized the limited resources at his command to fulfill the responsibilities of his office to the best of his ability.

The proximity of Spanish territory made law enforcement even more difficult. Criminals often sought sanctuary across international boundaries. Extradition agreements had not been concluded and American and Spanish frontier authorities viewed each other with contempt and suspicion. Nonetheless, as criminal elements increasingly took advantage of the situation, cooperation between American and Spanish authorities became a matter of necessity.

In February 1802 Governor Claiborne wrote to Don Juan Manuel de Salcedo, the governor general of Louisiana, about a robbery committed on the Mississippi River just a short distance below the confluence of the Arkansas River and the Mississippi. Claiborne pointed out that the crime came under Spanish jurisdiction, but expressed uncertainty as to whether the criminals were Spanish subjects. He declared that he had given his own law enforcement officers information regarding the crime, and hoped that Salcedo would do likewise. The governor general sent Claiborne a brusque reply about two weeks later, stating tersely that there was no means to determine the nationality of the criminals. Consequently, there was no reason why the crime should be attributed to Spaniards because it had occurred near a river controlled by Spain. For every six or seven Spanish boats that ascended the Mississippi River, Salcedo asserted, over two hundred American flatboats and barges descended it. But despite the contentious tone of the letter, Salcedo issued orders for the apprehension of the robbers and even reinforced a small Spanish garrison on the St. Francis River. When Claiborne replied to Salcedo about a month later, he apologized for leaving the impression that he thought the Spaniards alone were responsible for the outrage, and added diplomatically that both the United States and Spain had some "degenerate characters." [40]

At the time Claiborne notified Governor General Salcedo of the robbery, he had also alerted American authorities. He warned Captain Richard Sparks that the banditti might be heading toward Fort Pickering. On April 27 he wrote to Colonel Daniel Burnet in Claiborne County and spoke of pirates and robbers who infested the Mississippi River and the Wilderness Road. While assorted and numerous criminals haunted the roads and rivers, Claiborne attributed the robbery about which he had written to Salcedo to the Mason gang. The victim he identified as Colonel Joshua Parker, and the robbery attempt was made between Walnut Hills and the mouth of the Yazoo River. Claiborne warned that the nefarious activities of the notorious Mason gang had to be halted, and added: "while these Sons of Rapine and Murder are permitted to Rove at large, we may expect daily to hear of *outrages* upon the Lives & properties of our fellow Citizens." The governor asked Colonel Buret to take fifteen or twenty volunteers into the Walnut Hills and try to flush out the gang and bring them to Natchez for trial. At the same time, he instructed Lieutenant Seymore Rennick to provide Colonel Burnet with a sergeant and twelve men, while also alerting a small military unit at Bear Creek on the Tennessee River, should the banditti possibly move in that direction. [41]

Just who were the "Sons of Rapine and Murder" about whom Salcedo and Claiborne were exchanging communications? In a letter to Claiborne on March 3, 1803, Salcedo identified several members of the gang. He remarked that it was evident that "Old Mason [Samuel Mason] in the habits of robbery & crime for thirty years past," was the ringleader. Thomas Setton was identified as an Irishman and American army deserter. Wiley (Little) Harpe apparently joined the Mason gang as John Setton, or John Taylor. He and John Mason, one of Samuel's sons, were regarded as principal accomplices. John's brothers, Thomas and Magno, were also active, but in Thomas the "principles of virtue" had not been totally "extinguished." Salcedo further mentioned the names Basset, Collins, Glass, Philips, and Wood as members. The Mason gang presumably had abettors and connections in such strategically but widely separated places on or near the Mississippi

River as Natchez in the south and proceeding northward to Bayou Pierre, Walnut Hills (Vicksburg), Chickasaw Bluffs (Memphis), New Madrid, and on into Kentucky.[42]

Despite repeated attempts to apprehend members of the Mason gang, they continued to operate with impunity for several years. But about nine months after Claiborne sounded the alarm, most of the gang were taken into custody by Spanish authorities in the vicinity of New Madrid. However, the commandant of the post, Don Henry Peyroux, acted precipitately and consequently lost an excellent opportunity to break up the ring. After a trial of several days at New Madrid, a decision was made to send the prisoners to New Orleans, where Governor General Salcedo would decide their fate. Since the crimes had been committed in American territory, a decision was made in New Orleans to send the prisoners to the Mississippi Territory for trial in an American court. As the sloop in which they were traveling was passing Pointe Coupée, a storm erupted during which the prisoners escaped. On March 3, 1803, Salcedo wrote to Claiborne, told him of the debacle, and complained that Peyroux had failed to turn over some important evidence in the case when it was transferred from New Madrid to New Orleans. Moreover, Salcedo lamented, Peyroux acted too hastily in taking the banditti prisoners, which made it virtually impossible to apprehend the gang's accomplices and contacts. After promising his continued cooperation with Claiborne and the American authorities to break up the Mason gang, Salcedo alluded to expenses incurred in the apprehension of the criminals. He requested reimbursement, either from the Mississippi authorities, or from the $7,000 found on the prisoners at the time they were taken into custody.[43]

Although the Mason gang was able to extricate itself from this uncomfortable situation and resume its iniquitous crimes, Governor Claiborne continued to apply pressures. Having cause to think the Mason gang had taken refuge in Chickasaw or Choctaw country, the governor apprised his Indian agents of the possibility, and authorized the use of "confidential & active Indians" to assist in bringing the banditti to justice. Moreover, Claiborne sparked renewed and intensified efforts by offering a reward of $2,000 for the bandits.[44]

While several conflicting stories have been told of the ultimate destruction of the Mason gang, the reward offered by Claiborne was a potent factor in their demise. One story relates that John Setton, or Wiley Harpe, left the gang shortly after Claiborne offered the reward and returned to Kentucky. He later became involved in an "incident" and "paid the penalty." Mason and others of his gang robbed a traveler one day and found on him a copy of Claiborne's reward proclamation. When Mason later fell asleep, two of his henchmen cut off his head and set out to claim the $2,000. They appeared before the judge of the circuit court in Greenville to have Mason's head identified, make an affidavit, and lay claim to the reward. A stranger, who had been robbed some two months earlier on the Wilderness Road and had seen one of his companions killed by the gang, recognized the horses of the claimants. He strode into the courtroom and identified them as being parties to the robbery and murder. The two treacherous but audacious criminals were tried, convicted, and executed in Greenville.[45] The Mason gang had at last come to an untimely end.

During his two years in the Mississippi Territory Governor Claiborne was successful in two particularly important areas of responsibility: the establishment of law and order and the maintenance of stable relations with the Indian tribes. He worked to provide improved and expanded penal facilities, although they remained generally primitive and inadequate. The quality and effectiveness of law enforcement and the court system likewise underwent modest improvements under his supervision, and greater personal security was provided. The Mason gang was ultimately destroyed, due in no small part to the persistence and actions of the chief executive. And upon the demise of the Mason gang, travel became much safer in the Mississippi country where the gang had operated with impunity for years. Moreover, Governor Claiborne's actions as superintendent of Indian affairs generally contributed to improved white-red relations as he strove to carry out the humanitarian and sympathetic policies of the Jefferson administration toward the Indians. Aside from his land-grabbing proclivity and his attitude of condescension toward the Indians, Claiborne was considerably more progressive and enlightened than most of his frontier contemporaries. He worked long and patiently and with quiet determination to iron out differences that arose, and to improve the material well-being of the Indians. He strove to understand them better and, in turn, to have the Indians better understand the ways of the white man.

When problems arose, he viewed them as collective problems involving both whites and reds. Therefore, he sought to work with the Indian leaders to resolve outstanding differences and to remove suspicions. He worked to contain existing problems and to prevent potentially explosive situations from developing. The typical white approach in the frontier regions was to exercise a minimum of tolerance and suddenly to bare the mailed fist without warning. Andrew Jackson was a vigorous advocate and practitioner of this visceral claw-and-fang mentality, if not as callous and deceptive as "Nolachucky Jack" in attitude and conduct toward the Indians. And since it quickly emerged as the dominant philosophy, white-red relations in the more remote frontier areas were characterized generally by violence and bloodshed. William Claiborne was representative of the other and, unfortunately, less popular school of thought in the isolated frontier world. But in those areas where it prevailed, such as the Misssissippi Territory during his two years as chief executive, white-red relations were considerably less hostile and contentious.

IV

MISSISSIPPI: PROBLEMS ON BOTH SIDES OF THE RIVER

The threats posed by lawless elements, uneasy relationships existing among the Indian tribes, growing Indian resentment of the white presence in the Mississippi Territory, and the uncertain intentions of the neighboring Spaniards, had weighed heavily on the governor's mind from the time of his arrival in Natchez. If republican freedom, liberty, and justice were to be realized in the isolated, distant, and primitive Mississippi Territory, it would be possible only if the inhabitants were provided with reasonable security and safety. Fully cognizant of this fundamental principle, the chief executive went to work immediately to provide the necessary protection. In his maiden speech before the general assembly in December 1801, Governor Claiborne spoke briefly of the judiciary as an instrument intended to protect personal and property rights and then concerned himself at length with the problem of getting the militia organized. He called for a general militia law, enforced effectively, which would, with few exceptions, make service in the militia a requirement for all men not incapacitated by infirmities or age. To allow many exceptions, Claiborne believed, would be both injurious and unjust, for the "Social Compact" required that able-bodied men defend their country.[1]

Although Winthrop Sargent had served as governor of the Mississippi Territory from the time of its establishment in 1798 until the early spring of 1801, he had not succeeded in organizing a militia force. Governor Claiborne informed Madison that Sargent's failure to organize such a force had rendered the territory defenseless, except for a small contingent of regular army troops stationed at Fort Adams in the southwestern corner of the territory. This was a potentially dangerous situation when one realizes that Tennessee was six hundred miles away, that a foreign power bordered the territory, that the Indian threat was omnipresent, and that a large slave population constituted still another potential danger. Claiborne consequently emphasized to Madison that a well-armed, well-trained, and well-disciplined militia was essential.[2]

A few weeks later Claiborne expressed to General James Wilkinson, commanding general of the army, the fear that a mass slaughter might occur before the small unit of regular troops at Fort Adams could be thrown into action. He requested the general to build a blockhouse as a place of deposit for arms and ammunition. Greater safety would be insured and, ever mindful of the Republican virtue of economy, he added that the cost would be modest. About a week later Claiborne wrote to Madison and requested that spare arms for the militia be stored at Fort Adams. He used the occasion to mention the arsenal, or blockhouse, saying that it would not cost anything because the land and timber were free and regular troops would assume responsibility for the construction.[3]

Governor Claiborne not only continued to exert pressure for the construction of a blockhouse, but expanded his demand to include a regular military post. The governor's efforts ultimately proved successful, for within five months after arriving in Natchez, Claiborne learned that President Jefferson had agreed to the construction of the arsenal. The president advised the practice of economy, and Claiborne offered assurances that construction costs would be held to a minimum. On July 20 he reported to Dearborn that the blockhouse, located several hundred yards from his own place in Washington, was under construction and added that plans were being formulated for a regular military post. Early the next year he informed Dearborn that he was negotiating the purchase of some land for the fort. The land being considered was fertile, possessed sufficient timber for the necessary buildings, had firewood to last many years, and was in close proximity to the town of Washington. It had good spring water and was a healthy site for the camp. Claiborne reaffirmed that the fort would be built by regular soldiers, and that costs would be minimal. First suggesting that the seller's price of fifteen dollars per acre was exorbitant, the governor, fearful that Dearborn might indeed consider the price prohibitive, added hastily that the land would command an even higher price in a private sale. In due course, the governor acquired forty-three acres, submitted to Dearborn a design of the fort, and reported in early March 1803 that the installation was under construction.[4] Grateful for the support he had received, and never one to forego an opportunity to advance his own position with the national leadership, Claiborne dutifully named the newly completed installation Fort Dearborn.

From the time of his arrival in the territory, Governor Claiborne sought to end an obvious arms shortage. During his first month in office, he asked Madison to submit his request to President Jefferson for eight hundred muskets and rifles. The arms should be accompanied by information on their cost so that the federal government could be reimbursed. Failure to include invoices with the shipments that were received over the next several months posed a problem for Claiborne. The governor wanted to arm the militia as quickly as possible but, always attentive to costs, he obviously preferred not to be placed in the embarrassing position of selling them at less than their actual cost to the government. The following April he submitted a request for the loan of 1,000 stand of arms, although Dearborn had assured him earlier that he could expect five hundred rifles and three hundred muskets. The arms Dearborn had authorized were to be sold only to militiamen and at "reasonable" prices, although the "reasonable price" was not specified. Claiborne himself arranged the sale of the rifles, fixing the price at fourteen dollars. If the purchaser did not have the required amount of money, he was to give Claiborne a note through his militia captain in which he would agree to pay the sum in cash or cotton by February 1, 1803. Among the later arms shipments received was one authorized by General Wilkinson which included eighty stand of arms, a brass fieldpiece, and "Sixteen flannel Cartridges, filled with 1 1-2 pounds of powder each, for said piece of Ordnance."[5] Governor Claiborne could therefore claim reasonable success in his drive to arm the territorial militia.

The organization of the militia required time, patience, and perseverance, but of the three, time was the most critical because of the territory's potential problems. Even his most vocal critics never accused Claiborne of lacking patience and perseverance. Nonetheless, Claiborne, the consummate politician, normally availed himself of every opportunity to score the shortcomings of others, particularly if they, perchance, were Federalists. Thus he sharply criticized Sargent for his failure to organize the territorial militia. He admitted to Dearborn that the task was a trying, troublesome one. He attributed Sargent's failure to his refusal to let the militiamen elect their own officers. On this point Claiborne was correct, but what he failed to realize or, if he had more detailed information, neglected to admit candidly was that the Green-West faction had attempted to discredit Sargent by disrupting his efforts to establish a "well-ordered militia." In the unequal contest between Sargent and his local opponents, the latter's task had been made much easier by the fact that most Westerners were less than enthusiastic about service in the militia except as commissioned officers. Aside from this natural advantage, they had sought to undermine the authority of the militia officers by demanding that the militiamen themselves select their own commanders. Furthermore, they had encouraged militia officers to resign while encouraging the enlisted personnel to harass those officers who resisted until the officers grew weary and finally gave up their posts.[6] As a Republican, Claiborne favored the militia and, as a Republican, it was only logical that he endorse the policy of allowing the noncommissioned personnel to select their own ensigns, lieutenants, and captains. In early August 1802 less than nine months after his arrival in Natchez, Claiborne reported to Dearborn that he had just reviewed the militia in Adams and Jefferson counties, adding that the prospect of a well-disciplined and well-trained militia "exceeds my most sanguine expectations."[7] By that time the counties had been laid out into regimental, battalion, and company districts. The organization of the militia was proceeding apace, enabling the governor to feel a little more relaxed and adding to his confidence that sufficient forces were available at last to cope with problems that might develop.

    The legislature consistently cooperated with the chief executive in his efforts to organize an effective and viable militia system. In 1803 the lawmakers authorized the governor to organize in each battalion one or more volunteer companies under the designation of light infantry or rifle. In addition, the legislation instructed militia captains or commanding officers of the militia companies to take a census of all "persons free and bond" living in their company districts, to maintain up-to-date records, and to oversee patrols in their militia districts. A schedule of fines for non-attendance sought to insure attendance at militia musters. These fines, the proceeds of which were to be used to procure colors, music, arms, and ammunition, ranged from $1-2 for non-attendance by a non-commissioned officer or private at a company muster to $2-4 at a regimental muster.[8]

As was to be expected from his earlier record in Congress, Claiborne always preferred to rely on the militia, rather than the regular army, for safety. On the eve of his departure for Louisiana, Governor Claiborne addressed the territorial legislature and reaffirmed his unswerving faith in the militia. The speech bore a more than superficial similarity to President Jefferson's views on preparedness and the militia, as experessed by Jefferson in a letter to Claiborne on February 26, 1803. First speaking of the resumption of war in Europe and expressing the hope that the United States would be able to maintain its neutrality, Claiborne spoke of the necessity of being constantly prepared. The militia constituted the primary bulwark against both interal and external dangers, he contended, while standing armies threatened civil liberties. He solicited for his beloved militia the "fostering care of his Assembly," and informed the legislators that any militia laws encated by them would meet with his approval. A legislative committee responded to his address two days later, asserting that it saw no need to enact legislation beyond that enacted by Congress in 1792.[9] Although the residents of most frontier territories normally resented repeated musters and the added expense of arming themselves, Governor Claiborne apparently did not encounter any particularly difficult problems. Indeed, when it appeared that American force might be necessary to effect the transfer of the Louisiana Territory to the United States in late 1803, the secretary of war estimated that between six hundred and nine hundred Misssissippi militiamen would be available for immediate service.[10]

The establishment of a viable militia force was seen by Claiborne as being essential to the physical security of the Mississippi Territory. The development of an effective judicial system he regarded as equally essential to the welfare of the territory, both as a means of protecting the citizenry from threats to their persons, property rights, and civil liberties, and as a means of insuring an equitable redress for violations of constitutionally guaranteed rights. The former task was relatively easy since the need of a protective force was clearly visible in such isolated and remote country where real and potential dangers abounded. The establishment of an impartial and equitable judiciary, however, was more controversial and complicated. Because of the heated national debate concerning the role and scope of the judiciary, the quarrels that developed in the Mississippi Territory merely manifested the national dichotomy in less sophisticated terms.

Defeated nationally at the polls, the Federalists sought to use the judiciary as a vehicle to perpetuate their philosophy and ideology until they hopefully staged a political comeback. On the other hand, Jefferson, the chief architect and spokesman of the Republican party, remained deeply suspicious of the Federalist-dominated courts, viewing them as a Federalist institution of tyranny, oppression, and corruption. Consequently, the politically victorious Republicans rushed ahead with a measure of their own to replace the Judiciary Act of 1801 and largely succeeded in restoring the courts to their earlier status. The national controversy continued to swirl, culminating in the famous *Marbury v. Madison* case in 1803 in which Federalist Chief Justice John Marshall affirmed the doctrine of judicial review. The Republicans fought back by launching efforts to curb the partisanship of Federalist judges through the initiation of impeachment proceedings. Although successful in a few cases at lesser levels, they failed in their bid to impeach Supreme Court Justice Samuel Chase in 1805.

Against this broad national background of partisan thrust-and-parry, Governor Claiborne set out to establish a viable judicial system in the territory while allaying local suspicions of the courts.

However, his task was complicated by conditions peculiar to the frontier. Although most settlers were eager to establish systems of law and order, they generally displayed less interest and patience with legal formalities and intricacies. In fact, some few of the leaders and spokesmen in these wilderness outposts were fugitives themselves and therefore were less than enthusiastic about the development of a viable system of courts. Furthermore, Claiborne inherited a legacy of lively controversy surrounding the courts and the personalities associated with them. Governor Sargent and the judges were Federalist appointees and were resented by the territorial inhabitants and the lawmakers.

Knowing that the judiciary constituted a source of partisan friction when he went to Mississippi, Governor Claiborne chose to come to grips with it immediately. The judicial problem, as he interpreted it, essentially revolved around the earlier enactment of unpopular laws during the Sargent administration, disappointment with officials chosen to administer the laws, and dissatisfaction with certain persons associated with law enforcement. Thus, when the general assembly convened at Government House on December 19, 1801, Claiborne stressed the need and desirability to improve the courts. But aware of their strong feelings, Claiborne was not so optimistic as to anticipate constructive reform efforts on the part of the lawmakers. In a letter to Madison the following day, he admitted the need to improve the courts but doubted that it would be possible, for a great cleavage existed between the people and the courts, and over half of the territorial inhabitants had no faith whatsoever in the judiciary. Although newly arrived, Claiborne readily understood the fundamental problem: "I fear upon this Subject [the judiciary] they will be inclined to Legislate rather against Men, than upon principle; This is really an unpleasant State of things, and will not fail to be a source of much trouble to me."[11] His analysis of the problem was correct; he was also correct in his prediction that it would become a source of personal difficulty.

President John Adams had appointed the three members of the territorial supreme court. As Federalist officials, they were no more acceptable to the Mississippians than Governor Winthrop Sargent and had been under heavy verbal assault from much of the populace long before Claiborne's appearance on the scene. Claiborne was equally harsh in his criticisms of the judges. He noted an obvious lack of legal expertise in the territory, even on the highest legal tribunal. Seth Lewis, successor to William McGuire as chief justice in 1800, had been a practicing lawyer and Claiborne respected his excellent legal talent. But at the same time, the chief justice's two colleagues lacked the legal background and training necessary to serve in such a responsible capacity. Judge Peter B. Bruin was a merchant and had no legal training and experience whatsoever. Judge Daniel Tilton supposedly had "read" law for a few months but had never been a practicing lawyer. Claiborne assured Madison that if either Bruin or Tilton resigned, he would seek a replacement who had been trained in law. It was about nine months later when the opporunity arose.

Tilton left New Orleans for Liverpool in mid-1802 on a business trip and still had not returned several months afterward. Claiborne interpreted this action as an abandonment of his office.[12] In early November President Jefferson appointed David Ker, a lawyer and founder of the University of North Carolina, to replace him.[13]

Even before David Ker replaced Judge Tilton, discord had erupted between Chief Justice Seth Lewis and the territorial legislature. Claiborne shied away from the quarrel as much as possible because of its political implications. If he hoped his action would foster an abatement of the tug-of-war between the legislature and judiciary, he was disappointed. Complaints continued to be registered against Lewis, including charges that he was imposing exorbitant fines and penalties although the charges were not supported by evidence. The legislature conducted some hearings in an effort to accumulate enough evidence to support an impeachment effort, but this action proved fruitless.[14] Nonetheless, the chief justice's enemies were not to be denied. The matter came to a head when some Indians stole the judge's horse while he was holding court in the Washington District. He tried unsuccessfully to recover the horse and then petitioned the legislature for indemnity. The house finally approved the petition by a vote of 4-2, but the legislative council rejected it the following day.[15] Not wishing to carry on the running battle any longer with the lawmakers, Lewis bowed to the inevitable and resigned from the judgeship.[16] Thus, another Federalist pound of flesh was exacted. Although Governor Claiborne, who recognized that persons of Judge Lewis' legal talent and professional training were too few in the territory, had not joined in the unremitting attack on the judge, he nevertheless made no overt effort to defend the beleagured jurist or to influence the legislature to forego its partisan assault.

The members of the general assembly were just as displeased with the code of laws and system of courts established by the Sargent administration as they were with the governor and judges. The Ordinance of 1787 had authorized the governor, secretary, and three judges during the first stage of territorial government to adopt and enforce laws of the older states which appeared to suit territorial needs. However, the Sargent administration possessed copies only of the Northwest Territory's legal codes which Sargent readily admitted were inadequate. After their tardy arrival, the territorial judges finally adopted a criminal code which provided for such punishments as whipping and pillorying and authorized the forfeiture of estates when persons accused of arson, burglary, and treason were found guilty. They established a system of territorial courts, and legalized the probate court established earlier by executive proclamation and assigned such responsibilities as the probation of wills, the administration of estates, and the care of orphans.[17]

The territorial lawmakers unleashed a volley of criticisms, charging that the Sargent administration "made" rather than "adopted" laws in violation of the territorial ordinance. Moreover, they protested against what they regarded as exorbitant fees collected by the governor for marriage licenses and tavern permits. At the same time, they began to formulate laws to replace those enacted by the Sargent administration. The lawmakers, however, were hampered by a lack of experience. Claiborne, recognizing this weakness, acknowledged that it would lead to legislative irregularities and inconsistencies, but he was certain that time and attention would serve to correct them. With injustice therefore outweighing inexperience, the governor agreed with the general assembly that the laws enacted under the preceding administration were defective and should be repealed. Within a few weeks the lawmakers repealed them and replaced them with an almost entirely new set of laws. Although acknowledging that the new legal code was imperfect, Claiborne declared that it would "conduce more to the convenience & protection of the people" than the code it replaced.[18]

In late spring 1802, Governor Claiborne addressed the general assembly about some of the deficiences in the revised judicial system. While recommending measures to correct some of the weaknesses, he admonished the legislators to be more tolerant of popular criticisms of the revised system. He suggested staggered, rather than simultaneous, court sessions, and recommended that the more sparsely populated counties not be required to nominate the same number of jurors for service on the circuit courts as the more populous ones.[19] About eighteen months later the governor again discussed various judicial inadequacies with the lawmakers. According to Claiborne, judicial delays occasioned by the infrequent sessions of the courts constituted the most common complaint. The Washington District Court, he cited as an example, had not been convened at all during 1803. Moreover, the judges had to travel great distances to hold court, often through Indian country and at great personal danger. Citing the sums paid clerks and sheriffs he contended that the salaries of local officials were too meager; therefore, he urged modest salary increases for both members of the judiciary and law enforcement officers. Yet, having been a penurious congressman and having been advised pointedly by President Jefferson to hold costs to a minimum, Claiborne obviously had no intention of stepping out of character. While advising the lawmakers to be liberal, because "that economy ceases to be prudent, which denies to the labourer a price worthy of his hire," he nonetheless did not want them to be profuse. The legislature named a committee to review the governor's proposals, to study the existing judicial system, and to consider the possibility of establishing a scale of fees.[20]

The general assembly had acted favorably on several of the governor's proposals by the time he was ready to leave Mississippi.

They established schedules for district and county courts; to facilitate court action while accommodating the citizenry, the lawmakers provided for the admission of depositions taken from witnesses unable to attend court proceedings. In the interest of economy, as well as to protect citizens who became engaged in litigation, the legislators established a schedule of fees, including fees for legal representation. The legislature further provided for "attorneys general" for the territory's five counties. Each was to receive an annual salary of $700, except the attorney general of Washington County, whose salary was set at $250, because of the county's sparse population and reduced legal responsibilities. The attorneys general would receive, in addition, fees of $10 for felony convictions and $5 for "inferior cases." They represented the territory in all criminal prosecutions and in all civil cases in which the territory had an interest. The general assembly also authorized the acquisition of lands and the construction of necessary facilities, such as courthouses, jails, pillories, and stocks.

They stipulated further that the expenses entailed were to be met from taxes paid to the counties where such facilities were provided.[21] By the time Claiborne left the territory effective judicial and law enforcement systems had been established.

The establishment of a viable judicial system that would have the confidence and support of the people in frontier Mississippi was high on the governor's list of priorities and he achieved marked success. At the same time he readily recognized that the promotion of education was vital to longer-term territorial interests. The governor was also very much aware of President Jefferson's particular interest in education and therefore knew that his educational efforts in the territory would come under national scrutiny. His earlier experience in this field had been largely restricted to the short period in which he served as one of several incorporators of Washington College in Tennessee.[22] Preoccupied with more pressing matters upon his arrival in Natchez, Claiborne waited a few months before recommending to the lawmakers that a system of public education be established. The preservation of the republican form of government was dependent upon education, he asserted; every government having the general welfare and happiness as its objectives should strongly emphasize education. "A people involved in mental darkness become fit subjects for despotic sway," he reasoned, "but when Informed of *their* Rights, they will never fail to cause them to be respected by the Public Authority." Although an educational system would require substantial financial commitment on the part of the people, Claiborne was confident it would be forthcoming. If wealth were not used to promote education, he warned, there was the danger that it might "produce Luxury and Vice in the rising Generation and become the means of corruption both Public & Private." Claiborne then recommended the establishment of a "Seminary of Learning." The general assembly responded favorably and chartered Jefferson College nine days later.[23] Although the governor's active efforts to establish the college have been attributed to his desire to divert the attention of the people and to allay political opposition,[24] the evidence fails to support this charge. Claiborne's public record reflected a strong personal commitment to education, a commitment that was in the

Republican tradition, for Claiborne knew that here he was being held to strict accountability by his mentor in Washington. It is therefore unlikely that the Mississippi settlers motivated the governor's efforts to establish a college, preoccupied as they were with more direct and immediate problems. In any event, the establishment of the college was not an issue of such immediate significance that it swept away or even arrested appreciably popular currents of opposition to the Claiborne administration.

After the legislature chartered the new college, the issue of its location ensued. Various interested groups offered financial support contingent upon an agreement that the college be located at a predesignated location. The politically and socially influential Green family made a strong bid to locate it in Greenville. The college trustees reviewed and evaluated the offers and finally accepted the recommendation of David Ker, who had established a girls' school at Natchez the preceding year and later replaced Judge Tilton on the supreme court, to accept the Greenville site. Other powerful forces favored Natchez or Washington, the territorial capital located six miles north of Natchez. Claiborne, serving as spokesman for this group, accused Ker and his supporters of having a personal interest in the land involved at Greenville. Having tentatively accepted the Greenville site, the members of the legislature reversed their decision, and Claiborne appointed a committee to consider other possible sites. The committee favored a neutral location, but the Claiborne forces were not to be denied. The general assembly finally approved a Washington site on November 11, 1803.[25]

Having settled upon a location, the trustees turned their attention to the problem of financing Jefferson College. Several pledges of financial support were not honored because of the controversy over the school's location. An attempted lottery failed to secure funds and most of the tickets remained unsold. Private contributions likewise were inadequate, and Claiborne fretted about the college's precarious future. He suggested a tax on marriage licenses as one source of revenue.[26] The board of trustees, with Claiborne serving as chairman, also met upon the governor's suggestion to formulate a petition in which they appealed for a land donation to support the institution. They spoke of the people of Mississippi laboring under "peculiar impediments" in their educational endeavors since they had but lately "emerged from the lethargic Influence of arbitrary government." The trustees expressed a desire for financial aid from Congress for the support of the educational enterprise which would, they felt confident, "establish republicanism in the minds of the Youth of this Territory, and be the firmest bond of attachment to the Union." They alluded to the educational provisions of the Ordinance of 1787, and said that they should be granted the same privilege as the people of the Northwest.[27]

Congress acted favorably upon the petition from the trustees. On March 3, 1803, it passed "An Act regulating the Grants of Land and Providing for the Disposal of the Lands of the United States South of the State of Tennessee." The measure set aside a township of land and two lots in Natchez, not to exceed thirty acres, for the support of the institution.[28] Nevertheless, Claiborne and the trustees expressed disappointment because the stipulated sections then vacant included much land that was practically without value. They subsequently memorialized Congress to amend the law so that the land could be broken up into separate tracts, and requested that land superintendents be given authorization to select the lands that were to be donated to the college.[29] Congress apparently did not act upon the second memorial because the trustees later registered complaints about the unproductive lands appropriated by the federal government.[30]

Shortly before he left Mississippi, the governor again addressed the general assembly on the vital importance of an educational system. Science and literature should be promoted. The intrinsic value of personal liberties and a free government would be better appreciated. The most reliable safeguard against tyranny and bigotry, Claiborne proclaimed, lay in education. Education was a public, rather than a private, concern and it should be fostered and made available to every "growing family." To establish an educational system would be to render the greatest service to posterity, he said, and it would "establish an impenetrable bulwark around their civil and religious liberties." The house of representatives responded warmly to the governor's plea for an educational system, and agreed that tyrants relied upon the ignorance of their subjects to maintain themselves. That "precious jewel" called liberty would be safe, they asserted, only so long as society enjoyed the blessings of education. On the eve of Claiborne's departure from the Mississippi Territory, the general assembly incorporated The Mississippi Society for the Acquirement and Dissemination of Useful Knowledge.[31] Despite the strong vocal support and lip service offered by the chief executive and lawmakers, however, no further achievements appear to have been realized in the field of public education during Caliborne's two-year tenure in Mississippi.

While stressing the vital importance of education, Governor Claiborne was performing another valuable but complex and frustrating service. The chaotic state of land titles in the Mississippi Territory produced widespread apprehension among people that attempts would be made to deprive them of the lands they claimed. In fact, Governor Claiborne was aware that disputed land titles had contributed heavily to the frictions that developed between the people and the judiciary. At the same time, the chief executive defended the judiciary on the grounds that its decisions regarding land titles were based upon legality and fairness.[32]

Over a period of years the British, French, Spanish, and American governments and the state of Georgia had made numerous conflicting land grants. Having already relinquished parts of the region to a number of Yazoo land companies, Georgia had opposed the creation of the Mississippi Territory. Georgia and the federal government battled for many years over the contested lands. The conclusion of an agreement between the two parties on April 24, 1802, improved prospects for resolving the dispute. According to the terms of the agreement, the Georgia legislature relinquished claims to the land lying south of Tennessee and west of a stipulated line in return for a $1,250,000 payment from the federal government. Further, all persons who were actual settlers in the ceded territory before October 27, 1795, and whose land grants had been fully executed by the British authorities in West Florida or by the Spanish government before that date would have their grants confirmed. This provision was also to apply to persons whose claims resulted from survey or settlement before the 1795 deadline under the authority of a measure enacted by the Georgia legislature on February 7, 1785. According to this act, those lands on the Mississippi between the thirty-first parallel and the Yazoo River were to be incorporated into Bourbon County which was, in essence, a paper creation. After it paid Georgia the stipulated amount, the federal government was to use 5,000,000 acres of land or the proceeds from the sale of the lands to settle unresolved land claims. The federal government agreed to extinguish, at its own expense, all Indian land claims in Georgia, and promised to cede to Georgia any claim or right to lands located within the United States south of Tennessee, North Carolina, and South Carolina, and east of the territory ceded by Georgia. Finally, the territory ceded by Georgia was to become a state when it could fulfill the stipulated requirements.[33]

On July 26, 1802, Madison sent Governor Claiborne instructions regarding the newly acquired lands. The secretary of state directed Claiborne to supply the land commissioners with information on lands relinquished by the Indians on the Mobile and Mississippi rivers, the claims of settlers to lands relinquished by Georgia, claims under the Bourbon County Act of February 7, 1785, claims under the French government prior to the Peace of Paris of 1763, and claims under the British and Spanish governments before October 27, 1795.[34]

Governor Claiborne attempted to provide the federal government with as much information as possible on the land claims. About two weeks after he received Madison's directive, he sent out a handbill instructing the people to register their land claims with county clerks by November 1, 1802. The response, however, fell far short of the governor's expectations. On November 5, he reported to Madison that he knew a number of people who had not filed their claims, even though their claims were legitimate. Some neglected to file because they were unaware of the requirement. Many failed to do so "either through inattention, or from an unaccommodating position." Others refused to register their land claims because of rumors being spread deliberately by "designing men" that their rights would be greatly jeopardized by registration.[35]

Claiborne also reported on the land claims and turned over to Madison all of the relevant papers that he had accumulated. He informed the secretary of state that the extinguished Indian land claims in Adams, Claiborne, Jefferson, and Wilkinson counties amounted to 1,600,000 acres. In addition, the Indians gave up claim to some 3,000,000 acres on the Mobile River, of which only about one-third was valuable, and the rest was composed largely of pine barrens.[36] The land relinquished along the Mississippi, by general contrast, was fertile and valuable, he reported. Further, Claiborne pointed out that most British land grants had been made by the governor of West Florida, though some had been made by the king. Spanish applicants normally applied to the governor general of Louisiana or the governor at Natchez, although the Spanish king sometimes bestowed tracts of land on persons for meritorious service. In the course of the report, Claiborne urged that provisions be made for people who had settled on vacant lands, and expressed the hope that "these citizens may be secured in their improvements." He felt that small tracts of land should be sold to them at moderate prices. Distress would result if the government neglected to grant the settlers preemption rights, he predicted, and many would leave the Mississippi Territory and become citizens of a country that would bestow lands upon them proportionate to their needs. Only a few weak and defenseless people would remain, and speculators would greedily grab up the land. The result, Claiborne continued gloomily, would be the "introduction of a few wealthy characters, with a large increase of negroes; a description of inhabitants, already formidable to our present population." [37]

A few days later, Claiborne followed up his general report with one that dealt only with Washington County in which he again made an appeal in behalf of the squatters. In addition to turning over records of land claims that had been filed in Washington County, he reported that over one hundred families in that county alone had settled on unoccupied lands and had made improvements on them. He requested preemption rights for them, and asked that the land be sold at nominal costs. If not, Claiborne was convinced that the settlers would quickly migrate to nearby Louisiana.[38]

Governor Claiborne was the first person to make a comprehensive study of land claims in the Mississippi Territory, and his involved and lengthy reports made it possible for Congress to pass its first land act for the territory on March 3, 1803. The act confirmed all Spanish and British land grants issued to heads of families or persons over twenty-one years of age prior to October 27, 1795. In response to Claiborne's repeated recommendations that squatter rights be protected, the measure granted preemption rights on as much as a section of land to bona fide residents who had occupied and cultivated the lands before October 27, 1795. The act created two land offices to dispose of the nationally owned lands in the Mississippi Territory. One office was to be located in Adams County for lands lying west of the Pearl River, and another in Washington County for lands lying east of the river. Two registers, or land agents, and four commissioners were to be assigned to the two land offices, and a surveyor general was to be appointed for the territory.[39]

The appointment of persons to fill the newly created posts caused some dissension within the Republican party. Joseph Chambers was assigned as agent in the eastern land office. Edward Turner, a former aide-de-camp to Claiborne and son-in-law of Cato West was appointed to the western land office. Thomas M. Green, Mississippi delegate to Congress and a member of the influential Green family, had secured the post for Turner despite Claiborne's efforts to have his brother Ferdinand appointed. A petition against Turner was circulated shortly after the appointment, which led his supporters to charge that Claiborne and his brother were behind the "calumny." Turner declared heatedly to Senator John C. Breckinridge of Kentucky, who had also actively supported him, that Claiborne wanted to be "Governor over every thing in the Territory, even private affairs."[40] Although political passions boiled momentarily over the spoils of office, Governor Claiborne worked diligently to settle the problem of conflicting land claims. Indeed, Claiborne's success in coping with the difficult and delicate problems of land claims may have been instrumental in Jefferson's decision to reassign him to the newly acquired Territory of Orleans.[41]

Although very little health and sanitation legislation was enacted during his two years in frontier Mississippi, Governor Claiborne did try to protect the settlers as much as possible from communicable diseases. Diphtheria, typhoid fever, and smallpox routinely took a heavy toll, and Claiborne remained apprehensive that epidemics in nearby areas might spread to Mississippi. Inadequate medical knowledge about the cause and treatment of diseases required added vigilance. When the governor learned in the spring of 1802 that smallpox was widespread in New Orleans, he urged merchants and others who visited or engaged in business activities in that city to exercise every precaution to prevent the "communication of the contagion." Claiborne hoped, specifically, that the Natchez merchants would "forbear to Vend or expose for Sale, any *fur* Hats or woollen Cloths" imported from New Orleans during the epidemic because he felt that fur hats and woolen articles served to "nourish the Infection" and made possible its communication to distant places. About the same time, he advised the people to raise a subscription to send someone to Kentucky to procure smallpox vaccine.[42]

Despite precautionary measures, smallpox did creep into the Mississippi Territory. Claiborne ordered the erection of a temporary hospital, or "Encampment," to care for and to isolate smallpox victims. He was also very solicitous of the welfare of the patients. Although he discussed a wide range of subjects when he appeared before the general assembly on May 4, 1802, he devoted much of his address to the disease. Although the people were becoming alarmed, the governor hesitated to declare a quarantine because he believed he lacked specific authority to take that step and because he believed it would impede agricultural activities. Nonetheless, he called upon the lawmakers to enact a health law that would enable him to deal with the disease. The general assembly responded quickly by enacting the necessary legislation. Any person who willfully introduced the disease into Mississippi was subject to a fine and imprisonment. Acting under this authority, Claiborne sometimes ordered persons who had been exposed to the disease to be isolated in "some retired situation." While apologizing for such stern measures, he declared that the general welfare necessitated a rigid enforcement of the law.[43]

In the fall of 1802 Doctors David and William Lattimore drew up a comprehensive report to the governor on the prevalence of smallpox in the territory. They gave Claiborne credit for having curbed the contagion by trying to prevent its introduction and by having strongly encouraged vaccination. According to their report, filed about six months after the disease was first reported, an estimated two-thirds of the people had received the vaccination, and "in no one case, that we have heard of has it produced mortality." Had it not been for the vaccine, whose timely arrival the Lattimores thought providential, the disease might have been infinitely more serious. [44]

No recurrence of the disease was reported after the one outbreak. Shortly before he left Mississippi, however, Claiborne received some ominous reports from Samuel Mitchell, one of his Indian agents. In August 1803 Mitchell spoke of a considerable number of incapacitated travelers on the Wilderness Road. According to Mitchell, his home had been overflowing with patients for over three months. They were taking up much of his time, he complained, and were causing him much expense. Claiborne notified Secretary of War Dearborn of Mitchell's problem, and advised that the agent be supplied "by the publick" with an "assortment of medicine." [45]

At about the time the Lattimores were submitting their smallpox report, the governor's attention was jarringly diverted by the sudden and unexpected eruption of a problem of the first magnitude. On October 16, 1802, the Spanish intendant of Louisiana, Juan Ventura Morales, announced the suspension of the American right to deposit merchandise at New Orleans for transshipment. According to the terms of the Pinckney Treaty (San Lorenzo), concluded between Spain and the United States in 1795, the citizens of both countries had access to the Mississippi River. Moreover, American citizens were permitted the use of New Orleans as an entrepôt for their goods. After three years the Spanish king might continue the privilege, or he could designate another entrepôt on the lower Mississippi. Yet the intendant, subordinate in most matters to the Spanish governor of Louisiana, casually suspended the right of deposit without designating an alternate entrepôt and stubbornly resisted all pressures to rescind his action for seven tense months.

The intendant's action, seemingly taken on his own authority, momentarily muffled partisan polemics throughout the United States as Republicans and Federalists alike thundered against

Spanish arbitrariness. However, as expressions of extreme indignation reverberated across the land, visions of a resurgent and revitalized political party danced before the eyes of Federalist hopefuls. Sedate New Englanders joined assertive Westerners in a savage but therapeutic denunciation of the irresponsible Iberians who callously disregarded solemn treaty obligations. It even appeared for a brief moment that the issuance of a decree by an unknown Spanish colonial official in the remote Southwest would produce a degree of national unity, heretofore largely alien to the American experience. Furthermore, the Spanish action forced the Jefferson administration to consider foreign policy options hitherto incompatible with its traditions and inclinations.

Why Morales suspended the American right of deposit at New Orleans without making alternate provisions appeared, in some respects, to be an incongruous action. This is true despite the fact that the Spaniards had never officially received William E. Hulings, Evan Jones, or Daniel Clark as American consular representatives in New Orleans,[46] and were frustrated and distressed by American abuses of their commercial privileges on the lower Mississippi under the treaty of 1795. The intendant's action was clearly a violation of the Pinckney Treaty. Moreover, Spanish officials clearly knew that the action would arouse the Americans and possibly lead to a clash at a time when their defensive capabilities in and around New Orleans were almost nonexistent. The intendant's action appeared even more incredible since Spanish authorities had finally decided in mid-1802 to proceed with the retrocession of Louisiana to France under the terms of a secret agreement concluded between the two countries the preceding autumn. Consequently, some Americans, aware of Spain's close association with France since 1796, were convinced that Spain had acted under French instructions. Others were just as convinced that it was a deliberate Spanish effort to create problems for France since the retrocession was imminent.[47]

Morales casually turned aside the efforts of the Americans and Spanish colonial officials alike to rescind the order while speculation abounded as to whether the intendant had acted on his own authority or on order from the Spanish government. He explained his action by saying that the trading rights extended to neutral countries while the European war was in progress should now be terminated because peace had been restored under the Treaty of Amiens, concluded in the spring of 1802 after several months of negotiations. Very few, and least of all the Americans, were prepared to accept the intendant's explanation at face value.

Governor Claiborne first learned of the intendant's action from Vice Consul William Hulings, who had sent him a copy of the proclamation, and he asked Hulings to remind Morales that the measure constituted a treaty violation. A direct exchange of letters between Claiborne and Don Juan Manuel de Salcedo, the governor general of Louisiana, followed a few days later. In late October Claiborne reminded Salcedo of the Spanish obligation to provide the Americans with a place of deposit if New Orleans was no longer available.[48] Salcedo responded in mid-November that the Spanish king had not issued the order. Instead, the action, taken unilaterally by Morales acting in his capacity as intendant, was independent of the general government of Louisiana. Salcedo defended Morales by saying that the latter had taken the step against the Americans at the same time that he suspended the commerce of neutrals after the restoration of peace in Europe in the spring of 1802. Salcedo also contended that the westerners had repeatedly abused the privilege, citing the backlog of cases awaiting the Spanish king's decision. Much fraud had been perpetrated under the guise of ignorance, he charged, and Morales proposed to terminate it. Continuing his lecture, the governor general said that contracting parties ought to honor and respect treaties, but they should be annulled when they became pernicious and contained vicious principles. Considering the numerous American abuses of the privilege over a period of three years—a charge that undoubtedly had much validity because of the volume of the American traffic and the limited number of Spanish personnel assigned to enforce their traditionally mercantilistic regulations—Salcedo suggested that the action taken by Morales was logical and understandable. In fact, the governor general declared, he had himself initially opposed the action until Morales explained the reasons for it. Salcedo hoped nonetheless that the Spanish king would restore the right of deposit at New Orleans or at some other place on the lower Mississippi, provided such measure would not be "prejudicial to the interests of Spain." Salcedo ended his letter to Claiborne with an assurance of continued harmony between Spain and the United States.[49]

What Salcedo and other Spanish colonial officials did not know was that Morales had taken the action upon orders from Madrid. On July 14, 1802, Intendant Morales received a *muy reservada* (very secret) order from the Spanish secretary of the treasury, Cayetano Soler, to terminate the right of deposit, but not to divulge that he had received the order. Indeed, if pressed, he was to insist that he had acted independently. Spanish officials also directed the intendant to offer the explanation that he could not restore the privilege unless he received orders from the Spanish court. Morales' secrecy in carrying out his instructions from Madrid provoked a number of his associates in the Spanish colonial service. Although Salcedo defended Morales in his letter to Claiborne, he at one time considered intervening to prevent the issuance of the proclamation by which Morales closed New Orleans to the Americans. Moreover, the Marquis de Someruelos, the captain general of Cuba, expressed his displeasure, and the Marquis de Casa Irujo, the Spanish minister in Washington, ordered Morales to restore the right of deposit or to assign another entrepôt. The United States could not long restrain the westerners, Irujo warned, but Morales calmly brushed aside the order.[50]

As the intendant's nervous colleagues exerted pressures to force him to rescind his action or select another entrepôt in order to avert an imminent clash with the irate westerners and possibly with the American government, Governor Claiborne lost no time in notifying Washington of the intendant's action. Within hours of receiving the communication from Hulings, he forwarded the vice consul's letter and a translation of the proclamation to Madison and continued to keep him informed. In early November he reported that the "embarrassment" of American trade at New Orleans continued. American produce could be deposited, the governor added, but only after the payment of a duty of six percent. Claiborne asserted that it was inconceivable that the intendant had taken such action, fraught with such serious risks, without specific orders from the king.[51]

The governor's conclusion that the intendant's orders had emanated from Madrid was strongly supported by Daniel Clark, then serving as U. S. consul in New Orleans and may have been influenced by Clark. In a letter to Madison on March 8, 1803, Clark asserted that "there is among well informed People but one Opinion which is, that he [Morales] merely executes the orders received from his Government. He is too rich, too sensible, and too cautious to take such a responsibility on himself. . . . This determined Spirit of the Intendant is not natural to him, it is assumed because he feels himself supported. . . ." Clark, one of the best sources of information about Spanish policies and plans because of his numerous contacts within the Spanish colonial hierarchy in New Orleans, pointed out that Morales had not consulted with his Spanish associates. Normally, he did so and thus was able to place the onus on them when it was convenient. Several weeks later Clark reaffirmed his conclusion to Madison and provided additional reasons for his position, but added that the Spanish action was taken in concert with France. He reasoned that the assignment of a new series of code numbers to dispatches sent to Morales from the home ministry, the *muy reservada* classification, and the failure of Cayetano Soler, the Spanish finance minister, to discuss the intendant's action at all in subsequent dispatches were clear indications that the orders had been issued by the Spanish king. Finally, he pointed out that Morales had even ignored pressures from the captain general in Havana to restore the American entrepôt. Unless he was under specific orders from Spain, Morales would undoubtedly bow to the captain general because "I am persuaded from my knowledge of his [Morales'] Character, that the Intendant would shrink into annihilation at the Prospect before him."[52]

While Madison was receiving these reports, pressures were mounting for direct American action as western trade dwindled, having already been hurt by the momentary restoration of peace in Europe and the subsequent loss of markets for its agricultural goods. In an address to the territorial legislature on December 9 Governor Claiborne focused on the unexpected Spanish move. He expressed an awareness of the "anxious solicitude" of the people, but he held out no prospect of immediate relief and appealed to them to have faith in the federal government's ability to resolve the problem. In their response four days later, the territorial lawmakers alluded to the burgeoning hardships posed by the Spanish measure, and expressed their appreciation that the governor had acted with such dispatch in communicating with the national leadership on the matter. And as requested, the legislators assured Claiborne that they would rely upon the federal government for a speedy redress of their grievances against Spain.[53]

Although Governor Claiborne appeared calm publicly, he seethed inwardly over the imperious and provocative Spanish action. Even though the Spanish leaders in New Orleans had "put their nose out of joint" by barring American goods, he wrote to Madison that his own people were being hurt agriculturally and commercially, and a state of acute agitation pervaded Natchez. Shortly after his appearance before the general assembly, Governor Claiborne again wrote to Madison, indicating that Spanish officials had adopted a harder line. While American goods were received in the river, landing was *"unconditionally forbidden."* He reported that heavy winds had upset a boat loaded with cotton while it waited opposite the port of New Orleans. Spanish authorities only grudgingly permitted the cotton to be taken from the river to a nearby levee. As far as the irate and indignant governor was concerned, the Spanish court was responsible for the retraction of the right of deposit, despite Salcedo's denials.[54]

As American produce continued to accumulate, the westerners grew increasingly bellicose in demanding their rights to use the Mississippi River. It was theirs, they proclaimed, by their numbers, by their labors, and by the law of nature. "Our innumerable rivers swell it, and flow with it into the Gulf of Mexico." They had made no effort to prevent the French and Spaniards from ascending the Mississippi River and, conversely, the French and Spanish authorities had no power to prevent the Americans from descending it. Nervously recalling the Jay-Gardoqui negotiations several years earlier when eastern interests had been willing to "forbear" the American right to the use of the Mississippi River for as long as twenty-five or thirty years in return for a favorable commercial treaty, they added ominously:

"If Congress refuses us effectual protection, if it forsakes us, we will adopt the measures which our safety requires, even if they endanger the place of the Union and our connection with the United States. No protection, no allegiance."[55]

Both the governor and the Mississippi legislature continued to exert pressure on the national government to force the issue, having been given additional encouragement and support when the Kentucky legislature passed a resolution against Morales' act.[56] The general assembly memorialized the president and Congress, and declared emphatically that Pinckney's Treaty assured them free access to the Mississippi River and a place of deposit for western goods. Consequently, Morales' action represented a flagrant violation of their treaty rights, and they added forcefully that their privileges and rights were not to be violated with impunity. The memorialists concluded by pledging their lives and fortunes to support any measure that Congress might prescribe to vindicate the "honor and interests of the United States."[57] While the memorialists were pledging themselves to support Congress in any program that it devised to restore their rights, Governor Claiborne, although very careful not to convey his private thoughts to the legislators on possible retaliatory moves, made an interesting proposal to Secretary of State Madison. As a prelude, he declared that the Spanish action was "indeed extraordinary," and that the Spaniards had lately manifested a marked hostility toward the United States. The action taken by Morales constituted an "attack upon every principle of friendly intercourse" and was overwhelmingly responsible for the existing ferment. Having carefully set the stage, the governor then casually reminded Madison that there were about 2,000 militiamen in the territory who were "pretty well organized." Knowing the approximate strength of the Spanish forces in New Orleans and aware of the extent to which Spanish authority had been eroded, Claiborne estimated that he would need only about 600 men to take possession of the city, provided Spanish forces alone defended it. He also assured Madison that there were a number of inhabitants in the city and along the coast who would support the American occupation of New Orleans.[58]

It is quite possible that Claiborne's proposal to seize New Orleans had been influenced by Daniel Clark, in particular, and possibly to a lesser extent by Vice Consul Hulings. To these three men, the denial of deposit was merely the symptom of a more basic problem that could be resolved only by the American conquest of Louisiana. About three months after Morales issued his proclamation, Hulings told Madison that the restoration of the entrepôt would "only operate as an Opiate; palliating instead of eradicating the Evil." Restoring in perpetuity the deposit at New Orleans or at some other place on the Mississippi would not benefit the United States as much as ownership of all the land from the east coast of the Mississippi River to the Atlantic.[59] Clark was even more insistent and assertive. Declaring that France would be just as contemptuous of American capabilities as Spain after the retrocession of Louisiana, he continued: "I regret that we cannot be beforehand with them and take possession of a Place now offered us by the Inhabitants, without which we shall never be in safety, which we must one day occupy and the conquest of which may then cost much blood, lives and treasure." The local inhabitants were so disturbed that "Creoles, Spaniards and Americans would form but one body, they would now without bloodshed take the Government into their own hands and they would inseparably unite themselves to us; they cry out against our temporizing when our dearest interests imperiously call upon us to embrace the favorable moment for acting and they tremble when they see it pass and themselves on the point of falling under the lash of a Government they detest. . . ." The lethargic Spanish colonial government in New Orleans had no troops, no fortifications, and no money. Consequently, the United States could handily take Louisiana, "either by way of indemnification for past injuries or security for the future." Furthermore, Clark probably conveyed these impressions to Claiborne and discussed a possible American seizure of Louisiana when he visited Natchez during the latter part of March while New Orleans was still closed to American goods.[60]

The Jefferson administration had no intention of taking direct action against the Spaniards in New Orleans, hoping instead to overcome the impasse by diplomatic means and possibly resolving the more basic problem altogether if their efforts proved successful. In mid-January, 1803, Madison told Governor Claiborne that the federal government was acting to effect a satisfactory solution. Both the president and members of Congress were aware of the intendant's action, he said, and President Jefferson had appointed James Monroe as minister plenipotentiary and envoy extraordinary to France and possibly to Spain. Monroe would cooperate with the regular ministers of those countries, Madison promised, to secure more effectually and possibly to enlarge American rights to the Mississippi River "and the Territories Eastward thereof."[61]

Although expressing confidence in Monroe's capabilities, Claiborne's doubts mounted as his constituents experienced the full effects of the Spanish action. Vessels were taking on freight while lying at anchor in the river, and congestion was becoming an increasingly serious problem. He worried about the prospect of disposing of western produce, and gloomily forecast that few vessels would be entering the Mississippi in the future because of the denial of port facilities to the Americans and the prohibition of foreign trade with New Orleans. As a consequence of this, the surplus produce of the western country would be lost both to the nation and to the industrious farmers who produced it. There was no prospect, he told Madison, that Morales would restore the American right. While he came to be assailed by doubts as the days wore on as to whether Morales had acted under instructions from Madrid or on his own authority and had asked Vice Consul Hulings in New Orleans to find out, if possible, he was now more convinced than ever that it was the former. That Morales, a man "of handsome talents, and extensive fortune . . . should risque his reputation and estate by persisting in a measure of this kind without authority from his Court appears to me extraordinary."[62]

In mid-February Madison informed Governor Claiborne that the general consensus in Washington was that Morales had acted independently. Whether this was Washington's actual "reading" of the delicate situation, in fact, or was prompted by political and diplomatic considerations is open to conjecture. Having conveyed official Washington's view, Madison then spoke of the impending transfer of Louisiana from Spain to France and said that the French chargé d'affaires in Washington, Louis André Pichon, had been requested to interpose and prevent his government from denying the right of deposit to the westerners. Pichon responded favorably, Madison reported, and had even engaged a ship in Baltimore to convey the American request. The secretary of state enclosed a copy of the request and directed Claiborne to send it by hired express to Vice Consul Hulings in New Orleans. Hulings, in turn, was to inform the Spanish authorities who, hopefully, would then relent.[63]

In the meantime, the westerners began making alternate arrangements. Recognizing that Spain might not restore the right of deposit and uncertain of the extent to which the national government would insist upon Spanish adherence to the treaty, the westerners selected Natchez as a logical substitute for New Orleans. In early March, Claiborne informed Madison that western boats were arriving daily at the former Mississippi capital. The markets were low, according to the governor, but no difficulty was being encountered in the export of goods to the Atlantic seaboard and Europe. Although the adjustments had been made and tempers had begun to subside, the westerners insisted stubbornly that full indemnification would be demanded for commercial losses ensuing from the denial of a place of deposit.[64]

Speculation persisted concerning the origin of Morales' proclamation and whether it would be retracted. It appears that Morales, in fact, did relent before receiving official instructions. In a letter of March 3, 1803, Claiborne told Madison that the port of New Orleans had been partially reopened to western trade, but added that much was yet to be done before the trade would be restored to its "Stipulated Channel."[65] According to one account, the royal order by which Morales was directed to reopen New Orleans to the Americans was drafted on March 1. The order was then sent to Irujo in Washington so he, in turn, could notify the federal government as quickly as possible. Irujo received the directive on April 19, informed Secretary of State Madison, and then dispatched it to Intendant Morales. The Spanish order reached New Orleans on May 17, and a proclamation was issued within two hours announcing the reopening of New Orleans to American trade.[66] After a disruption of seven months in which tempers flared, a backlog of boats laden with western goods impeded the flow of traffic, and negotiations continued both locally and among Washington, Madrid, and Paris, western trade on the Mississippi finally resumed its normal course. Governor Claiborne at last was able to breathe a sigh of relief.

While the governor stubbornly labored to have the commercial rights of westerners restored, American diplomats had been engaged in more encompassing diplomatic maneuvers which would have a profound effect upon the westerners. These negotiations would affect Governor Claiborne even more directly. The lucky American mastermind who had initiated the negotiations, of course, was the suddenly wily Thomas Jefferson who suggested informally that the restoration of New Orleans to the French would compel a conjugal alliance of the United States with the British fleet and nation. And all of this from one who felt a particularly strong spiritual and intellectual attachment to the French, was patently anti-British, and was naturally disposed toward pacifism and isolationism. Robert R. Livingston, his minister in France, engaged in delicate negotiations with the imperious Bonaparte and enduring Talleyrand. In March 1803 the president commissioned James Monroe as minister plenipotentiary and envoy extraordinary to France, as Secretary of State Madison had informed Governor Claiborne, and he joined with Livingston to consummate a gigantic real estate deal that would double the territory of the United States. As the success of the American diplomats in Paris became a certainty, Claiborne, now beginning to round out his second year as governor of the Mississippi Territory, could put himself in readiness to move from Natchez down the river to New Orleans. After all, the newly acquired territory would need an experienced overseer.

V

LOUISIANA: ACQUISITION, APPOINTMENT, AND AN AMERICAN INTRODUCTION

The acquisition of Louisiana by the United States has been likened to an overripe watermelon dropping into the American lap. The surface application is sufficiently innocuous and admits of an elementary validity. At that level, one is at liberty to assume that almost any country could just as easily have fallen heir to Louisiana. The United States *just happened* to be there at the right time and the melon was so ripe that Uncle Sam was not even required to shake the vine. Beneath the casual veneer of this colorful but unlikely metaphor, however, lurks an implication of historical prescience and certitude. Louisiana was predestined to slip from the grasp of Madrid and Paris, just as it was predestined to be pulled into Washington's fold. It dons the nineteenth-century "divine right" raiments of God and the American nation. That is, the divine constancy and preferment redounding to the founding fathers at Independence Hall in the City of Brotherly Love was also available to those who negotiated the Louisiana Purchase sixteen years later.

Louisiana was the subject of much diplomatic discourse and intricate maneuvering from the time of its transfer to Spain at the conclusion of the Seven Years' War to its ultimate acquisition by the United States forty years later. During those four decades the protracted and often delicate course of events sometimes attained incredible proportions. Selfish ambition, bold intrigue, and a common duplicity frequently marked the conduct of the principals. Even weather conditions intruded and added to the drama at a

Louisiana Purchase Transfer Ceremonies

Juan Morales

critical juncture. Louisiana's fate was linked inextricably to the European political and diplomatic climate as well, and its story reads like a narrative of poorly kept secrets, broken promises, and recurring dreams of empire. It is a narrative of lofty idealism and strict construction bowing precipitately before the forces of opportunism and expedience. It is a narrative of steadily mounting casualties among French occupational forces on a lonely Caribbean island, and it is a narrative of explosive American anger engendered by Spanish violations of a solemn treaty. In essence, a vast and indefinite land and its heterogeneous peoples awaited an uncertain outcome.

Only the United States benefited from the strange course of events. It doubled its territory and used the heady momentum of its acquisition as a springboard for further conquests. Hapless, helpless Spain saw its empire further eroded, and its weakened position in the Western Hemisphere only invited further predatory advances and colonial upheavals. Persistent Gallic dreams of a reestablished and resurgent empire in North America flickered and faded but they did not vanish completely until three generations later when Emperor Maximilian, pawn of French dreams and ambitions, lay dead in the hot Mexican sun.

Although at the end of the Seven Years' War France ceded Louisiana to Spain as compensation for the loss of the Floridas, French interests and aspirations regarding Louisiana never completely subsided. During the closing years of the eighteenth century the Committee of Public Safety, the Directory, and ultimately the Consulate pressed for the retrocession of Louisiana. Spain finally bowed to Gallic perseverance and retroceded it in a secret treaty concluded at the small Spanish village of San Ildefonso on October 1, 1800, although Louisiana remained under Spanish administrative jurisdiction for over two years. Spanish Minister Manuel de Godoy acknowledged his country's inability to defend it, saying: "No es possible poner puertas al campo (You can't lock up an open field)."[1] Both parties attempted to shroud the negotiations for retrocession in secrecy. French Finance Minister Barbé-Marbois feared that news of the transfer of Louisiana to France would precipitate a British attempt to conquer the territory. Within a short time, however, rumors of the French acquisition openly circulated in Mississippi and Tennessee. In fact, the week that the transfer agreement was concluded, Governor Claiborne informed Secretary of State Madison that he had information which seemed to confirm the retrocession and that he expected French occupation to follow shortly. [2]

After concluding the agreement for retrocession, First Consul Napoleon Bonaparte entertained grandiose visions of a French empire in America. He ordered immediate preparations for the occupation of Louisiana, but the events of the next few months brought only repeated disappointment. Although General Victor Collot, who had conducted a survey in the Mississippi Valley, had advised him that Louisiana could be occupied and defended by 1,500 troops and an artillery company, Bonaparte issued an order to organize secretly an expedition of several thousand troops. He selected Dunkirk as the port of embarkation for the French forces, but repeated Spanish delays in arranging the actual transfer of Louisiana hampered the preparations. The two governments finally came to terms on October 18, 1802, but another week elapsed before officials in Paris received notification. In the meantime, French officials had switched the point of embarkation from Dunkirk to the Dutch port of Helvoet Sluys, located some thirty kilometers southwest of Rotterdam. This necessitated a transfer of troops and equipment. While preparations continued, General Claude Victor replaced General Victor Collot as captain general of Louisiana. Denis Decrès, minister of navy and colonies, told General Victor in November and again in December that the expedition was ready to embark, but his assurances proved to be premature. High winds damaged some ships intended for the expedition and the families of French officials took their time in preparing for the voyage. The continuing delays prompted French officials to send Pierre Clement Laussat, colonial prefect and second in command to General Victor, to Louisiana to make advance preparations to receive the expeditionary force. The colonial prefect left La Rochelle on January 10, 1803. [3]

But further delays were yet to come. Just when it appeared that the expedition finally would embark—over six months after Bonaparte directed Decrès to begin immediate preparations—severe winter weather caused the small harbor to freeze over and the ships were icebound. Conditions did not improve until March. Another two-week delay occurred in April when high winds again damaged several French transports. By this time it no longer mattered. Prompted in part by the delays resulting from the impossible weather conditions, Bonaparte had changed his mind. Irrespective of this unanticipated problem,

Bonaparte's decision was still a logical one and he knew it. The European truce arranged under the Peace of Amiens seemed unlikely to last, and the resumption of hostilities in Europe would require the Corsican's full attention. Moreover, Bonaparte needed a friendly United States to reestablish French sovereignty over Louisiana, and President Jefferson already had communicated his opposition to the proposed transfer to the French government. Finally, French forces continued to suffer losses in men and material at the hands of Toussaint L'Ouverture and his partisans in Santo Domingo. A violent struggle between the island's planters and slaves and the scourge of yellow fever further aggravated the deteriorating French position.

Two months before Bonaparte ordered Denis Decrès to begin immediate preparations for the French occupation of Louisiana, President Jefferson had instructed Robert R. Livingston, the American minister in Paris, to propose the American purchase of New Orleans and West Florida. Jefferson also used Pierre du Pont de Nemours, a recent French immigrant, to promote the transaction. On December 31, 1802, du Pont informed Jefferson from France that he thought Bonaparte might be willing to sell New Orleans and West Florida for $6 million. Du Pont's letter indicated that Bonaparte was at least considering alternatives to the French occupation of Louisiana several weeks before the beginning of the neutralizing cold wave. Indeed, having had sufficient time in which to make a comprehensive assessment of the plan, Bonaparte probably had largely decided against it and the cold wave merely confirmed his decision. British naval might could easily make a shambles of his Caribbean dream, and President Jefferson, aware that a French occupation of Louisiana could hardly be viewed in the same casual and patient light as the Spanish overlordship, conveyed the impression that he was serious about a conjugal alliance with the British fleet and nation. Jefferson secured $2 million from Congress to conduct the negotiations and appointed James Monroe as special envoy to assist Livingston in Paris. But lest French leaders take his threat lightly, he instructed his two diplomats to proceed to London and negotiate an alliance if the French proved obdurate, and he underscored his intentions by personally making friendly overtures to the British chargé in Washington. Having firmly made up his mind, the First Consul peremptorily ordered his finance minister to negotiate the sale of Louisiana immediately.[4] Consequently, President Jefferson, the wily diplomat and consummate actor who had already planned the Lewis and Clark expedition, acquired Louisiana for approximately $15 million. This amounted to a mere $5 million more than the United States had been willing to pay for New Orleans and West Florida.

Despite the reservations and problems which accompanied the transaction—the French promise not to relinquish Louisiana to a third party without Spain's consent, the indefinite boundaries, the constitutional reservations, and the vociferous Federalist protests—it was, as Talleyrand declared, a "noble bargain." By agreeing to sell Louisiana, Bonaparte acquired additional funds needed to prosecute the war against England. At the same time, the acquisition added immensely to the size and resources of England's only serious rival in North America.[5] A hard-riding courier brought news of the sale to the French troops at Helvoet Sluys just as they were finally ready to set sail for Louisiana.[6] Napoleon simply had not bothered to notify Decrès and General Victor of his earlier decision not to occupy Louisiana.[7]

The French officials assigned to oversee the occupation of Louisiana were not the only ones who remained uninformed. Neither Governor Claiborne nor the fastidious French prefect Laussat learned officially for some time of the sudden burst of diplomatic activity in Paris. From his distant and remote station on the lower Mississippi, the handicapped governor sought to learn as much as possible and to keep Washington posted. At about the time that Denis Decrès erroneously informed General Victor that the expeditionary force was ready to depart for Louisiana, Claiborne advised Secretary of War Henry Dearborn that according to reports from the Spanish governor, Victor would arrive in about a month with 3,000 men and that an additional 7,000 troops would follow shortly.[8] In late March, when the harbor at Helvoet Sluys had reopened, Claiborne received reports from Joseph Chambers, Choctaw factor, and Silas Dinsmoor, Choctaw agent, that Pierre Clement Laussat had arrived on the Mississippi River two days earlier and that the Spanish governor had left to meet him.[9] Meanwhile, following his arrival Laussat prepared to take control of Louisiana, blissfully unaware that within a month a Gallic-American agreement would reduce his mission to a ceremonial level.

For the moment the salient concern in both Natchez and New Orleans was whether Spanish colonial leaders would acquiesce in the retrocession of Louisiana to France. Officials in Madrid had been less than enthusiastic and had agreed to the transfer only after two years of negotiations following the agreement at San Ildefonso. The influential but controversial Daniel Clark, who came to New Orleans from Ireland in 1786 to join his wealthy uncle, feared that the French prefect's conduct would compound Spanish obdurateness. Despite the widespread apprehension, the formal transfer was concluded without Spanish-inspired impediments or embarrassments on November 30, exactly seven months after the French sale of Louisiana to the United States. The commissioners, Laussat representing France and Manuel de Salcedo and Casa Calvo representing Spain, met at the Cabildo, the distinctive Spanish government building constructed in 1795 and located across the street from the Place d'Armes. Ignoring the inclement weather, many citizens gathered in the public square facing the Cabildo to witness the ceremony. The French prefect, described by Daniel Clark as a kindred spirit to Edmond Genêt and one who assumed an air of authority that "disgusts the rich and frightens the poor," issued a proclamation declaring that Louisiana would remain only temporarily under French jurisdiction.[10] The embarrassed Laussat, who had learned of the sale of Louisiana to the United States only a short time before, had previously branded rumors to that as "an improbable and impudent lie" created by President Jefferson as an election maneuver.[11] Forced to reverse his course the prefect now exuded an ingratiating generosity toward the new owner whose rights would be formally confirmed in another twenty days. According to Laussat the Louisianians would acquire the rights and immunities of American citizens, and they would be protected in the enjoyment of their liberty, property, and religion. They would unite with a people distinguished for their industry, patriotism, and understanding. Manifesting no awareness of the complex judicial problem that soon would confront the American leadership, Laussat assured the Louisianians that they would enjoy an "upright, impartial, and incorruptible jurisprudence." Trade monopolies would disappear, duties would no longer be levied on exports, and only uniform duties would be imposed on imports. The Mississippi River would become the Nile of America, he predicted, and "the wharves of this other Alexandria will be crowded with ships from all quarters of the world." At the same time, Laussat, who from the moment of his appearance in New Orleans had antagonized Spanish colonial leaders, continued to exacerbate Spanish sensibilities. According to the fastidious Frenchman, no longer would the natives of Louisiana be inconvenienced by representatives whose malpractices could be easily concealed by geographic circumstances from the mother government. This must have sent Mediterranean blood pressures and pulse rates soaring, adding to the existing displeasure of Salcedo and Casa Calvo. The prefect ended by proclaiming expansively that France was voluntarily emancipating the colony.[12]

In the three-week interim between the termination of Spanish rule and the transfer of Louisiana to the United States, Louisiana was officially under the jurisdiction of France. During that time the haughty and pretentious prefect administered Louisiana without advisors, administrators, or even a meaningful security force. Virtually unknown by the people of Louisiana and ignorant of the territory and its inhabitants, he repeatedly offended and embarrassed the Spanish dons who remained sullen and resentful. Under these uncertain circumstances, the Americans moved quickly and decisively.

Rumors of the American acquisition of Louisiana from the French had been circulating and generating excitement among the Americans and uncertainty among the Louisianians for several months. On July 17, 1803, President Jefferson had written Governor Claiborne to confirm the agreement. He enclosed a set of questions about Louisiana which he had sent to Daniel Clark in New Orleans. He requested that both men respond to as many of the questions as possible. The president wished to make the information available to Congress so that it, in turn, could "take understandingly the best measures for incorporating that country with the Union." The exuberant president hailed the acquisition as the greatest achievement since the attainment of American independence. The transaction, he exclaimed, was "the more fortunate as it has not been obtained by war & force, but by the lawful & voluntary cession of the proprietor, a title which nothing can hereafter bring into question. It secures to an incalculable distance of time the tranquility, security & prosperity of all the Western country." In a follow-up letter Jefferson informed Claiborne that the transfer of Louisiana would occur immediately after the two governments ratified the treaty sometime late in October. Delicacy and skill would be necessary, he advised, in working with the French and Spanish officials. Then the personally exciting news followed:"I had had it in contemplation to get you to repair thither at the time to transact it, and to hold the place some little time until Congress shall direct what is to be done more particularly."[13]

On August 12, Governor Claiborne who earlier had requested permission to visit Tennessee for a few days informed Jefferson that he would gladly postpone the visit and would remain in readiness to proceed immediately to New Orleans upon receipt of orders. Claiborne added that "I know of no mission which would be so grateful to my feelings."[14] In a subsequent letter to Secretary of State Madison, Claiborne expressed deep appreciation for his selection as a commissioner and the resultant opportunity to contribute "tho even in so small a degree, to the peaceful and happy establishment of the American Government in Louisiana." Displaying a studied but characteristic humility, he continued: "I lament that I have too much reason to distrust my Talents for the high station to which I am called. But if honest views, zealous and faithful attention to the duties instructed to me, will be accepted in lieu of more Brilliant Abilities, I hope to retain that confidence of my Government which at this time constitutes a principal Happiness of my life."[15] Although Claiborne did not intend for officials in Washington to accept these professions of modest capabilities too literally, his self-evaluation was remarkably accurate. He was not a man of overwhelming brilliance or rare talent. Yet he combined average abilities with strong ambitions and an almost unlimited commitment to the responsibilities of his office to achieve a consistently superior record of public service.

In the weeks following his communication from President Jefferson, the governor proceeded to inform the legislature, his Indian agents, and factors of the acquisition. When he wrote to Joseph Chambers at Fort St. Stephens and heaped praise upon the "amiable and able Statesman" who had made it all possible, he accurately predicted that the American flag would be flying over New Orleans by Christmas. In early October the governor appeared before the Mississippi legislature to announce the impending transfer and, borrowing heavily from the president's earlier correspondence, expressed his gratitude that Louisiana had been secured by "honest purchase" rather than by "the precarious tenure of force." It would unite the American family, he continued, in interests and affection, "a union which I pray to my God may exist co-equal with time." The lawmakers responded two days later and agreed that, aside from the realization of independence, "all other objects of inferior concern, sink from view, and are eclipsed by the magnitude and grandeur of this acquisition."[16]

On the last day of October Jefferson signed the congressional act giving the president authority to take possession of Louisiana under the terms of the Franco-American agreement and authorizing him to employ army, navy, and certain militia forces to maintain American authority. While the act made no provision for a permanent system of government, it vested civil, judicial, and military powers in the territory with such person or persons selected by the president until the end of the current legislative session or until Congress provided for a temporary government. On the same day President Jefferson issued commissions to Governor Claiborne and General James Wilkinson to receive Louisiana jointly or separately, but he gave Claiborne exclusive authority to govern the ceded territory. Having earlier expressed some worry that France, dissatisfied with its "late bargain with us," might find some pretext to void the agreement, the president refused to relax until the agreement was executed and the territory was in American hands. He was fully aware that Carlos Martinez de Irujo (Yrujo), Spanish minister to the United States, had responded to Madison's blunt assertion that the dons would have to decide whether they wanted "a garden of peace or field of war" with the ominous rejoinder that Louisiana might well cost the Americans more that $15 million if they "undertook a quarrel."[17]

The president had initially intended for Claiborne alone to receive Louisiana, but rumors of possible Spanish opposition to the transfer induced him to appoint General Wilkinson as well. Whatever his reasons for selecting them, Jefferson could hardly have chosen two more disparate persons. Claiborne was impeccably honest; Wilkinson hardly knew the meaning of the term. Claiborne had an uncompromising commitment to his government and republicanism; Wilkinson steadfastly maintained a commitment only to self-interest. Claiborne was by disposition candid and forthright; Wilkinson was congenitally devious and deceitful. The transfer brought this ill-assorted pair together into a "conspicuous but distrustful association"[18] that would be maintained intermittently for several years. Laussat remarked later that the transfer could hardly have begun more inauspiciously, and that the American government would have been hard-pressed to send two representatives less suited to win the support and confidence of Louisiana's "ancient inhabitants."

However, in fairness to the inexperienced commissioners, Laussat probably would have found ample reason to question the qualifications of any persons chosen for the task. While conceding that Claiborne possessed some "charming private qualities," Laussat characterized him as a person of great awkwardness and few means. As for Wilkinson, the prefect accused him of being illogical, eccentric, and an inebriate.[19] The shared responsibilities and Wilkinson's personality sometimes annoyed Claiborne who jealously guarded his own prerogatives to the point that he occasionally appeared petty and picayune. When preparing to go to New Orleans, he wrote to Jefferson about his associate's superior military pretension. He was apprehensive that the "Rank attach'ing to the station, in which I am now placed, might excite some jealously." Although Claiborne considered himself to be the senior partner, he realistically acknowledged a logical delineation of responsibilities. He assured the president that he would studiously avoid any pretense of military command, even with the militia, but he was fully prepared to act with energy and dispatch in the "diplomatic proceedings." A few months after the transfer was concluded he declared to Madison that he would never again share a responsibility equally with another official. "*Three* may accord, but *two* never can; and in this latter case, nothing will be done, or the business will be conducted in a way that will not be pleasing to either, and *perhaps* not satisfactory to the government."[20]

On the day that Jefferson appointed him to be a commissioner, Madison sent Claiborne some general instructions and guidelines. Although Claiborne would have almost unlimited powers, the secretary of state advised that prudent judgment would dictate moderation and "conciliatory deportment." Since the Americans assumed the Spanish governor to be favorably disposed toward the United States, Madison directed Claiborne to allow him to remain in his quarters and to show him every courtesy. However, Madison instructed Claiborne, in the event of Spanish opposition, to "give effect to our title which is clear and just, by employing force for the purpose." Should the Spaniards offer active resistance, the commissioners were to decide whether the force they would lead to New Orleans, joined by those inhabitants in the city who would support them, would be sufficient to overcome the Spanish forces. If a *coup de main* became necessary, General Wilkinson was to direct it, according to instructions from the War

Department. The force would consist of regular troops stationed in the vicinity—those stationed at Fort Adams which was located on the Mississippi River just north of the thirty-first parallel—as many Mississippi militiamen as could be organized for the mission, and "as many volunteers from any quarter as can be picked up." Moreover, 500 mounted militiamen from Tennessee would be instructed to proceed to Natchez to join the expedition. However, Madison thought the Tennessee militiamen would not be necessary if Claiborne moved quickly to effect the transfer and if Spanish reinforcements were not dispatched to New Orleans. Finally, Madison advised the use of psychological warfare. Claiborne was invited to "add the effect of terror to the force of arms" by disseminating information, "which is a truth," that an overwhelmingly powerful force was being assembled in the western states that would be capable of stamping out all conceivable resistance. Laussat's support was desirable but not essential.[21]

Secretary of War Dearborn wrote to General Wilkinson to tell him essentially what Madison had told Claiborne. He authorized the two commissioners to proceed to New Orleans without loss of time with six companies of regular troops and one hundred volunteer militia, but the two men were to make their own assessment and decide, after consulting with Clark, Laussat, and other leaders in New Orleans, what their precise course of action would be. Some three hundred to four hundred regular troops would be available, along with six hundred to nine hundred militiamen from the Natchez vicinity. Moreover, some six thousand militiamen were to be held in readiness in Kentucky, Tennessee, and Ohio for possible use. Speed, he felt, would increase the probability of a peaceful transfer and make the additional forces unnecessary, but they would be ready for any eventuality.[22] General Wilkinson could not be located at the time, however, and was unaware of his appointment and this directive from the War Department.

Intent on utilizing every possible resource to effect a quick and peaceful transfer, Madison wrote to Daniel Clark at the same time he and Dearborn sent instructions to Claiborne and Wilkinson. The two commissioners would have to determine the feasibility of a *coup de main*, he stated. They could not wait for reinforcements to be assembled from the western states, therefore, or allow the dons to make defensive preparations. The secretary of state solicited assistance from Clark for the task ahead. First, he wanted the Irish immigrant, now established in New Orleans and sensing real opportunities in the fluid political climate, to provide the two commissioners with as much information as possible since their actions would be based on intelligence data available to them. Second, if a *coup de main* became necessary, he wanted Clark to rally local support. He hoped, moreover, that Laussat would use his influence to promote a peaceful transfer.[23]

As he began preparations to carry out the directive from Washington, Governor Claiborne solicited Clark's active assistance and support. He wanted Clark's estimate of Spanish military strength in New Orleans and vicinity and of the approximate size of the American force that would be required to suppress any resistance that might materialize. He invited "any hints which you may be able to give as to the most adviseable move of proceeding with an Army and Approaching the City," and inquired about the intentions of the "high officers now at Orleans." Also, Claiborne said he had been informed that Clark was prepared to organize and lead pro-American forces in New Orleans. He advised caution and discretion on Clark's part, but wanted to know the numbers, strength, influence, and reliability of these elements.[24]

Responding to the flurry of requests, Clark flooded Claiborne with almost daily missives over the next few weeks. Initially, he felt the transfer would proceed peacefully, asserting contemptuously that Casa Calvo was incapable of a "deep laid plan." However, his reports increasingly reflected uneasiness. While he did not wish to convey the impression that Louisiana's heterogeneous peoples were hostile or dangerous, he cautioned the Americans to be prepared for any eventuality. In his estimation the people were grossly ignorant and might be influenced by designing persons. Since Clark believed that if the Spanish leaders acted they would do so without support from Spain, he remained confident they could not succeed. Spanish military forces were weak and ineffective, the fortifications were crumbling, and the militia was unreliable. Indeed, many of those people upon whom the Spaniards relied for support, Clark believed, would join the American ranks. But to insure this, a strong and visible American presence was necessary; otherwise the people would not run the risk of exposing themselves to possible Spanish reprisals. If the Spaniards, having a regular force of only about three hundred men, of whom seventy-five were then in the hospital, should make threatening gestures, the Americans could confidently advance against them. Clark estimated that three hundred of the city's male inhabitants were ready to attack any force that opposed the American entry. Clark reported that his personal differences with Laussat had been resolved, but added that he and the prefect would continue the appearance of coolness toward each other for effect. By doing this, Clark pointed out, he would be received by the "opposite side and admitted to a knowledge of their secrets and intentions from which I would otherwise be debarred."[25]

Much of Daniel Clark's optimism subsided and gave way to alarm when friction developed between the Spanish and French leaders in New Orleans. Clark reported on November 23 that Madame Laussat had denounced some Spanish officers as "Souls of filth" because they had declined to attend a fete she had given. This, plus Laussat's explosive temper and peremptory attitude toward the Spaniards was altogether too provocative, Clark felt, and he implored Claiborne: "for God's sake lose no time in marching this way to put an End to the horrid situation we are in—We are placed over a Mine that may explode from one moment to another and the effect may be dreadful beyond conception."[26] Almost a week later Clark informed Claiborne and Wilkinson that Louisiana would be retroceded to France on November 30 which would be necessary before the ultimate transfer to the United States. On the day of the transfer Clark reported to Claiborne that he had organized a company of around one hundred American volunteers in the city to help the prefect maintain the peace while Louisiana would be technically under French jurisdiction.[27] But about two weeks afterward Clark expressed a real sense of urgency: "every delay is a day of fear and suspence for the whole Country and . . . you cannot possibly make use of too much expedition to arrive & put an end to it."[28]

Hampered by inadequate communications, President Jefferson eagerly awaited news of the transfer from his officials in Louisiana. Confidently assuming that preparations for the transfer had proceeded apace, he informed Thomas M. Randolph, his son-in-law, that the two commissioners probably had arrived in New Orleans on December 6-7 and if so, news of the transfer should reach the national capital by the first of the year.[29] In fact, Jefferson did not receive word until mid-January. Had he known the difficulties confronting his commissioner in Natchez, he might well have been nervous and agitated. Preparations were not progressing to Claiborne's satisfaction, and the elusive Wilkinson's whereabouts remained unknown. In Wilkinson's absence, the harried governor attempted to press ahead with preparations for the transfer. He finally decided that if he failed to locate Wilkinson, he would work out a course of action based on reports from Clark, Laussat, and other available sources in New Orleans.

Federal authorities had selected Fort Adams as the staging area for the American forces. As early as the preceding July the War Department had contacted Captain Edward Turner, commandant, to "prepare materials for the construction of boats, and to collect provisions for the increased number of troops," estimated at three hundred to four hundred. At the end of October, Dearborn directed him to finish the boats needed and to complete all necessary preparations for the trip, if Wilkinson had not taken command by then.[30] Nonetheless, little progress was being made. In early November Claiborne reported to Dearborn that he and Turner were making arrangements, "with a sincere wish that I may be soon joined by my experienced Coadjutor," who reportedly was in the vicinity of Pensacola. Buoyed by a report from Clark that the Spaniards did not plan to oppose the transfer and another from an unidentified source in New Orleans that the defenses in New Orleans were inadequate and that there were too few Spanish troops even for garrison duty, the governor added: "Were General Wilkinson now here, I therefore should not hesitate to urge an immediate descent, with such troops as are already prepared, and a small Body of Volunteers from the Territory." Since Wilkinson had not yet arrived, he would continue preparations and try to muster a "respectable" territorial militia force. He followed this report with another to Madison on November 20 in which he said that preparations at Fort Adams were not in "such forwardness." This was an understatement. Captain Turner would be ready after November 27 if muskets alone were necessary, but he would need ten days at least if artillery was required. As if this was not enough to create uneasiness in Washington, he further reported that volunteer militia enrollments had been disappointing because of cotton crops and business "at this particular season of the year." Four days later he reported to Madison that he had sent the Natchez Artillery Company, the Natchez Rifle Company, and a militia company from Natchez Landing to Fort Adams by boat. Over the vocal protests of its owner, he also impressed the schooner *Bilboa* to help transport the troops to New Orleans.

Claiborne said he would leave Natchez by land on December 2, and he hoped to receive another eighty volunteers along the way.[31]

Meanwhile, General Wilkinson, who had been making a boundary survey, learned of his appointment as a commissioner and began a leisurely and circuitous journey to join his associate at Fort Adams. He reportedly left Fort St. Stephens, located north of Mobile on the Tombigbee River, on November 11 and proceeded to Pensacola. From there he went to New Orleans, arriving on November 25. He conferred with French and Spanish officials there and then headed northward on the following day. He finally arrived at his destination on December 4, almost a month after he learned of his assignment. Governor Claiborne, having set out from Natchez on December 2, also reached Fort Adams on December 4.[32] The commissioners quickly learned that much work was yet to be done before the voyage to New Orleans could begin.

General Wilkinson, who previously had shown no disposition to hurry, now vigorously pressed preparation while ignoring Claiborne. Wilkinson ordered the troops to remain on fatigue duty until preparations were completed. He directed the issuance of ammunition and flints and the necessary equipment for field operations to the hastily assembled expedition of approximately five hundred men, which included some two hundred Mississippi militiamen, and he supervised the assembly of a flotilla of nineteen boats to transport them to New Orleans.[33] Heavy rains on December 6-7 hampered operations and added to the confusion and discomfort of the men. Since his superiors in Washington had charged his associate with responsibility for directing the military operations, Claiborne patiently remained in the background during the week of preparations. On December 7 he informed Madison that he had not conferred with Wilkinson about their mission, but he assured the secretary that he expected that the "utmost harmony in opinion and action will exist between us." In effect, Claiborne had decided to make the best of a potentially disruptive problem while at the same time alerting officials in Washington to the situation in the event it worsened. In a letter to Jefferson the following day, he repeated much of what he had said to Madison, but he how *hoped* that "the utmost *harmony* in opinion and action" would obtain between them. He stated that he had so studiously avoided participation in the military preparations then in progress at Fort Adams that General Wilkinson could have no possible cause for resentment or antipathy toward him. He then added pointedly: "If therefore I do not succeed in conciliating the confidence of the General in this particular, I shall only have to regret, that my best efforts towards that object have been fruitless." Ever economy-minded and never having participated in such a field experience, the expenses incurred in the preparations appalled Claiborne. Considering the possible implications for the nation's future, he exclaimed: "I . . . shall therefore pray to my God more fervently than ever, that our country may never be forced to the ruinous necessity of extensive armaments." He further concluded that the owner of the schooner *Bilboa* had protested its impressment in order to "enhance the price of her service." Although Wilkinson had estimated that the expedition would be ready to embark from Fort Adams on December 8, it did not begin the descent to New Orleans until three days later and it did so in a driving rain.[34]

A lively race ensued which, in a sense, portended the personal rivalry that would come to characterize relations between the two men. The *Bilboa*, transporting Claiborne and his party and the artillerists who were to return salutes offered the expedition as it descended the river, led the flotilla part of the way. However, the schooner ran aground near the mouth of Bayou Tunica at Pointe Coupée on the evening of December 12 while Wilkinson and the main force continued southward on their barges and flatboats. Claiborne quickly secured a barge and the trip was resumed, but crowded conditions and exposure to the weather caused some discomfort. They pressed ahead in an effort to recover the time lost as a result of the accident and to rejoin the flotilla. By December 15 the flotilla was only about three leagues from the city and its flag was discernible from the city by the next morning. Wilkinson and the troops disembarked and encamped outside the city itself. Claiborne and his party arrived about twenty-four hours later and joined the main force on the afternoon of December 17. Reporting to Madison on the same day, the governor expressed satisfaction that his separation from the flotilla had caused no delay or inconvenience. The weariness and fatigue of the trip quickly disappeared when an "animating hum of joy" from the townspeople greeted the Americans. The city remained calm as the French prefect and the American commissioners exchanged visits over the next two days.[35]

The official ceremony by which the vast Louisiana country was transferred from France to the United States occurred on

December 20. Activities began at eleven o'clock when the municipal militia paraded before the crowds of spectators who had gathered to witness the momentous occasion. Prefect Laussat duly observed that the balconies of the square—Place d'Armes—were filled with "beautiful women and fashionable men" and Spanish officers wearing plumes.[36] At noon the two American commissioners rode into the square at the head of their military contingent whose members were attired in dress uniforms. Directly behind the advancing commissioners were the cavalry, followed by four artillery pieces with the American flag draped from the first howitzer, followed, in turn, by the infantry and additional cannons.[37] These forces drew to attention facing the municipal militia which had previously assembled in the public square before the impressive Cabildo. The American officials exchanged credentials with their French counterparts, and Laussat presented Claiborne the key to the city.[38] The French flag was lowered slowly as the American flag was being raised aloft. The latter was stuck momentarily "as if it were confused at taking the place of that to which it owed its glorious independence." When the American flag was hoisted, shouts and the waving of hats were noted among "one particular group," and the enthusiasm they displayed made "more gloomy the silence and quietness of the rest of the ... spectators."[39] Claiborne, the central character in the brief but epochal drama, provided a less detached view. Reporting to Adams a few hours later, he proclaimed with pardonable exaggeration that: "The Sandard of my Country was, this day unfurled here, amidst the re-iterated acclamations of thousands. And if I may judge by professions and appearances, the government of the United States is received with joy and gratitude by the people."[40]

In the official proclamation which Governor Claiborne delivered to the assembled officials and citzenry, he stressed that the transfer was mutually advantageous. He enjoined the people to commit themselves to the United States. The transfer represented a "connexion beyond the reach of change, and to your posterity the sure inheritance of freedom." In return for the many benefits they would receive, the Louisianians would be expected to "cultivate with assiduity . . . the advancement of political information; you should guide the rising generation in the paths of republican economy and virtue." The United States would be amply remunerated, he continued, if the citizens of Louisiana attached themselves to the American Constitution in proportion to the many blessings that the document provided. Claiborne concluded by pledging himself to the promotion of their happinesss and welfare "during my continuance in the situation in which the President . . . has been pleased to place me." [41]

Certain measures had to be instituted immediately to provide governmental continuity and to insure a smooth and orderly transfer of authority. Consequently, Governor Claiborne reinstated the Conseil de Ville, the municipal body established by the French prefect to replace the Spanish Cabildo. It consisted of a mayor, recorder-secretary, and twelve councilmen. To provide security, General Wilkinson moved quickly following the ceremony to assign eight detachments of troops to positions throughout the city. Three mobile patrols were also set up and Wilkinson himself was "on Horse frequently." Moreover, he imposed a nine o'clock curfew, after which strangers and unauthorized persons, particularly slaves not carrying lights and written passes from their masters, were to be challenged and possibly taken into custody. While insisting that there was no imminent danger, Wilkinson requested a few hours later that the War Department dispatch a five-hundred-man force of regular troops to New Orleans for garrison duty. Rumors of a plot to burn the city and of a slave revolt, as well as lingering doubts about Spanish intentions, had made the general apprehensive. [42]

Following the transfer ceremony Claiborne assumed the responsibilities for governing the territory. Numerous public and private functions marked the occasion. The Marquis de Casa Calvo, bowing to these developments and outwardly suppressing his personal antipathy toward his archenemy, honored the French prefect with a lavish ball. Laussat reciprocated with an even more elaborate and festive ball in which hundreds of guests ate, danced, drank, and gambled throughout the night. Now it was the Americans' turn, but financial considerations handicapped Governor Claiborne. At the time he was appointed commissioner, he was authorized to draw up to $400 per month from the War Department, beginning with his departure from Natchez to New Orleans. About two weeks later, Madison authorized him to draw up to $10,000 from the State Department for the administration of Louisiana, but this amount was to be paid out of monies collected at New Orleans. Aside from this budgetary limitation, the economy-minded Republican leader, always the stalwart champion of fiscal austerity, doubted the widom of drawing upon the 'public treasure" for such unseemly purposes. However, General Wilkinson, subscribing to his own oblique system of fiscal accountability and unburdened by pangs of conscience, was more than equal to the occasion. The War Department would be able to attest to the general's facility in about four months. Wilkinson used the occasion of the transfer and the opportunities it afforded to inaugurate a celebration which lasted until the latter part of April and cost the government the tidy sum of $6,619.72. Among the random refreshments enjoyed by the commissioners and their guests were 162 pounds of coffee, 196 gallons and one quarter-cask of Madeira, 4 gallons of sherry, 144 bottles of champagne, 60 bottles of white wine, 100 bottles of "hermitage" wine, 588 bottles of red wine, 6 bottles of cordials, 67 gallons of brandy, 81 bottles of porter, 1 case of gin, 258 bottles of ale, 3 barrels of cider, 5 gallons of rum, 2 gallons of whisky, and 11,360 "Spanish Segars." Although Governor Claiborne did not authorize these expenses and undoubtedly felt very uncomfortable about them, he was, in effect, an accomplice. Several years later when John Randolph of Virginia charged Wilkinson in Congress with having received advances of rations beyond his legal advances, the hapless and embarrassed Claiborne attempted to defend their "table expenses." Although it would be difficult to convince the Congress of their frugality, he said, he and Wilkinson had practiced the most prudent economy. "The Wine, *as well as the Segars* were used by the Sovereign people," he asserted in proper Republican form, and added that he and the general "could not avoid receiving with hospitable attentions, the many respectable strangers, which political events had (at the time) drawn to New Orleans." Many other expenses were necessarily incurred, he told Secretary of the Treasury Albert Gallatin, which he had paid himself. Although he had considered requesting reimbursement, his only wish was "to have as few Accounts as possible to adjust with the government."[43] The archetype of solid Republican "oeconomy," having been "mauled" by congressional watchdogs for his fiscal transgression, if more indirect than that of the general, was not likely to repeat the mistake. But this was merely the first major embarrassment produced by his association with the free-wheeling Wilkinson.

Although major interest was centered in New Orleans for the transfer of December 20, 1803, Upper Louisiana was likewise surrendered to the Americans during the succeeding months.

Jefferson wrote to Captain Meriwether Lewis on November 16, 1803, to tell him that orders for its transfer would be sent out at about the time Claiborne and Wilkinson were receiving Lower Louisiana.[44] Captain Amos Stoddard, a New Englander and Revolutionary War veteran who had practiced law in Maine for several years before returning to the military service, was selected as acting commandant and received his orders from Governor Claiborne and General Wilkinson. The formal transfer of Upper Louisiana to the United States was scheduled to be held in St. Louis. Captain Stoddard arrived in the city on February 24, 1804, where he was greeted by Spanish Lieutenant Governor Carlos Dehault Delassus and a number of citizens. Stoddard planned to assume control almost immediately, but ice on the river delayed the arrival of some of his men and Delassus was indisposed for a time. As a consequence, the transfer ceremony was not held until March 9-10, 1804. Prefect Laussat, who elected not to make the trip to St. Louis, commissioned Captain Stoddard to receive Upper Louisiana from Delassus. The transfer from Spain to France, with Stoddard serving as the French agent, occurred on March 9. Captain Meriwether Lewis, then in the city to complete preparations for his upcoming expedition to the northwestern coast, witnessed the exchange for the United States. On the following day Captain Stoddard transferred Upper Louisiana from himself as the French commissioner to himself as the American agent. Following the formal ceremony, Stoddard addressed the inhabitants, as Governor Claiborne had done earlier in New Orleans. He assured them that they could expect fair and equitable treatment and that they would enjoy full rights and privileges of American citizenship. The only other formal transfer observance in Upper Louisiana was held at the small Spanish post at New Madrid, where Captain Daniel Bissel assumed command eight days afterward.[45] Although Governor Claiborne was interested in the relinquishment of the various posts in Louisiana to American authorities, he simply could not send emissaries and troops to receive and occupy them. To have done so would have weakened and depleted his own altogether too meager security force in New Orleans. General Wilkinson had released the volunteer companies of the Mississippi militia about two weeks after the transfer in New Orleans, leaving only the approximately three-hundred-man contingent of regular troops from Fort Adams and a small volunteer force organized by Daniel Clark to assist the

American commissioners. Fortunately for all concerned, the various individual transfers proceeded as smoothly as the one at New Orleans.

Not until the completion of the transfer of the Louisiana territory in fulfillment of the terms of the Franco-American treaty could American officials seriously ponder the magnitude of their great acquisition. This would not be fully determined for another half century, during which there would be tedious and exhausting diplomatic exchanges, threats and counterthreats, and finally decisions arrived at in the crucible of war. Initially, the average westerner did not concern himself with the question of the great boundaries; he was elated that he now had full and complete control of the Mississippi River, so vital to his economic wellbeing. In time he expanded his horizons. The Jeffersonian vision was a more encompassing one and it antedated the Franco-American treaty. From his station in New Orleans, Governor Claiborne assumed a vitally important position, both in terms of the greater vision of the Sage of Monticello and his disciple and successor, and the influence he would exert upon their strategic and tactical plans to make the vision of an expanded Louisiana a reality.

Uncertainty about the boundaries of Louisiana did not originate with the Franco-American treaty. The secret Treaty of San Ildefonso, concluded some nineteen months earlier, stated that Louisiana consisted of the same extent which France had ceded to Spain in 1762, and "such as it should be after the treaty subsequently entered into between Spain and other states."[46] Bonaparte himself had encouraged the boundary ambiguities and Talleyrand responded to American inquiries by advising them to rejoice in the noble bargain they had won for themselves. Governor Claiborne, having earlier exhibited expansionist propensities, seized upon the ambiguities to press vigorously at every opportunity for an expanded interpretation of American claims.

Even before the actual transfer, Jefferson had questioned Claiborne and Clark about Louisiana's boundaries. Claiborne responded that an earlier attempt had been made to determine the western limits. The mouth of the Sabine River was the point of departure for the party attempting to establish it. The party proceeded up the Sabine to a point some five leagues northwest of Natchitoches where the effort was discontinued. To the president's inquiry about the distance from the mouth of the

Mississippi to the western boundary line, Claiborne was less than helpful, stating that it had never been measured, but added: "an old Inhabitant here who calculates by day's journey's, supposes it to be about 160 miles." In a postscript, he said he had just been informed that the jurisdiction of Louisiana ended and that of Texas began ten or twelve miles west of Natchitoches on the Red River.[47] Then a week after the formal transfer of Louisiana to the United States, Claiborne and Wilkinson wrote to Madison about the southwestern boundary. They had conferred with Laussat and had been told that France had claimed the land from the Rio Bravo (Grande) northward to the thirtieth degree north latitude. The country beyond this point had not been explored by even the most "Enterprizing travellers."[48] The Spaniards insisted that the Sabine River, rather than the Rio Grande, was the western boundary. Indeed, they later laid claim to some territory east of the Sabine but pulled their troops back across the river after a few nervous hours when war with nearby American forces became imminent. Captain Amos Stoddard attempted to resolve the problem by drawing a boundary line based on French pretensions, but it was hardly an improvement upon the vague clause in the Treaty of San Ildefonso. He recognized the Perdido River as being the eastern boundary, while the western one was "partly on the rio Bravo, and partly on the Mexican mountains; north and northwest, partly on the shining mountains, and partly on Canada." Stoddard identified the Shining Mountains as the Andes. The Mexican mountains began north of the Gulf of Mexico, near the left bank of the Rio Bravo, and extended northwesterly until they intersected with the Shining Mountains, according to the captain.[49] Despite the inquiries, the American authorities attached no immediate importance to the western boundaries. Rather, their attention was focused mainly to the eastward. This followed naturally since Jefferson had given West Florida a priority second only to the Isle of Orleans. With Stoddard, officials in Washington provided strong support for the Perdido "pretensions" which Spain rejected categorically. Although the Louisiana Territory was divided into the Territory of Orleans and the District of Louisiana by Congress a little over two months following the official transfer, both the eastern and western boundaries remained lively sources of disagreement and conflict in the ensuing years.

The undetermined boundaries were subject to interpretation, but the principals agreed that Louisiana constituted a substantial territorial acquisition. They also agreed at the time that the "vitals" of Louisiana consisted of the Isle of Orleans, including the city of New Orleans, the coastal stretches along the Gulf of Mexico, and the lands lying adjacent to the Mississippi River. Contributing to the momentary frustration and confusion of the incoming Americans were "old country" geographic designations, reflections of the Gallic and Iberian continental and colonial experiences. Approximately three-fourths of the territory's total population and an estimated seven-eights of the total wealth were located within these narrow limits. The pulsating heart was the bustling port city of New Orleans, sprawling for a mile along the east bank of the Mississippi and claiming about one-fifth of the total population. Encircling the Crescent City and affording it a false sense of security were five forts, built during the four decades of Spanish occupation but in a state of abject disrepair in 1803. The only other settlement on the "island" south of New Orleans was Terre aux Boeufs, or San Bernardo, twelve miles away. The "island" itself was bounded by the Mississippi River on the west and south, and on the east by the Gulf of Mexico. On the north and beginning at the Mississippi River, the Isle of Orleans was bounded by the Bayou Manchac, known at the time as the Iberville River, the Amite River, lakes Maurepas, Pontchartrain, and Borgne, and the Mississippi Sound. The Lower Coast encompassed those lands lying along the Mississippi River and extending northward from the Balize at its mouth on the gulf to New Orleans. The Upper Coast extended northward from the city to the settlements at Pointe Coupée, a distance of about seventy-five miles. From Bayou Manchac on the north and extending southward to within some fifty miles of the Balize and broken only by the city of New Orleans, great plantations extended in an almost unbroken line on both sides of the Mississippi River.[50]

When Jefferson appointed Claiborne to preside over the newly acquired territory, even the normally perceptive president did not fully appreciate the responsibility he had vested in his young frontier disciple. Aside from the undetermined boundaries, Louisiana was "an American enclave in an otherwise solidly Spanish-held area extending all along the Gulf of Mexico from Florida to Mexico itself."[51] The cultural heritage, economic life, and political institutions of Louisiana differed markedly from those in any other territory under American control. The economic and cultural center of Louisiana was the flourishing port city of New Orleans. The institution of slavery and a slave-holding aristocracy were already established and entrenched. Cotton and sugar were grown on the great fertile plantations lining the banks of the river, producing a staple-crop agricultural economy. Although the American influence rapidly increased after 1803, the Americans at the time of the transfer were a decided, if somewhat vocal, minority. Governor Claiborne's most formidable task was the introduction of American institutions and the "Americanization" of the inhabitants which he was expected to accomplish without producing any serious local disruptions. Moreover, the governor's inability to communicate with the inhabitants in any language other than English compounded his problem.

According to a census taken in 1806, the total population of the Territory of Orleans, not including the District of Louisiana created two years earlier, was 55,534. Almost half of this number consisted of Negro slaves and "free men, women and children of colour."[52] Inhabitants of French extraction made up the single greatest element of the dominant white population, followed by inhabitants of Spanish ancestry, although almost every conceivable national type was represented in the territory. Moreover, social gradations extended from primitive herdsmen and hard-scrabble farmers to pretentious barons and haughty chevaliers. And as was to be expected, democracy-oriented Americans poured into the territory in ever-increasing numbers in the years following the acquisition of Louisiana. Indeed, the vigorous sweep of the enterprising Americans into the new territory has been likened to the inundation of Rome by the barbaric Germanic tribes. The "ancient inhabitants" would have agreed with and appreciated the comparison. That the cauldron sometimes threatened to spill over before any real degree of homogeneity was realized, then, should have occasioned no particular surprise.[53] Indeed, it is surprising, in view of the basic cultural, social, and political disparaties that far greater turbulence and antipathy did not accompany the "Americanization" process.

If the natives looked with suspicion and contempt upon the American newcomers, the latter were anything but impressed with the Louisianians. Even the normally positive Claiborne, especially when stung by unkind local barbs, was at times harshly critical. The greatest of their "mischiefs," he observed starchily to

Madison about four months after his arrival in New Orleans, was their moral depravity. Love of wealth and luxurious dissipation, he charged, "had nearly acquired the ascendancy over every other passion."[54] Claiborne, who conveyed this impression in a moment of personal pique in reaction to local criticisms, was usually more generous and laudatory in his assessments of the Louisianians.

At the time he offered his premature and narrow criticism of the "ancient inhabitants," Governor Claiborne had no particular reason to believe nor did President Jefferson intend that his appointment would become a permanent one. It was a recess appointment and the president had merely asked him to serve until Congress decided upon the status of Louisiana. The acquisition produced a number of loaves and fishes and competition for them, as always, was very keen and often distasteful. Some candidates made strong bids; others were encouraged to make themselves available. The juiciest political plum was obviously the governorship, and Jefferson was deluged with applications. In mid-1803 Jefferson seemed to favor Thomas Sumner, Jr., for the post. Sumner, who was then in Paris, had worked for a time on James Monroe's staff. A disagreement with Robert Livingston, however, appears to have eliminated Sumner as a candidate. About a month afterward Secretary of the Treasury Albert Gallatin informed Jefferson that William Lyman of Massachusetts was interested. The president responded a few days later that Lyman's "measure of himself differs so much from ours that it is not likely we shall agree in a result." Fulwar Skipwith, who was later active in trying to secure the separation of West Florida from Spain, was mentioned as an aspirant, and Daniel Clark seems to have had some hope of appointment.[55] Even Aaron Burr's name was bruited about for a time and New Orleans newspapers quoted eastern newspaper sources as reporting that Burr had been appointed governor before speedily retracting the accounts. Apparently Burr did have some friends and confederates who actively supported his candidacy, and who wished to "send to the devil that idiotic boaster W. C. C. Claiborne."[56] Nonetheless, the president's vivid memories precluded any consideration of his old political ally turned nemesis in 1800.

The president seriously considered several candidates for the Louisiana post. He made a special effort to secure the services of the Marquis de Lafayette. Jefferson asked him to accept the post, and Congress gave the marquis a land grant in Louisiana, which

Lafayette interpreted as an effort to entice him to go there. In fact, Jefferson told Claiborne several months before the formal transfer of Louisiana that the post was intended for Lafayette, whose services and fame made him "Peculiarly acceptable to the country at large." But circumstances—Lafayette was imprisoned at Olmütz at the time—prevented Lafayette's nomination, and Jefferson thought that the marquis probably would never accept the post.[57] James Monroe was Jefferson's second choice. In early 1804 the president wrote to Monroe, who was then in London, and said that the salary of $5,000 would be several thousand dollars less than he was then making, but added hastily that living expenses in New Orleans would be substantially less. As added allurements, the president mentioned the "richest lands in the world" and the "extraordinary profitableness of their culture." Monroe responded that his responsibilities in London and Madrid required too much time for him to consider the post. When Claiborne remained in the position and came under heavy fire from Daniel Clark and his allies in New Orleans and from John Randolph on the floor of the House of Representatives, Jefferson again broached the subject in a letter to Monroe. He wrote that the Territory of Orleans was still without "such a head" as he desired, and added that it was a post second only to the presidency. While both Lafayette and Monroe repeatedly rejected the administration's overtures, Andrew Jackson quietly explored his own chances when he visited Washington in early 1804. However, he refrained from discussing the post directly with Jefferson for fear that he would be regarded as a "courteor."[58] There is no particular reason to believe that he would have received serious consideration even had he formally applied. His record in both houses of Congress had been mediocre and he had yet to emerge as a prominent national figure.

Governor Claiborne was not as passive and reluctant as his former associate. Much of the local support he received in his efforts to secure the regular appointment bore the Claiborne imprint and indicated active solicitation and collusion. This included an address of appreciation from the citizens of Washington and Wilkinson counties in the Mississippi Territory drawn up on March 18, 1804. The citizens of the two counties congratulated Claiborne for his Louisiana appointment and thanked him for the leadership he had given them. They spoke of his simplicity of manners and dignified conduct as commissioner, and added that it would "remain a lasting monument of honest fame not to be rusted by the breath of faction." If Jefferson decided to retain him, they said, the loss would be regrettable, but they pledged their esteem for him in whatever capacity he served. Claiborne responded that their approbation was a testimonial to his good intentions rather than superior public service.[59] Additional support came from Isaac Briggs, who served as surveyor general in the Mississippi Territory and later went to the Orleans Territory to serve in the same capacity. About two weeks after the official transfer, Briggs wrote to President Jefferson that the existing situation in Louisiana demanded a leader of "Inflexible integrity, mild yet firm, a virtue superior to temptation—Intelligence to discern what is right, and resolution to do it, however unpopular for the moment—and Patience unconquerable by perverseness in others." Louisiana was a land of paradise converted into "a pandemonium," he observed, and the person best suited to cope with the situation was Governor Claiborne. Almost two months later Briggs again wrote to Jefferson and stated that Claiborne's replacement would appear to be a triumph for Claiborne's political enemies and would imply that the president had lost faith in him, "which I firmly believe he values above every other thing on earth, except the consciousness of deserving it." In both letters Briggs implied that the position should search out the man, rather than the reverse, hinting that Claiborne was contemplating retirement.[60]

Eager to win the appointment and leaving nothing to chance, Claiborne made a direct bid in late February to influence the president's decision. He informed Jefferson that an aspiring clique, which he declined to identify, was promoting a candidate for the governorship while attempting to make his own administration unpopular. They were circulating rumors that Jefferson had lost confidence in him, and that he would be replaced shortly. Claiborne made the point that when a Spanish officer was replaced, he was assigned to a higher post unless he had been disgraced. If ordered back to the Mississippi Territory, therefore, the impression would be that he was in disgrace. Claiborne informed the president that excessive expenses, low salary, incessant application, and mental anxiety had caused him to view the governorship in a less appealing light than many people, but he added quickly, lest Jefferson accept what he was saying at face value, that the president's confidence in him was an "inestimable treasure." This letter of February 25, when compared with Isaac Briggs' letters of January 2 and February 27, indicates strongly that the two men worked closely in a determined effort to win the appointment for Claiborne. [61]

Finally on August 30, some ten months after he appointed Claiborne commissioner to receive Louisiana, Jefferson wrote to Claiborne and enclosed his commission as governor of the Territory of Orleans. But even as he did so he made it clear that the appointment was largely *ad interim* by saying that it would afford Claiborne additional experience and allow him to determine the proper time and manner of withdrawal from the post if he desired. [62] When Claiborne's name was submitted to the United States Senate for approval in December, some opposition was anticipated. The nomination was approved, however, with only one dissenting vote. [63]

Although Claiborne received the appointment, both Jefferson and Madison continued to canvass the field and kept their options open. They never reconciled themselves completely to the Claiborne appointment, but nevertheless retained him in the post throughout Louisiana's territorial period. But why Claiborne? The most obvious explanation was that Jefferson and Madison failed to evoke any interest in the post from their first and second choices, Lafayette and Monroe. Of the available candidates none was demonstrably superior to Claiborne which was in itself a tribute to his abilities. Jefferson's preference for Lafayette and Monroe could hardly be interpreted as diminishing Claiborne's reputation. In fact Jefferson had confided to Secretary Dearborn that Claiborne's conduct had been so prudent and conciliatory that "no secondary character could have a better right." [64] Claiborne was convenient and available and he had previous political and administrative experience in the Misssissippi Territory, in the Congress, and in the Southwest Territory. Moreover, his incumbent status and a satisfactory record of performance during the interim period strengthened his candidacy. Claiborne was steady and reliable, if not a charismatic leader of instantly recognizable and overwhelming administrative capabilities. Indeed, if not initially, both Jefferson and Madison probably came to recognize that the particular leadership qualities possessed by Claiborne were preferable in that particular environment, embracing as it did an alien people and culture, to the more traditional territorial leadership. It required a leader possessed of almost infinite patience, perseverance, understanding and empathy, in addition to the usual administrative and political skills.

The American frontier was not the birthplace of such personal attributes. Claiborne's "reliability" was political and ideological. He was the embodiment of Republican virtues and values, a fact not taken lightly by Jefferson and Madison, who easily combined lofty idealism with pragmatic politics. One writer stressed "economy" as a reason for Claiborne's selection, saying he was willing to serve for a smaller salary. Although economy was a Republican trademark and Claiborne's affinity for economic stringency had been clearly established, the gubernatorial salary *per se* was of little consequence. In view of the importance Jefferson attached to the post, even if he exaggerated it in his effort to lure Monroe to Louisiana, it is hardly likely that the president was that parsimonious. The element of political gratitude inevitably surfaced as a consideration. While it may have been a factor, its influence was minimal. Having appointed Claiborne governor of the Mississippi Territory, Jefferson probably felt that he had largely discharged his political indebtedness. These factors in varying degrees contributed to Claiborne's appointment.

Selecting a chief executive to preside over the newly acquired territory was, in fact, secondary to the issue of what form the government of Louisiana should assume. Jefferson, ecstatic about the purchase, although he personally had never traveled farther south than his native Virginia or farther west than the Shenandoah Valley, exclaimed in the glow of his recent triumph: "The world will here see such an extent of country under a free and moderate government as it has never yet seen."[65] But this was the idealistic philosopher speaking at the time, not the president of the United States. Louisiana was new to the American experience, hardly fitting into the typical territorial mold. Instead of a few American frontiersmen intent on establishing tomahawk rights, a few traders and trappers, small and thinly scattered forts, and disparate Indian tribes giving way sullenly before them, Louisiana was a land of over 50,000 people, 5,000 more than resided in Ohio at the time. Moreover, they were a foreign people who knew little, if anything, about evolving American institutions, and what little they knew often evoked feelings of contempt. The issue before the president and Congress at the time, then, was potentially divisive. Jeffersonian idealism clashed head-on with practical reality, and the latter won handily. Prior to the American acquisition, the government of Louisiana was vested in a Spanish governor and intendant. They were independent of each other but were responsible to Havana and ultimately to Madrid. Commandants, whose powers within their respective jurisdictions were as complete as those of the governor and intendant, implemented the policies and orders of their superiors. Such concepts as popular sovereignty, representative government, and due process of law, therefore, were largely meaningless to Louisiana's masses.

Hesitation in Washington about the form of government that should be established in Louisiana embarrassed the Jefferson administration generally and Governor Claiborne in particular. Jefferson had solicited information from Claiborne and Clark about Louisiana in mid-July 1803, to assist in determining the kind of government Louisiana should have. Claiborne, who reported that the Spanish government in Louisiana was "partly Civil, partly Military, and in some degree ecclesiastical," took the pragmatic position that the territory should not be accorded statehood because the inhabitants were unfamiliar with the American political and governmental system. When the Congress authorized the president to take possession of Louisiana in October, the authorization stipulated merely that the existing form of government in Louisiana would be maintained until Congress could establish a new government. Consequently, Claiborne became the unwitting victim of a colossal irony. Claiborne, the stanch Republican who professed an utter abhorrence of absolutist government, was suddenly catapulted into a position of almost unlimited authority. Aside from two congressional limitations—he could not grant land titles or levy new or additional taxes—Claiborne was responsible to the president. As chief executive of Louisiana, Claiborne was vested with the powers of governor and intendant; in addition he retained his position as governor of the Mississippi Territory for several months. The governmental structure of Louisiana, in effect, remained basically unchanged for nine months after the transfer.

Both the failure of Congress to provide for the immediate establishment of a governmental system radically different from anything the Louisianians had known and the selection of William Claiborne as chief executive were major windfalls for the inhabitants, even if they failed to recognize and appreciate the fact at the moment. A virtual governmental paralysis would almost certainly have ensued had Congress sought to introduce far-ranging changes immediately. Although Claiborne admittedly exercised executive, legislative, judicial, military, and economic and commercial authority, as well as having responsibility for the Indian tribes in Louisiana, his approach to government was measured and methodical; he used his powers sparingly and judiciously. When decisions and actions were necessary, he demonstrated that capacity; when not required by conditions and circumstances, he placated, compromised, and deferred decisions which would have caused serious or potentially serious repercussions. In short, he exercised only those powers that were necessary to maintain stability and insure peace and order. Clearly the Actonian Maxim did not apply to this modest Jeffersonian exemplar.

Having reestablished the Municipality, or municipal council, in New Orleans, Claiborne diligently sought to work closely with it. He presided over weekly sessions of the governor's court, hearing civil and minor criminal cases only because it was necessary. In doing so, he was very uncomfortable, not only because he inherently opposed the basic policy but because he was unfamiliar with prevailing laws and customs and because of his inability to speak and understand the French language. Upon the recommendation of the municipal council, he established a temporary court of pleas in New Orleans almost immediately after the transfer. He hoped at the time that this body, empowered to accept cases involving sums up to $3,000, would replace the governor's court, but both courts were essential. The court had no jurisdiction in cases involving disputed land titles, and cases involving in excess of $500 could be appealed to the governor. Each of the seven judges serving on the court of pleas was to serve as a "conservator of the peace," and was empowered to hear civil cases involving up to $20 and criminal cases involving up to $200 and prison terms up to two months. At the local level of government, Governor Claiborne retained the civil and military commandants. These officials traditionally were responsible for the maintenance of security and order and could hear cases involving up to $100 in their respective districts. When selecting officials to serve in these various capacities, Claiborne generally reappointed those who had served earlier and were willing to continue under the new government. The only major exceptions were the military appointees in Natchitoches, Ouachita, Concordia, Opelousas,

Attakapas, and Upper Louisiana because "their commands were on the frontier." Although ability was desirable, the primary prerequisites for appointment were integrity and loyalty to the new authority.[66]

A little less than a month after the transfer, Claiborne recommended to Jefferson the first grade of government for Louisiana, as set forth in the Northwest Ordinance. Although some people preferred a military government, he said, he personally opposed it because the people would have gained nothing by the transfer. A few weeks afterward he reported that Laussat was encouraging the admission of Louisiana to statehood and that the people had come to expect it. But even those who favored it, he added, doubted that the people were capable of governing themselves.[67] While Claiborne was transmitting his report and recommendations to Washington, President Jefferson secretly worked to construct a feasible government for Louisiana. He, too, was convinced that the Louisianians were incapable of governing themselves since they were totally inexperienced. While Claiborne had recommended the first grade of government, Jefferson worked out a modification that fit loosely between the first and second stages of government. To apply the Northwest Ordinance to Louisiana "would turn all their laws topsy turvy." He pondered the frustrating question at length before he finally made his decision, saying at one point: "What kind of government would at first be most suitable & proper god only knows. It would be farcical to see a lawyer in a court of justice addressing a jury of them at present. With a few exceptions, they have no other idea of any kind of government than a Commandant with both civil & military jurisdiction." He finally concluded that the government should consist initially of a ruling governor and "Assembly of Notables," the latter being "a thing more familiar and pleasing to the French." In essence these appointed officials would constitute a ruling oligarchy charged with the responsibility of introducing American institutions, traditions, and customs to the native Louisianians. Nonetheless, Jefferson viewed this government as an improvement over the first stage of government under the Northwest Ordinance because the appointive "Assembly of Notables" would be better than a territorial legislature and would "not be a greater departure from sound principle."[68]

Although written personally by Jefferson, John Breckinridge of Kentucky, a reliable and discreet associate, introduced the bill in the United States Senate. Political pragmatism determined Louisiana's initial form of government, but the president's name under no circumstance was to be associated with the "Breckinridge Bill." Had the president's authorship been divulged, this would have called forth a torrent of vituperation and ridicule from the Federalists whose political assaults Jefferson felt keenly and personally. At the same time, his open identification with the bill would have caused his own disciples and adherents to doubt his basic commitment to the philosophical principles with which he had come to be identified. Following the bill's introduction in the Senate, it underwent some minor changes and its more controversial features were discussed and debated. Opponents of the bill charged that it contravened both the federal Constitution and the Franco-American treaty. Nonetheless, the Congress adopted "An Act for the Organization of Orleans Territory and the Louisiana District." Although the president approved the measure on March 26, 1804, it did not go into effect until October 1. It provided for the separation of the Louisiana Territory into the Territory of Orleans and the District of Louisiana, with the former consisting of the region south of a line drawn at the 33⁰ north latitude. The act vested executive power in a governor appointed for a period of three years. The secretary, appointed for a four-year period, had the normal secretarial responsibilities but he became acting governor whenever that office became vacant. The governor and thirteen-man legislative council, whose membership was chosen annually, constituted the legislative authority. The president appointed all of these officials. The measure vested judicial power in a superior court consisting of three judges, in such inferior courts and justices of the peace as the territorial legislature decided to establish, and a federal district court presided over by one judge.[69] The act differed from the Northwest Ordinance in certain other essentials, most of which were intended to meet the particular needs of the native inhabitants. Slavery was not forbidden in the new territory, but it was restricted. The territorial legislature was authorized to enact "new" legislation rather than merely adopt laws previously enacted by the state legislatures. Finally, the bill failed to authorize a non-voting territorial delegate to Congress. The size of the population and territory certainly justified congressional representation, and the experience it would have afforded a people who had never experienced representative government and "democracy in action" would have been invaluable.

The disappointment of the native inhabitants surfaced quickly following news that Louisiana had not been given statehood. Handbills calling upon the people to revolt were posted clandestinely. Claiborne was not unduly concerned, but he had them taken down and quietly increased general security measures. However, he acknowledged that "adventurers" then pouring into New Orleans might try to use the discontent to serve their own purposes.[70] The press reflected local dissatisfaction. A "fellow citizen" denounced a supporter of the act as one who had taken "leave of his senses." It constituted a violation of the Franco-American treaty, in his view, and had resulted in great inconvenience to the people. The result was the establishment of a government more oppressive than the one against which the American colonists had revolted in 1776.[71] Local leaders, the most active and vocal of whom were Americans rather than natives, attempted to take advantage of these early feelings of resentment by organizing the more influential citizens and drawing up a formal statement of protest. In a memorial to Congress—an American device that would have been unthinkable under French or Spanish rule—they protested the denial of statehood, restrictions on slavery, the introduction of the American legal system, unfair appointments, the governor's excessive powers, and Claiborne's inability to speak the language. The group chose three local Frenchmen, Pierre Derbigny, Jean-Noël Destréhan, and Pierre Sauvé, to present the memorial to Congress, a shrewd move by the local American leaders most responsible for the memorial. The day after he was inaugurated as governor, Claiborne told Madison that although the memorial reflected some genuine patriotism, it was tinged by a foreign influence. The memorialists included some Bonapartists, and he added that J. Etienne Boré, a wealthy sugar planter, had threatened to appeal to Napoleon if Congress rejected the memorial. According to Claiborne the people of Louisiana were a pacific and uncommonly credulous people who could easily be swayed by Louisiana's abundant supply of designing men. According to the governor, few people attended the meeting to draw up the memorial. When the memorial was later circulated, many signed it without reading it; others signed it without understanding it, and others' names were attached to the memorial without their knowledge. As Claiborne continued to make reports to his superiors about the memorial and some of the key figures who inspired it, Derbigny, Destréhan, and Sauvé presented it in

Washington.[72] The three Louisianians, who had but little of the "French frippery" about them and "resembled New England men more than the Virginians,"[73] impressed a number of congressmen. Although the memorial produced no immediate results, it may have influenced the administration's decision to advance Louisiana to the intermediate, or second stage, of government the following year.

Although the government act of March 1804 did not take effect until October 1, Claiborne needed more than six months to make the necessary preparations, and as a result the new territorial government got off to an unsteady and uncertain start. When he was inaugurated on Tuesday, October 2, the governor declared that he anticipated major assistance from the legislative and judicial branches, "and the kind indulgence and support which a generous people always extend to the honest efforts of a public Officer."[74] His decision to proceed with the inaugural activities at that particular time was a difficult one but he was beginning to feel a sense of urgency and further delays would merely complicate his tasks. Six days earlier his wife and infant daughter had died from yellow fever. Claiborne was himself ill with the disease and would not recover for several months. Furthermore, despite the conciliatory and optimistic tone of his address, Claiborne faced mounting opposition to his administration. He was hampered by the refusal of a number of persons to serve in the new government.

Also, inadequate salaries and the inability of a number of prominent planters to spend the required amount of time away from their plantations made recruitment difficult. Others declined because they resented the congressional refusal to admit Louisiana to statehood immediately. Real or imagined grievances and a desire to obstruct governmental processes and thereby embarrass both Claiborne and the leaders in Washington caused still others to turn down appointments.

Governor Claiborne was one of the very few senior territorial officials in New Orleans at the time the new government went into effect. James Brown, a lawyer and linguist, served as territorial secretary only until December 11, 1804, when John Graham of Kentucky replaced him. Officials appointed by the president to serve on the superior and district courts straggled into New Orleans over the next several weeks, and one appointee died en route. Moreover, judicial instability continued when a number of judicial officers served only briefly both because of low salaries and the difficulties and complexities of the task.[75] Establishing the legislative council proved both difficult and embarrassing. The president made appointments to this body from a list of candidates presented to him by the governor. However, some of the president's initial appointees refused to serve and some even used their influence to entice others to do likewise. On November 19 Claiborne reported to Jefferson that only five of the thirteen nominees had accepted commissions to serve on the council. Since he needed seven councillors for a quorum, the governor finally resorted to the expedient of filling in blank commissions and having the president approve them later. Jefferson sanctioned the practice shortly afterward but he reiterated guidelines which he had conveyed earlier to Claiborne. In making appointments, the Americans were to have a bare majority over the natives, persons should be chosen who knew both the French and English languages, and a majority of the positions should go to persons representing the agricultural interests, while still insuring representation for the mercantile community. Following delays caused by the lack of a quorum and an outbreak of yellow fever in New Orleans, the legislative council finally convened on December 4. The meeting, Claiborne noted, had served to check a spirit of anarchy, and had increased local confidence in the new government. Nonetheless, the problem of securing legislators to serve on the council continued to plague the governor, particularly during the next two years. In fact, Claiborne developed a sensitivity about the matter and sometimes hesitated to fill out commissions despite President Jefferson's permission lest his feelings be "subjected to the mortification of a refusal."[76]

With the legislative council finally convened, Governor Claiborne appealed to the lawmakers to pass vitally needed measures to insure a sound and efficient government. He urged that priority should be given to the establishment of a system of jurisprudence, pointing out that he had instituted only limited judicial measures during the provisional period. He also asked for "seminaries of learning," an effective militia law, internal improvements, the incorporation of New Orleans, and the enactment of health laws and police ordinances. Julien Poydras, president of the council, responded to the governor's short address in French, and in a carefully phrased statement assured the governor that priority would be given to the establishment of "a system of jurisprudence suited to the interests, and as much as possible, to the habits of the citizens." In alluding to the almost unlimited authority vested in Claiborne during the provisional period, he complimented the governor for exercising that authority with a "moderation unexampled." In view of the demands made on the governor and his accessibility to all, whether for serious or trivial reasons, he continued, "we are more surprised that so much has been done, than that more has not been effected." Poydras assured the governor that the agenda he had presented would be duly considered.

During the five months that it remained in session and under Claiborne's experienced leadership, the council enacted fifty-two laws. Among the more essential measures were laws providing for the organization of the militia and the establishment of an educational system, although both defied effective implementation for several years. They divided the territory into twelve counties, and authorized the selection of a sheriff, clerk, treasurer, coroner, judge, and as many justices of the peace as the governor decided were needed for each county to replace the former Spanish officials. In an effort to inform and educate their constituency, the lawmakers also passed a resolution early in the session calling for the printing in both the French and English languages of five hundred copies of the Constitution, the Franco-American treaty, and the territorial act of March 26, 1804. Claiborne's infrequent use of the veto indicated a reasonably harmonious working relationship between the governor and legislature. He did veto a bill which would have permitted any interest rate agreed to by the contracting parties because he believed it would give the lender an unfair advantage. He also vetoed a measure providing for the creation of a court of commerce in New Orleans and including regulations for the formation of juries in commercial cases on the ground that it was too favorable to the commercial community. Finally, he vetoed a bill which would have prevented persons from holding office under the government of the Orleans Territory except those who were inhabitants of Louisiana on or before April 30, 1803, or were citizens of the United States. While the governor agreed in principle with the proposal, he doubted whether the bill was the "rightful object" of territorial legislation. Congress had given the president an "uncontrouled discretion as to certain appointments to office," and he questioned the constitutionality of any act of the territorial legislature "which would abridge the powers of the office I have the honour to hold...." [77]

After the council adjourned in May, Governor Claiborne made his first extended trip into the countryside, traveling from New Orleans northward along the Mississippi River to Pointe Coupée in an effort to implement the judicial measures passed by the legislative council and to introduce the American system of jurisprudence. He also wanted to get to know the people and to feel the public pulse, as well as to use the trip to relax and regain his health. The "raging" fever of the previous year had left him in a state of debility. By mid-June Claiborne was able to report that each of the twelve counties had a judge. Furthermore, he had appointed other county officials from among the ranks of the territory's most influential citizens, usually upon the recommendations of judges and ex-commandants.[78]

Following his return to New Orleans, the governor called the legislature back into a brief ten-day session to deal with some routine but nonetheless important problems. He had shown some inclination during the first session of the legislative council to act in the interests of the working class and it became even more obvious as he opened the second session with a short five-minute address. Acting in response to complaints from the public, he asked the lawmakers to set a scale of fees for notaries public, having earlier approved a measure whereby judges were to regulate compensatory rates for clerks, criers, translators, counsellors, and attorneys provided costs did not exceed $100. Of even greater concern was the standard practice of creditors having debtors imprisoned until they made full disclosures and surrendered their properties under oath. While the legislators had passed legislation during the earlier session to protect "the industrious classes of the community against imposition and deceit, I am persuaded you will esteem it a duty to protect the honest debtor, who gives up all he possesses, and not in that case to suffer the loss of liberty to be added to his other misfortunes." The legislature enacted both measures in accordance with the governor's recommendation. One measure exempted women, ministers, persons over sixty years old, and all other persons whose health would be endangered from imprisonment for indebtedness. The lawmakers also made some additional judicial provisions, including the establishment of a probate court and arranging for the superior court to go on circuit. The rest of the session was devoted to more routine activities, such as the establishment of regulations for taverns and other places of public entertainment, as had been done earlier by the Mississippi legislature.[79]

Governor Claiborne, who had announced earlier that Congress had passed a measure to advance the territorial government to the intermediate stage, appeared before the legislative council to bring the session to a close on July 3. He had enjoyed a sound working relationship with the cooperative legislative council, but local criticism of the governor and of his administration had increased substantially. As a consequence, he used the closed session to defend his administration. Only rarely during his years in Mississippi and Louisiana did the chief executive feel inclined to defend his administration directly and this was generally to his superiors in Washington or indirectly through surrogates. However, stung by the rising voices of protest, the governor alluded to party spirit and the particular traditions and culture of the people as forces which would make the administration of the territory both painful and perplexing for a number of years. In view of the French and Spanish backgrounds of the inhabitants, changes of allegiance, and ties of birth, history, and language "where like causes every where produce, the man indeed must be little acquainted with human nature, who has supposed that in a territory thus situated, the principles of the American government, could have been introduced without difficulty, or that the public functionaries could have discharged their duties in such a way, as to conciliate the good opinion of all." He admitted to the lawmakers that unavoidable inconveniences to the people had occurred. Moreover, he acknowledged having made possible errors during the provisional period, but he believed that they had been exaggerated by the "malevolent and designing." Striking a posture of moral indignation, he continued: "but in relation to the *calumnies* to which I have been subjected, and *their authors*, I look down upon them with contempt, from that eminence on which conscious rectitude has placed me." Although Claiborne may have been well advised to display firmness at the beginning of his administration, this was hardly the time and place for such an intemperate outburst. It only gave encouragement to his critics, some of whom soon served in the territorial legislature. Furthermore, Claiborne's experience in the homogeneous Mississippi Territory should have prepared him to expect some dissent. Although it was unusual for Claiborne to react as emotionally as he did on July 3, his sensitivity to criticism, manifested by an attitude of great moral self-righteousness, was one of his greatest weaknesses. Although his critics might be expected to engage in intemperate conduct, the governor could ill afford such luxury as leader and spokesman for the new American authority in the territory.[80]

On March 2, 1805, a little less than a year after the first territorial act was passed and during the first session of the legislative council, Congress passed and the president approved "An Act for the Government of Orleans Territory." It provided for the second stage of government for the Orleans Territory which Governor Claiborne had recommended in late August of the previous year. The older legislative council was to give way to a general assembly, consisting of an elective house of representatives and an appointive legislative council. The latter was to consist of five persons chosen by the president of the United States from a list of ten candidates submitted by the territorial house of representatives. To allow time for the governor to make the necessary arrangements, including the holding of territorial elections, the new legislative body would not be convened until the first Monday of the following November.[81]

Despite his momentary agitation, Governor Claiborne could take pride in the events of the previous eighteen months. The transfer of the Louisiana Territory had proceeded smoothly despite American apprehensions, and Claiborne had won his coveted appointment as territorial governor. The Orleans Territory would be functioning under an intermediate level of government within a few months, and the people could reasonably anticipate admission to statehood in due course. By midsummer, the work of the territorial government in New Orleans was becoming more routine, and county governments were beginning to take form.

The American influence could be increasingly observed at the local level. The legislative council had cooperated with the governor by enacting laws which made possible the introduction of American institutions. To be sure, there had been harsh criticisms of the American newcomers and some embarrassments, but the governor had charted a steady course and much had been accomplished. At the same time, it was increasingly obvious that the governor could expect an intensified opposition in the days immediately ahead. Moreover, the opposition could be expected to take advantage of the diminished controls resulting from the creation of a more representative territorial government. With such challenges looming ahead, the governor would have to mobilize his full resources to surmount them. And, most assuredly, the attitude and demeanor of the governor, as reflected in his intemperate address of July 3, would necessarily undergo an immediate transformation. Fortunately for him, the outburst was but an aberration that rarely surfaced publicly.

VI

ORLEANS TERRITORY: THE DYNAMICS OF POLITICS

On July 26, 1805, approximately three weeks after he prorogued the legislative council, Governor Claiborne issued a proclamation calling for the election of twenty-five delegates to the new house of representatives. Each county was designated an election district and each district was assigned a specific number of delegates. The governor did not mention franchise or delegate qualifications in the proclamation, although he instructed local officials to adhere to requirements of the Northwest Ordinance of 1787 for both. Following the September elections, the newly elected members of the house of representatives convened at the hôtel de ville in New Orleans on November 4. The house organized itself on the following day and the delegates selected Jean-Noël Destréhan as speaker. The legislators then turned their attention to the selection of ten nominees from which the president would appoint the five-member legislative council. On November 8 they submitted their nominations and, after drawing up a number of memorials to Congress on such subjects as land titles and education, they adjourned to await presidential action on their nominations. In making their nominations for the legislative council the territorial lawmakers had ignored Governor Claiborne's recommendation that they select candidates who represented all sections of the territory, thus reflecting a reasonable economic and urban-rural balance. All but one of the nominees were from Orleans County which included New Orleans and which already had seven representatives in the twenty-five-

Julien Poydras

Jean-Noël Destrehan

member house. The day before the session ended Governor Claiborne sent Jefferson the list of candidates and in response to the president's earlier request included some brief commentary on each nominee. The only candidate Claiborne refused to recommend was Evan Jones, a New Orleans merchant and political opportunist who emerged as an avowed enemy of the governor's administration. Those ultimately confirmed as counsellors were Joseph Deville D. Bellechasse, Jean-Noël Destréhan, who was then succeeded by John Watkins as speaker of the house of representatives, Jean (John) B. Macarty, Pierre Sauvé, and Julien Poydras, the last of whom was selected following the Senate's rejection of John W. Gurley.[1]

The general assembly convened in New Orleans on March 25, 1806, and remained in session until June 7. Initially the lawmakers appeared to be in a courteous and cooperative mood, with the native inhabitants easily dominating both houses of the legislature. Unlike the earlier appointed legislative council which relied upon, and worked effectively with, the experienced chief executive, a cadre of delegates now came to New Orleans determined to exercise their legislative prerogatives. Inexperienced in democratic processes and politically naive, a number of these basically well-intentioned native legislators were also manipulated by such newcomers to New Orleans as Daniel Clark and Edward Livingston. Men like Clark and Livingston, whose driving political ambitions were blunted by the governor, now put forth a sustained effort to paralyze the Claiborne administration. The governor had occupied center stage and was the locus of power since the earlier legislative council had been appointed. Although statehood had not been conferred, a new era at least had dawned with the territory's advancement to the second stage of government. Governor Claiborne's opening address on the second day resembled his opening remarks the previous year. Again he requested legislative action in the fields of judicial revisions, the criminal code, penal facilities, roads, inland navigation, and education.[2] But, to the assertive and determined legislators, a reordering of the territory's political power structure was the primary order of business. The governor had clearly signaled in his closing address to the legislative council almost eight months earlier that he was prepared to pursue a policy of firmness and decisiveness against those who attempted to reduce his administration to a state of impotence and to embarrass him personally. The lines therefore were clearly drawn. Skirmishes shortly ensued which quickly gave way to ferocious encounters. The solons deliberately invited vetoes by the governor and they were not disappointed. The result was legislative sterility and the single least productive session of the territorial period.

Aside from the unscrupulous machinations of ambitious newcomers who dreamed of personal political fiefdoms in the fertile Orleans Territory, a confrontation was inevitable. The exectutive-legislative fireworks of 1806 were the natural culmination of native resentments which had mounted steadily after the Louisiana transfer. They represented more than a mere struggle among strong personalities or competing branches of government although both were contributing forces. Two widely different cultures were suddenly thrown together as the result of distant diplomatic and political initiatives, and when they began to interact, to knit together, sparks were certain to be generated. The surprise was not that sparks flew during the earlier years of the territorial period but that the sparks failed to ignite an explosion. The legislative session of 1806 was the first real opportunity afforded the native inhabitants to give vent to their resentments and frustrations against the alien authority and they took full advantage of it. Nonetheless, the political atmospherics had a positive effect because they cleared the air to a marked degree.

Following the turbulent legislative session of 1806 relations between the two branches of government improved slowly during subsequent sessions. The lawmakers retained their independence, but the charged atmosphere of 1805 and 1806 increasingly gave way to a seriousness of purpose and spirit of cooperation on the part of the governor and the legislators. When the governor exercised the veto power in the ensuing years, even his more uncompromising critics in the legislature were not inclined to question his motives. Increasingly after the critical months in 1806 the lawmakers came to accept Claiborne's basic integrity, while the governor demonstrated more skill and diplomacy in working with the lawmakers. From the legislative side, the solons became more responsible and responsive, and as they acquired more legislative experience, they showed a greater willingness to cooperate with the chief executive in coping with territorial problems. Furthermore, such potential outside threats as the Burr conspiracy and Spanish-American frictions over the boundary between Texas and the Orleans Territory provided an additional impetus for greater cooperation between the two branches.

The second legislature, whose first and second sessions in early 1808 and 1809 each lasted for over two months, enacted a number of measures which reflected basic improvements in the legislative process. The lawmakers' decision to appoint permanent committees enabled them to dispense with the earlier practice of waiting until problems developed and then appointing ad hoc committees to cope with them.[3] The establishment of permanent committees also permitted a more thorough study of territorial problems, long-range planning, and greater continuity in governmental operations. At the same time, the legislature finally came to grips with the problem of excessive absenteeism among members. Illness routinely cut down on attendance, but a substantial number of legislators were planters and found it difficult to stay away from their plantations for extended periods of time without risking considerable financial hardship. Also, some lawmakers absented themselves from the legislative chambers to express disappointment with the territorial and national administrations. To insure better attendance, the legislators passed and the governor approved a measure whereby delegates who failed to appear within fifteen days after the beginning of a session, unless detained specifically by illness, would not be reimbursed for mileage and expenses.[4] Such a measure would have been inconceivable two years earlier.

Infringements upon American national interests resulting from the continuing European conflict also contributed to a more positive executive-legislative relationship. This was particularly true of the third legislature which met during the first four months of 1810 and from late January until the end of April 1811. Although his proposed legislative program included the usual appeals for educational measures, health provisions, more stringent militia laws, and judicial revisions, Governor Claiborne's opening addresses dealt at length with the growing estrangement between the United States and both England and France. The United States had attempted to impose economic sanctions against England and France in an effort to force the two warring coalitions to cease preying upon American shipping and respect Yankee neutrality. Governor Claiborne appealed to the legislators to support the national policy of economic coercion by promoting domestic agricultural and industrial growth, thereby relying less on European goods. The spectre of war made the resolution of outstanding differences much easier, even if to a lesser extent than in other American territories because of the declining but still pronounced European influence upon many of the native inhabitants of the Orleans Territory. At the same time, the addition of a part of West Florida to the Orleans Territory and the growing awareness that statehood was at last about to be realized added significantly to executive-legislative compatibility.

The chief executive also had the monumental task of establishing the American judicial system in the territory. The territorial government act of March 26, 1804, provided for the organization of the government in October, but no judicial changes could be made until the legislature convened and passed the necessary legislation. When a legislative quorum was finally secured in December, Claiborne requested that first priority be given to the establishment of a system of jurisprudence. He explained that he had sought largely to maintain the status quo until the exact status of the territory had been determined by Congress. The legislators enacted the judicial measure and Governor Claiborne established the superior court. Congress had provided for the tribunal in the government act of 1804—this was the first time Congress included specific provisions for such a court in a territorial act—and President Jefferson had already appointed the three justices. The superior court finally replaced the governor's court, a tribunal retained by Claiborne from the Spanish colonial administration until a court system was established. In April of the following year the legislature divided the Orleans Territory into twelve counties, each possessing a county court presided over by a judge. The measure also authorized the governor to appoint as many justices of the peace for each county as he deemed feasible. The law further stipulated that the county courts were to be convened four times per year to exercise both judicial and administrative responsibilities. The county judges had cognizance in cases involving amounts over $50 and less than $100; the justices of the peace had jurisdiction in cases involving up to $50. In July the legislators enacted and Claiborne approved a measure providing for the superior court to go on circuit, although its permanent seat was in Orleans County. The court was required to hold a session in ten of the twelve counties sometime between June 1 and November 1 of each year. Sessions held in Pointe Coupée and Rapides counties were to serve Ouachita and Concordia counties as well because they were sparsely populated. Moreover, the act provided for the establishment of a probate court for the territory, with the magistrate of Orleans County serving as ex-officio judge. The court was to be convened monthly to carry out its functions, including the taking of proof of wills.[5]

No judicial provisions were made by the legislature the following year because of the executive-legislative impasse. However, substantial changes were made during the second session of the first territorial legislature which lasted from mid-January until April, 1807. In his address Claiborne reminded the legislators that he had earlier recommended revisions of the judicial system because the existing one was "exceptionable, and illy adapted to the present state of the Territory" and needed an *"immediate* and *radical* change." According to Claiborne, the county courts presented major problems because there were not enough of them to handle their assigned tasks, and it was difficult to secure jurors and qualified judicial personnel to staff the existing courts. Claiborne also accused the county courts of extravagances although he made no attempt to support the charge. Moreover, he pointed out that sessions of the superior court in New Orleans constituted a major inconvenience for those citizens who had to travel great distances, an indication that the earlier legislation stipulating that the superior court was to go on circuit annually had not yet been implemented. The legislature responded positively to the governor's appeal and effected some basic changes. It divided the territory into nineteen parishes, but it retained the existing counties for purposes of representation in the territorial legislature, taxation, and the organization of the militia. Each parish was to have a judge who exercised civil, criminal, and police jurisdiction. The governor appointed them for a four-year term to replace the county judges. The lawmakers also made more realistic provisions for the superior court. Whereas the earlier measure had required the superior court to go on circuit annually and to hold ten sessions over a five-month period, the new law provided for the establishment of five superior court circuit districts.[6]

When he addressed the first session of the second territorial legislature on January 18, 1808, the chief executive reported that the parish courts were organized and functioning and that men of character and integrity were serving as parish judges. Although the basic judicial structure was satisfactory, Claiborne recommended some refinements. Because he believed that the superior court would be more impartial in such a complex and sensitive area of litigation, he suggested the parish courts be denied jurisdiction in cases involving disputed land titles. He also recommended that the responsibilities of the justices of the peace be defined more explicitly, and that legal forms be simplified as much as possible for the convenience of the people.[7] By this time—some four years after the first measure was enacted which provided for the organization of the judiciary—the territorial court structure was established and functioning. No further substantive structural changes were made during the territorial period. However, in his address to the second session of the second legislature in early 1809 the chief executive suggested that the legislature petition Congress to increase the number of justices on the superior court from three to five. Claiborne's message also revealed hints of a growing personal attachment to the territory, a continuing Republican apprehension of the judiciary, and a personal frustration with the territorial courts. The governor publicly challenged the act by which Congress vested in the superior court "original and final jurisdiction." He asked the lawmakers to enact a measure in which the superior court's functions and duties would be explicity defined; yet, even as he did so, he expressed doubt as to whether the territorial legislature had sufficient power to curtail the authority of the superior court.[8] Although both the second and third legislatures worked rather closely with the chief executive, these recommendations were not pursued, probably because Claiborne had second thoughts on the delicate subject and because preoccupation with the West Florida revolution and the American drift toward war with England overshadowed such matters.

Establishing the territorial courts was one problem, finding persons both qualified and willing to accept appointments, particularly for service on the superior court, was another. Of Jefferson's first three appointees to the superior court, only John B. Prevost, a native of New York and nephew of Aaron Burr, actually came to New Orleans to assume his duties. Other appointees either declined the offer or served only briefly because of the enormous difficulties of the task and the necessity of knowing both French and English. The climate and the high mortality rate from yellow fever during the summer months discouraged others. Furthermore, the $2,000 annual salary was too modest to attract many outstanding jurists. James Brown of Kentucky served briefly as territorial secretary and was offered an appointment to the superior court but he resigned shortly afterward in favor of a private law practice in New Orleans. In fact, Claiborne had predicted to President Jefferson in mid-1804 that appointees would not serve long because of the low salaries. Later he told Madison that Prevost's large family could not subsist on the judge's low salary. Following Dominic A. Hall's appointment as judge of the Federal District Court of New Orleans, Claiborne asserted that Hall's expenses in New Orleans would exceed his professional income. To underscore the point, Claiborne explained that his own table expenses for two months exceeded $1,300 even though he practiced "prudent oeconomy."[9] Despite Claiborne's concern for their inadequate salaries both Prevost and Hall remained in their posts, and Hall emerged as a powerful judicial figure who dared to challenge and penalize Andrew Jackson several years later. Nonetheless, the court suffered from this high attrition rate during the territorial period. The same weakness pervaded the lesser courts but requirements for service in the judiciary at the subordinate levels were more informal and casual. The frequent changes in personnel contributed substantially to the instability of the judicial branch of government during the territorial period.

Claiborne's decision to introduce the English common-law system, familiar only to the small minority of newcomers from the United States and other English-speaking countries, provoked intense local opposition. President Jefferson, aware of the complex problem confronting Claiborne, instructed him to introduce the American system of jurisprudence. He then asked the impossible by directing Claiborne to bring the native Roman law system into conformity with it without causing undue uneasiness. Claiborne strove diligently to carry out the task. Indeed, it may well have been in this specific area of responsibility that Jefferson's choice of Claiborne as governor proved most prudent and efficacious. In compliance with the president's wishes, Claiborne largely maintained the traditional legal system for almost a year while effecting only those changes which the exigencies of the moment required.

Despite the governor's empathy with the native Louisianians, they severely criticised every decision he made regarding the judiciary. Moreover, he had to combat the natural tendency of the Creoles, frustrated and bewildered by the dizzying course of events which placed them under American jurisdiction, to view with nostalgia the "good old days" of Spanish colonial rule. Admittedly absolutist and autocratic, it was still a system with which they were familiar; the new one may have held great promise but at the time it engendered fears and apprehensions, causing some natives to brace themselves for an immediate defense of their customs and traditions. Within a week of the transfer, a newspaper critic warned ominously that Louisianians would require political and legal maxims that suited their particular circumstances.[10] Governor Claiborne had retained the governor's court, a Spanish institution, only because of necessity during the provisional period. Yet he delayed and deferred action whenever possible to avoid charges of arrogating to himself "a plenitude of power which the haughtiest of my predecessors had never employed."[11] Claiborne also came under fire when, in response to pressures from local mercantile and commercial interests, he established the court of pleas less than two weeks after his arrival in New Orleans. The decision to create the new tribunal had appealed to Claiborne in part because he thought it might enable him to abolish the governor's court. Local elements appealed directly to national leaders to force the governor to rescind his action and abolish the newly established court and to reverse some of the decisions he had made while presiding over the governor's court. President Jefferson responded bluntly that it was a mistake to assume that appeals could be made to the president. While he, Jefferson, might suggest that the governor review a given case, the president did not wish to convey the impression that he questioned or opposed the governor's decisions.[12]

Thus Jefferson supported the verdicts handed down in the governor's court and Claiborne's decision to create the court of pleas. Yet when Claiborne learned that the court of pleas was creating hardships for debtors, particularly for the planter class, he made the necessary adjustments. Although the planters usually had sufficient security in land and property to cover their indebtedness, the court of pleas at first acted too speedily, handing down decisions before the planters could raise sufficient funds to meet their financial obligations. As a result, the properties of the planters were subject to legal seizure and sale. When the problem was brought to the governor's attention, he established a longer time period between the issuance of writs and ultimate judicial sales.[13]

The governor, nonetheless, was criticized for both courts. Although a "Louisianian" admitted that the ills afflicting the native inhabitants were largely the result of circumstances rather than administration, he criticized Claiborne for introducing the American legal system without having sufficiently prepared the people for the change. Just imagine, he said, a citizen, constable, or sheriff being given orders he did not understand and in an alien language. Just imagine the embarrassment of the judges who had no substantive knowledge of the new legal system if they attempted to combine it with traditional Spanish laws. The decisions of the judges, he charged, were like the toss of dice. If a litigant were displeased with a judicial decision, his appeal was only to one person, the governor, and this offered little consolation to the oppressed client. The "Louisianian" concluded his bitter diatribe with an impassioned appeal to Congress to put an end to the existing evils and insure justice for the people of the territory.[14]

Probably the same critic declared caustically that the governor's legal decisions would be a source of merriment if reviewed by the legislature.[15] The "Louisianian" apparently thought such a legislative review was possible, which underscored his lack of familiarity with the newly introduced American governmental system and provided some insight into the scope of the task facing Claiborne as he sought to explain the new system to the native inhabitants.

Ignorance of English legal procedures and language difficulties readily explained the native Louisianian's frustrations and apprehensions during this critical period. Utter confusion reduced judicial processes to near paralysis. Trial by jury and the use of lawyers in criminal and civil cases were previously unknown. Cases were often introduced in English. Lawyers pleaded their cases in different languages before judges who understood only one language, and the judges sometimes dozed and slept during judicial proceedings. Jurors who did not understand English left their boxes when the proceedings were in English. When the case was concluded, the jurors retired together to the jury room. Each juror was convinced that the particular argument he had heard and understood was conclusive and insisted that the verdict be determined accordingly.[16]

At the time Claiborne called for legislation to create a court system in late 1804, he also requested a new legal code since the existing one was unsatisfactory in his view. He wanted an energetic system, he said, but not one that was cruel or sanguinary. The governor expressed his progressive penal philosophy succinctly when he told the lawmakers: "Laws are not weaker for being merciful. It is not the severity, but the celerity of punishment that repels crimes." The detection of crimes should be followed, he continued, by prompt court decisions in which "light suffering" would be imposed.[17] Judge Prevost also appealed to the lawmakers to establish a system of practice for the superior court. He added that the "difficulty of combining trial by jury with the ancient practice, without legislative aid, will tend much to impede that speedy distribution of justice, which would otherwise take place." The legislators referred the judge's written appeal to the committee assigned to draw up a legal code and system of practice for the supreme court.[18]

When he addressed the short session of the territorial legislature on June 22, 1805, the governor announced that the courts which were to be established would have common-law jurisdiction. However, grasping the inherent difficulties of implementing this policy and wishing to be as reasonable and conciliatory as possible with the Louisianians, he added: "I recommend it to you to consider how far this constitutional provision will innovate upon your present system, and what measures will be expedient to prevent the inconveniences that might attend an unprepared transition from one mode of practice to another."[19] In short, Claiborne insisted upon adherence to his basic policy but allowed for a substantial degree of latitude and flexibility within the broader policy framework. Time and experience would hopefully make the transition palatable to Louisianians, and compromises would produce a mutually satisfactory hybrid system of jurisprudence.

In the meantime, the legislature enacted measures dealing with criminal procedure. No defendant would be forced to answer questions regarding the offense of which he was accused, but judicial officers would be permitted to take voluntary statements. These statements, including responses to specific questions, could be put in writing and signed by the accused, but only if agreed to voluntarily by the alleged criminal.[20] A few months afterward, the legislature enacted a measure which set forth prescribed punishments for stipulated crimes and misdemeanors.[21]

While these measures moved toward passage, efforts to formulate a new legal code continued. Prompted by Judge

Prevost, who was a brother-in-law of Evan Jones, the legislative council approved the appointment of two lawyers to work with a legislative committee to prepare a civil and criminal code. Governor Claiborne opposed the measure because of enmity toward the two lawyers, James Brown and Moreau Lislet, according to Judge Prevost, and because he considered the laws of Tennessee were "fit for every state of Society in whatever clime." James Brown, who had resigned from the superior court a few weeks earlier, pointed out that everything was available to draw up a code of laws—Spanish ordinances, British statutes and common laws, and state codes. The people, he said, were ready to accept a code compiled from these several sources. Brown predicted that the legislature would draw up a code based on French laws and Spanish ordinances which the governor would reject. Claiborne would then formulate a code founded on English common law which the legislature would reject, and an impasse would result. Seizing upon the emotionally charged issue to discredit Claiborne, Brown referred to daily criticisms of the governor and declared that even the governor's friends admitted he lacked capacity and firmness.[22]

As Brown predicted, a bitter clash occurred between Claiborne and the legislature in 1806. In his opening address, the governor stressed the need for a civil code and called for the construction of a "penitentiary house." He pointed out that it was virtually impossible to work inmates sentenced to confinement and hard labor until such an institution had been provided, and he recommended the "adoption of every expedient which may tend to the prevention of offences." Especially concerned by a mounting vagrancy problem, he noted that some communities had dealt successfully with vagrants by confining them temporarily to "some laborious occupation, by which the indolent and dissolute are at the same time prevented from annoying society by their mischevious example, and made to defray the expenses of their subsistence."[23]

Although the governor stressed the problems confronting the judiciary and made some recommendations, the legislators were determined to air their views while moving toward legislative supremacy. They began by enacting a measure which established qualifications for membership in the legislature favoring the "ancient inhabitants" and disqualifying certain duly elected members. The governor vetoed the act and thus set the stage for the contest over a more fundamental issue. The battle was joined when the legislators enacted a bill confirming Roman legal concepts and principles as bases for judicial decisions, thereby precluding the use of English common law. The lawmakers thus invited the executive's veto, and he obliged. But in vetoing the measure Governor Claiborne merely grasped the gauntlet hurled at him by the strident solons. Indeed, they probably would have been far more disappointed had the bill been signed submissively. The legislative council then countered the governor's action with a ringing resolution on May 28 calling for the dissolution of the general assembly. A majority of the councillors charged that the governor had repeatedly thwarted legislative prerogatives and wishes. They believed the general assembly's dissolution would save the taxpayers the expense of maintaining a legislative body unable to accomplish anything because of executive obstinacy.

Only the preservation of their laws, customs, and traditions could soften the transition from one governmental system to another. The lawmakers insisted the territorial government act of March 2, 1805, preserved their laws because it allowed them to retain laws that were not in conflict with the federal Constitution. The common laws of the American colonies had varied greatly, they pointed out, and Congress made no effort under the federal government to impose a uniform system of laws upon all the states. Aside from the right of trial by jury and the writ of habeas corpus, the lawmakers felt they could accept or reject common laws as they wished. They contended that they had the prerogative to preserve their "ancient laws" provided they did not contravene the Constitution or measures enacted by Congress for the Orleans Territory. Their own Roman law provided the bases of the civil and political laws of all civilized European nations, they proclaimed proudly and defiantly, and presented "an assemblage of grandeur and of prudence that is above all criticism. How pure these decisions drawn from the source of natural equity. How luminous this digest, the work of the greatest lawyers, animated by the encouragement of the wisest emperors. How simple the forms of these contracts, and how sure and how prompt the means of obtaining the remedies prescribed by law for the reparation of civil evils of every description."[24] They did not wish to contrast Roman law with English common law, for virtually the entire territorial populace recognized the wisdom of the former. They believed that uncertainty and fear would ensue if the traditional legal customs of

Louisiana were replaced. The legislature's responsibility, as the members viewed it, was to establish fundamental legal bases, with secondary laws being enacted later. The lawmakers proceeded to elaborate upon the mass confusion surrounding the courts. Over half of the lawsuits of the succeeding thirty years would involve contracts entered into under the traditional legal system, they estimated, and the English legal system would be inapplicable. If the governor alone reigned supreme by virtue of the veto power, the legislature should not "serve as a rattle to amuse the people." The lawmakers ended by asking if it was necessary to spend $30,000 to present to the people the spectacle of a scandalous struggle in which the will of the majority was thwarted by the minority.[25]

The governor responded to the resolution calling for the adjournment of the legislature with the observation that the legislators had that prerogative. However, Claiborne may have quietly used his influence to have the resolution defeated in the lower house where he commanded greater political support. Nevertheless, several legislators had already resigned or had expressed their intention to resign at the close of the session. When the term ended on June 7, Claiborne declared that he had no objection to the adjournment but he attempted to minimize the impasse. Unlike his closing address a year earlier, the governor asserted that differences of opinion among lawmakers were to be expected in a society where people were free to think and act for themselves. "If, therefore, on some occasions, the executive did not approve the proceedings of the two houses, all that can with truth be said is, that our object was the same, but we differed as to the means of promoting the general welfare."[26] Although gracious and publicly conciliatory, Claiborne expressed personal doubts, bitterness, and indulged in self-pity. Territorial legislatures invariably attempted to embarrass the executive, he lamented, but this was especially true of one dominated by a majority of Frenchmen. He had always felt that the premature introduction of democracy into the Orleans Territory was hazardous and his experiences provided confirmation.[27]

Work continued on the formulation of the civil code despite the executive-legislative deadlock of 1806. However, the governor's position on the volatile problem underwent a marked change between the end of the legislative session in mid-1806 and the beginning of the second session in mid-January of the following year. His moderated stance was probably due in part to a realistic and dispassionate appraisal of the problem during the interim and the consequent realization that failure to achieve a compromise would result in a total collapse of the judicial system and cause further popular alienation. Another contributing factor was undoubtedly a wish to placate the local inhabitants who were enraged over General Wilkinson's abuse of civil authority during the Burr controversy and Claiborne's failure to curb Wilkinson's outrageous conduct. Now more subdued and conciliatory, Governor Claiborne denied any intent to innovate. Rather he wished to retain those principles of the civil law which were essential to the security of property and were "in unison with the interests of a free people."[28] The completed work, much of which was drawn from the Napoleonic code, was presented to the legislature the following year. While the code was inferior to the parent document, it was nonetheless superior to anything "two individuals could have produced, early enough, to answer the expectation of those who employed them."[29] Governor Claiborne readily agreed that it possessed many excellent principles, but he pointed out that certain features of the code would require modification. Later legislators, he said, would have a view of the "whole ground," and would make improvements. In the meantime, it would serve as a guide for both citizen and magistrate. He expressed his particular appreciation that the adoption of the civil code had finally removed a source of embarrassment to all.[30]

In the autumn of 1808 Claiborne sent instructions to the judges for implementing the code. In his letters Claiborne pointed out that there would still be legal uncertainties and sources of confusion for both judges and citizens, but the legislature, he promised, would make the necessary modifications in time. In his letter to William Wykoff, a Pennsylvanian who had migrated to the Orleans Territory where he became a civil judge, the governor said that a number of American newcomers would be disappointed and critical of the legal system. Nonetheless, the "old inhabitants" constituted the vast majority of the population, he continued, and they were very proud of their customs, institutions, and traditions. As a consequence, additional time would be required to introduce the new system, and the "work of innovation must progress slowly and cautiously, or otherwise much inconvenience will ensue and serious discontents will arise." Claiborne anticipated that both the Americans and Louisianians would create problems for the judges, but he advised Wyckoff to be patient and administer the adopted laws according to justice and mercy.[31] In essence, the Creoles had scored a victory by their insistence upon the retention of their legal customs. At the same time, Governor Claiborne's willingness to accede to their wishes and to recognize the possible consequences of a forced and precipitate adoption of the English common-law system constituted a valid measure of the chief executive's own substantial abilities in effectively dealing with an extremely complex and disruptive problem.

Several functional aspects of the common-law system, as well as basic legal concepts and principles, baffled most Louisianians. The use of attorneys was an innovation to them and a source of resentment and complaint. Governor Claiborne himself had developed some reservations about attorneys while in the Mississippi Territory, viewing them as a disruptive force. His experiences in New Orleans tended to reinforce these feelings. He told Madison that the attorneys were "harbingers of many vexatious Law-suits," and described them to Jefferson as a restless and turbulent element in the territory. During a moment of exasperation in 1807, he regretted that he no longer had the powers he possessed three years earlier. If so, he would probably send the lawyers "one & all to Washington."[32]

Governor Claiborne had been instrumental in establishing a scale of fees for attorneys while in the Mississippi Territory and he worked with the territorial legislature to devise similar legislation for the Orleans Territory. A measure, enacted on January 22, 1805, empowered judges to regulate the fees of clerks, criers, counsellors, translators, and attorneys in superior court cases, provided costs did not exceed $100.[33] About three months later the legislature approved a specific scale of fees for court officials and attorneys.[34] The legal profession resented the regulation of fees and criticized the governor for having favored such legislation. Governor Claiborne not only encouraged the regulation of attorneys' fees—he received numerous complaints from citizens who had paid what they regarded as exorbitant fees—but he felt that lawyers should be required to acquire licenses to practice law. However, in 1808 the lawyers mobilized enough support to defeat a measure which would have established a scale of fees and required a license to practice law.[35]

Claiborne's growing feud with attorneys reached a climax in the summer of 1808 when he proposed that lawyers be barred from serving in the legislature. The attorneys successfully blocked Claiborne's proposal and issued a newspaper broadside in their defense. "Misnomus" declared satirically that laws had been trampled upon the previous year and that the time had come to trample upon the lawyers. Alluding to the Burr conspiracy, the writer declared that nothing on a comparable scale had been uncovered since in the territory, but "fortunately for the harmony and comfort of society, a new and formidable conspiracy, which threatens to make every thing the prey of their rapacity, has been ingeniously, found out, and, beautifully, developed to your eyes— A CONSPIRACY OF ATTORNIES." The legislature should censure attorneys for making it possible to administer laws with a celerity that was most inconvenient for many worthy people. Laws should be passed to banish attorneys, and their books should be burned by the public hangman as tools of chicanery. Trial by jury should be abolished, witnesses should be excluded for incompetence, and the superior court should be abolished as an agency of despotism. The fortunes of the attorneys should be confiscated, the critic continued sarcastically, and utilized to abolish reading and writing. When the "reforms" were enacted, maybe a few scriveners would be allowed, but they would not be entitled to fees. Instead, they would be expected to live on what they could steal.[36] The harrassed Claiborne was in the unenviable position of earlier bearing responsibility for the use of attorneys in the judiciary, and later of being the object of attacks by the lawyers when he came to oppose them for what he considered to be grasping fee excesses and an undue exercise of influence and power.

If the denial of immediate statehood and the introduction of an alien system of justice disappointed Louisianians, they clearly resented the governor's seeming inclination to favor the American newcomers when making appointments. Although Claiborne was frequently charged with partisanship in appointments, he nevertheless made a sincere effort to select qualified persons for posts of public trust. He held explicit instructions from President Jefferson to choose men of integrity and understanding, but loyalty to the United States was to be the most fundamental criterion in making appointments. Furthermore, Jefferson had directed Claiborne to see that the majority of appointments in the legislature go to Americans. In early 1805 a critic compiled a list of eleven newcomers appointed by Claiborne. A number of them were inebriates and persons with low morals, the critic charged indignantly, and one was the proprietor of a grog shop who had been convicted of fraud. He estimated that "at least a triple portion" of Americans were serving on the court of pleas and the board of health. While admitting that Americans comprised only one-third of the municipal council, he charged that it was only because the governor was afraid to meddle with Laussat's *"sacred institutions."* [37] Shortly afterward another newspaper critic accused the governor of favoring foreigners and Federalists. The latter charge was patently false in view of Claiborne's highly partisan Republican preferences. According to his critic, the governor ignored honest, upright citizens in order to favor "every villain if he can cringe and flatter a little." [38]

Governor Claiborne strove to reassure his critics that he was wisely using the power of appointment, and he categorically denied that he favored the Americans. If a preference was displayed, he asserted, it was in favor of the Louisianians. The mayor and most members of the municipal council were natives, and he did not think that a single "modern Louisianian" held an appointment in the militia except in the volunteer units. Most of the district commandants appointed following the transfer were natives. Indeed, few posts had been given the Americans, he insisted. Rather, most of the jobs that "cou'd safely confide to Citizens indiscriminately" had been conferred upon the natives. [39] The governor's record of appointments during the territorial period generally substantiated this contention.

The Creoles often seized upon minor incidents to heap criticism upon Claiborne and did so within weeks after his arrival in New Orleans. They refused to allow him to forget that a near riot had threatened to disrupt a public ball he attended. Both Claiborne and Wilkinson attempted to restore order following a stormy dispute which arose over whether a French or English dance should take precedence. Wilkinson tried first to restore calm by addressing the participants in a "mixture of English and bad French." When the clamor increased he and Claiborne led the American partisans in singing "Hail Columbia" and "God Save the King." The Creoles replied with "Enfants de la Patrie" and a resounding "Vive la Republique." Quiet seems to have been restored only after the two American commissioners withdrew from the ballroom. Charges and countercharges ensued over responsibility for the incident, with the American leaders attributing it to some visiting French officers and enlisted men from Bordeaux. The New Orleans social leaders temporarily suspended the traditional public balls as a result of the melee. Native sensibilities received further affronts in the ensuing months and critics frequently identified Claiborne as the primary culprit. A critic who identified himself as the "Louisianian" assailed Claiborne for having interfered with the manners and customs of the people and reminded him of the earlier public incident. Even the most barbarous conquerors respected the customs and opinions of conquered people, he asserted. Although he hoped that such improprieties would end, he said, every day some new mischief or "act of clownishness" transpired. The governor was even seen wearing his hat during performances at the theatre, the critic charged indignantly, and asked: "Does he think he is among Indians or Yahoos?" Even the president did not insult his audiences in such a disgraceful manner. Did the governor feel that his title allowed him to insult and offend a polished and cultured people? About the same time another critic sought to portray Claiborne as an uncouth and ignorant intruder into the cultured and sedate New Orleans society. He recalled in particular Governor Claiborne's attendance at a public ball held at Madame Le Gendre's residence the preceding winter. Unable to converse in French, unfamiliar with French country dances, and embarrassed by the "insignificant part he acted in the circle," the governor amused himself at brag, lost substantially, and "sneaked home at sunrise." [40]

Although the frequent victim of newspaper criticism, Claiborne was accused of attempting to control the press, particularly *The Union: New Orleans Advertiser*. The editor, Joseph Kidder, retorted that Claiborne had no more control over his newspaper than the emperor of Morocco. The editor inquired if the charge stemmed from a refusal to abuse the governor and the federal government. If nothing had been published against either in his newspaper it was because it was not justified. [41] Several months afterward Joseph Kidder certified that he at no time consulted with Claiborne about what he should or should not publish. Rather, when "Serpent d'eau" had made the charge during the preceding summer of 1804 that Claiborne had sought to control the publication, the governor had merely expressed the hope that nothing would be published which would agitate or divide the people. [42] "Laelius" also defended the governor against the varied criticisms appearing in the newspapers while at the same time putting them in perspective and reflecting a more basic understanding of the underlying forces producing the torrent of criticism. Disclaiming as little disposition to flatter Claiborne as some of his detractors to do him justice, "Laelius" observed that "the possession of great power is in its nature calculated to excite dislike." The governor's duties were so numerous and varied that no one person, however talented, could be expected to perform them all to the universal satisfaction of the people. If unable to approve everything he did, "Laelius" continued, all must admit that Claiborne at no time had played the role of tyrant. In view of the difficulties confronting Claiborne after his arrival in New Orleans, "its changes of Government, which are always attended with some derangement and discontent; the discordant mixture of its ancient and its new laws; the variety of its inhabitants differing in opinion, in language, and in nation; the disputes between the principal Foreign Agents [Laussat and Casa Calvo]; the natural impetuousity of the public mind, often exasperated by the licentiousness of the Press; the multiplicity of the complaints to be received and the impossibility of giving satisfaction to those whose interests were jarring and incompatible; we may be permitted to congratulate ourselves that good order has been so well preserved in Louisiana since it came under the dominion of the United States." [43]

Claiborne may have inspired some of the support received from such sources as Joseph Kidder and "Laelius" although no tangible proof surfaced. Neither did he respond publicly to newpaper criticism during his first several years in the territory. However, he knew that some of the criticism would ultimately reach Washington, and he attempted to defend himself privately to his Washington superiors. He admitted to Madison that the "newspaper scribbling" and "licentiousness" aroused his sensibilities. Yet his own conscience was clear and he vowed never to threaten the freedom of the press. [44]

In addition to charges of attempting to muzzle the press, the governor was sometimes accused of indecisiveness. This was particularly true of those who became impatient with his inclination to placate and to defer decisions which, in the governor's view, did not have to be made immediately or were especially controversial or divisive. Nonetheless, there were times when Claiborne should have made prompt decisions but failed to do so. Claiborne's sensitive and intuitive perception of the unusual and sometimes unique problems prevailing in the territory and his disposition to act accordingly constituted one of his greatest strengths as territorial governor. Yet unfortunately there were times when he rationalized belated actions or failure to act at all because the problems or situations were ostensibly peculiar to the Creole society. One critic observed that any action taken by Claiborne during the earlier years of his territorial administration would have been accepted without audible protest. Indeed, he said Claiborne could have imprisoned the most influential citizen in New Orleans initially without fear of opposition. By the late summer of 1805, however, the people seized upon the slightest pretext to complain and protest. The critic attributed this to the governor's irresolute temperament, as well as to political inexperience, native disappointments, and his ignorance of the French and Spanish languages.[45]

When Claiborne declined to defend himself publicly or to take action to silence his critics, the right to criticize sometimes developed into license and abusive personal attacks appeared in the newspapers. A detractor noted that the governor occasionally complained of an inadequate $5,000 annual salary. Why did he not resign then, the critic asked rhetorically. According to rumor, he continued, Claiborne had sought to overcome his "pecuniary difficulty" by offering marriage to two wealthy women in the city. Although the writer said he was skeptical of the rumor at first, Claiborne's acceptance of the regular gubernatorial appointment in 1804 tended to confirm it, he concluded, and added bitingly that "nine or ten thousand dollars per annum ought to content a plain republican Governor." At about the same time, "Fidelis" wrote about "A Dream" in which he passed at night near the governor's home when the city was hushed and quiet. Suddenly he heard music and dancing and great revelry. A rustling of silk arrested him and a tall and graceful lady with a perfect symmetry of features—a description of the late Mrs. Claiborne who had died from yellow fever less than five months earlier—appeared out of the mist. When the revelry from the governor's home became louder, she clasped her hands in agony, gazed toward heaven, and then "bent her willing steps toward the graves of Louisiana." When Micajah G. Lewis, the late Mrs. Claiborne's brother and a private secretary to the governor, learned that the author was a Mr. Sterry, he issued a challenge. Lewis, whose death from yellow fever had appeared imminent at the time Mrs. Claiborne and her daughter died, was subsequently killed in the duel.[46]

The Claiborne administration was the object of individual and isolated attacks but most of the opposition centered increasingly in Evan Jones, Edward Livingston, and Daniel Clark. Each was a newcomer to the territory and each sensed personal political opportunities when the United States took control of Louisiana, but Claiborne was the primary impediment to their ambitions. Jones, a merchant and former United States consul, was a leader among those who refused to serve on the legislative council. Claiborne unequivocally opposed Jones's candidacy and declared bluntly that he did not merit the confidence of the national leadership. When Jones gave the local newspapers a statement explaining his reasons for declining the post, a newspaper critic accused him of political opportunism and self-interest. Jones, the critic charged, would not accept any governmental appointment unless it included a lucrative salary. Another critic in the same newspaper incorrectly asserted that Claiborne had recommended Jones but added that it was probably best for Jones and the nation that he declined. Yet another critic who identified himself as "Flagellus" accused Jones of refusing for publicity purposes. Even though personal friends might regard his refusal as clever and spirited, "Flagellus" assured him that the people were amused by his impertinence and folly. As for the person who offered Jones' name in nomination, "Flagellus" snorted: "Rely on it, sir, it was someone who knows you as little as the President does." Noting that political neophytes often miscalculated their importance, he assured Jones that he was guilty of a gross miscalculation, saying: "Long Sir, might you have passed in silence and safety among the crowd, unnoticed, unmolested, had not your evil genius impatiently hurried you out of obscurity to which you were so much indebted for protection." Regarding Jones' ardor for his fellow man as unusual, "Flagellus" asked if such heroic principles were imbibed from the British at Pensacola or the Spaniards in Louisiana. Jones went to Pensacola during the American Revolution, "Flagellus" noted, and he ended his attack by charging flatly that Jones' patriotism began when Laussat removed him from the post of consul in New Orleans.[47] Whether Claiborne was instrumental in the concentrated assault on his political nemesis is conjectural, but a major effort was made to discredit Jones. It may have been more than coincidental that a few weeks earlier critics accused Claiborne of controlling the newspaper that attacked Jones.

The second member of the opposition triumvirate was Edward Livingston whose brother had negotiated the Louisiana Purchase. His public career in New York appeared to be assured until the discovery of a $60,000 deficit in his accounts. Livingston's talent, erudition, and almost immediate success as a lawyer following his emigration to New Orleans impressed Claiborne who felt initially that he would be an "acquisition to Louisiana, where men of Science & political Information are so much wanting." He abruptly changed his opinion when Livingston quickly emerged as a self-seeker and labelled him an obstructionist and opponent of the Jefferson administration's territorial policies. As governor of the Orleans Territory, Claiborne had to contend with Livingston's "Talents, Address, Intrigue, and ... Influence." Livingston was a key figure in the drafting of the memorial to Congress in 1804 which Claiborne unsuccessfully discouraged. A long and protracted legal struggle over the batture, some land built up by the Mississippi River in front of the levee in New Orleans and covered by water from four to six months each year, intensified animosity between the two men. The batture was used as a common beach and wharf by the local inhabitants and had an appraised value of $200,000. Claiborne contended that it was the common property of the people. President Jefferson ultimately recommended that Congress claim the property in the name of the United States on the grounds that the city's claim to it had passed to the United States at the time of the transfer.[48] Litigation continued for several years and the courts ultimately confirmed Livingston's claim. Although Livingston won title to the property, Claiborne won the popular esteem. This easily translated into political support at the time Claiborne was engaged in political warfare with his adversaries and later when he stood for elective office. It was concomitantly an object lesson for the Louisianians in the fundamentals of democratic government. Confronted by a popular protest following receipt of news in mid-September 1807, that the United States Supreme Court had ruled in favor of the claimants, Edward Livingston and John Gravier, Governor Claiborne carefully explained the decision to the local citizens. Further inquiries about their claims could be made, but they had to be initiated in compliance with the laws. Having made his basic point, he asked the people to retire peacefully to their homes.

Although Livingston was a political enemy and the local citizens had the more legitimate claim to the batture, in his view, Claiborne declined to take unfair advantage of an unpopular legal decision to mobilize local support against his political foes.[49]

The third member of the triumvirate, often referred to as "Clark, Livingston, & Company," was the Irish immigrant Daniel Clark. All three contributed initially to the peaceful transfer of Louisiana to the United States. Clark was particularly active in providing information and organizing elements in New Orleans to maintain the peace during the brief period of French control under Laussat and keeping them in a state of readiness to assist the modest American force if Spanish opposition developed. Clark has been described as a "molelike individual, who burrowed his way through the life of his generation in the Southwest, leaving many surface indications of his activity but seldom giving any sign of what the activity was all about." While there was no hard evidence of his rascality, "one would hardly employ such terms as honor, probity, fidelity in describing him."[50] A contemporary, either Evan Jones or a Frenchman named Labigarre who had been in New Orleans several months, described Clark in mid-1804 as one who panted for power, was mortified by disappointment, and was capable of doing more good or harm than any other person in the territory.[51] Pierre Clement Laussat detected in Clark a distinct talent for intrigue and an uncommon perspicacity. General Wilkinson, hardly a reliable judge of character, contended that Clark tried to achieve control over Claiborne by trickery and turned against him when he failed. In the autumn of 1804 Clark told Wilkinson that he had just returned from a trip through much of the territory to mobilize opposition to Claiborne, and a few months later he rebuked Wilkinson for encouraging Claiborne's retention as governor. At the same time, he said that the "wretch" was distressed because of growing political opposition and the loss of his brother-in-law who had been active politically in his behalf and had been killed in a duel. Claiborne and the people were mutually sick of each other, Clark reported, and reiterated his intention of getting rid of the governor.[52]

Governor Claiborne was not disposed to remain passive in the face of Clark's sustained assault. He attributed Clark's opposition to disappointment because he felt that he had not been adequately rewarded for the assistance he provided in the Louisiana transfer. This explanation, in addition to later frustrations resulting from his inability to get rid of the "wretch" while advancing his own personal aspirations, was probably valid. The governor kept national leaders fully informed of his adversary's activities. From the time of his arrival in New Orleans, Claiborne charged, Clark and his supporters had been confirmed obstructionists of the federal government's territorial policies and of his territorial administration. In early November 1804 Claiborne charged flatly and correctly that Clark was involved in land speculation in West Florida with Morales and was "Decidedly in the Spanish interest." In a letter to Jefferson the following month Claiborne warned that if "particular individuals," an oblique reference to Clark and his colleagues, continued to excite insurrection that "the energies of the law must lay hold of them." The running battle continued over the next several months. When Clark was elected territorial delegate to Congress he accepted the post "in order to oppose Governor Claibornes Creatures and schemes." Having no intention of being outmaneuvered because of his adversary's new advantage, Claiborne told Jefferson in July that Clark was busily engaged in gathering information against his territorial administration for use in Washington.[53] Further, he reported that Clark was relying upon John Randolph of Virginia, who had criticized Claiborne in Congress on March 5, 1806, to press the anti-Claiborne campaign. The attack to which Claiborne alluded was Randolph's criticism of unpreparedness in the Orleans Territory when Spanish-American tensions developed over the Texas-Louisiana boundary in 1805-06. The caustic Randolph blamed "the miserable Governor you have set over them" for the unpreparedness while admitting that his information was provided by Clark, "an enlightened member of that odious and imbecile Government."[54] In December Clark himself launched an attack on Claiborne in the House of Representatives while taking personal credit for the peaceful transfer of Louisiana because of the volunteer militia force he had organized. He charged Claiborne with having shown a preference for a Negro militia unit over some white contingents following the transfer, and complained that the Orleans militia was completely unorganized.[55]

When Clark's charges were published in the *Orleans Gazette*, Governor Claiborne demanded a retraction. Clark refused and Claiborne demanded satisfaction. Seconds were chosen, John W. Gurley for Claiborne and Richard R. Greene for Clark. The duellists and their seconds crossed into Spanish territory and selected Fort Manchac, south of Baton Rouge. On Monday, June 8, 1807, challenger and challenged confronted each other with pistols at a distance of ten paces. Weapons were raised upon signal and the governor took a bullet in the right thigh but the congressional representative was unscathed. The wounded Claiborne returned to New Orleans on the following evening and his condition was reported as being "as well as can be expected."[56] Claiborne told President Jefferson about a week later that he was still confined to his room and was in much pain "but the wound suppurates profusely." He assured the president that his private secretary would perform the duties that were required until he was able to resume work.[57] President Jefferson was very much upset for a time, fearful that Claiborne had been mortally wounded. The problem was compounded because John Graham, the territorial secretary, had resigned and the president was concerned that the territory would be without effective leadership. In fact, he asked Benjamin Morgan, who had served on the legislative council, if he would serve temporarily as territorial secretary, but Claiborne's recovery made an immediate appointment unnecessary. A short time later Jefferson appointed Thomas B. Robertson to replace Graham as territorial secretary.[58]

Clark won the *affaire d'honneur* but Claiborne won the political war. When Clark went to Washington as territorial delegate, ties with his local constituency loosened. His political base in the territory was further eroded when he was succeeded in the congressional post by Julien Poydras. Since Poydras and Claiborne had maintained a sound working relationship, Clark's replacement by Poydras was interpreted as a Claiborne victory. Clark nonetheless continued to obstruct the Claiborne administration and to make his opposition felt keenly whenever possible. Although Claiborne had clearly outdistanced his political foe by the latter part of the territorial period, the scars of battle were yet too painful and the cunning and resourcefulness of his antagonist too unrelenting for him to relax and savor his triumph. A few months before the territorial period ended, Claiborne travelled to Baton Rouge, by then under American jurisdiction, to organize the parish courts and militia. While there he wrote to Thomas Jefferson, then retired but still active as an elder statesman, remarking that he dreaded returning to New Orleans where he would again be subjected to "all the intrigues & all the malice of Clarke, Livingston & Company."[59]

Governor Claiborne experienced moments of weariness but at no time did he despair in his continuing conflict with the formidable triumvirate and their adherents. He never allowed the sound and fury of partisan warfare to divert him unduly from his assigned task. He had been directed to introduce American governmental and political institutions among peoples of Gallic and Iberian heritage and temperament and who had been largely insulated from the steadily advancing American influence until the nineteenth century. Claiborne charted his general course in conformity with Jefferson's policy directives, but he maintained tactical options. He tacitly accepted two fundamental but related truths inherent in the existing situation in order to insure the success of his mission: a specific timetable or schedule of achievement was to be studiously avoided, and there were practical limits to the substitution or alteration of native institutions. That is, it was by necessity a process of cultural fusion gently encouraged and prodded along by the chief executive. Native resentment was encountered which sometimes impeded the work of the Claiborne administration. Yet the most formidable opposition came from ambitious and designing American newcomers who tried unsuccessfully to harness local disappointments and frustrations to serve their personal ambitions. The fundamental issue was not so much the "ancient" versus the "modern" inhabitants. Although it was decidedly a factor of some significance, it was subordinated markedly to the thrust and parry between Clark, Livingston & Company and the Claiborne administration. When the governor came to this conclusion, he adjusted to it and was more successful in carrying out his more basic aims. His own skills were refined in the process and this, combined with the attainment of some political and governmental experience by the native leadership, resulted in a greater compatibility between the two. Furthermore, this experience convinced the native leaders that the fears conjured up by the transfer of Louisiana to the United States were without substantive basis. As all of this became more apparent, the machinations of the Clark coterie dwindled and faded away to a state of relative impotence.

VII

ORLEANS TERRITORY: MILITIAMEN, INDIANS, AND SLAVES

Governor Claiborne's primary task was to establish a viable system of government in the Orleans Territory. And one of the most fundamental responsibilities of the Claiborne administration was to provide safety and protection for the territory's 50,000 inhabitants. The task was not an easy one. Doubts concerning the intentions of the Spanish colonial forces in the territory and local rumors of a possible Negro revolt and conspiracy to put the torch to New Orleans produced great uncertainty locally. In view of the modest number of regular troops, mainly Mississippi militiamen and local volunteers, this responsibility must surely have weighed heavily upon the shoulders of William Claiborne as he affixed his signature to the transfer document in the Cabildo at noon on December 20, 1803.

Claiborne relied chiefly upon regular American troops assigned to the territory to maintain local order. The Mississippi militiamen returned to their homes in March, but additional reinforcements joined the 300 regular troops stationed in the Orleans Territory. By mid-year Lieutenant Colonel Constant Freeman arrived and assumed command of ten companies of regular troops and two companies of marines. Although death and illness from yellow fever decimated their ranks during the warmer months, over 700 regular troops were on station in the territory by autumn. These included over 500 in New Orleans; 74 at Ouachita, Opelousas, and Attakapas; 70 at Natchitoches; and 73 at Plaquemines.[1] These troops were sufficient to cope with minor disorders and to maintain internal security in the absence of serious external threats. Thus, the presence of several hundred regular troops, together with the absence of foreign intervention, contributed to a general air of security. Governor Claiborne's consequent tardiness in organizing the local militia produced a sense of apathy which impeded his later attempts to reorganize the militia.

Claiborne's reports to Washington concerning the militia reflected his casual attitude. On the day of the transfer, he advised Madison that the militia was a subject of some considerable interest among the people, but he was not inclined to do anything until he learned about "the nature of the establishment."[2] A few days later he told the secretary of state explicitly that it was not a pressing matter although he planned to commission two or three militia companies which had offered their services.[3] The governor's decision to accept the services of the Orleans Volunteers, however, stirred local criticism. The "Louisianian" charged that he accepted it while declining others because it consisted chiefly of Americans and that such action tended to divide the Louisianians and the American newcomers.[4] In a rejoinder to the criticism, "Laelius" pointed out that the Orleans Volunteers had served during the three-week retrocession to France, and that Claiborne would have conducted himself unworthily and offensively toward his fellow countrymen had he refused. Instead he organized them into a battalion of four companies and gave the battalion command to "*an ancient Louisianian whose native language was French.*"[5]

Claiborne's acceptance of some free Negro militiamen, organized as the Battalion of Free People of Color, drew even heavier fire than the organization of the Orleans Volunteers. A week after the Louisiana transfer Claiborne told Madison about two Negro companies previously in the Spanish service. To re-commission them would be regarded as an affront to some, and opposed "to those principles of policy which the safety of the Southern States has necessarily established." Yet to disband them might offend and make enemies of them.[6] Confronted by this dilemma Claiborne sought guidance from Washington. Secretary of War Dearborn advised their acceptance as a matter of expedience. He recommended that their officers be chosen carefully and that the size of the unit be reduced as inconspicuously as possible whevever opportunities developed. The governor accepted the free Negro volunteers shortly afterward, choosing Majors Michael Fortier and

Lewis Kerr, both whites, to command the battalion.[7] And as Claiborne anticipated, reaction was almost instantaneous and several protests were made. One indignant critic demanded to know why the Negroes were given a standard similar to that of the Orleans Volunteers.[8] Criticisms of the governor's acceptance of these two battalions, the territory's only militia units for about a year, and charges of negligence in the organiztiion of the militia produced the Claiborne-Clark confrontation at Fort Manchac in the summer of 1807. In addition to the racial problem and charges of favoritism toward the newcomers, language differences hampered efforts, and militia musters constituted a real inconvenience for inhabitants living in outlying settlements. Many Louisiana farmers were unwilling to serve except at the higher levels. Moreover, the drafting of French subjects into the territorial militia because they were not registered as French nationals long posed problems for local officials. The French commissioner of commercial relations in New Orleans urged French subjects to register immediately, and then he asked Governor Claiborne to exempt from service those holding French certificates of registration.[9]

When Governor Claiborne addressed the legislative council in December 1804, he recommended the enactment of a militia law with the admonition that "neither moderation, nor wisdom, nor justice, can protect a people against the encroachments of tyrannical power. The abundance of agriculture; the advantages of legislation; the usefulness of the arts—in a word, every thing dear to a *free people*, may be considered as insecure, unless they are prepared to resist aggression."[10] The lawmakers agreed to enact the necessary legislation, and they subsequently accepted the Orleans Volunteers militia. Provisions were also made for a volunteer cavalry troop in New Orleans, and a short time afterward the legislative council authorized the formation of volunteer militia companies on the condition that those who enrolled provide their own uniforms and equipment. Members were not permitted to withdraw from such units without the consent of their commanding officers or the governor; those who were expelled were not to be admitted for service in other militia companies. The lawmakers subsequently passed a militia law which remained essentially unchanged until 1811. All physically fit free white males between the ages of sixteen and fifty were to be enrolled in the militia within four months after the passage of the law. Militia captains or commanding officers were made responsible for registrations. The new law exempted city and territorial officers, school teachers, doctors, apothecaries, stage drivers, ferrymen, postmasters, mariners, and ministers from militia service. The militia was to be organized into brigades, regiments, battalions, and companies, and the territory was to be divided into militia districts. Acting under this authority, Governor Claiborne divided the territory into three militia divisions by proclamation on August 23, 1805.[11] He also established quotas for the parishes, and drew up detailed descriptions of the uniforms that were to be worn by the militia officers. Aside from his insistence upon the appointment of both Americans and Creoles, the governor did not interfere with the selection of militia officers. In late 1806 Claiborne reported to the legislature that some progress had been made in the organization of the militia, but he recommended that greater fines be imposed for non-attendance at militia drills and that punishments for improper conduct while on parade be more severe. Although these weaknesses were generally acknowledged, the lawmakers ignored the governor's recommendations.[12]

When he addressed the legislature in early 1807, he again asked the lawmakers to pass a more stringent militia law to insure a disciplined militia, and again they ignored his request. He also asked them to accept the Battalion of Free Men of Color as an integral part of the militia. Two years earlier in accepting the Battalion of Orleans Volunteers, the legislators had ignored the Negro battalion. The lawmakers finally agreed to accept it in late January 1807.[13] Unlike the sharply negative response from some elements when the governor accepted the service of the battalion in 1804, the absorption of the Negro battalion into the regular militia provoked no criticisms. Its local acceptance was probably attributable in part to its length of service but more particularly to the growing prospect of American involvement in the European war and local crises produced by border tensions and the Burr conspiracy.

When the governor appeared before the legislature in early 1808 the prospect of war with England was very real and he attempted to convey a sense of urgency to the lawmakers. Reviewing the conflict in Europe, he pleaded with the legislators to work with him in an effort to create a viable militia force while admitting candidly that efforts to establish a dependable militia had failed. The defect was in the militia law, he declared, not in the officers. Musters were irregularly attended and there was no visible evidence of discipline. To remove these weaknesses, he recommended more stringent penalties for infractions, and further suggested that the militia officers familiarize themselves with the Baron Steuben treatise on tactics.[14] But again his appeal fell on deaf ears.

Concern with the growing international crisis was much more evident in Washington than it was in New Orleans. On March 30, 1808, Congress passed a militia act authorizing the president to raise a militia force of 100,000. The measure assigned a quota to each state and territory and it further stipulated that the units were to be prepared to march almost immediately. The quota assigned to the Orleans Territory was 837 militiamen. On December 23, 1808, Governor Claiborne issued a proclamation to the militia calling upon them to fulfill the quota requirement by volunteering for service. Appealing to their patriotism in the face of the crisis, he reminded them that Americans were being killed, their property was being destroyed, and American seamen were being impressed by foreign powers. He exhorted them to rally, add discipline to their native courage, and "be ready at a moment's warning to receive with your bayonets the enemies of our rights and independence."[15] Here was their opportunity, he implored, to prove that they appreciated serving under a system of freedom and democracy.[16] Although privately doubtful of the native response, Governor Claiborne met the quota with voluntary enlistments. Improving American foreign relations in the succeeding months, however, prompted Claiborne to release the volunteers in mid-June 1809.[17]

Although the territorial quota had been met, the atmosphere of crisis hanging over the land did not have a positive effect upon either the dismal state of the militia or the inclination of the lawmakers to cooperate in the establishment of an effective militia force. In his address to the solons on January 14, 1809, the governor again recommended measures to cope with the situation. Militia officers needed to be given authority to enforce discipline, exemptions from the militia service should be reduced, musters should be held more frequently, and stiff fines needed to be imposed for absenteeism. He resorted to cajolery and appealed to the basic virtues of the Louisianians in his request for a law which would remove these weaknesses. The preservation of individual rights required "that we should engraft the character of the soldier on that of a citizen." He denied that the local youth had suffered from degeneracy. Instead, they had inherited the virtues and spirit of their fathers, but "to give this spirit energy; to make it subservient to the defense of the country they must be armed and disciplined."[18] The legislators again shrugged off his appeal and the festering problem continued to embarrass Claiborne. A few months afterward the frustrated governor made the humiliating admission that even the Orleans Volunteers and Orleans Troop of Horse, the oldest and most visible militia in the territory, were also in a deplorable state. The agitated governor then ordered the dissolution of the units and their absorption into the regular militia.[19] The adjutant general, Colonel Henry Hopkins, likewise conceded that the militia was "in a deranged and feeble state." Hopkins explained it in part by saying that no one language was intelligible to a given militia company, discordant manners and prejudices were common, and no mutual friendship and confidence existed, all of which were necessary to a viable militia force. Local charges that the situation was due to Governor Claiborne's neglect, Hopkins declared, were both "ungenerous and unfounded."[20]

It seemed that the lawmakers would never comply with the governor's repeated requests. In his opening address to the first session of the third legislature on January 12, 1810, he admitted that a "contrariety of views" had prevented enactment of badly needed militia legislation. He again enumerated the defects in the militia law of 1805 and cited as supporting evidence the adjutant general's report of the previous year.[21] In addition to the weaknesses cited repeatedly by the governor, it seems that militia enrollments were substantially less than they should have been. According to the annual report submitted by Adjutant General Hopkins on June 30, 1810, there were 6,209 militiamen, organized into thirteen regiments, the Battalion of Orleans Volunteers which was still listed on the rolls, and five troops of horse. This reflected an increase of only sixteen militia enrollments over the previous year.[22] The fortunes of the militia were at low tide, the threat of war still hovered over the nation's capital, and unstable conditions prevailed in the territory.

Governor Claiborne predictably appealed again for a "more energetic" militia system in early 1811, whereupon a newspaper critic who identified himself as "Zeno" assailed him for having recommended heavy fines and even imprisonment as measures intended to overcome the militia problem. This might be possible, "Zeno" suggested, in a "strong armed aristocracy, or an absolute monarchy." But if the militia law enacted several years earlier could not be enforced, he wondered "how, in the name of common sense, are we to enforce those *Napoleon* edicts contemplated?" The weakness of a legislature was demonstrated by the enactment of unenforcable laws, such as the Embargo Act passed by Congress, and he predicted the same result with the militia law then under consideration by the territorial legislature. The development of an effective militia system would be possible only when self-preservation, self-love, and love of country served as incentives. "So long as men of wealth shew a supineness and apathy to any thing like defense," the critic contended, "so long will the other grades of society be indifferent. Let a martial spirit be diffused amongst those who have the most to defend—let them shew the example and it will ensure success." It was essential therefore for the lawmakers to convince the people that their safety, property, and independence were contingent upon defensive preparations. [23]

A slave insurrection in St. John the Baptist and St. Charles parishes in January 1811 finally convinced the solons that both their safety and property were endangered. The resulting anxieties quickly broke the long impasse and the governor's appeals for an effective militia at last fell on receptive ears. The lawmakers, suddenly feeling a sense of urgency, amended the militia law of 1805 and adopted most of the provisions which Claiborne had requested annually since 1806. These included more frequent musters and fines for non-attendance ranging from $20 for officers to $7 for non-commissioned officers and privates. Money collected from the fines was earmarked to buy arms and ammunition. [24] When the governor sent a copy of the law to the secretary of war, he expressed the hope that the militia could at least be placed on a "good footing." [25]

The legislation had at last been enacted but unfortunately no qualitative changes resulted; the quick and decisive suppression of the slave revolt removed the momentary danger. "Zeno" was correct after all. The basic weakness was a lack of enforcement. Nothing further was done following enactment of the law to develop a respectable militia force, partially because of popular preoccupation with the territory's imminent admission to statehood. Claiborne had clearly failed in his efforts to establish a viable militia force, and his repeated efforts to absolve the officer corps of responsibility were wrong. The legislative authorizations he sought were deferred altogether too long, but no significant improvements were produced following their long-delayed enactment. Numerous problems, some of which were unique to the territory, admittedly impeded his efforts but they also became rationalizations for failure. And the failure was a collective responsibility. As "Zeno" correctly contended, the territorial leaders, especially the planter class, pursued their private interests and their nonchalant demeanor influenced popular attitudes toward service in the militia. Moreover, the consistent refusals of the lawmakers to display any significant commitment to the development of a respectable militia had not gone unnoticed among the masses. Nevertheless, ultimate responsibility for the plight of the militia must be assigned to Governor Claiborne as commander of the militia and to his officer corps. The exasperated Claiborne appealed to the territorial legislatures for five years to make the requested changes, yet there is absolutely no evidence to indicate that he made any meaningful effort to infuse discipline and order in the militia ranks.

Not once did he take forceful measures against offenders even during times of tension and crisis. Thus he relied almost completely upon regular military forces in the territory to cope with internal disturbances and external threats.

Although an enfeebled militia at best emerged during the territorial period, such a security force was needed to provide internal security as well as to provide some protection against external threats. The Indians constituted a possible danger, just as they had in the Mississippi Territory. Although he did not hold the specific title of superintendent of Indian affairs, Governor Claiborne's responsibilities in the realm of Indian affairs nonetheless were comparable to those exercised while serving earlier in that capacity in the Mississippi Territory. Moreover, the basic philosophy which had dictated his Indian policies while in Natchez was readily evident in New Orleans. In turn, it was commensurate with President Jefferson's benevolent national policies toward the Indian tribes.

Claiborne sought to cultivate friendship with the Indians and to reassure them of his commitment to their general welfare. He instructed Captains Amos Stoddard in Upper Louisiana and Edward Turner, commandant at Natchitoches in the northwest, to treat the peaceful Indians with kindness and consideration and to protect them against misdeeds and violence. The best way to insure the friendship of the Indians, he declared, was by an impartial administration of justice. He also recommended the distribution of some rations to honest and well-disposed Indians which would hopefully provide tangible evidence of the government's interest in their welfare. The governor indicated to President Jefferson that efforts should be made to contact the Indians living west of the Mississippi for the purpose of promoting friendly relations. In fact, with the president's approval, he decided to meet personally with the Indian leaders at Natchitoches.[26]

Well aware of the legendary greed of many white traders and its corrosive effect upon white-red relations, Claiborne regulated the Indian trade within the limits of his resources in an effort to protect the Indians from unscrupulous practices. He pointed out to Madison that since he had not been designated superintendent of Indian affairs, he lacked specific instructions from Jefferson for coping with the problem of unregulated trade. Nevertheless, Claiborne independently instructed his commandants to be certain that the white traders posted bond with security amounting to $4,000 and that persons of dubious character not be permitted to engage in the trade at all. Moreover, the traders were to accept only peltry from the Indians for their goods. Absolutely nothing else was to be accepted by the traders. Claiborne explained that this was essential to prevent persons from going into Spanish territory and taking horses or encouraging the Indians to do so and thereby creating unnecessary disputes with the neighboring Spaniards.[27]

While the governor was trying to cultivate friendly relations with the Indians and prevent incidents which might provoke the Spaniards, some of the Spanish leaders were busily engaged for a time in activities intended to undermine the American authority and create difficulties. This included efforts by Casa Calvo and some of his associates to incite the Indians against the United States. In early September 1804, the governor received a report from Captain Turner who, in turn, had just heard from William Graham, who resided in the Casada Nation. According to Graham, the Aish Indians were bringing pressures to bear on the Casadas to force them to move into Spanish territory. A grand council was scheduled to be held under Spanish auspices on the Sabine River for the purpose of encouraging Indian warfare against the United States. Graham also reported that the threat of war was intensified by Spanish rumors, particularly from priests at

Natchitoches, that Louisiana would soon be restored to Spain. Further, the priests purportedly were telling the Indians that the United States offered no protection to religion, and that association with the American infidels would "dishonor the Shades of their ancestors, who had lived and died in the true faith." Governor Claiborne questioned Calvo about the rumors and received assurances that Calvo would consult with other Spanish officials in an effort to insure harmony and understanding.[28]

American-Spanish relations took a turn for the worse in succeeding months, and Claiborne moved quickly to insure Indian neutrality in the event of war between Washington and Madrid. Recognizing the influence that the Cadoquia (Caddo) Indians exercised over the tribes residing in the vicinity of the Red River, the governor delivered a speech to the Caddo chief and a few warriors at Natchitoches on September 5, 1806. Claiborne assured them the president wished to promote the happiness of all mankind, and to improve the lot of the "Red Children." The president wanted the Indians to live in peace, and to cultivate their fields in safety. Claiborne advised the Caddoes to distrust those persons of forked tongues who dared proclaim that the president was not their friend. "Brother. Let your people continue to hold the Americans by the hand with sincerity and friendship, and the Chain of Peace will be bright and strong; our children will smoke together, and the path will never be covered with blood." Although the president desired peace, he was unafraid of war. The Americans had driven back the king's forces during the Revolutionary War, he reminded the Indians, and added: "We were then a young people, but have grown to manhood, and could strike an enemy with a heavier hand, and a stronger arm." American troops, he proclaimed expansively, were stretched out over a vast territory, from regions where snow seldom fell to others where armies could cross ice-covered rivers. The governor then spoke of possible conflict with Spain, and informed them that negotiations were in progress. Should the negotiations break down and war ensure, Claiborne asked nothing more than neutrality on the part of the Indians. "When white people enter into disputes, let the red man keep quiet, and join neither side." In closing his address to the Caddoes, Claiborne asked them to inform other tribes of what he had said. Grand Chief Dehahuit responded with comparable eloquence and promised that he would forever remember Claiborne's words and advice. He spoke of the cordial

Cadoquia-French relationship of the past and of America's acquisition of the land owned formerly by France, and added: "We being on the land of course go with it, so we regard you in the same light as we did them." Chief Dehahuit promised that Caddo hands would never be stained with the blood of white men, and that Claiborne's words would be remembered and passed on from one to another until they reached the setting sun. The Caddo chieftain proclaimed that he had been embarrassed earlier as the Americans stood on one side and the Spaniards on the other, and he himself knew not "on which foot to stand." Now he knew. Chief Dehahuit asserted in closing that while his skin was red, his heart was white, and he committed the Caddoes to friendship and kindness.[29]

The threatened American-Spanish conflict did not occur and the Caddoes' commitment to their new patrons was not put to the test. However, they remained peacefully inclined and maintained friendly relations with the whites. The Caddoes were a pacific people by nature, but the governor's eloquent address probably influenced them. Although the United States had at the time hardly more than a token force at Natchitoches, the most exposed forward post in the northwest, and although the Spanish forces at one time crossed the Sabine River and approached the isolated and dusty little settlement itself, Governor Claiborne at no time displayed an inclination to enlist Indian support for the American cause. Rather, he adhered scrupulously to the policies he enunciated at the time of his conference with Chief Dehahuit and his advisers.

Some of the other tribes were not as peacefully disposed as the Caddoes and Governor Claiborne, fully aware of the greater truculence of some, remained alert to prevent isolated problems from developing into real sources of conflict. The Choctaws had displayed a certain bellicocity in Mississippi, for example, and Governor Claiborne acted quickly when incidents occurred in the Orleans Territory which involved the Choctaws and could have given them cause for offense. When he learned that a white man had wounded a Choctaw warrior, he immediately sent the Choctaws a "talk." If the warrior died, he promised that the murderer, identified only as Thomas, would be brought to justice. He also utilized the occasion to speak of Spanish-American differences, and advised the Choctaws to remain aloof from the quarrel. Following the death of the warrior, Claiborne wrote to the family and told them that their lamentations would not bring their loved one back to life. The murderer had fled, but orders had been sent out for his arrest and he would be punished. In the meantime, Claiborne asked the family's forbearance and patience and appealed to them not to shed innocent blood. As he had sometimes done earlier, he tried to pacify the relatives with gifts but they refused since acceptance would have amounted to a compromise from their point of view. Although there is no evidence that the murderer was captured and brought to justice, the incident did not provoke further problems with the Choctaws and relations remained generally stable.[30] In fact, when it was rumored that the Couchatta Indians on the Sabine River were menacing the frontier and committing depredations, the Choctaws offered their services to punish them but Claiborne wisely declined. [31]

The murder of a member of the tribe by a white man identified as Watson sparked the Couchatta eruption. The Couchattas, a small tribe of about 200 persons living along the Sabine River, in retaliation, killed two whites in the vicinity of Natchitoches. In an effort to head off further strife, Governor Claiborne sent the Couchattas an address asking if the rumors that they wanted to raise their tomahawks against the Americans were true. He reminded them that the Americans were regarded by their enemies as "men and warriors." The "great American chief" wished his "red children" well, Claiborne assured them, but he advised them to desist from "mischief" or the president would send his warriors against them.[32] John Sibley, Indian agent at Natchitoches, reported to Claiborne that the angry and uneasy white settlers had threatened to march against the Couchatta village and wipe it out. Governor Claiborne, who continued to fret because he had never received specific instructions about his Indian responsibilities, made a report to Secretary of War Dearborn and expressed the fear that such a move would spark an all-out "Indian War West of the Mississippi." To prevent further violence, Claiborne instructed Colonel John Thompson of the Eighth Militia Regiment to keep his men in a state of readiness and he alerted cavalry units at Opelousas and Natchitoches. If the Indians committed any further outrages or continued their predatory incursions, the governor authorized the militiamen to apprehend them or pursue them as far west as the Sabine River. At the same time, he advised caution and added that "Forebearance and moderation under minor wrongs, are not unfrequently means of averting greater evils.[33] Fortunately, no further violence occurred and relations between the Couchattas and white settlers improved and returned to normal in the succeeding months.

Although forced to take precautionary measures when the threat of conflict and violence developed, the compassionate Claiborne sought to protect the Indians as well as the whites. When four Alabama Indians were sentenced to be hanged for murder in the autumn of 1808, the governor pardoned two of them because they apparently had been only accessories to the crime and because their deaths might have provoked the Indians to seek revenge which would only "hasten their extirpation from among the Nations of the Earth." The governor then repeated a prophecy made earlier by an anonymous Indian chief: "The time will come, and it is not far distant, when in this whole tracts [sic] of Country there will not be left, one solitary Indian for a White man's dog to bark at." [34]

The governor was concerned generally with the welfare of the small Indian tribes in the Orleans Territory but the plight of the Alabama Indians in particular caused the governor to intercede with the federal government on their behalf. At about the time the four Alabama Indians were to be hanged, Judge George King informed Claiborne that the Alabamas were without land. Although the white settlers had actually recommended pardons for two of the four prisoners, they demanded at the same time that the Alabamas leave the Opelousas region. Judge King pointed out that the Alabamas had lived among the whites for forty years, their men were hunters, boatmen, and cattle drovers, and their families picked cotton for a livelihood. Having lived among the whites for such a long time the Alabamas wanted to remain with them. King recommended that they be given title to 2,000 to 3,000 acres of land which Claiborne approved and transmitted to President Jefferson. In turn, the president appeared before Congress on December 30, 1808, and requested that the Alabamas be accorded the opportunity to establish "fixed habitations." [35] As a result, the Alabamas were not uprooted from their homes and forced to relocate in the more isolated and unsettled lands to the westward.

Although he had not received specific guidelines from Washington, Governor Claiborne faithfully carried out the benevolent and paternalistic Indian policies of his Washington mentor. He sought to preserve a "good understanding with the

Indians West of the Mississippi,[36] and his treatment of the Alabamas, Caddoes, Couchattas and others served precisely that purpose. Although Claiborne realized that the Indian chief's prophecy about the ultimate extinction of the red men might indeed come to pass, it would not be because of Claiborne's policies or his lack of concern for Indian welfare. Not only did he seek to prevent or contain disputes between the whites and Indians, but he insisted that the local Indian tribes remain aloof from disputes among the whites in which the Indians stood only to lose. Yet condescending toward the "red children" as he had been earlier in Mississippi, he nonetheless was their abiding friend.

The maintenance of stable relations between white settlers and the small Indian tribes proved far less demanding on Governor Claiborne than the problems associated with the institution of slavery. The Spanish colonial authorities had permitted traffic in slaves, and the labor needs on the great plantations lining both sides of the Mississippi River had made it a thriving business. During the three-week retrocession of Louisiana to France three French ships delivered 463 African slaves to the Louisiana market, and American authorities made no effort to prevent their entry. Moreover, immediately following the transfer of Louisiana to the United States Governor Claiborne did not attempt to curb the slave traffic.[37] However, when Congress passed an act for the organization of the Orleans Territory in March 1804, it included a provision prohibiting the importation of slaves into the territory. Yet it did permit legitimate owners going into the territory for permanent settlement to take their slaves with them.[38]

Most Louisianians strongly resented the restrictions on slave importations, and they complained bitterly about them. Since Claiborne was expected to enforce the law, local residents frequently blamed him for the policy. Although he pointed out that a continued influx of slaves could produce a slave insurrection comparable to the bloody slave revolt which had erupted earlier in Santo Domingo, he told Jefferson that the people would be satisfied with nothing less than a resumption of the foreign slave trade for a few years. Claiborne squirmed uncomfortably under the criticism directed toward him for the restriction while privately expressing his personal feeling to Jefferson: "The Searcher of all Hearts, knows, how little I desire, to see another of that wretched Race, set his foot on the Shores of America. How, from my Heart, I detest the Rapacity, that wou'd transport them to us."[39]

The governor reported an almost insatiable demand for slaves, and said that Louisianans were almost unanimously agreed that the territory would be "ruin'd for ever" unless slave imports were continued. Even the most respectable citizens were unable to "suppress the Agitation of their Tempers" when the prohibition was mentioned.[40] With local emotions thus aroused, a formal protest was shortly forthcoming. The planters, merchants and other interested persons held some meetings and formulated a memorial enumerating several grievances. Pierre Derbigny, Jean-Noël Destréhan, and Pierre Sauvé presented the memorial to Congress on January 4, 1805. The memorialists argued the need for Negro laborers and field hands on the basis of local climatic conditions and the nature of agriculture in the territory. Negroes were essential, they contended, for the cultivation of such crops as cotton, indigo, rice, and sugar. The levees could be kept in repair only by "those whose natural constitution and habits of labor enable them to resist the combined effects of a deleterious moisture and a degree of heat intolerable to whites." Unless slave imports were permitted, the petitioners predicted gloomily, cultivation would cease "and the great river resume its empire over our ruined fields and demolished habitations."[41]

Even though the memorialists presented what they regarded as a persuasive case and Governor Claiborne pointed out that the restriction constituted a major source of discontent among the Louisianans, Congress refused to remove the restriction. As a result of the congressional refusal to yield on the controversial matter, Governor Claiborne had to contend with the difficult and emotionally charged problem of slave smuggling. Many ordinarily law-abiding citizens defied the ban and added slaves illegally to their working forces. John Watkins, mayor of New Orleans, told John Graham, the territorial secretary, flatly that even the most effective government would be unable to prevent the smuggling of slaves into the territory. Watkins declared that the slaves would be smuggled in from Jamaica, Martinique, and Santo Domingo instead of Africa because of the reduced risks.[42]

The mayor's assertion that the slave trade would continue despite governmental attempts to halt it was generally conceded; the only realistic question remaining was whether the Claiborne administration and the federal authority in the territory would be able to appreciably reduce the volume of traffic. The existence of innumerable bayous with sea outlets, such lakes as Borne,

Maurepas, and Pontchartrain, and the endless swamps, were all an open invitation to adventurous slave traders. Furthermore, Spanish-owned West Florida lay to the northeast and Texas to the west. Pensacola, Baton Rouge, and Mobile, in particular, beckoned to the slavers who used such places as centers from which to smuggle slaves into Claiborne's domain. Since he was unable to take direct action against the slave depots, the governor asked Gallatin in 1811 about the possibility of taking Mobile. Less than a week later, Claiborne asserted to James Monroe that the American occupation of those lands running eastward to the Perdido River would help eliminate the illicit slave traffic.[43] The United States was not then ready to move directly against Mobile and Pensacola, but Baton Rouge did come into American possession shortly afterward and this helped combat the illicit slave traffic.

Governor Claiborne instituted several measures to reduce the volume of the slave traffic. He had Colonel Constant Freeman station a subaltern officer and a small complement of men at the Balize. The officer boarded ships ascending the river to check their papers and to find out how many Negroes were aboard. The ships then proceeded northward to the Plaquemines where they were detained until permission was granted to proceed to New Orleans and checks of the ships were again made. If there were no discrepancies between the Balize and Plaquemines reports, the authorities assumed that the ships were not engaged in smuggling.[44]

The governor also prevailed upon Captain John Shaw, who headed up the naval command at New Orleans, to extend his cruising patrols as far eastward as the Perdido River. All foreign ships found hovering off the coast which had Negroes aboard were to be intercepted and taken to New Orleans where an inquiry and trial would be conducted. Moreover, the governor gave orders to examine all ships arriving from foreign ports. When slaves who were not a part of the regular crew were found aboard such ships, the vessels were held until final dispositions of their cases were made.[45]

The territorial authorities faced a formidable task under normal conditions but the impact of the French Revolution and Napoleonic wars on many of the Caribbean islands greatly compounded the problem. Thousands of refugees—whites, free Negroes, and slaves—principally from Cuba and Santo Domingo, poured into the Orleans Territory during the territorial period.

Thirty-four vessels crowded with 5,800 refugees, including 4,000 free Negroes and slaves, arrived in New Orleans during a three-month period in 1809.[46] Although the slaves were held temporarily aboard the ships, Claiborne released them in the care of their masters on the condition that they would be made available when required by the authorities. He informed Julien Poydras, then serving as territorial delegate to Congress, of the influx and recommended that Congress relax existing restrictions on the admission of exiles seeking haven in the territory.[47] The governor also sought relief for them and worked closely with a hastily formed Committee of Benevolence which was established during the major exodus from the islands in 1809 to provide emergency relief.

Some of the native inhabitants became alarmed when the refugees first began arriving shortly after the American acquisition of Louisiana. One critic accused the governor of being unconcerned about the dangers resulting from the admission of the "brigands." Although the governor did not respond publicly, he assured Madison that he had taken every precaution to prevent the import of dangerous slaves by which he meant mainly those who had participated in the Santo Domingo revolt. Although he admitted some probably had been able to evade the authorities, he did not feel personally responsible.[48] A "Louisianian," probably Derbigny, insisted nonetheless that the governor should have enforced the municipal ordinance against the admission of "bad characters" and could have authorized the municipal authorities to expel dangerous refugees. He then launched a more personal attack on Claiborne, asserting that there was no point in speaking of expelling dangerous exiles when Claiborne himself was uninterested. He accused the governor of pardoning a slave accused of murder in another territory because he was owned by one of the governor's relatives. According to the accuser, Claiborne then permitted the relative to sell the slave "under his own eye, as if nothing was to be apprehended from such example."[49] Personal criticisms resulting from the admission of refugees were not uncommon during the early days of the Claiborne administration but they subsided after the bitter recriminations of 1805 and 1806.

The authorities sought generally to prevent the emigration of free Negroes and mulattoes into the territory as a matter of policy. This was done initially under the authority of municipal ordinances and a legislative measure which forbade the entry of free Negroes from Hispanola and "the other French islands of America." However, a more comprehensive act was passed by the legislature and approved by the governor in the spring of 1807 which excluded free Negroes and mulattoes from entry into the territory. According to the measure, such persons who entered and settled in the territory were subject to a fine of $20 per week after the first two weeks. If they refused to pay or provide security to the judiciary for departure within two weeks, they were to be committed to jail. The parish judge was then authorized after a ten-day notification to sell them for a stipulated period in order to pay the fine and costs levied by the courts. If unable to sell them, the prisoners were to be employed on public works for the same number of days they had remained in the territory after the two-week period of grace.[50] However, inadequate and incomplete local records made it virtually impossible to ascertain the extent to which the law was enforced.

Governor Claiborne not only had responsibility for the prevention of the illicit slave traffic and of keeping "bad characters" from entering the territory, but citizens also appealed to him whenever their slaves escaped. One of the more convenient places of refuge for runaway slaves was the Spanish settlement of Nacogdoches. Casa Calvo and some of his colonial associates were convinced that American restrictions on slave imports would preclude the assimilation of the Louisianians. They remained in New Orleans for two years following the transfer, covertly encouraging slaves to run away. By hastening the anticipated slave shortage, the Spanish dons hoped to undermine the tenuous American influence among the natives. They also circulated a rumor in 1804 that the Spanish king had issued a decree in which he promised freedom and protection to slave escapees. When Governor Claiborne learned of the purported decree and its local circulation, he immediately corresponded with Casa Calvo, Don Juan Manuel de Salcedo, who replaced Calvo as governor of Louisiana in 1801 and later served as governor of Mexico, Don Joaquin Ugarti, the Spanish commandant at Nacogdoches, and Antonio Cordero, captain general of Texas. He warned them that Spanish encouragement and protection for deserting slaves might have serious repercussions. In fact, he declared that he was already having to restrain some of the irate settlers at Natchitoches who were threatening to go to Nacogdoches to claim their slaves. When Calvo attempted to elicit a promise from Claiborne that no harm would be inflicted on returning slaves, the governor replied firmly that nothing short of unconditional surrender of the escapees would relieve existing tensions. While he personally did not favor harsh punishment for the fugitives, he preferred to leave the question of leniency to the slaves' masters. Despite occasional displays of temper and recriminations, Claiborne and Salcedo finally agreed to a policy of mutual cooperation in the return of slave escapees on January 15, 1809. When the governor announced the agreement to the legislature shortly afterward, he suggested that the solons might wish to enact a law which spelled out the powers and duties of the territorial officials in coping with this particular problem.[51] However, the agreement resolved the problem and thereby precluded the need for legislative action.

Governor Claiborne and his associates were likewise concerned about the attitude and demeanor of the black population in the territory. While the governor and lawmakers recognized the necessity of formulating civil and criminal codes to cope with offenses committed by the whites and free blacks, they also enacted legislation dealing with the behavior of the slave population and slave-master obligations and responsibilities. Moreover, when they imposed an annual tax of fifty cents per slave in 1805 and increased it to seventy-five cents two years later, they also required the slave owners to keep detailed records on their slave forces, including such information as age, state of health, and marital status. The act doubled the tax rate for slaves not listed on the roles and specified fines of up to $100 for failure to provide information.[52] The legislation provided a source of revenue while at the same time it enabled parish authorities to remain generally informed about the number, location, and status of the slave population.

The legislature also passed the first of three slave laws at about the same time. It retained the Spanish laws providing for the punishment of Negro slaves, except that it forbade cruel and unusual punishments. It also stipulated that the county courts had jurisdiction over all crimes, except murder, committed by slaves and that such cases were to be heard by a county judge and four householders. The superior court had original jurisdiction in cases involving slaves accused of murder. The following legislature passed a Black Code and a measure specifying the penalties for slaves found guilty of various crimes.[53] The Black Code, based on the earlier Spanish and French codes, included approximately forty sections dealing with master-slave relations. The master's responsibilities included caring for the ill, aged, and disabled, and it stipulated that the master was to provide the slave with clothing, rations, pay for work on Sundays, and a schedule of work and rest. Penalties were prescribed for owners found guilty of neglect toward their slaves. Moreover, the code provided some penalties for offenses committed by slaves, and denied to slaves the right to carry arms, engage in civil suits, and testify against whites. The accompanying act prescribed the death penalty for persons who encouraged or incited slave revolts, and fines of $1,000 to $2,000 and a year's imprisonment for persons found guilty of transporting slaves out of the territory. [54]

In the spring of 1807 the lawmakers passed a measure setting forth "rules of conduct to be observed with respect to negroes and other slaves of this territory." If the overseer or any other white person representing the plantation owner was threatened, insulted, or attacked by a slave employed on the plantation, the offense was to be punished by "the judge and the inhabitants." The law charged them with responsibility for the punishment of crimes committed by slaves "at their discretion, according to the gravity of the case." A person found guilty of concealing a slave in his house or receiving and hiring a slave without the permission of the slave's master was subject to a fine of $2 per day for each day of concealment or employment, and he was responsible for any damages committed by the slave during such time. If the offender was unable to pay the fine, he was subject to imprisonment from fifteen days to three months. Moreover, slave owners were not to permit other slaves to visit their slave forces in the slave quarters, or to permit their slaves to dance at night. [55]

The territorial legislature also passed an act regulating the emancipation of slaves. No owner could emancipate his slaves unless they were at least thirty years old and had a record of good conduct for the preceding five years. However, this requirement was waived if the slave or slaves had saved the life of the master or a member of his family. A notice of intent to emancipate had to be posted and persons opposing the action were required to file their opposition with the county court within forty days from the date of the notice. The owner could then free his slaves if no opposition had been filed. However, the act could be nullified later if the authorities learned that the act was intended to defraud creditors, minors, or persons who had a possible interest in the act but were not then present. This condition did not apply if the emancipator had the financial resources or other property to satisfy possible creditors. Every act of emancipation not meeting the requirements of the law was to be declared null and void. Also, the proprietor and public officer would each forfeit $100 for the failure of the emancipator to meet the stipulations of the law. Half of this amount was to be paid to the informer and the rest was to be paid to the territorial treasury. Finally, the emancipator had the tacit obligation to maintain such emancipated persons in the event they required it, "owing to fickelness [s.c], old age, insanity, or any other proved infirmity." If the person refused, the judge could require a monthly payment which would be used to sustain the emancipated slaves until they were able to care for themselves.[56] The primary aim of this legislation obviously was to discourage the general practice of emancipation since there was a constant demand for slaves in the territory. Second, if all legal requirements were fulfilled and slaves were emancipated, the authorities sought to prevent them either from suffering unduly or becoming objects of public charity.

During the years in which Governor Claiborne grappled with slave problems, he consistently urged the solons to enact laws intended to keep the slave population submissive. The underlying motive for such legislation was the spectre of a slave revolt. This was understandable in view of the suppressed state of the slaves and fairly persistent rumors of revolt. In fact, on the day of the Louisiana transfer Claiborne was informed of a possible slave revolt and clandestine plans to put New Orleans to the torch. When General Wilkinson requested another five hundred regular troops the day after the transfer, he based the need on the threat posed by armed Negroes. Apprehensions were increased because of the size of the black population. The total territorial population was fixed at 55,534 in 1806. This number included 22,701 slaves and 3,350 free Negroes,[57] collectively amounting to some forty-five per cent of the total number. The influx of blacks from the Caribbean islands which included some "bad characters" despite the screening of incoming refugees added to the edginess of the white inhabitants. Moreover, the unstable political situation, the heterogeneous character of the territory's inhabitants, foreign intrigue, and the inclination of designing elements to fish in troubled waters increased the likelihood of a slave uprising. Just as Toussaint L'Ouverture led the blacks in revolt against the

French authority in Santo Domingo and thereby influenced Bonaparte's New World ambitions, a black revolt had also erupted in Louisiana in 1795. Dissension among the Negro leaders led to a disclosure of the plot, and consequently fewer lives were taken by the insurrectionists. The whites lashed back, hanged twenty-three of the conspirators, and exhibited their bodies at conspicuous points along the Mississippi River between Pointe Coupée, where the outbreak occurred, and New Orleans.[58]

Continuing rumors following the transfer and reports submitted to the governor heightened the concern. John Watkins, dispatched by Governor Claiborne in early 1804 to visit several districts and to appoint commandants, filed an ominous report upon his return. The Negroes were idle and insubordinate. They were wandering about at night without passports, he continued, and were stealing, drinking, and rioting.[59] In September some New Orleans residents petitioned the governor to appoint an "Extraordinary Commission" to investigate a rumored slave conspiracy. Although aware of the rumors but not as disturbed by them, Claiborne nonetheless strengthened night patrols in the city, alerted the local militia, and declared that he would arm every white man in New Orleans if necessary to meet any developing threat.[60] Rumors of a possible slave revolt shifted shortly afterward to more remote Pointe Coupée whose inhabitants called upon Claiborne for a military force to cope with the problem. According to the Pointe Coupée settlers, the slaves had learned of the Santo Domingo revolution, and "a Spirit of Revolt and mutyny [sic] has crept in among them—A few days since we happily Discovered a Plan for our Destruction." The governor wrote to Captain Turner, the commandant at Natchitoches, and promised to send twenty-five or thirty men immediately, in addition to one hundred muskets. At the same time, he advised Turner to organize all male citizens between the ages of sixteen and fifty for possible militia service. Claiborne's action in part was attributed to his knowledge of the revolt about a decade earlier, but he was also convinced that the slaves in the Pointe Coupée area were being encouraged by the Spaniards at Nacogdoches.[61] Again, no serious outbreak occurred, but rumors persisted of possible slave violence. A free Negro, identified as Stephen, warned Claiborne in early 1806 of a Creole plot in New Orleans which was ostensibly spearheaded by Calvo who was then out of the city. "They only wait the return of the Marquis to give the WHOOP to commence the massacre."

According to Stephen, the conspirators planned to free the slaves and have them join them in the uprising. Should there be a sudden cry of "fire" some night, Stephen warned, the Americans should not go out to investigate.[62] Again, Claiborne was not unduly disturbed by the warning, but public safety again demanded that he take certain precautionary measures.

Rumors of imminent slave uprisings persisted over the following years but nothing happened until early 1811. Then very suddenly a violent insurrection erupted about forty miles north of New Orleans in the German Coast parishes of St. John the Baptist and St. Charles. Estimates of the total number of slaves involved ranged from less than two hundred to as many as five hundred. The revolt was well organized and led with most of its senior leaders directing the movement from horseback. The insurrectionists advanced southward toward New Orleans hoping to persuade other slaves to join their ranks. Many of the planters and their families fortunately received some advance warning of the impending outbreak and managed to escape. The planters organized swiftly to meet the onslaught and then struck back savagely. A planter named Manuel Andry reported that some of the avenging whites caught the insurrectionists at Francis Bernoudi's plantation and indiscriminately slaughtered a number of Negro captives.[63]

In the meantime General Wade Hampton, who had replaced General Wilkinson, assumed direct command of two companies of volunteer militia, thirty regular troops, and a company of seamen from Captain John Shaw's naval command to suppress the revolt. They moved northward and were joined by some volunteer cavalrymen, presumably a militia unit but without leadership, and they made initial contact with the insurrectionists at the Fortier plantation. The slaves had occupied Colonel Fortier's sugar works, consisting of two brick buildings, where they elected to make a major stand. Hampton and his men killed "fifteen or twenty" and wounded several in the ensuing battle and the others fled precipitately. The slaves afterward attempted to reorganize at the Bernoudi plantation, but were dispersed and further broken up.[64]

Sixty-six Negroes were killed during the slave insurrection and several were captured and hanged. Sixteen of their leaders were taken to New Orleans where they were tried, convicted, and executed. Their heads were placed on poles and exhibited along the river as a grim reminder to the slave population, just as the aroused and avenging whites had done in the revolt of 1795. Two white persons, one of whom was Manuel Andry's son, died at the hands of the insurrectionists. A few others were wounded. Manuel Andry, struck by an axe-wielding slave, recovered and led the assault on the slaves at the Bernoudi plantation. Property losses were moderate.[65]

After the insurrection was suppressed and the emergency had ended Governor Claiborne followed a typically moderate course. He was convinced that a display of ruthlessness was necessary to produce the desired effect, but he opposed the execution of all the slaves who had participated in the outbreak. When the trials were in progress in New Orleans, he expressed the hope that "the list of the guilty may not be found still greater." The governor later granted pardons to some of the prisoners.[66]

The governor also sought to indemnify owners whose slaves had been killed during the course of the revolt. The legislature passed a compensatory act, as Claiborne had hoped, but a new problem developed. The costs of indemnification amounted to $29,000. When the treasurer reported that the territorial treasury contained only $19,500 in unappropriated funds, Claiborne called for and received a supplementary bill authorizing the payment of the full amount in regular installments.[67]

Even as Claiborne and the lawmakers were finding a means to reimburse the slaveowners, rumors of another threatened slave revolt continued to circulate. The governor received information that the slaves in the German Coast area and in New Orleans seemed to be restless. Although Claiborne was convinced that many of the rumors were without foundation, he nonetheless alerted local militia units and had arms and ammunition distributed.[68] The situation fortunately cleared up over the succeeding months and a state of normality again prevailed in the territory.

In the wake of the uprising, the municipal council enacted an ordinance intended to tighten security measures against the slave population of New Orleans. It forbade slaves to congregate either publicly or privately, except for funerals, sports, and dances. But sports events and dances were restricted to Sundays and had to be held before sundown. Only blind or infirm slaves were permitted to carry canes or sticks in the streets. Slaves found guilty of any of these offenses were subject to a penalty of twenty-five lashes. Moreover, slaves were denied lodging or sleeping quarters in houses other than those of their masters, overseers, or persons to whom they were hired out except by written permission. In addition, slaves could not rent rooms, apartments, or houses, even with the permission of their masters. Proprietors who rented places to them and masters who gave their permission were subject to fines of from $10 to $25.[69]

The last legislative session of the territorial period was convened on January 28, 1811, having been delayed for several days by the slave revolt. In his opening address on the following day, Governor Claiborne discussed the insurrection and reported that it had been quelled completely. He expressed appreciation to the regular forces, militia units, and volunteers for their prompt and effective action in the restoration of order. The speed with which the revolt was stamped out and the examples made of the principal leaders, he hoped, would have a stabilizing effect. Nonetheless, he sought to use the violent outbreak to spur the legislators into the enactment of measures needed to provide greater security. He again stressed the necessity of militia reforms but his refrain was ignored with a comparable regularity by the lawmakers. He also appealed for a more discriminate admission of slaves into the territory, declaring: "It is a fact of notoriety that negroes of all characters the most desperate and conduct the most infamous; convicts pardoned on condition of transportation—the refuse of jails are frequently introduced into this territory."[70] Although the authorities were a little more vigilant in the denial of admission to such undesirables as criminals and convicts from the prisons of other states and territories, no meaningful effort was made to curb the slave traffic because of the continuing heavy demand for slaves. In short, the governor admitted in his address before the legislature that his efforts to curb the flow of slaves into the territory had failed.

The abortive slave revolt was not a real test of the territory's security capabilities, but the resources at hand had proved sufficient to cope decisively with it. The territorial militia was still a fragile, uncertain, and untried force. Moreover, slaves continued to be brought into the territory despite the governor's efforts. In seeking to accomplish these two objectives, Claiborne's efforts clearly ran counter to what the native white inhabitants regarded to be their greater interests. Therefore, in these specific areas of responsibility, his was at best a record of limited and indifferent success and more frequently of outright failure. Yet given the unique environment in which he functioned and the concomitant problems peculiar to that environment, Governor Claiborne's achievements exceeded surface indications. Beyond this, they were but a part of his greater charge which was to direct, lead, push, and coax an alien people into the fold and make them an integral part of the American political, social, economic, and cultural fabric without creating, as President Jefferson admonished, undue uneasiness. After all other candidates for the territorial post were considered and the uncertainties about Claiborne himself were measured against this fundamental responsibility, it seems increasingly plausible that William Claiborne just might have been the right person in the right place at the right time.

VIII

ORLEANS TERRITORY: THE ROUTINE OF ADMINISTRATION

Governor Claiborne had a wide range of tasks less exciting than slave uprisings and Indian threats but more significant to the overall success of his administration. The Americanization of Louisiana was contingent upon several factors, including the development of an educational system. Indeed, when viewed in terms of Claiborne's preeminent objective, education assumed a significance second only to the maintenance of internal security.[1]

Claiborne, fully cognizant of President Jefferson's interest in education, made a special effort to keep officials in Washington informed. Prior to the Louisiana transfer Jefferson had requested information from Governor Claiborne and Daniel Clark concerning Louisiana's educational system and the literacy levels of its inhabitants. Claiborne reported that New Orleans had only one public school, supported principally by the Spanish king, which served only the city's wealthiest families.[2] He also mentioned the Ursuline convent in New Orleans which had been established during the preceding century and provided educational opportunities for girls. At the end of 1803, the convent had seventy-three "boarders" and a hundred "day students," each of whom contributed financial support according to her means.[3] Claiborne concluded his report by saying that a majority of the people supposedly were able to read and write, but that some few had had additional educational training.[4] According to the governor the Spanish government had discouraged education. Even members of the upper classes lacked any real interest in education, preferring instead to parade their power and wealth before the masses. Claiborne pledged to make the introduction of an educational system a primary objective. New Orleans had ample resources, he was certain, to support an educational system. Although the "Sons of ignorance and affluence" preferred to maintain the status quo, in the governor's view, he hoped to convince leaders in Washington that the federal government should erect some schools and "some superior seminaries of Literature in this Province." Claiborne believed that as long as education was left to private foundations, no real improvement could be expected. Carefully setting the stage for his proposal, the governor told Madison that the success of the American experiment in the territory was contingent upon a diffusion of knowledge. To effect this, Claiborne recommended that Congress appropriate $100,000 annually for educational purposes. When he wrote to Jefferson a few months later, he suggested that some federally owned buildings and lands in the territory be relinquished to local authorities to assist in providing for public schools.[5]

Claiborne questioned his commandants about the status of education in their respective districts, inquired whether French or English schools existed in these locales, and solicited advice about the best means for introducing and supporting education. Parents should be encouraged to educate their children, he urged, and stressed knowledge and virtue as vital factors in the promotion of happiness, prosperity, and liberty. An address Claiborne delivered to a delegation of students from Abbé Roland's Academy emphasized the necessity of education. If permitted one favorite wish, he said, he would like to see "Science rear her Lofty head throughout United America." Neither time nor expense should be spared, he was convinced, to enrich youthful minds with "correct morals and correct information."[6]

In his maiden speech before the newly convened legislative council in December 1804, the governor called for mass education. He pointed out that several of the states were encouraging literature and literary institutions, some of which were beginning to compare favorably with those in Europe. He hoped the legislature would serve as a generous patron of "seminaries of learning." Julien Poydras, president of the council, assured the governor that public education would be given serious attention. About three months later the legislative council passed and the governor approved a measure providing for the creation of the University of Orleans which embraced a system of collegiate and public schools. The governor, federal judge, justices of the superior court, president of the legislative council, mayor of New Orleans, and other territorial leaders were to serve as university regents. The regents were authorized to establish the College of New Orleans whose administration and staff would consist of a president and four professors. The college would provide classical instruction, French, Spanish, and English, ancient and modern history, natural and moral philosophy, mathematics, logic, and rhetoric. Moreover, the regents were to establish a library and, one or more academies for boys in each county, and as many academies as necessary for "the youth of the female sex." The academies for boys would offer instruction in French and English, reading, writing, arithemetic, grammar, and geography while the academies for girls would provide language instruction and "the polite branches of literature." Two lotteries which were authorized to raise $50,000 annually would finance the university system, but it was hoped that the transfer of unused federal lands in New Orleans to the city would provide additional support.[7] In the end, however, the lotteries proved wholly inadequate, and the legislature declined to make any financial appropriations. As a consequence, the education act of 1805 was not implemented for some time.

During the next four years the legislators made some revisions in the proposed educational system. In his address to the legislature on March 25, 1806, Governor Claiborne pointed out that some states had established tax-supported schools in every neighborhood. He recommended the same for the territory, declaring that the tax should "bear alike on every individual, in proportion to his wealth."[8] The governor was particularly concerned that people who lived in the more remote areas would not have access to the academies and therefore would be denied the benefits of education. Acting on the governor's recommendation, the legislature adopted a measure providing for "neighborhood schools." Except for Orleans County, which was excluded from the terms of the act, the lawmakers shifted control of the schools from the board of university regents to the counties. "Fathers of families" in each county were to select five county commissioners who were to determine the number and location of the schools, and each county was to provide the necessary support for its schools.[9]

When he addressed the legislature in 1808, the governor pointed out that no substantive educational progress had been made because the schools had been left to the "precarious support of private bounty." Although he recommended one or more free schools in each parish, the governor, whose relations with the legislature had improved markedly, told the solons that they should determine the means of financing them.[10] The legislature enacted a new measure which stipulated that a jury of twelve to twenty-four "respectable" county citizens would determine the "mode, place and amount of tuition money" for the county schools. A commission of five trustees was to be selected from the jury which would have control of the schools. However, ambiguities in the law, especially the means of financing education, merely added to the existing problems, with some interpreting the law to mean that the county juries were authorized to raise funds for school support.[11]

Addressing the lawmakers a year later, the governor offered a discourse on the continuing European wars and their impact upon the United States, and then once more directed the attention of the legislators to the territory's educational inadequacies. He noted that parents were beginning to recognize the importance of education for their children, and remarked that the number of private schools had increased, and that Pointe Coupée Parish actually had made provisions for some schools. Again seeking to generate support for education, the governor declared that instruction should be accompanied by efforts to inculcate ardent patriotism and principles of morality. Children reared in such a climate became sources of parental and societal pride and "the pillars of their country's glory."[12] Nonetheless, all hope the governor may have had of developing a viable educational system vanished when the legislature passed an act which forbade the imposition of taxes for school support from persons who opposed it. Now convinced that the public would not provide the necessary funds, the dejected governor expressed the faint hope that Congress would subsidize public education in the territory.[13]

When he appeared before the last territorial legislature in early 1811, the governor had no particular reason to think the legislators would be any more receptive to education than their predecessors. Nevertheless, Claiborne made his usual appeal, declaring that education was the bulwark of liberty. He alluded to a treasury surplus and suggested that the legislature appropriate "a moiety at least of that surplus to objects of public utility." He recommended the establishment of four academies, so located as "to reconcile local prejudices and to enlist in their favour the pride and interest of the Citizens generally, that they also be so conducted as to excite among the professors and Students a great and constant rivalship."[14] The governor probably was taken aback when the legislators responded with a declaration that aside from its intrinsic merits, the "peculiar situation of this Country forces the consideration of this subject upon us." The general assembly appropriated $39,000. Of this amount, $15,000 was to be used to establish the College of Orleans, and $2,000 was appropriated to establish an academy in each of the twelve counties. The solons also authorized annual appropriations of $3,000 for the College of Orleans and $500 for each of the county academies. At the same time, the legislators stipulated that fifty indigent students were to be accepted free of charge in the College of Orleans. The university regents were also authorized to appoint three administrators for each county academy.[15] In essence, after a lapse of six years, the legislature provided the means necessary to implement the education act of 1805. Despite the governor's persistent prodding, very little educational progress had been achieved. The most significant gains had been registered in the increased number of private educational institutions and the gradual development of a more receptive public attitude toward education. Nonetheless, as the territorial period drew to a close, the legislators had at least accepted an educational responsibility and commitment, and they had established the foundation of a viable educational system. The governor almost single-handedly had achieved a substantial educational triumph which would be of incalcuable importance in the territory's Americanization processes.

    The College of Orleans finally opened its doors in late 1811. The basic obstacle to its establishment had been a lack of funds, but controversy over its location had also caused some delay. Finally on May 3, 1811, Governor Claiborne notified Mayor James Mather of New Orleans that the university regents had agreed to erect the college on the Trême plantation, and suggested at the same time that the city donate the lots and buildings on the plantation to the institution.[16] When the college began operation about six months later, it reported an initial enrollment of seventy students. Then in April 1812 the university regents memorialized Congress to donate to the institution the grant of land on which Government House was located. The regents anticipated a rapid expansion of the enrollment, and wished to erect additional buildings. Hoping to persuade Congress to respond favorably, the regents pointed out that the college would offer instruction in the English language, "the only medium by which can be understood the laws and principles that govern the different States." Moreover, according to the petitioners, the tranquillity, the "permanency and vigor of a Government composed of Free States, depend essentially upon the virtue of the Citizens—or, in other words, upon the general diffusion of knowledge throughout the Community."[17] Apparently Congress declined to act on the petition.

The university regents were also responsible for the selection of a competent college staff. When the education act of 1805 was passed, President Jefferson recommended Du Pont de Nemours for the presidency, but the nomination was premature since financial support was not forthcoming. Six years later when the college finally became a reality a writer advised the regents engaged in the selection of a faculty to require more proof of educational talent than the "exhibition of voluminous compilations." Those who excelled along these lines, he concluded, were "void of every thing like genious or fancy." He submitted a list of candidates for the presidency and for the various chairs to be filled.[18] The regents made their selections, and the first class was subsequently admitted to the College of Orleans. Although modest in size and educational goals, the college had emerged, albeit belatedly, as a viable institution of learning.

Governor Claiborne was often disappointed and suffered some setbacks in his efforts to introduce a system of public education, but the difficulties and perplexities associated with territorial land titles proved more worrisome and frustrating. Fortunately for Claiborne, his earlier experiences in the Mississippi Territory proved to be of great help in dealing with these problems. To President Jefferson's query about land titles in mid-1803, Governor Claiborne responded that many people in Louisiana possessed land under French and Spanish patents. Most of the patents had been granted to actual settlers, he surmised, and were conditional upon the maintenance of levees and land improvements. Claiborne responded negatively to Jefferson's inquiry about possible feudal rights, but he added that another person had suggested, perhaps facetiously, that there were some self-appointed nobles.[19]

The decision of Spanish authorities to retain their land records after the Louisiana transfer aggravated the already troublesome land title problem. James Brown, then serving as a United States attorney, reported to Secretary of the Treasury Gallatin in late 1805 that some of the records had been sent to Pensacola during the preceding summer where they would "grow or dwindle" according to avarice or interest. Madison warned Claiborne shortly afterward that the Spanish authorities were about to remove the land archives from New Orleans. Since it would constitute a violation of the American treaty with Spain, he directed Claiborne to take any legal action necessary to acquire them. A few weeks later Madison again stressed the importance of acquiring the records since many people would be greatly inconvenienced if they were transferred from New Orleans and the opportunities for fraud would be increased.[20] Despite promptings from Washington and Governor Claiborne's repeated appeals, the Spanish colonial authorities withheld many of the land records from the Americans.

While still serving in Mississippi Governor Claiborne had kept a watchful eye on those Louisiana lands lying immediately west of the Mississippi River. In early September 1803 he told Daniel Clark that a number of people from the Mississippi Territory had been locating and surveying lands in that region for some time. He warned Madison that much of the land in the trans-Mississippi was being acquired fraudulently. He suspected that Don José Vidal, a Spanish commandant west of Natchez, was attempting to secure lands in that area for his friends. He reported also that people from Natchez and Jefferson County were surveying and improving lands west of the Mississippi River in the belief that the American government would confirm their claims. In fact, Claiborne expressed the opinion that land frauds were rapidly becoming as common in Louisiana as they had been in Mississippi before 1795. Information from Clark that the Spanish colonial government had not given any person permission to locate or survey lands west of the Mississippi River relieved some of Claiborne's fears. All such locations and surveys were null and void, Clark declared, and persons making them were subject to prosecution. Spanish commandants earlier had been given the right to make land grants, subject to the approval of the Spanish government, Clark pointed out, but Intendant Morales had withdrawn it. Clark assured Claiborne that most of Captain Vidal's land grants were invalid. The governor immediately forwarded this information to Washington.[21]

Recognizing the complexities of the problem and the resultant local apprehensions, Claiborne exercised his powers as governor and intendant in 1804 to authorize Bartholomew Lafon to resurvey French and Spanish land grants. This was to be done upon the request of land claimants who would pay the same fee for such services as the Spanish colonial government had charged. Then, on March 2, 1805, Congress passed an act to ascertain and adjust land titles in the Orleans Territory and District of Louisiana issued by the French and Spanish governments prior to the transfer of Louisiana to the United States on December 20, 1803. The act authorized the president to divide the Orleans Territory into two land districts. The president was to appoint a register and two commissioners for each of the districts. The district commissioners and registers were to meet as a board to ascertain the rights of claimants under French or Spanish grants, as stipulated in the first two sections of the act. The boards were to be convened on December 1, 1805, and function until they completed their work on March 1, 1806. The secretary of the treasury was authorized to appoint one agent for each board who would investigate land claims and titles. Finally, the act stipulated that the powers vested in the surveyor of lands owned by the United States south of Tennessee would be extended over all public lands of the United States in the Orleans Territory to which Indian titles had or would be extinguished.[22]

Ferdinand Ibañez, engaged by John W. Gurley as land register and James Brown as agent to prepare an abstract of the lands granted in the District of Louisiana and the Western District of Orleans, compiled and turned over to Brown a voluminous abstract in late 1805. The impressive but incomplete abstract listed some 370 land claimants, mainly in the western districts, representing a land aggregate of about 350,000 acres. At the same time, Ibañez pointed out that many of the land records were held by Morales, Don Andre de Armisto, a former secretary, and Don Juan Carlos Ximines, a former notary for the Spanish government. Ibañez also reported to Brown that the French and Spanish authorities had issued around three thousand land warrants and orders of survey in the districts of Louisiana and Orleans. Ibañez's abstract, however, represented only a small portion of the total lands to which claims were laid. In his own report to Gallatin on

December 11, 1805, Brown pointed out that a number of land settlements had been made under written orders from Spanish commandants, the only evidence of which was held by the claimants themselves. Moreover, many of the land titles were held by Juan Ventura Morales and some of his associates, Brown emphasized, and no real effort had been made by the American authorities to secure either the original land titles held by the Spaniards or copies of them.[23]

Many claimants became understandably apprehensive, as they had in the Mississippi Territory, when the provisions of the congressional act to ascertain land titles were carried out. And as he had done in Mississippi, the governor and his associates offered reassurances. John W. Gurley was inclined to execute immediately the law to adjust and regulate land claims, but he toured his district for several weeks to explain and discuss the land law to prevent undue alarm by the people.[24] Governor Claiborne assured Louisianians repeatedly that they had nothing to fear from the land act; on the contrary, their legal claims would be confirmed "according to the equity of their situation and not to rigorous law." The governor frequently made appeals to the federal government as well in behalf of the claimants. He further recommended that people living along the Mississippi River be given certain preemption rights, an act reminiscent of his appeals several years earlier for settlers in the Southwest Territory. Many people refused to settle along the frontier, Claiborne pointed out, because of the fear that settlement would constitute a violation of the law. In 1809 a number of people requested permission to settle upon some of the federally owned lands lying west of the Mississippi. While Claiborne cautioned that Congress alone could grant preemption rights, his declaration that no effort had been made to remove previous squatters on government lands implied his tacit approval for those desiring to settle on the public domain. Claiborne was genuinely interested in facilitating means for settlers to acquire moderate land holdings through preemption, but he was at the same time on guard against the threat of vast land steals by selfish speculators. While pointing out to Gallatin that a fear of violating the law made many people reluctant to settle on unclaimed lands, he reminded the secretary of the treasury that speculators displayed no such hesitancy. In letters to Jefferson and Madison, Claiborne lashed out savagely at the speculators, charging that they profited from the distresses of others, especially the native inhabitants of Louisiana. According to the governor, some speculators even courted local support by denouncing the United States. The old inhabitants, he proclaimed, were thus nurturing "Vultures who would not willingly leave them the path which leads to the Grave of their ancestors."[25]

Despite Claiborne's efforts, land claims in the Western District of Orleans remained a source of friction as the territorial period drew to an end. A critic who identified himself as "Camillus" contended that land claims were still a source of constant irritation to the people. Several incidents connoted an organized system of governmental injustice. The people agreed to register their land claims because of governmental encouragement, "Camillus" declared, and some had traveled up to two hundred miles to do so. According to "Camillus," when Congress learned that the uncertainty surrounding Spanish land policies threatened to jeopardize legitimate land claims, it attempted to resolve the problem by establishing a land board composed of understanding men and then giving the board discretionary authority. Although the people were pleased with this action, "Camillus" stated, Madison accused the board of sometimes acting illegally. Later, according to the critic, Madison demanded that the board alter some of its opinions and refuse to recognize certain types of land titles. "Camillus" suspected that Governor Claiborne had already received orders to dismiss the land commissioners if they refused to comply with Madison's demands, adding: "No matter where, when, or by whom tyranny is exercised—chains are no less galling for being guilt." Despite this trenchant denunciation, "Camillus" had the temerity to suggest that his respect for Madison's position and age had caused him to temper his criticisms.[26] Land claimants in the Western District of Orleans presented a petition to Congress a few months after the "Camillus" missive appeared in print. Although they held legal land claims, many of them for a variety of reasons had declined to register their claims during the time limit set by Congress. The petitioners pleaded their case on the basis of ignorance, unfamiliarity with the "views of the Government," and unsound advice from people who opposed the federal government. Some refused to register their land claims because of fear that they would be invalidated, others because they had mislaid their records, and some because their records were retained by the Spanish authorities. Still others declined because of the distance they would have had to travel and because of the registration expenses. The memorialists pointed out that the Mississippians had been indulged repeatedly and they desired the same consideration. In fact, they suggested, language difficulties and limited knowledge of the new government entitled them to even greater consideration.[27] The federal government, in fact, did accord them the usual indulgence as it had in Mississippi.

While doing his best to protect valid land claims in the Orleans Territory, Governor Claiborne also sought to prevent the Spaniards from disposing of lands in West Florida since the federal government claimed West Florida as an integral part of Louisiana. The governor asked Calvo if Morales planned to persist in the sale of lands in West Florida and if he had authorization from Madrid. Calvo responded that no sales would be made at the time, and added that he hoped the United States would make a similar concession regarding the lands west of the Mississippi. In early August 1805 Claiborne told Madison he had informed Calvo that he would regard the Spanish sale of lands claimed by the United States as being "highly indecorous." At the same time, he told Calvo that he did not think the United States would then dispose of lands lying beyond the "acknowledged limits of the Ceded Territory." In essence, Claiborne's position was that both sides should desist, although he admitted to Madison that he was not quite sure what to do if Morales defied him and continued to sell vacant lands in West Florida from his land office in New Orleans. He was convinced that such action constituted a violation of the "Law of Nations," and to sell lands to Americans for purposes of encouraging emigration from the United States was an "offence at Common Law." The governor's uncertainty, however, vanished quickly. Less than a week later he wrote to Calvo and demanded that Morales' land office in New Orleans be closed; another letter followed almost immediately in which Claiborne demanded written assurances from Morales that he would not dispose of lands lying west of the Perdido River, "as well in relation to those lands said already to be sold as those which remain unsold." Calvo requested that Morales be permitted to continue working in New Orleans in his official capacity, and to continue collecting money on lands sold earlier. But Claiborne was adamant and refused to budge. Instead, he had passports prepared for Morales and told Calvo, whose relationship with Morales was strained, that he would assist him in the transfer of Morales to a Spanish post. Morales gave written assurances that he would not sell lands west of the

Perdido, and would not complete the titles to lands sold earlier under the Spanish government.[28] Even as he bowed to the determined Claiborne, Morales protested against the "violence and Contempt with which the regal authority has been treated thro' my person, my own authority emanating from that Source."[29]

Even though he won out over the resourceful Morales, Claiborne continued to grapple with the land problem in West Florida, particularly after the eastward extension of United States authority in 1810. West Florida inhabitants holding land titles and patents from the Spanish government became uneasy about their legality, but Governor Claiborne offered them the same assurances he had given earlier to the landholders west of the Mississippi River. The United States, he said, had been traditionally liberal and indulgent toward actual settlers. In early 1812 he told Gallatin that ignorance of registration requirements, difficulty in locating records, the expenses involved, and apprehension as to how their land claims would be received by the new American authority had kept many persons from registering their claims. Governor Claiborne also used his influence to have the land offices reopened for the convenience of the people, as he had earlier in the Mississippi and Orleans territories.[30] As the result of Governor Claiborne's sympathetic supervision of land claims and titles, popular fears were allayed and no serious problems developed. Moreover, while offering assurances to actual settlers whose land claims were generally modest, he sought by every means at his command to curb the activities of the land speculators who constantly jockeyed for advantages and privileges. In short, the primary beneficiaries of Claiborne's land policies were persons of modest means and circumstances. This was particularly noteworthy in view of his earlier association with such notorious land barons as William Blount.

While Governor Claiborne struggled with the delicate and complex problems of land claims, he also established and expanded postal routes and postoffices in the Orleans Territory. Postmaster General Gideon Granger wrote to Claiborne about a mail line between Washington and New Orleans in September 1803. A temporary express mail had already been set up between Washington and Natchez, and President Jefferson wanted the line extended from Natchez to New Orleans. The governor complied with the directive and he received subsequent instructions to continue the emergency mail service between Natchez and New Orleans. In early 1805 Jefferson informed Claiborne of plans to establish regular mail service between Washington and New Orleans by way of Fort Stoddert on the Mobile River. This route required carriers to travel through seventy miles of Spanish-controlled territory, much of which the United States also claimed. To prevent a possible incident in West Florida which might disrupt James Monroe's current efforts in Madrid to acquire the disputed territory, Jefferson suggested that Claiborne secure travel permission for the mail carriers from Casa Calvo. Claiborne outlined the proposed post road to Calvo and asked not only permission but for protection as well for the carriers, and Calvo agreed. However, Vicente Folch was governor of West Florida, and Madison directed Claiborne to remind Folch of the military road the Spaniards were constructing between Pensacola and Baton Rouge which, in view of American claims to the region, Madison felt was far more serious than the "harmless" mail route through West Florida.[31] Folch, like Calvo, agreed to the American postal route. By mid-1806 Jefferson reported to Claiborne that the postal route from Washington to New Orleans had been largely completed to Fort Stoddert and could be traversed in thirteen days. He hoped that the remainder of the line would be completed by the following year and that the entire trip from Washington to New Orleans would not take more than two weeks. By the time the route was completed, Jefferson was hopeful that all of the territory through which the postal route passed would be "honestly ours." When the United States and Spain almost came to blows over the Sabine boundary in 1806, Governor Folch threatened to discontinue the route through West Florida but no serious disruption occurred.[32]

The erection of postoffices in the Orleans Territory continued in conjunction with the establishment and expansion of postal routes. In the spring of 1804 Claiborne recommended the establishment of four postoffices between Fort Adams and New Orleans, but most remained unconstructed for several years. In September 1811 the only postoffice in the 190-mile stretch between New Orleans and Pinckneyville, Mississippi, was located at Donaldsonville, about sixty-five miles from New Orleans. Claiborne again recommended the establishment of a postoffice at Baton Rouge, and another at St. Francisville. The latter place was suggested because Claiborne considered the postoffice at St. John's Plains, located twenty-two miles from St. Francisville, inadequate. However, he learned a few days later that postoffices had been erected at both places.

Several months later he recommended a further expansion of the postal service through the creation of two postoffices between Blanchardville and New Orleans.³³ Although much work remained to be done as the territorial period drew to a close, a regular network of postal routes and postoffices at least had begun to take form.

Even though Governor Claiborne made persistent efforts to establish and insure an effective postal service, the postal system was only rudimentary and uncertain at best. Lawless elements sometimes attacked, robbed, and killed the riders. High water often caused delays. Violence along the Wilderness Road between Natchez and Nashville hampered the mail service, and complaints about mail irregularities were often registered. In mid-1807 Governor Vicente Folch, then in Baton Rouge, complained that he had not received letters which had been written to him from New Orleans and Natchez. In the spring of the following year Claiborne himself complained to Madison about a failure to receive any "intelligence" from Washington, and suggested that it might be better to use mail schooners between New Orleans and the Atlantic Coast.³⁴ Similar complaints continued to be registered through the remainder of the territorial period, but the delays and uncertainties persisted.

While Governor Claiborne continued efforts to improve and expand the territorial postal service, he also labored to establish a satisfactory banking system. From the time of the Louisiana transfer local inhabitants pressured Claiborne to establish a bank to alleviate problems created by constricted credit policies and a greatly restricted circulating monetary medium. The termination of Spanish silver imports from Vera Cruz and the Spanish suspension of the redemption of certificates then in circulation in the Orleans Territory caused a severe specie shortage.³⁵ On March 11, 1804, less than three months after the Louisiana transfer, Claiborne told Madison that the people were displaying an "uncommon Solicitude" for a bank, and that a petition calling for it had been signed by almost every respectable person in the vicinity of New Orleans. He was inclined to "indulge" them because the bank would serve a good purpose, he said, even though he had personal doubts about his authority to take such action and about the legality of the bank itself. Three days later, Claiborne, acting in his capacity as governor and intendant and without authorization from Washington, issued an ordinance for the establishment of a bank. Capital stock in the bank was not to exceed $600,000 and was to be divided into 6,000 shares which were to be sold at $100 each. Although Claiborne contended that the bank's utility justified his action, he candidly admitted that political expediency had also played a part in his decision. Always sensitive to criticism and usually inclined to appease his critics, the governor confessed to Madison after the issuance of the ordinance that the bank would allay discontent among the Louisianians.[36]

Claiborne's apprehensions about the bank were well founded, even though its establishment was easily justifiable commercially and politically. President Jefferson notified Claiborne almost a month after the ordinance had been issued that Congress had passed a law authorizing the Bank of the United States to establish a branch bank in New Orleans. Under the charter of the United States Bank, no other bank under the authority of the federal government was to be established. As a consequence, Claiborne's action was illegal because the bank to be established would not be a branch bank of the Bank of the United States. Confronted with this dilemma, the governor whined to Madison about the extreme embarrassments to which he had been subjected and the great difficulties facing him. Even though his action might be illegal and difficult to explain to the authorities in Washington, Claiborne claimed a purity of motives and added that "my Conscience will acquit me of intentional error."[37] The governor obviously was in an uncomfortable situation. The proposed bank lacked legal authorization, but the repeal of the ordinance calling for the creation of the bank might further arouse Louisianians. By May the governor sensed that his dilemma might be resolved. He told Madison that $140,000 had been subscribed almost immediately, but "the rage of Subscription cooled with almost incredible rapidity and the Eagerness with which the Citizens at first hurried into the Speculation, was quickly equalled by the neglect into which it sunk." Not a single share had been sold in weeks, he reported, and the required capital probably would not be secured. Thus, if the Bank of the United States decided to create a branch bank in New Orleans, it would not encounter any competition. Claiborne hoped that the failure to raise the necessary capital subscriptions would spare him the embarrassment of repealing the ordinance. Although elated by this prospect, Claiborne nonetheless again whined to Washington that the ordinance "was rather extorted from me by imperious circumstances." In mid-

June he wrote to Gallatin that the bank ordinance called for the necessary capital to be subscribed fully by the first Monday in January 1805, and he was certain that the subscription would not be met by that time.[38] In August he reported to Jefferson, who was upset because the projected bank contravened the congressional measure, that "The Bank continues to sleep." By the first of the year, however, Claiborne's elation quickly subsided as "Clark, Livingston, & Company" mounted an intensive drive to raise the required subscription. The governor spoke of Livingston's financial speculations, one of which netted a profit of $30,000, and predicted gloomily that the money probably would be raised after all. The defensive governor rationalized that the failure of the Bank of the United States to erect a branch bank in New Orleans had encouraged the subscriptions, although the Louisianians knew that he personally opposed it.[39]

The necessary money was finally raised and the territorial bank went into operation in 1805. The directors of the United States Bank did not seriously protest the action, although they decided later to establish a branch bank in the city. In fact, a second local bank was created during the territorial period and business interests pressed for yet another one. In early 1811 the governor informed the legislature that if a third territorial bank was needed to encourage commerce and agriculture, he would approve it.[40] Thus adequate banking facilities were provided to meet growing territorial needs at minimal embarrassment to the sensitive governor.

Just as the territorial populace looked to the governor to meet their financial and credit needs, they also turned to him for leadership and direction when disease threatened widespread illness and death. His earlier experience in combatting a threatened smallpox epidemic in the Mississippi Territory made it easier for him to cope with the ravages of disease in the Orleans Territory. However, the annual yellow-fever outbreaks, the cause of which remained a mystery, posed a much more serious threat than the health problems he had encountered in Mississippi. Native Louisianians, though still susceptible, had developed a certain immunity to yellow fever, but newcomers to the territory were particularly vulnerable and death tolls sometimes achieved staggering proportions. In early 1804 Claiborne told Jefferson that the disease had been exaggerated, but he quickly developed a profound respect for its devastating effects with the coming of the summer months, often referred to as the unhealthy season. In the early autumn he told Jefferson that a third of the Americans who had migrated to New Orleans in the preceding year had succumbed to it, "and nearly every Person from Europe who arrived in the City during the Summer Months."[41]

Regular troops sent to the Orleans Territory for military assignments suffered from a variety of illnesses, but yellow fever was one of the most prominent causes of illness and death. Less than a month after his arrival in New Orleans, Claiborne told Jefferson that the American forces had already suffered much sickness and added that it would probably increase during the spring and summer months. As he anticipated, disease decimated the military ranks during the "unhealthy season." In mid-September he told Jefferson that the troops removed from the city had shown some improvement, but eleven of the ninety troops remaining in New Orleans had died during the preceding three days. Two weeks earlier he had reported that seven to eight persons were dying daily in New Orleans from the yellow fever.[42] According to one source, ninety-four soldiers had died by October. Twenty-two were ill in New Orleans and another eight soldiers were ill at a nearby camp. Moreover, only three officers were physically fit for military duty at the time, and construction and repair work on the city's fortifications had been largely suspended because of sickness.[43] Although they suffered from a number of diseases, most of the casualties resulted from yellow fever.

The military buildup in 1808 and 1809, as the prospect of war with Great Britain mounted, resulted in augmented military forces in the Orleans Territory. About twenty-five per cent of the approximately two thousand regular troops sent to New Orleans by the spring of 1809 were incapacitated when General Wilkinson arrived to assume overall command in April. Learning of the mounting illness and fatalities among the troops, Secretary of War William Eustis ordered them moved northward to Fort Adams or to Natchez. Before he received the order, however, Wilkinson moved them to Terre aux Boeufs, a marshy site located twelve miles south of New Orleans, later reporting to Eustis that he had done so for reasons of health, morals, and discipline. Then, when he received Eustis' order, Wilkinson chose to hold fast, arguing that the troop removal would leave the city unprotected in the event of a British attack, the expense of moving them would be substantial, and it would endanger the health of the men unnecessarily because of the unhealthy season and the time it would take to transport them northward. The onset of rains in mid-summer caused sickness and mortality rates to rise sharply among the men at Terre aux Boeufs, and the secretary of war sharply ordered Wilkinson to obey his directive. The general finally began the evacuation of Terre aux Boeufs in September; those who were indisposed were transported by boats provided by the navy and the remainder slowly moved northward along the banks of the river in a veritable death march. More than two-thirds of the 935 men who began the ill-fated trip became ill, and 240 had died by the time the march was completed in late October. Wilkinson had 1,953 regular troops under his command during the summer of 1809. Of this number, 764 died and 166 deserted, representing an overall loss of about fifty per cent. Although the deaths were attributed to a number of causes, the "raging fever" apparently was the principal cause. Alarmed over the high mortality rate, officials in Washington replaced Wilkinson with General Wade Hampton and ordered the establishment of a congressional committee of inquiry. A general court martial in 1811 considered charges of neglect of duty against Wilkinson as a result of his decision to station the regular troops at Terre aux Boeufs and the staggering casualties sustained by his men.[44] The court martial board, however, failed to sustain the charge against the controversial general.

In addition to wreaking havoc among the regular troops dispatched to the territory, the "prevailing fever" also frequently impaired governmental operations. Under the terms of the congressional measure enacted in March 1804, the provisional period was to end with the establishment of the new territorial government on October 1, 1804. The legislative council was not convened and organized until early December, however, because Governor Claiborne was unable to locate enough lawmakers to constitute a quorum. A number of factors caused the delay, but the indisposition of some of the legislators or members of their families was a major one. Similar problems persisted throughout the territorial period and compounded Governor Claiborne's woes as chief executive. In mid-September 1804 Claiborne told Jefferson that his three clerks were confined to their beds, and he reported the death of Joseph Briggs, his private secretary, five days afterward. Indeed, the death toll from yellow fever was particularly high in 1811 and resulted in a brief delay of the statehood convention. At the same time, James Mather, mayor of New Orleans, suggested that the governor request financial assistance from Congress for the Charity Hospital which extended medical care and services to numerous persons stricken with yellow fever, including a number of persons discharged from the armed forces.[45]

Governor Claiborne and members of his family fell prey to the disease. Claiborne had an attack during his first summer in New Orleans, but was able to write President Jefferson in late August that he was "represented as the only American who has yet recovered." He confessed to Jefferson several months afterward that his "constitution" had not become acclimated and feared that he might have to relinquish the governorship. Other attacks followed in the ensuing years and he reported to James Monroe in late 1811 that he was recovering slowly from the yellow fever because of "a debility of the body, which generally follows the fevers of this climate."[46]

Although Governor Claiborne survived the yellow fever, his health remained impaired. Other members of his family were not so fortunate. While he was a young congressman, Claiborne had ridden to Tennessee between sessions to marry Elizabeth ("Eliza") W. Lewis, daughter of William Terrell Lewis, a prominent Nashville leader. When he went to Natchez in late 1801 as governor of the Mississippi Territory, he was accompanied on the arduous trip by his wife and infant daughter, Cornelia Tennessee. President Jefferson dispatched him to New Orleans two years afterward to receive Louisiana. The new responsibility had forced him to forego a trip he had planned to make to Tennessee. Mrs. Claiborne and her daughter, however, went to Nashville and visited with relatives while her husband was preoccupied in New Orleans. Despite the uncertainty of his selection as governor of the newly acquired territory, Claiborne nonetheless decided to send for his family after a few months. His wife and daughter joined him in early June. A short time afterward the entire family was stricken with yellow fever. Weakened and debilitated by the fever, Claiborne informed Jefferson on September 13 that his wife was suffering from an "Affection of the Liver, and in her enfeebled State, no medicine can prudently be administered, which would reach this disorder." Mrs. Claiborne rallied momentarily but she and her three-year-old daughter died on September 27. Although he had earlier intimated to Jefferson that he was considering retirement from public life—a hint intended in part to spur his appointment as governor since the president had spent several months canvassing the field of possible candidates for the post—he told Madison that he would continue to serve in a public capacity since he had no one to care for after the death of his family.[47] In his inaugural address on October 2, he repeated essentially what he had written to Madison, saying: "All the felicity which a recent domestic calamity has left for me to seek or enjoy, is in contributing to the happiness of those over whom I am called to preside."[48]

The yellow fever had snuffed out the lives of his wife and daughter but further personal tragedy lay in store for the governor. Two years later he married Clarissa Duralde of Attakapas, daughter of Martin Milony Duralde and Marie Josephe Perrault Duralde. The governor happily reported his marriage to President Jefferson, saying that Clarissa was "born and educated in the Prairies of Opelousas." His wife felt a close attachment, he continued, to the United States and the "American Character." The compatible marriage was further cemented by the birth of a son in the summer of 1807. But the yellow fever was particularly virulent during the summer and fall of 1809 and an unusually large number of deaths resulted. Clarissa was stricken and died after a brief illness on November 29, a little over three years after Elizabeth's death. On December 17 the saddened governor wrote to President Madison:

> On the 29th of last month, it pleased Almighty God to take from me my beloved wife, than which a greater calamity, could not have befallen men,—She was in the Bloom of life, and uniting to a graceful person, the sweetest disposition and the most enlightened understanding, her Smiles relieved anxiety & Sweetened every care.—I am not conscious Sir, of unbecoming weakness; but this misfortune has nearly undone me.—I have however one great source of consolation; it consists in a sweet little son about 18 months old whom providence in its mercy, has thought proper to spare me.—I could wish to live to rear him up in the paths of virtue & patriotism; & my prayer to heaven, will be granted if at some future day, his virtues, talents & attachment to civil & Religious freedom should recommend him to the patronage of his Country.[49]

About a month afterward Claiborne informed Jefferson of his personal bereavement. Jefferson responded in early May, strove to console him, and asserted that the only sources of relief were time, silence, and occupation. "Of occupation, you have enough and of the highest order; that of continuing to make a worthy people happy by a just and parental government, and of protecting them from the wolves prowling around to devour them."[50]

When he addressed the opening session of the legislature on January 12, 1810, Governor Claiborne alluded to the heavy mortality rates of the preceding year and recommended the enactment of some health measures. He favored enactment of quarantine regulations for incoming shipping and greater emphasis upon cleanliness, and suggested that careful study be given to a proposal made by President Jefferson in 1804.[51] Jefferson had proposed a plan that year to combat yellow fever, saying that "genuine" yellow fever was uncommon to the country and "even to the outskirts or open parts of a close-built city." Jefferson consequently proposed that each inhabited square of a city be surrounded by open squares, with each inhabited square constituting, in essence, an independent town. The president advocated essentially open air and proper drainage to combat yellow fever.[52] Some tentative steps in that direction were taken at the time and later. One of the city newspapers encouraged a campaign to clear away the animal and vegetable filth as a means of combatting the "prevailing fever."[53] Municipal leaders later recommended that the forts and batteries surrounding New Orleans be destroyed because the ditches were filled with water, "the contagious exhalations of which are the very cause of epidemical diseases." When the citizens of New Orleans petitioned Congress at the end of 1808 to keep the batture from falling into the hands of Edward Livingston, they spoke of disease generating on the water side of the batture and suggested that an open space be left between the buildings and the water. In the absence of free air circulation, the petitioners pointed out, New Orleans would "probably be often visited by the dreadful scourge of The Yellow fever." Although greater interest was generated momentarily when the governor's second wife died in late 1809, no concentrated effort was made to put the Jeffersonian plan into operation. Thus the yearly arrival of the "unhealthy season" continued for many years to engender feelings of apprehension and dread among native inhabitants and newcomers alike.

Governor Claiborne's close attention to such important but mundane problems as health and sanitation, banking and credit, conflicting land titles and claims, and postoffices and postal roads reflected a tenacious devotion to the demands of public service. In fact, the patient, deliberative manner in which Claiborne approached these problems indicated two things. First, President Jefferson had selected a leader to govern the Orleans Territory whose earlier experiences in frontier Tennessee and the Mississippi Territory had given him some insight into the problems and needs of his new and more heterogeneous constituency. Second, he was able to apply his earlier experiences to good advantage in the Orleans Territory. But even as the governor utilized his earlier experiences to cope with these problems, more exhilarating and portentous developments unfolded to challenge his resources and resourcefulness. The dons, frustrated by a crumbling empire and the duplicity of the imperious Corsican, rattled their sabers along the Sabine. Moreover, the Weehawken duellist, whose political fortunes collapsed as his mortally wounded antagonist slumped to the ground, retreated westward and dark rumors of a Burr conspiracy circulated wildly in the Crescent City. Even as he girded to meet these challenges, the governor must have reflected pardonably upon his earlier experiences in the Mississippi Territory and viewed them as the good old days.

IX

THE SABINE FRONTIER AND THE BURR CONSPIRACY

Governor Claiborne's aggressive policies toward the Spanish colonial authority in Louisiana, West Florida, and Texas influenced Spanish-American relations to a far greater extent than has been acknowledged heretofore because attention has usually been riveted on Washington and Madrid rather than remote New Orleans. Moreover, his recommendations influenced administration leaders and their policies toward Spain. James Monroe, who negotiated the acquisition of Louisiana in Paris and was later dispatched to Madrid to negotiate a settlement of the disputed Louisiana boundary with Spain, had access to Claiborne's reports.

Governor Claiborne's demeanor toward the Spanish colonial leaders was frequently assertive and peremptory, quite unlike his conciliatory and permissive policies toward elements within the Orleans Territory. This was, however, in character for the governor and reflected to a considerable extent his concept of official priorities. That is, he viewed matters of external politics and diplomacy as a special responsibility in which he was expected to act aggressively and decisively by comparison with internal affairs which permitted more informality and tolerance. The firmness he consequently displayed toward Calvo, Morales, and Folch contrasted sharply with his hesitation when confronted by the blandishments of Generals Wilkinson and Jackson. From the governor's perspective, this did not constitute a philosophical inconsistency. Thus he had been able to stifle his personal disappointment when General Wilkinson arrived late, as usual, at Fort Adams and then proceeded to make preparations for the transfer of Louisiana to the United States while ignoring his fellow commissioner. But at the same time Claiborne vowed to the Jefferson administration that he fully intended to assert himself diplomatically with the French and Spanish officials when he and Wilkinson arrived in New Orleans.

In the absence of explicit instructions from Washington, the confident governor often acted forcefully and independently. He had reacted sharply to the temporary Spanish denial of the American right to deposit at New Orleans in late 1802 and early 1803, and had boldly suggested to President Jefferson that he was prepared to march into New Orleans at the head of an American force. He was likewise forceful in asserting expanded American claims to both the eastern and western boundaries of the Orleans Territory. Indeed, Governor Claiborne may well have been ahead of administration leaders in sensing the confusion and near paralysis which gripped Spanish foreign policies at the time, and he was eager to take advantage of the situation. The American acquisition of Louisiana left Spanish colonial policy essentially unchanged. Failing to comprehend the "rearranged international boundaries in North America," the Spanish still hoped to push back the Americans from the Gulf of Mexico and contain them east of the Mississippi River. Instead of a realistic retrenchment commensurate with Madrid's limited capabilities to defend its territorial holdings and concomitant acceptance of the loss of the Louisiana territory, Spanish colonial officials sought petulantly but feebly to sow discontent among the Louisianians and to undermine the new territorial administration with a view to rolling back the American gains. The result was a continuing erosion of the Spanish authority and further territorial losses, and Governor Claiborne remained alert and eager to press the developing American advantage.[1]

Although the prospect of war between the United States and Spain reached a new high in 1806, tensions had long characterized relations between the Americans and Spanish colonial authorities in the lower Mississippi. Morales' denial of port facilities at New Orleans to the Americans in the autumn of 1802 had accentuated the problem. Although France had transferred the Louisiana territory to the United States in late 1803, the Spanish authorities gave way only grudgingly. Under treaty provisions, the Spanish

The Sabine Frontier

Aaron Burr

leaders in Louisiana had three months to evacuate their troops, but Claiborne and Wilkinson were impatient with them almost from the moment of their arrival in New Orleans. A week after the transfer they told Madison that they would retain the Mississippi militia units in New Orleans until the Spaniards had completed their evacuation. They complained that the Spanish soldiers were continuing to occupy the barracks while their own men were being subjected to unnecessary inconveniences.[2] Despite the departure of a small Spanish unit in early March and Spanish assurances that the evacuation would be completed by March 20, almost a month elapsed before the three hundred remaining troops left for Pensacola. Several Spanish officers who remained in the city seriously considered resigning from the Spanish service in order to establish residence in Louisiana. Almost another year elapsed before Colonel Don Carlos Dehault Delassus of Upper Louisiana passed through New Orleans with some thirty men on their way to Pensacola.[3]

The Spanish withdrawal from Louisiana had been largely completed within a year after the transfer, but the Marquis de Casa Calvo and Juan Ventura Morales and their retinue of sixty men managed to delay their departure for over two years. Although exasperated with both men, Claiborne particularly distrusted Morales, who defiantly retained a land office in New Orleans and continued for a time to sell land in West Florida despite American claims to it. The irritated Claiborne pointedly told Madison that he would resort to any legitimate means to force the ex-intendant's removal without violating "any principle which ought to be respected on such an occasion." Although Washington severed diplomatic relations with Madrid in the spring of 1805, Madison did not explicitly order the expulsion of the Spaniards from the Orleans Territory until mid-November. By insisting that he was awaiting the arrival of three vessels which were coming for him, the defiant Morales withstood intensified pressures to leave. He complained that the American order to leave constituted an infringement upon the "Laws of Hospitality" and "wounded" Madrid's right to permit its agents to remain long enough to complete their business. When Claiborne told him bluntly in early 1806 that the Jefferson administration wanted him out of the territory, he retorted that the reminder was unnecessary. Moreover, he wanted assurances that the vessels coming for him would be permitted to proceed as far as Bayou St.

John "without any apprehension of being incommoded by the Artillery of the Fort, or of being proceeded against by any other means, by which they may run the risque of being detained or captured." He ended by requesting passports for himself, his family, and entourage. Claiborne immediately provided them and authorized the vessels to proceed to Bayou St. John. At this point thirty-one merchants and businessmen in New Orleans declared that they were creditors of Spain and feared they would lose their money if Morales departed.[4] Nonetheless, Claiborne refused to defer his redoubtable adversary's departure any longer. Morales and his entourage departed almost immediately afterward for Pensacola.

The Marquis de Casa Calvo, posing as a "boundary commissioner," displayed a comparable resourcefulness. On November 18, 1805, Madison informed Claiborne that the United States had not accredited Calvo and that neither Washington nor Madrid had proposed the creation of a boundary commission. He directed Claiborne to insist that both Calvo and Morales leave immediately and to indicate to Calvo that as long as the two countries differed over the territorial boundaries a commission was not feasible. At the time Calvo had travelled westward to the Trinity River where he apparently was considering the establishment of a settlement for discontented Louisianians who did not wish to remain under American authority. Determined to prevent Calvo's return to New Orleans because he might influence "characters well suited for mischevious and wicked enterprises," Claiborne assigned Captain George T. Ross to deliver a dispatch to Calvo directing him and others holding Spanish commissions to leave because of the failure of Monroe's mission to Spain and the provocative conduct of Spanish troops to the west. Claiborne believed that the present situation necessitated their speedy exodus. Ross traced the Calvo party to Attakapas and on to Natchitoches, only to learn that it had left the settlement five days earlier. Ross reported to Claiborne that Calvo was spreading the rumor that Louisiana would remain under American authority only temporarily, encouraging the settlers not to register their land titles or run land surveys, and attempting to incite the Indians. Nevertheless, Ross continued his search and delivered the message to the elusive Calvo. Although the Calvo party returned to New Orleans, the relieved governor reported to Madison that Calvo had departed for Pensacola on February 15, 1806,[5] about two weeks behind Morales.

Relations between Spain and the United States continued to deteriorate following Claiborne's expulsion of the troublesome Spanish colonial leaders. The uncertainty of Louisiana's southwestern boundary brought the two countries to the verge of war. Since the transfer of Louisiana to the United States, Spanish and American forces had eyed each other warily across the disputed territory. A week after the transfer, Pierre Clement Laussat told Claiborne and Wilkinson that France had claimed lands extending westward to the Rio Grande and northward to the thirtieth parallel but no serious effort had been made to determine the boundary beyond that point. Laussat's suggestion that the Rio Grande constituted the western boundary had upset Calvo, and Governor Vicente Folch of West Florida accused the French of deliberately encouraging Spanish-American hostility so that the French could capitalize upon the differences at a future date.[6]

As the boundary differences assumed more serious proportions, Governor Claiborne became apprehensive over an ominous Spanish military buildup in Baton Rouge, Mobile, Pensacola, and East Texas. When reports of anticipated Spanish reinforcements continued to circulate, Claiborne confronted Calvo and told him that the president did not want either side to take actions which might jeopardize the negotiations then in progress between the two countries. Calvo responded that the Spanish posts had not been strengthened except insofar as Spanish forces were relocated after their evacuation of Louisiana. He added, nonetheless, that Spain was dispatching a fleet and 4,000 troops to Mexico to protect Spanish territorial possessions against possible American threats implied in congressional debates and in statements made by the American minister in Madrid. Although Claiborne hoped that peace could be maintained, he felt that Spain would yield to America's "just claims," especially if several thousand American troops stood in readiness along the western border. If war came, he felt that the western people would rally together in the face of danger. At the time, however, there were not enough regular troops in the territory to reassure the inhabitants or to prevent "mischevious machinations" by those inclined to treachery. If war appeared inevitable, he urged Madison in early 1806 to organize a cavalry unit since the lands west of the Mississippi were largely prairie and an army would need cavalry support.[7]

The Spanish-American waltz of the Sabine had actually begun long before Governor Claiborne recommended a major American military buildup on the western frontier. Before the transfer, in fact, John Sibley had warned that the Spaniards were preparing to occupy Adais, located forty miles east of the Sabine. If permitted to do so, the Americans would be confronted by a fait accompli and it would be more difficult to dislodge them later. Captain Turner reported Spanish movements close to Natchitoches although he did not think they were prepared to station a strong force east of the "river Grand at present" because of logistic requirements. He pointed out that Natchitoches was the only settlement in the general area extending to the Rio Grande where inhabitants could secure provisions.[8]

While the Americans speculated about Spanish intentions and continued to press for the acquisition of West Florida, the Spaniards seized the initiative in the west. They claimed the lands extending to Arroyo Hondo, a tributary of the Red River located east of the Sabine. Colonel Antonio Cordero was appointed governor of Texas in October 1805, serving under Don Nemesio Salcedo as captain general of the Interior Provinces of Mexico. Shortly afterward several hundred Spanish troops swept across the Sabine and occupied Bayou Pierre, located about fifty miles west of Natchitoches, and Adais, and Spanish troops extended their patrols to Arroyo Hondo. Under orders from Major Moses Porter, commandant at Fort Claiborne, located on the Red River near Natchitoches, Captain Turner and about sixty men forced the Spaniards from Adais. Both sides subsequently withdrew from the disputed area. Governor Cordero appointed Lieutenant Colonel Don Simon de Herrera commandant of the Louisiana frontier and assigned him and six hundred militiamen to the Spanish post of Nacogdoches. Spanish troops resumed patrols as far east as Arroyo Hondo in the early spring of 1806. Herrera and about four hundred troops then occupied Bayou Pierre in early August.[9]

The increased aggressiveness of the dons had followed a substantial augmentation of forces on the Louisiana frontier. By the time the boundary crisis peaked in September, the Spaniards had committed almost 1,300 troops to the western frontier, over half of whom were stationed at Nacogdoches.[10]

American officials generally attributed Spanish aggressiveness on the western frontier in 1805 and 1806 to Spanish reluctance to accept the "rearranged international boundaries" resulting from the Louisiana transfer, but other factors contributed to Spanish apprehensions. Rumors persisted of an expedition being raised in

Kentucky to conquer Mexico. The so-called Mexican Association, composed of an estimated three hundred members, had been organized in New Orleans to work for the removal of the Spanish authority from Mexico. Increased American activity in the frontier area, including the dispatch of an American expedition up the Red River, also worried the Spanish. When Jefferson first mentioned the projected expedition to Claiborne in the spring of 1805 he explained that it was to gain geographic and scientific data. The president instructed Claiborne to invite Calvo to send along one or two representatives, with the United States assuming their expenses. If Calvo refused, he should be made aware that any possible violence committed against the party would not be taken lightly by the American government, but the president cautioned Claiborne not to convey this sentiment in such way that it could be interpreted as a threat. In March 1806, about the time the Spaniards resumed their patrols to the Arroyo Hondo, Claiborne reported to Jefferson that Colonel Constant Freeman had virtually completed preparations and he and his party were about ready to leave New Orleans. The governor feared the Freeman party might encounter Spanish resistance.[11] In late July Freeman reported to Claiborne that a Spanish force of 140 to 150 men under Don Francisco Viana had intercepted the expedition and forced it to turn back to Natchitoches on July 29. Freeman also reported that a Spanish force, headed by Viana, had ridden into a Caddo Nation village, torn down an American flag, and threatened to treat the Freeman expedition as it had the American flag.[12] In late August Claiborne complained to Herrera, who was then at disputed Bayou Pierre, about the interception of the expedition and the outrage committed against the American flag. Further, he asked why the Spaniards had captured three Americans, identified as Brewster, Irvin, and Shaw. Herrera's reply, issued two days later, insisted that the Caddo and Red River incidents occurred in Spanish territory, and that the three Americans were caught spying on Spanish positions. Claiborne sent Herrera a sharp rejoinder, rejecting his explanations and pointing out that the incidents had occurred in a region which the French previously had controlled. In demanding the release of the three men, he explained their observation of Spanish forces in terms of idle curiosity and pointed out that Spaniards visited Natchitoches daily and thus were free to observe American troop positions and movements. Claiborne terminated his dispatch to Herrera with a warning that he would issue no further communications on the subject. Instead, he would report to the president, "who will Know what measures to direct, when wrongs are offered to the American nation."[13]

While Claiborne traded missives with Herrera and the Spaniards became more assertive, the Americans began augmenting their own forces. In a special message to Congress on March 19, 1806, President Jefferson, who had informed Congress of Spanish-American tensions in his annual address of the preceding December, reported on the earlier Spanish occupation of Adais and invited Congress to institute security measures.[14] The message was delivered only one day after Spanish forces had again temporarily occupied Adais. Upon recommendations from Governor Claiborne, who estimated that 1,200 troops were needed because of the Spanish difficulties, the American government acted to increase American military capabilities in the Orleans Territory. Secretary of War Dearborn ordered the repair of fortifications in New Orleans, and made additional gunboats available for use on the Mississippi River and the nearby lakes. He dispatched more troops to the Orleans Territory and augmented the forces at both Fort Adams and Natchitoches. Dearborn also instructed Claiborne and Governor Robert Williams of the Mississippi Territory to place their militia forces on the strongest footing possible.[15] In early May 1806 Dearborn placed General James Wilkinson, then serving in a civil capacity as governor of Upper Louisiana, in command of the American forces in the region. Dearborn told him that neither side was to occupy the disputed territory. Nonetheless, a "quiet possession" of the lands east of the Sabine, "with the trifling exception of the small place called Bayou Pierre," would be justifiable and logical since the area was regarded as American territory. Although Wilkinson was to be in command if military action became necessary, Dearborn instructed him to consult with Governor Claiborne and possibly Governor Williams.[16]

Even though officials had ordered General Wilkinson to proceed from St. Louis to his new assignement as quickly as possible, he took his time for a number of reasons. He was deeply involved in the Burr conspiracy but its outcome was highly uncertain and he awaited further developments. Moreover, he suspected that the Jefferson administration was attempting to use the assignment as a means of removing him as governor of Upper Louisiana but he wanted to remain in the post at the time. Furthermore, the prospect of waging war against his former financial benefactor was less than appealing to the general, and he did not relish the idea of having the forthright Claiborne as an associate. Finally, his wife was ill at the time, and the more southern climate was less comfortable during the summer months.[17] As a consequence, he tarried as long as possible and did not put in an appearance on the tense frontier scene until the latter part of September. The controversial general obviously moved at his own pace and employed his own independent and oblique style of action which, even more incredibly, appeared as a matter of course to have official Washington's tacit endorsement. No rebukes or even sharp slaps of the wrists were forthcoming, at least, from Dearborn and other national leaders. In large measure he continued to be strictly his own man, acting purely in accordance with his own personal interests and inclinations.

Between the issuance of Wilkinson's orders on May 6 and his belated appearance at Natchitoches on September 22, the primary responsibility of dealing with the assertive dons was left to Governor Claiborne and Colonel Thomas H. Cushing. The latter had been ordered to Natchitoches with three infantry companies, two field pieces, and supplies as the boundary controversy came to assume more serious proportions. Both Claiborne and Cushing vociferously protested the Spanish incursions, but Herrera replied that the territory in dispute was a dependency of Texas and had been held by Spain from "time immemorial." Herrera acknowledged that he had crossed the Sabine on orders from Captain General Cordero, and insisted that the responsibility would fall on the United States if war erupted or negotiations bogged down between Spain and the United States.[18]

Unlike the leisurely general, Governor Claiborne moved with dispatch and vigor to cope with the developing crisis. On April 17, 1806, he met with Acting Governor Cowles Mead of the Mississippi Territory in Natchez and they worked out a joint plan. The decisions made in Natchez clearly bore the Claiborne imprint. If Dearborn had not rescinded earlier orders to Colonel Cushing, then in command at Natchitoches, regarding the Spanish thrusts into the disputed territory, they agreed that it would be advisable to dislodge the Spaniards. Second, if Colonel Cushing's regular force at Natchitoches was inadequate to the task before it, the Orleans militia should be called into service. Third, if the Orleans militia were needed at Natchitoches, Governor Claiborne should proceed there at once. Fourth, the Mississippi militia should be held ready and used to defend New Orleans if the Spaniards threatened the city. Fifth, if additional troops were needed in Natchitoches, Mead would send one hundred mounted infantrymen. Finally, the two governors expressed regret that Wilkinson was absent, but promised to place at his disposal any portion of their militia that he required.[19] When Herrera again swept across the Sabine and on to Bayou Pierre at the head of several hundred Spanish troops in July, Claiborne and Mead met near Natchez on August 17 to reaffirm their earlier agreement.[20]

Governor Claiborne continued to work feverishly to get the militia ready during the emergency but, in view of his continuing problems with the organization of the militia, his efforts met with mixed reactions. According to one report, Claiborne and his militia officers called out and addressed two militia regiments and a part of a third one. They asked for volunteers during the crisis, and instructed those who declined to step back one pace. When they stood fast, the governor accepted their services and left. Following the appearance of an account in a newspaper extra, a swarm of men reportedly confronted Claiborne and insisted that they had misunderstood and had not intended to volunteer at all.[21] Indeed, Claiborne was never quite certain as to how much support he would be able to command from the people of New Orleans. In a letter to Dearborn from Natchitoches on August 28, four days after his arrival at the settlement, he stated that the Americans in the exposed region were willing to serve, but that many of the ancient inhabitants were attached to Spain and probably would remain neutral in the event of conflict. In the same letter, he asked that four additional militia companies of Mississippi cavalry be called into service on the frontier. Such counties as Attakapas, Opelousas, and Rapides could be "deprecated upon with impunity, by an active Enemy." The parishes were located in prairie country and Spanish forces, composed mainly of cavalrymen, he pointed out, could make "predatory incursions" without serious risk. He was in Natchitoches at the time, he said, to animate the militia and call them to duty if necessary. The American troops were in excellent shape and would attack if the Spaniards moved into American territory. Claiborne reported that the Spaniards had just made a "retrograde movement," having pulled back to Bayou Pierre from east of Bayou Funda, located about seventeen miles from Natchitoches. At the time, he estimated that the Spanish force numbered about one thousand men.[22]

Colonel Cushing experienced intense pressures as the crisis approached a climax. The secretary of war had ordered him to force the Spaniards back across the Sabine, but Wilkinson, who had yet to put in an appearance, had instructed him to avoid hostilities. He had explained to Herrera that the American troop reinforcement had been purely defensive and proposed a mutual removal from the disputed area. Herrera had replied defiantly that he was defending Spanish territory and warned against American infringements, and shortly afterward Governor Cordero set out from San Antonio with one hundred troops to reinforce Herrera.[23] Claiborne, who had rushed to Natchitoches from Natchez upon learning of Herrera's aggressive action, pressed Cushing to move against the Spaniards. Aggressive American action was necessary, he felt, not only because of the Spanish thrust into the disputed territory but because the loyalty and respect of the Louisianians for the American authority were contingent upon forceful action. Moreover, inaction by the American forces would invite further contempt by the dons, and it would make the governor's conduct appear ridiculous in view of his feverish preparations for the imminent showdown. Disappointed and personally embarrassed by Colonel Cushing's refusal to act forcefully, Governor Claiborne sullenly slipped out of the dusty American settlement. Recognizing the continuing possibility of war, he paused long enough on his return route to check on militia strengths and capabilities in the western counties of Attakapas, Opelousas, and Rapides.

In early September the nonchalant Wilkinson belatedly entered the picture. On September 8 he told Dearborn that Claiborne had "arranged" the militia in the western counties. He proposed, however, to hold the militiamen and regular troops in abeyance while draining the "cup of conciliation to maintain the peace of the country ... in opposition to the ardor which I think I discern in the executive officers of these territories." This was an obvious allusion to Claiborne and Mead whose aggressiveness toward the Spaniards worried the general. Wilkinson also reported the slight "retrograde" movement of the Spanish forces, suggesting that it was possibly due to the ill health of the Spanish troops, lack of forage, or lack of provisions. The bombastic general concluded his communication to Dearborn by proclaiming imperiously that he would plant the American flag on the left bank of the "Grand river" if the Spaniards dared to strike a blow.[24]

General Wilkinson met Governor Claiborne at Rapides on September 19 while on his way to Natchitoches and as Claiborne was returning to New Orleans. They conferred briefly and Wilkinson assured the governor that he would insist upon the Sabine River as the boundary line. He inquired about the number of militiamen that were available, and Claiborne responded that he probably would be able to place in excess of four hundred at his disposal. Wilkinson continued on his way following the conference and arrived in Natchitoches three days later.[25]

Having hitherto shown no inclination to hurry, General Wilkinson lost no time in communicating with the Spanish military leaders after his arrival in Natchitoches. He proposed to Governor Antonio Cordero that both sides refrain from acting precipitately while their respective governments continued their negotiations, and expressed a sense of repugnance at Herrera's rejection of the "reasonable and rightful demands" made earlier by Claiborne and Cushing. Cordero acknowledged the dispatch five days later and informed Wilkinson that it had been forwarded to Captain General Nemesio Salcedo. The Spaniards, nevertheless, withdrew to the west bank of the Sabine at about this time. Then on October 11 Cordero wrote to Wilkinson from Nacogdoches and observed that Wilkinson had moved his forces toward the Sabine. Cordero pointed out that he had not received a reply from Salcedo, but added that he had no choice as a soldier but to repulse any hostile move by the American forces. A few days later Wilkinson injected a new element into the tense situation. On October 21 he wrote Jefferson hinting ominously of a "daring enterprise"—a reference to what came to be known later as the Burr conspiracy—and declared that he would compromise with Salcedo and pull back to New Orleans and put the city in a state of readiness if the information he had was true. Eight days later, as American troops continued to inch westward toward the Sabine, Wilkinson proposed to Cordero that both sides yield and pull their forces back to Natchitoches and Nacogdoches. He was prepared to do this, he proclaimed expansively, to "perpetuate the tranquillity of these inhospitable wilds, where waving the point of honor, the subject of contest is scarcely worth the blood of one brave man." The next day Wilkinson told Cordero that he had heard from Salcedo but that the captain general had ignored his proposal and confined himself to a discussion of civil matters. It is conceivable that Salcedo was aware of the strained relationship between Wilkinson and Claiborne and was attempting to exploit it. Since Salcedo had ignored him, Wilkinson wished to know what Cordero thought of his proposal of a mutual withdrawal. Cordero responded on November 1 that he wished to avoid conflict but he disclaimed authority to act independently. Now exceedingly eager to effect a rapprochement, Wilkinson expressed complete satisfaction with Cordero's reply, stressing that his earlier suspicion of Spanish hostility toward the United States had proven to be unfounded. Disregarding his earlier proposal of a simultaneous withdrawal, the unctuous general broke camp and withdrew his forces to Natchitoches as a signal of his desire for conciliation. But at the last moment, Herrera, who had been largely ignored, notified Wilkinson that he had learned of his proposal and was breaking camp himself and pulling back to Nacogdoches.[26] When Salcedo learned of Herrera's apparently independent action, a surprising step for a lesser Spanish officer to take on his own authority, he directed Cordero to abide by Herrera's decision.[27]

Although Wilkinson stole the spotlight from Claiborne after his arrival in Natchitoches and claimed credit for converting the "haughtiness of the Dons into a temper most conciliatory,"[28] the governor played a respectable role. He concluded a working agreement with the Mississippi governor to cope with the Spanish threat, and carefully coordinated his plans with Mead to preclude the possibility of a misunderstanding. He also rushed to Natchitoches to advise and counsel Colonel Cushing long before Wilkinson put in his tardy but dramatic appearance. Moreover, he displayed a firm attitude in the face of Spanish blandishments and was intent on forcing the Spaniards to evacuate the disputed areas east of the Sabine River. If the Spaniards agreed to the same terms with Wilkinson which Claiborne had proposed several weeks earlier, the governor's conduct, at least, was never questioned and made the subject of suspicion, as Wilkinson's was. Finally, Claiborne was successful in raising troops to cope with the threat, even though his critics accused him of being unable to rally the militia. This was reflected in his estimate on September 19 that he could provide Wilkinson with about four hundred militiamen. But three days later he told him that he could allow him five hundred men without weakening other areas.[29]

The Burr conspiracy explained General Wilkinson's haste in arranging the Sabine compromise and the Spanish alacrity to accept the agreement. The ambiguous and uncertain plot appeared to threaten both the American western states and territories and Mexico. In early November officials in Washington instructed Wilkinson to compromise with the Spaniards and to pull back the American forces to meet the Burr threat, but acting on his own initiative Wilkinson had already begun to withdraw. "General" William Eaton of Tripolitan lustre had already divulged the plot to President Jefferson. According to Eaton, Burr had taken him into his confidence and told him of his plan to separate the western states and territories, to take Mexico, and to establish a monarchy over which he, Burr, was to preside. Burr alluded to a trip he had made into the west in 1805 to procure maps and to consult with influential persons willing to participate in the plan. He believed that the federal government was too weak to offer much opposition, and he was prepared to capitalize fully on political differences between Federalists and Republicans. Further, Eaton predicted that many people would join Burr because of the dullness of civil life and the prospect of double pay and double rations, in addition to the allurement of Mexican silver mines. Jefferson initially attached little credence to Eaton's story, but later reports of a secret expedition and Burr's order with a western firm for several boats tended to authenticate Eaton's report.[30]

Burr's coded message to Wilkinson, dated July 29, 1806, and delivered to him in Natchitoches by Samuel Swartwout, indicated that the general was a party to the conspiracy and lent added credence to Eaton's report. Burr told Wilkinson that he planned to leave Philadelphia on August 1 and would reach the falls of the Ohio by mid-November. Boats were under construction for the expedition, and he would secure men and supplies along the way. He expected a rendezvous with Wilkinson at Natchez in mid-December to complete their plans. Burr apparently hoped to launch an invasion of Mexico by way of the Sabine River with volunteers and General Wilkinson's force. He intimated that he would have some British and American naval support for an expedition against Vera Cruz which would be launched by February 1, 1807, although Burr appears to have been deliberately deceiving Wilkinson about the availability of naval units. He also entertained hopes of mobilizing support in the Orleans Territory for his plans through influential associates in New Orleans, and to seize the money in the New Orleans bank to help finance the enterprise.[31]

Wilkinson sent President Jefferson two ominous but vague warnings about the plot, the first of which indicated a tentative but hesitant decision to abandon Burr and alert Washington. In the first, written on October 21 and received about a month later by Jefferson, Wilkinson alluded darkly to plans which staggered even his own imagination, but he declined to mention specific names because it might influence prematurely a "salutory design." He was uncertain of the "prime mover and ultimate objects of this daring enterprise," but indicated that a western revolt or separation from the federal government would be auxiliary to a conquest of Mexico. Wilkinson proposed to Jefferson that gunboats and sloops be stationed at the mouth of the Mississippi, that troops be concentrated to apprehend the expedition, and that artillery emplacements be erected some fifteen miles below the mouth of the Ohio. On November 12, after he pulled back from the Sabine, Wilkinson warned of "an explosion which may desolate these settlements, inflict a deep wound on our republican policies, involve us in a foreign conflict, and shake the government to its very foundation." The conspiracy would be given strong support in New Orleans, he predicted, and he indicated that he would proclaim martial law in the city. The controversial brigadier cagily suggested that he would "resort to political finesse and military stratagem. I must hold out false colours, conceal my designs." He would probably sacrifice his own life by leading a "handful of veterans" against Burr's 7,000-man force. The redoubtable general would smile at obvious dangers, but he confessed ostentatiously to the president that he dreaded "the stroke of the assassin" after suggesting that the conspirators would threaten his life.[12] Jefferson, who under other circumstances may have been amused by the general's theatrics, issued a proclamation two days after receipt of Wilkinson's initial warning in which he called upon federal, state, and local officials to use all lawful means to break up the conspiracy.

Governor Claiborne, having shamefacedly slipped back into New Orleans after his aggressive efforts to prepare for a military showdown, lacked time to luxuriate in self-pity for his personal rebuff in the barren and remote northwest. As Wilkinson reached an easy accommodation with the dons and American forces were pulled back, the governor was suddenly bombarded with ominous and usually oblique warning about the rapidly developing danger which, according to the reports, threatened to sweep New Orleans before it and engulf Mexico while dismembering the federal union. When Wilkinson sent his second warning to Jefferson, he also warned Claiborne. The storm would erupt in New Orleans, Wilkinson proclaimed, and he would himself either conquer the conspirators or perish in the attempt. Unknown dangers surrounded the governor. Wilkinson declared that his friends as well as those of Claiborne were involved, and the general cautioned the governor: "You have spies on your every movement and disposition—and our safety and success depends *vitally* on the concealment of our intentions ... do not breathe or even hint it." On the same day Andrew Jackson warned Claiborne that treachery had become the order of the day. Jackson, who suspected that Wilkinson was a Burr associate, feared the Spanish force on the Sabine might link up with Wilkinson and in turn unite with the Burr force.[33] Jackson reminded Claiborne of their friendship, and advised him to put New Orleans in a state of readiness and to be prepared to cope with both internal and external enemies. He advised the governor to "keep a watchful eye on our General," and to "Beware of the month of December." He cautioned against an imminent effort to separate the Orleans Territory from the United States. With a flourish reminiscent of Wilkinson, the aroused and vigilant Jackson added a grim note of determination: "I would delight to see Mexico reduced, but I will die in the last ditch before I would yield a part to the Dons or see the Union disunited."[34] Almost two months later, with the situation still unsettled but assuming more concrete proportions, Jackson again wrote to Claiborne. He informed the governor that he had called out twelve militia companies for possible use against the conspirators, and had dispatched a messenger to Fort Massac near the confluence of the Ohio and Tennessee rivers to investigate the rumor that Burr was at the mouth of the Cumberland River with about one thousand men and one hundred boats. Jackson reported that Burr had left Nashville on December 22 with two boats, eight oarsmen, two families, six horses, and one cow. He added that Burr had been tried and acquitted in Kentucky before going on to Nashville. Jackson criticized the War Department for its handling of the threat, proclaiming stoutly that nerve was needed to purge the American political system of conspiracy and treason. He cautioned Claiborne to keep Wilkinson and his cohorts under surveillance, saying that they might be desperate to "procure a country and a home." If a real threat materialized, Jackson asked Claiborne to notify him. He would hasten on the wings of patriotism to the danger point, wreak vengeance upon Spanish insolence, and strike down those who would dare conspire against the United States.[35]

Acting Governor Cowles Mead also dispatched warnings to Governor Claiborne and offered assurances of his support. He, too, charged that New Orleans was seething with conspirators, and added that they were being trained by "the active and restless Daniel Clark—he is their head, father, and promoter." About a month later Mead assured Claiborne that the Mississippi militia could be relied upon to put up a fight when the Burr expedition swept southward on the Mississippi River. However, if Burr managed to get through Mississippi with his reported force of two thousand men, Mead reminded Claiborne that Wilkinson would be Claiborne's worst enemy. "Consider him a traitor, and act as if certain thereof. You may save yourself by it." [36]

On November 25, 1806, the day that President Jefferson issued a proclamation about the conspiracy and two weeks after Wilkinson sent oblique warnings to the president and Governor Claiborne, the general appeared with a flourish in New Orleans. For the next several days Wilkinson was a study in motion. He had pulled back eleven companies from the Sabine, leaving only one company at Natchitoches, and sent Major Moses Porter and one hundred men ahead to New Orleans to begin defensive preparations. As he withdrew toward New Orleans, he asked Acting Governor Mead to provide five hundred militiamen. When he declined to explain why he needed them, the wary Mead refused. He directed the commanding officer at Fort Adams to move his men and equipment to the city, where he planned to make his defensive stand, and he instructed Captain John Shaw to concentrate his naval forces in the vicinity of New Orleans to confront Burr's "flotilla." Warned repeatedly of the presence of Burr accomplices and sympathizers in the city, Governor Claiborne logically proposed calling out the militia and marching northward to intercept the conspirators. Wilkinson vetoed the proposal and countered with a recommendation of martial law and suspension of the writ of habeas corpus in the city which Claiborne in turn refused. To meet the attack, Wilkinson concentrated approximately one thousand regular troops in New Orleans and vicinity and he called the Orleans Volunteers into service in January 1807 and they remained on active duty until early March. While busily erecting defenses and deploying his men, Wilkinson engaged in a whirlwind of private conferences with Burr accomplices who were avowed enemies of the Claiborne administration. These activities perplexed Claiborne who also conferred with Wilkinson, but the general disclosed nothing to him in their initial meeting.[37]

Over Wilkinson's protests, Governor Claiborne called a meeting of the merchant community at his residence on December 9 to inform the businessmen of the reasons for the military preparations. Even then they were told only because the two leaders needed to enlist their support, not because they wished to share the confidence with them. Claiborne spoke first and warned of a "premeditated attack on the Territory, by a formidable party of men assembling on the Ohio, headed . . . by some of the first characters of the union," and of the presence of traitors in the city. He then excused himself to confer with his militia officers, and left the decisions necessitated by the threat to the general and the merchants. At no time did the governor mention Burr's name specifically, nor did the general when he addressed the group after Claiborne's departure. Wilkinson told them that some two thousand men were expected to reach Natchez on December 20, and they were expected to move southward from there against the city itself. Moreover, he warned that disguised but armed vessels would "come into our river in order to serve as a convoy to the expedition to be made against Vera Cruz." He informed them that sailors were needed to help man Captain Shaw's flotilla to defend against the enemy craft. Wilkinson favored impressment as a means of securing naval personnel, but the merchants chose instead to impose an embargo on all ships in the port of New Orleans thereby freeing sailors in the city to volunteer for service. The merchants hoped to recruit three hundred sailors for temporary service, and they subscribed $4,500 to defray expenses.[38] After the meeting Wilkinson reported the action taken at the meeting to President Jefferson. Now, he exclaimed suspensively, much would depend on the "Wind and weather."[39]

A week later Claiborne issued a proclamation to the populace stating that an attempt was being made to subvert the authority of the United States and to invade Mexico. For the former, Claiborne cited the law against treason as stipulated in the Constitution; for the latter, he pointed out that any participant would be charged with a high misdemeanor which could result in imprisonment up to three years and a fine of up to $3,000. According to a local newspaper account appearing on December 23 Burr was "made the vehicle." Alluding to the numerous rumors associated with the plot, the writer observed sagely that "it might be criminal either to treat them with indifference, or receive them absolutely as true."[40]

In the meantime, Wilkinson continued to exert heavy pressures on Claiborne to proclaim a state of martial law and suspend the writ of habeas corpus so that he could move against alleged Burr agents in the city. Claiborne quietly but firmly refused because it would be unconstitutional and the danger was not sufficiently critical to initiate such extreme measures. As an alternative he recommended that the Burr agents and accomplices in New Orleans be dealt with through regular civil processes. Wilkinson rebuked the governor and sarcastically inquired if all defensive preparations were to be nullified by "our reverence for our civil institutions, . . . or shall we lose the house because we will not break the windows?"[41] Frustrated and impatient, Wilkinson decided to act independently and in defiance of the civil authority. Two days before Claiborne issued his first public proclamation, the general arrested two alleged Burr abettors who were members of the Mexican Association. Committed to the abolition of Spanish authority over Mexico, the Mexican Association was not linked directly with the Burr conspiracy. In fact, although Daniel Clark and Edward Livingston had warmly received Colonel Burr the preceding year, they studiously avoided any direct association with the conspiracy as it began to take form. More arrests followed. Among those arrested or implicated during the growing controversy were Justus Eric Bollman, whom Burr sent to New Orleans as his personal representative; Samuel Swartwout, who delivered Burr's coded message to Wilkinson in Natchitoches; Peter V. Ogden, another Burr courier; James Alexander, an attorney who applied for a writ for Bollman; James M. Bradford, editor of the *Orleans Gazette*; and General John Adair, who had written two years earlier to Wilkinson that "Mexico glitters in our eyes. . . ." and had ostensibly solicited militia support for Burr in the western counties of the Orleans Territory. Even Judges James Kerr and James Workman were arrested and detained briefly on charges of having plotted to revolutionize Mexico.[42] In ordering these arrests, Wilkinson contended that he conferred with Federal District Judge Dominic A. Hall and Superior Court Judge George Mathews, Jr., and they advised him to use his discretion. He also contended later that Governor Claiborne had agreed to share responsibility for his actions.[43]

Rumors of Burr's imminent appearance on the lower Mississippi at the head of a formidable military force continued to swirl throughout the city as Wilkinson trampled on the civil authority and prepared for the expected onslaught. To the north, Acting

Governor Cowles Mead addressed the Mississippi legislature following receipt of dispatches from Washington about the plot. He exhorted the lawmakers to "convert the pen of legislation into the weapon of war, and suspend the elegance of debate for the clangour of military array." Mead then prorogued the legislature in order to cope with the emergency. According to prevailing rumors in late January 1807, Burr and a three-hundred-man expedition had moved as far southward as the mouth of Bayou Pierre on the Mississippi River and several miles north of Natchez. Colonel Ferdinand Claiborne, the governor's brother, stood ready to challenge Burr with a force of comparable size.[44]

After all the frenzied preparations and elaborate precautions taken by the leaders in the Mississippi and Orleans territories, the so-called Burr threat simply failed to materialize. Indeed, it increasingly assumed the proportions of comic opera and climaxed with the belated appearance of Burr and a handful of men in Mississippi on January 10, 1807. Judge Peter B. Bruin, an old acquaintance who had served earlier in the judiciary under Governor Claiborne, informed Burr that Mead had ordered his arrest. The colonel quietly submitted to a farcical trial before the superior court on February 2 with Bruin and Thomas Rodney serving as presiding judges. Burr disappeared the next day, but Lieutenant Edmund P. Gaines, the young commanding officer at Fort Stoddert, later apprehended him at the home of Major John Hinson. Nicholas Perkins, registrar of the local land office, and eight guards escorted Burr to Richmond, Virginia. He was tried for treason several months afterward in the United States Circuit Court, with Chief Justice John Marshall presiding. Much to the anguish of the Republicans, the judicial proceedings acquitted Burr of the charges against him.[45]

About a week after Burr had appeared before Judges Bruin and Rodney in Natchez, Governor Claiborne sent the Orleans legislature a message informing them of Burr's apprehension. Having steadfastly resisted Wilkinson's demands, he recommended at last that the legislators temporarily suspend the writ of habeas corpus. He did so on the ground that many of Burr's adherents who remained in the Mississippi and Orleans territories constituted a security threat, and he speculated that many well-meaning and honest citizens may have been "seduced" by various means to engage in an *"unauthorized expedition* to Mexico." To support his request, he enclosed a copy of Secretary of War

Dearborn's dispatch in which he discussed the conspiracy and directed Claiborne to act immediately against those who threatened the laws and peace of the United States and to arrest immediately persons who aroused suspicion. The lawmakers refused for the same reasons Claiborne had refused Wilkinson, having received opinions from the leading judicial officers in the territory that such action would contravene the Constitution.[46]

As the threat of invasion vanished with Burr's apprehension and removal, any immunity Claiborne and Wilkinson may have enjoyed was cast aside precipitately and a torrent of criticism ensued. Judge James Workman, having been personally humiliated, led the assault on the general and the governor. Both "their civil and military excellencies" had accused Workman of supporting an independence movement in the territory and identification with the Mexican Association, to which the judge now retorted scathingly: "Great God! How degrading it is to be engaged in a contest with such adversaries" as "a little nameless brigadier, and an underling clerk of Mr. John Beckley's." The irate judge declared that Claiborne was paid $5,000 annually to enact laws with the advice and consent of the legislature, "but congress might as well have ordained that his excellency should speak French, or write English, or act with wisdom, or dignity, or courage." Workman said he had reminded Claiborne repeatedly of his responsibility to enforce judicial decisions and protect the civil liberties of the people. When Claiborne refused repeated requests to curb the general's arbitrary conduct, Workman pointed out that he adjourned the court sine die.[47] Finally despairing completely, he had resigned his judicial post.

A number of Louisianians, including Judge Workman, criticized Claiborne and Wilkinson for an unauthorized use of the territorial militia. On January 13, 1807, the day before his own arrest, Workman protested against putting the Orleans Volunteers on active service under Wilkinson. He recommended the rescission of the order.[48] Then in May a newspaper critic who identified himself as "Centurio" castigated Claiborne unmercifully. He questioned the governor's authority to transfer the militia into the federal service without the militia's consent and in the absence of a federal or territorial law that authorized such a move. If it could be done, the critic proclaimed, then this was not a free country. Claiborne pretended that he acted on orders from the president, "Centurio" said, but he challenged the right of the president to take such action unless Congress gave him the authority. If the president himself lacked the authority, he obviously could not grant authorization to someone else. "Centurio" conceded that Claiborne had acted properly in assisting Wilkinson when the latter hurried to Natchitoches to meet the Spaniards, if Wilkinson ever hurried, he added caustically. But the transfer of the Orleans Volunteers to the federal service did not occur until after the prospect of invasion had vanished and was "for the most odious purposes of domestic oppression." Much had been said about the assemblage of rebels, but "Centurio" saw no real evidence of it. The only evidence of such rebel assemblages, he charged, was that which Jefferson had communicated to Congress, "to which even he himself does not seem to give implicit credit." Moreover, he demanded to know why the militiamen had been held so long in active service when it became clear that the Burr plot had no substantive basis. "Centurio" also accused the press of having supported Claiborne and Wilkinson and labelled the members of the territorial press as "Volunteers par force." The press had earlier remained silent, prim, and prettily behaved, he charged, when the public mind had been greatly agitated. In effect, "Centurio" accused the governor of having muzzled and controlled the press.[49]

Some of the territorial lawmakers also joined the ranks of the indignant critics after the legislature was convened on January 13, 1807. They grumbled about the temporary embargo. Some demanded to know why the decision was made to confront the enemy in New Orleans rather than northward on the Mississippi as Claiborne had advocated. They objected to Wilkinson's arbitrariness and the continued state of emergency after the danger had disappeared. Some of the solons supported a petition to Congress on the matter, but it was voted down 14 to 7.[50]

Buffeted by criticism, the beleagured twosome offered a varied range of reactions both during and after the emergency. The general sometimes assumed a posture of imperious silence and disdain, or when his actions were challenged he responded with the cavalier retort that he accepted all responsibility. But bombast sometimes gave way to a seemingly humble effort to defend his character and motives. In a newspaper statement at the end of 1806, he said he had left family and friends in New York three years earlier to return to the national service on the frontier. He had done this, he said, because of an "unsettled account" of $30,000 to $40,000 owed to the federal government.[51] In making this disclosure he wished to convey the impression of a modest and dedicated public servant whose motives were impeccably honest. Governor Claiborne usually did not take "ground quite so high" as his blemished associate when confronted by critics, but he invariably asserted a purity of motives. Moreover, when pressed, he sometimes moved to the attack himself and forced his critics onto the defensive. When some of the legislators questioned the conduct of the two leaders, for example, Claiborne complained that the legislature had contributed nothing to the suppression of the conspiracy.

Despite recurring rumors of personal animosities, Claiborne and Wilkinson appear to have closed ranks to combat their critics. Andrew Jackson told an unidentified general that a serious quarrel between the two had been rumored, and that Claiborne purportedly slapped Wilkinson. While uncertain of this Jackson nonetheless was certain that a "violent dispute" had occurred.[52] General Wilkinson himself mentioned the rumor to President Jefferson, admitting that he and Claiborne had differed on "some subordinate points," and noting that it was his enemies who charged that he was attempting to replace Claiborne. The accusation, he declared innocently, was "opposite to every inclination in my breast." The general claimed that Claiborne deserved far more from the people of the territory than they were willing to concede. Unable to maintain a modest posture for very long, Wilkinson proclaimed that he really had saved the day by his decisive action on the Sabine and by his later arrest of Adair and other Burr accomplices which prevented an insurrection in New Orleans.[53] When all reports were in and passions subsided, he was certain he would be exonerated. His conduct defied inquiry, and if "tested by the sunbeams of investigation . . . pensions, conspiracies, and verbal conventions will vanish before the truth like the mist of morn before the rising day."[54]

Governor Claiborne offered a comparable defense, telling the secretary of war that both he and Wilkinson had been maligned. While modestly admitting his own limitations, he declared that Wilkinson deserved well of the United States, a statement which sounded suspiciously like Wilkinson's assertion to the president about Claiborne. Even though the general's actions were sometimes exceptionable, the governor believed that Wilkinson had little choice and that the safety of New Orleans was attributed to him. When he wrote to Jefferson a month later, Claiborne stated that he had been an eyewitness to the general's conduct, and to his official and private correspondence. He was convinced that Wilkinson "opposed Burr from principle & that his Acts, were directed by the purest motives of patriotism." Although admitting his associate's errors, Claiborne attributed them to zeal, and added that Wilkinson's assertiveness was justified "by the Magnitude of the danger, as it appeared to him." Had Burr descended the Mississippi with a large expedition, as planned, all would have applauded "and eulogized in grateful Language the promptitude and energy of the Commander in Chief." His own personal support of Wilkinson was based on conviction, he admitted candidly, because mutual confidence was lacking. Wilkinson was "an honest, zealous and Active Agent in the suppression of a Conspiracy, which had for its objects the subversion of our Government, and the dismemberment of the Union."[55]

The governor and general were not devoid of support in the controversy. In late March 1807, Claiborne sent Madison two addresses by "many respectable citizens" in which they expressed their gratitude and approval for the leadership provided by the two men.[56] In addition, Jackson sent Claiborne a letter containing the names of a number of persons who supported them. Jackson, too, conceded that Wilkinson had opposed Burr from principle and that his intentions were sound.[57] However, the conduct of both men during the emergency displeased President Jefferson who admitted readily that Wilkinson had abused the judiciary and had "trodden the law in the dust." In addition, Jefferson lamented that Wilkinson had "swaddled" the governor and "laid him to bed like a great baby."[58] For the president, then, one of his ex-commissioners had been unconscionably assertive; the other had been revoltingly pliant.

Governor Claiborne's conduct during the Burr episode must be evaluated in much the same vein as the perceptive local newspaper writer who observed that it might be criminal to treat the conspiracy rumors with casual indifference or to accept them unconditionally. The governor, inundated by a flood of oblique warnings, had to make some difficult decisions. As far as the conspiracy was concerned, Claiborne had to assume that it did constitute a threat to the national government generally and to Orleans Territory in particular, especially in view of Jefferson's proclamation and the secretary of war's urgent dispatches to the territorial governors directing them to use every lawful means to preempt the plot. Jackson became alarmed, sent Claiborne two ominous warnings, and called out some militia units for possible use. For several weeks not one major figure, either at the national level or in the lower Mississippi region, was prepared to label the Burr conspiracy a gigantic hoax. By spring Claiborne could look back on the episode with a certain detachment or even amusement, but to have treated the threat lightly or ignored it altogether in its formative stages would have been both reckless and irresponsible.

Claiborne also had to decide quickly whether Wilkinson's loyalties to the national government were fixed, or whether he was indeed an integral and essential part of the audacious conspiracy. His loyalties had been and would continue to be suspect. Doubts must have assailed Claiborne before he resolved the issue in his own mind. Nonetheless, unfolding events confirmed the governor's decision to work with and support Wilkinson's military preparations to defend New Orleans.

Following Claiborne's decision that Wilkinson could be relied upon to defend national and territorial interests, he had to determine the latitude Wilkinson would be permitted in the implementation of defense plans. Here Claiborne was ambivalent. Both leaders conceded the general gravity of the situation, but they differed about the degree of the danger. This determined their respective positions on what they considered to be the most feasible course of action to cope successfully with the emergency. Wilkinson entertained absolutely no doubts about the magnitude of the threat and he pressed hard for a declaration of martial law and a suspension of the writ of habeas corpus. Claiborne disagreed, but he was less certain of his position. Wilkinson quickly sensed the hesitancy and moved boldly to exploit it by seizing and detaining a number of suspects. Claiborne, as Wilkinson, was aware that a number of Burr accomplices and sympathizers were in the city, and he knew that they could easily spring into action as a fifth column if the Burr expedition became a reality. Claiborne even tacitly endorsed some of the arrests and detentions, but he was still inclined to think that the disposition of the cases should be the prerogative of the civil authority. At the same time, he knew that some of the leading figures in the judiciary were Burr acquaintances and held membership in the Mexican Association. Thus Claiborne's decision that justice would be best served by reliance upon the civil authority was undermined to some extent by this knowledge. The emboldened general therefore seized upon Claiborne's doubts and uncertainties to trample upon the civil authority and treat the judiciary with brutal contempt. Claiborne acquiesced in this reprehensible and vulgar course of action. Moreover, his recommendation that the legislature temporarily suspend the writ of habeas corpus on the basis of the secretary of war's warning about the Burr threat after the threat had been removed invited further public contempt. His later defense of Wilkinson's conduct to the president and secretary of war compounded his error. After the threat had disappeared and from a distance of a thousand miles, President Jefferson could easily conclude that the tarnished warrior had laid the governor to bed like a great baby. But even so, a significant condition was that he laid him to bed under extenuating circumstances.

Finally, Governor Claiborne committed a more obvious error and his culpability was not softened by extenuating circumstances. The concentration of forces in New Orleans and the concomitant flurry of activity contributed to an atmosphere of crisis and apprehension. Yet neither Wilkinson nor Claiborne offered a public explanation for several weeks. Even more inexcusable, they made no effort to take the public into their confidence and mobilize popular support for the task before them. The closest Claiborne came to doing so was when he met with the business community, sought its advice about the best means of securing sailors for Shaw's flotilla, and the merchants provided a solution within the hour. Morover, when he belatedly disclosed the plot in a public proclamation, he concentrated primarily on the penalties that could be imposed for complicity in the conspiracy or support for Mexican independence from Spain. Furthermore, failure to inform the public for some time lent credence to unfounded rumor and invited strong public reaction against the secretive twosome when the local citizenry came to realize that no substantive basis existed for the alarm after all. Thus Claiborne's two major mistakes were his unwillingness to support the civil authority against the Wilkinson blandishments and inroads, and his failure to confide in the public and mobilize popular support. Reflecting even more unfavorably on the governor, a more serious but comparable development occurred eight years later and Governor Claiborne's response was again almost identical. In short, he failed to learn from the mistakes of the Burr conspiracy.

X

THE WEST FLORIDA CONTROVERSY AND STATEHOOD

Obfuscations in the Franco-American treaty about the eastern boundary of the Louisiana territory were just as worrisome as the western boundary ambiguities and they produced a more persistent source of contention. While Napoleon and Talleyrand had no intention of promoting American territorial interests by providing a more precise boundary delineation, the American leaders did not hesitate to take advantage of Talleyrand's "noble bargain" to press for a larger Louisiana, east and west. The uncertain boundary, combined with American proximity and Spanish preoccupation resulting from the resumption of the European war after a brief respite, provided the Americans with tantalizing opportunities to enlarge their domain. These factors, in addition to Spain's failure to adjust to the geopolitical realities resulting from the loss of Louisiana, enabled the Americans to chip away at Spain's dwindling continental holdings east of the Mississippi River and south of the thirty-first parallel. In view of the existing circumstances, the surprise was not so much that Spain lost some territory but that its losses did not come sooner and were not much greater. That is, in view of the American advantages and, conversely, Spanish disadvantages, it is hard to conceive of the voracious American appetite having been sated temporarily by the acquisition of a mere part of West Florida. The matter assumes even more incredible proportions when one considers that American policies toward the Spanish government, especially as they related to contiguous Spanish colonial territories, were influenced by Governor Claiborne's reports and recommendations. Claiborne was the American government's man-on-the-scene who vigorously pressed the American claim to West Florida.

Governor Claiborne insisted noisily even before the Louisiana transfer that West Florida was an integral part of Louisiana. In mid-1802—over three months before Morales became the target of his wrath for having temporarily denied the port of New Orleans to the westerners—Claiborne encouraged the United States to take advantage of European preoccupations to extend its holdings, saying to Madison: "In the course of the negociations [sic] among the great nations of the Earth for Territory, I wish to God the U. States could possess themselves of East & West Florida, including the Island of Orleans."[1] When the governor learned of the American acquisition of Louisiana, one of his immediate concerns was whether it embraced West Florida. He suggested cautiously that it was included in the earlier Spanish retrocession to France, and asserted that the French had exercised jurisdiction over those lands extending as far eastward as the Perdido River prior to the cession to Spain in 1763. If the terms of the Treaty of San Ildefonso were essentially the same as they had been conveyed informally to him and Spain had "*ceded Louisiana to France as the same was previously possessed by France*," there was no doubt in Claiborne's mind that "the greater part of what is now termed west Florida is included."[2] However, Laussat told the two American commissioners a week after the transfer that while under Spanish jurisdiction Louisiana's eastern boundary passed mid-stream from the Mississippi River to the Iberville River, and on through Lakes Maurepas and Pontchartrain to the sea, thereby excluding West Florida.[3] A few weeks after the transfer Claiborne and Wilkinson told Madison they had not protested against the non-delivery of West Florida as far as the Perdido to the United States because it was "to [sic] near the Close of the Business, lest it might create some Embarrassment."[4] Nonetheless, the commissioners were careful to concede nothing. On March 26, 1804, they registered a "protestando" with Laussat declaring that they did not intend to investigate Spanish claims to West Florida or to state their own beliefs. They wished, however, to make clear that nothing they did was to be construed as an abandonment of American claims. Their "protestando" dealt with "that Portion of West Florida, which formerly constituted a Part of Louisiana as France possessed it." In short, the two commissioners were

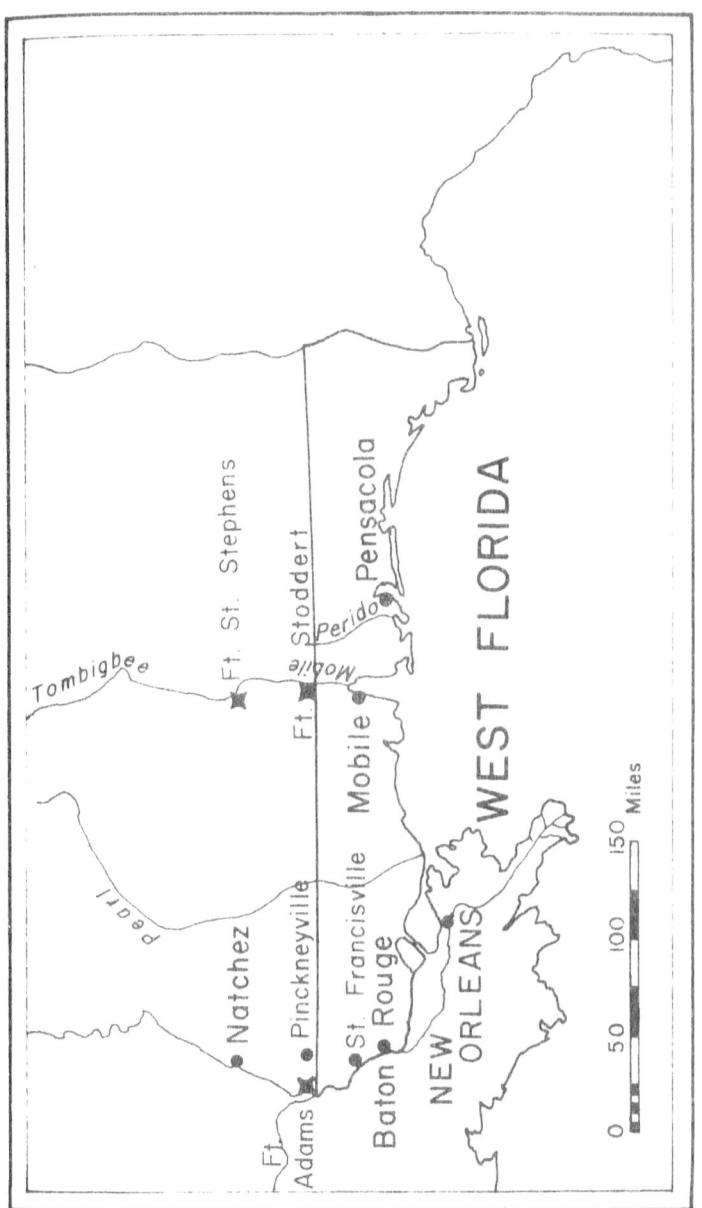

West Florida

James Wilkinson

engrossed in the immediate tasks associated with the transfer and they had only a small force to support the new American authority at the time, but they fully intended to press for the expanded eastern boundary when it was most appropriate.

A number of leaders associated with the transfer regarded the ambiguous boundaries as only a temporary problem. A week after the transfer Laussat expressed the belief that the Spanish government would relinquish the Floridas in return for some land west of the Mississippi. A short time afterward Claiborne told Madison that Spain probably would give up the lands to the Perdido upon American insistence unless encouraged by France to hold fast. He also mentioned the possibility of acquiring the Floridas in return for the relinquishment of American land claims beyond the Sabine River.[5] Favoring the exchange himself, but cautiously inviting the president's response, Claiborne told Jefferson in late 1804 that the Spanish colonial leaders were inclined to think that Spain would give up the Floridas if the United States would forego its claims to the lands lying west of the Mississippi.[6]

Governor Vicente Folch of West Florida, having made a realistic appraisal of the developing situation and its implications for Spain, also encouraged the exchange. He did this in a treatise called "Reflections on Louisiana," which he apparently wrote in 1804. Folch readily recognized the importance of the Floridas to the United States both in terms of American trade and the "ascendency" the national government would attain over the Indian nations in the region. The Spanish government should employ a "most careful combination of art and force" with regard to the Floridas. He felt that Spain should reject all American offers unless the Americans were willing to exchange their trans-Mississippi holdings, or that portion of those lands needed by Spain to block all communications between the United States and Mexico. If Spain agreed unconditionally to American pretensions under the Franco-American treaty, Folch warned, the keys to the New World would be in the hands of Spain's most dangerous neighbor. Propelled by their "insatiable avarice" and "boundless designs," the Americans would quickly subdue Mexico and Peru. The recovery of the trans-Mississippi lands was as important to Spain, Folch reasoned, as the Floridas were to the "peace, prosperity, relief and profit" of the United States. If the Americans were permitted to retain the trans-Mississippi lands, they, like the Goths and Vandals, "would overrun Mexico and everything in their path." And in the wake of their conquests, the Americans would "propagate in their course the pestilent doctrines that have desolated the most valuable part of Europe, and which have deprived whole kingdoms of their foundations." In the face of such a fearsome possibility, Folch recommended the exchange with Spain tossing in a "sum of money which seems suitable to attract the attention of the people and tempt the government of the United States." He noted that the American public debt amounted to 70,000,000 pesos. If Spain agreed to exchange the Floridas for the lands west of the Mississippi and to pay the American indebtedness over a period of time, the people of the Atlantic states would support it and force the government to accept it. But the offer should be made, he advised, only when less prohibitive attempts to find a solution had failed.[7] Folch's profound "Reflections" clearly indicated that he had come to know the strengths and weaknesses of his American competitors fully during his years in West Florida. None of his colonial associates displayed a comparable insight and knowledge, either of the Americans themselves or of the inherent implications for Spain's precarious colonial holdings. Folch's greater perspective was matched, at least, by the perceptive and calculating Thomas Jefferson. The president had also made an accurate appraisal of the dons, and his expansive overview of American national interests just as obviously precluded any serious thought of relinquishing Washington's trans-Mississippi claims. In essence, why should the Jefferson administration make a choice when both easily fell within the American reach? Time and circumstances favored the Americans.

    The United States appeared ready to enforce its claim to West Florida about two months after the Louisiana transfer. Congress authorized the president to establish a customs district with Mobile as its port of entry. When the president created the Mobile customs district at the end of May, however, it only embraced those lands lying within the United States, with Fort Stoddert selected as the port of entry. Both the Spanish and American governments assumed threatening postures and Jefferson ordered military reinforcements rushed to New Orleans. The American intent, however, was not to provoke war. Some six weeks before the customs district was created, Madison had quietly instructed James Monroe, then serving as minister to Great Britain, to open negotiations with the Spanish government for the acceptance of the Perdido River boundary and for the sale of Florida to the United States.[8]

President Jefferson, his country's realtor *par excellence*, appeared for a time to be on the verge of arranging a second "noble bargain." Again, Napoleon needed money and Spain, having become a French ally against England in late 1804, was the convenient vehicle as it had been earlier. Talleyrand informed the American minister in Paris that Spain would sell Florida to the United States for $7,000,000. To establish a conducive climate, the versatile Talleyrand hinted that the American offer be preceded by timely American threats. Jefferson readily obliged in his annual message on December 3, 1805. In an otherwise conciliatory address Jefferson assumed a truculent posture toward Spain for its failure to respond to Washington's amicable overtures and the hostile actions and conduct of Spanish colonial forces toward peaceful American citizens in the Orleans and Mississippi territories. This had compelled him, he growled, to station American troops in the frontier areas to protect American citizens and to repel the aggressive thrusts of hostile forces. But behind the scenes a tentative understanding had already been reached between the French and American officials. Spain would accept the Perdido boundary claim of the Americans and would receive $5,000,000 for the rest of Florida. Moreover, the Americans would accept the Colorado River of Texas rather than the Rio Grande as the southwestern boundary. On December 6 the president sent Congress a special message in which he intimated that France would promote a settlement between the United States and Spain. Jefferson declined to divulge the terms of the agreement, but John Randolph, chairman of the committee to which Jefferson's special message was referred, declined to cooperate when he learned that Jefferson wanted $2,000,000 for "diplomatic purposes." The House nonetheless approved the special appropriation and the money was taken to France by Fulwar Skipwith, the American consul general in Paris. When, however, the American minister in Paris notified the French leaders that the United States was prepared to fulfill its obligations under the tentative agreement, Napoleon transmitted to him a declaration by the Spanish king stating that Spain would not alienate the Floridas. Spanish leaders, probably learning of the Franco-American agreement from Federalist sources after Jefferson was forced to ask for money from Congress to support his initiatives, therefore refused to accede to its terms.[9]

Although frustrated by Spain's unwillingness to cooperate with its French ally, the resourceful Jefferson quickly shifted to viable alternatives, one of which emerged as a result of swiftly changing developments in Europe. After France and Spain partitioned Portugal and a French army was stationed in Spain, Napoleon placed his brother Joseph on the Spanish throne. The Spanish people then rose in revolt against the foreign intruders. Jefferson, who envisaged a possible Anglo-American rapprochement despite the *Chesapeake* affair of the previous year, wrote to Madison on August 12, 1808, that "a moment may occur favorable, without compromitting us with either France or England, for seizing our own from the Rio Bravo to Perdido, as of right, and the residue of Florida, as a reprisal for spoliations." [10]

In late October Jefferson conveyed his views to Claiborne so that the governor, in turn, could transmit them to leaders in West Florida. The United States was a warm friend of the Spanish patriots and would have no objection to continued Spanish sovereignty over Cuba and Mexico. The United States would not, however, allow the two possessions to fall into the hands of either Britain or France. Jefferson concluded his letter to Claiborne with the statement that American and Spanish interests were the same, "and that the object of both must be to exclude all European influence from this hemisphere." Thus the later Monroe Doctrine had its genesis in the president's letter to his representative and spokesman in New Orleans. [11]

The establishment of a political climate conducive to the extension of American authority over a part of West Florida was preceded by a number of incidents and confrontations between the Americans and Spanish colonial authorities. Governor Vicente Folch labelled the establishment of the Mobile customs district in 1804 as "ill-grounded pretentions," and warned Claiborne that American intrusions into West Florida would be resisted by force. Claiborne responded pacifically that the issues raised by Folch were for their respective governments to resolve. He added that he was only an executive agent charged with the administration of his government's laws and instructions. While his response was polite and conciliatory, he conceded nothing but he studiously avoided using the issue to provoke the Spaniards at that particular time because the Jefferson administration hoped to achieve its objectives by diplomatic means.[12] Nevertheless, American settlers to the northward who were adversely affected by Spanish control of the river outlets, especially Mobile, were incensed and frustrated by Spanish policies. Agent Joseph Chambers at Fort St. Stephens complained that he could not pay the duties levied by the Spanish customs officials at Mobile. Governor Claiborne importuned Folch to remove the restrictions, arguing that the American factory at the fort kept the Indians pacified. Chambers later persuaded Casa Calvo to exclude the factory from the payment of duties, having earlier paid them under protest as he had been instructed by Claiborne. Yet private traders were given no relief from the import and export duties levied by the Spaniards on goods moved by way of the Mobile River. The Spanish authorities sometimes seized American vessels when their captains refused to pay the exactions, and the local American settlers threatened to retaliate by destroying Spanish ships venturing up the Tombigbee River.[13] Governor Claiborne, having corresponded several times with Spanish officials about the problem, sent John Graham, the territorial secretary, to confer with Folch. Folch promised to suspend the practice and refund duties paid by the Americans during 1805 provided Spanish vessels were permitted to take their cargoes duty-free to Baton Rouge. Claiborne informed Madison of Folch's proposal, but he feared that the refusal to permit ships loaded with slaves to pass beyond New Orleans would cause Folch to withdraw the offer. In late March 1806 Claiborne reported to Madison that the free navigation of the Mobile was still prohibited and causing hardships for the Tombigbee settlers. Although the settlers had agreed not to trade with the Spaniards as long as the restriction was in force, he stated, the decision proved only their patriotism and spirit since it did no injury to Spain. To force the Spaniards to comply, Claiborne recommended that "the intercourse of our Seaports, and particularly New Orleans with Pensacola and Mobile, be interdicted," since the two Spanish settlements secured most of their supplies from New Orleans. Claiborne also reported about the same time on Spain's military strength and asserted that Mobile could be taken with minimal losses if national leaders issued the order.[14] Yet such orders were not transmitted from Washington and Claiborne dutifully continued to work toward a peaceful settlement of the problem. During this tense period in 1805 and 1806 when a clash was clearly possible, Secretary of War Dearborn ordered the Pascagoula River to the west of Mobile cleared of obstacles up to the thirty-first parallel so that Fort Stoddert in the Tombigbee district could be supplied "under cover of a Gunboat ... through that channel."[15]

While the Americans and Spaniards exchanged missives over the creation of the Mobile customs district and Spanish customs exactions on the Mobile River, events around Baton Rouge alarmed Spanish colonial leaders and convinced them that the Americans planned to seize West Florida. The Baton Rouge "revolt" was sparked by Nathan, Samuel, and Reuben Kemper who had settled on an estate in Feliciana Parish near St. Francisville which was owned by Senator John Smith of Ohio. The Kempers had been engaged by Smith to develop the estate, but the partnership proved unsatisfactory and Smith initiated legal action to have the Kempers removed forcefully when they defied his orders to vacate the estate. Don Carlos de Grand Pré, the Baton Rouge commandant, decided in favor of Smith after nearly three years of litigation. Nathan and Samuel and four companions barricaded themselves and resisted initial efforts to expel them while Reuben promoted their interests in New Orleans. The Kempers had hoped to enlist the support of other local American settlers, but they, holding lands under Spanish grants, supported Grand Pré. Faced with a superior militia force organized by Grand Pré, the Kempers fled to Pinckneyville, located in the Mississippi Territory southeast of Fort Adams.[16]

Morales and his real estate associates in New Orleans, particularly Daniel Clark and Edward Livingston, then attempted to use the incident to promote their own landed interests. Their agent in St. Francisville, Edward Randolph, organized an independence movement in West Florida. A small, nondescript band, including the Kempers, marched toward Baton Rouge to take the fort, capture Grand Pré, and proclaim independence. Having done this, they would offer West Florida "to some government accustomed to freedom." The attempt failed, however, and the insurgents were forced to retreat to the Mississippi Territory after a few weeks. After receiving assurances of local support, Governor Vicente Folch began construction of a military road from Mobile to Baton Rouge and personally led a two-hundred-man force to Baton Rouge. When he arrived, he discovered the "revolt" had subsided, but he reinforced and repaired the fort and forbade further land sales to Americans.[17]

The abortive "revolt" could have been used as a convenient pretext to occupy West Florida, but the Jefferson administration carefully avoided identification with it. When Calvo appealed to Claiborne on August 11 to prevent American assistance to the insurgents, the governor sent him a conciliatory response fifteen days later explaining that he and his family were suffering from yellow fever and this had caused the delayed response. Although his authority was restricted to the Orleans Territory, he assured the marquis that he would act to prevent the Kempers from receiving assistance from American territory and he promised to investigate Reuben Kemper's conduct. Claiborne told Madison several months later that only a few ignorant and uninformed people had participated in the "insurrection." After Carlos Martinez de Irujo, the Spanish minister to the United States, reacted sharply to the incident, Madison told Claiborne that, if such incidents were launched from American territory and American citizens were involved, those who participated in them violated American laws and should be punished. On orders from Jefferson, Madison directed the governors of the Orleans and Mississippi territories to prevent expeditions against Spanish territory and he authorized them to use their militia forces if necessary. Madison and Jefferson feared that Spanish leaders would react to the Baton Rouge "revolt" by suspending the boundary negotiations which were then in progress. The secretary of state sent Claiborne's correspondence on the Kemper affair to George Erving, the American chargé d'affaires in Madrid, so that he in turn would show it to the Spanish officials to prove that there had been no official complicity in the local incident.[18]

Although the abortive Kemper "revolt" had largely ended upon the withdrawal of the insurgents to the Mississippi Territory in mid-September 1804, Spanish colonial officials remained nervous for several months. On May 6, 1805, Calvo told Claiborne that the insurgent elements were about to become active again. He warned that a recurrence could upset the critical negotiations then in progress between their governments and that the "repose and Tranquillity" of both territories would be disturbed. Calvo proposed a joint effort to quell any recurrent outbreaks, and Claiborne assured him that he would view "with no common regard" a renewal of disturbances at Baton Rouge. Moreover, he vowed to do everything possible to prevent American citizens from assisting the Kempers, whom he regarded personally as ruffians, and would insist that American accomplices be punished according to existing laws.[19]

The Kempers and their handful of accomplices created no further difficulties, but Spanish-American relations took a turn for the worse in 1805 and Claiborne's conciliatory disposition gave way to truculence. Diplomatic relations between the two countries were suspended, and Madison at last directed Claiborne to expel Calvo and Morales from the Orleans Territory. In his reports to Washington, Governor Claiborne advocated a "forceful settlement" of outstanding differences with Spain. Furthermore, the governor appeared eager for the Spaniards to initiate military action in the border regions which would enable the United States to retaliate and overrun the disputed territories. Whereas Claiborne had been inclined earlier to report developments to Washington, he now encouraged the Jefferson administration to react aggressively and decisively to Spanish initiatives. Hence, Morales' denial of the port of Mobile to the Americans for a time during the summer of 1805, purported Spanish reinforcements at a number of posts such as Baton Rouge, Mobile, and on the western frontier, and Folch's disruption of the United States mail service through West Florida in mid-March 1806, aroused Claiborne's wrath. American inaction in the face of such deliberate provocations, Claiborne fumed, merely invited further indignities. The dons would display proper respect for American rights only by the application of force, he exclaimed to Jefferson, and the "sooner this expedient is resorted to, the better." [20]

Although Claiborne's official conduct toward the Spaniards had been generally reserved and conciliatory throughout most of 1804 and 1805 and his attitude became visibly more bellicose in later 1805 and 1806, he at no time retreated appreciably from his role as a war hawk and proponent of manifest destiny. He viewed Spain's military capabilities on the troubled frontiers with ill-concealed contempt, and he repeatedly urged administration leaders to take advantage of existing opportunities. On November 20, 1805, he wrote to Jefferson about the resumption of war in Europe and suggested that it might be well to settle the boundary dispute while the Spanish government was preoccupied. Three months later he informed Madison that local sentiment in New Orleans favored occupation of the lands lying west of the Perdido. The inhabitants of the disputed area would acquiesce, and the Spaniards were too weak to resist. Similar urgings followed and Claiborne ostensibly submitted a plan to take Baton Rouge, but national leaders continued to follow a moderate course. [21] Even when the Sabine crisis erupted in 1806 Jefferson and Madison declined to make an overt bid to take West Florida. Then when Napoleon placed his brother Joseph on the Spanish throne, national policies shrewdly shifted to take full advantage of the new situation. The Jefferson administration imperiously applied the non-transfer principle to the Floridas and Cuba, and informally conveyed assurances of American friendship and sympathy to the local leaders in West Florida.

The political climate in West Florida came increasingly to favor an American takeover. The deposition of the Spanish king and competition among rival juntas for the loyalty of the Spanish people swept away the political moorings of Spanish subjects in West Florida. The Spanish government could no longer provide them with more than token protection. American settlers in increasing numbers had migrated to and established residence in West Florida. Moreover, the popular and able Carlos de Grand Pré had been succeeded by Don Carlos Dehault Delassus whose administration was both inept and corrupt. At about this time leaders in Washington decided to send emissaries into the troubled territory to read the public pulse and nudge the local inhabitants to initiate action themselves.

When Governor Claiborne visited Washington in 1810 he consulted at length with President Madison about intervention in Florida. To the insistent governor, nature had "decreed the union of Florida with the United States, and the welfare of her inhabitants demands it." He expressed the hope that American intervention would come in response to an invitation from the West Florida inhabitants and he inquired about the possibility of arranging the invitation. In mid-June the president authorized Claiborne to write to Judge William Wykoff, Jr. of Pointe Coupée and request that he go to West Florida and inform the inhabitants that the United States would welcome them. Having offered such assurances, Wykoff would encourage them to arrange a popular convention and make a formal request for annexation to the United States. Madison wrote to Wykoff and William H. Crawford of Georgia six days later, enclosed a letter explaining the president's Florida policy, and solicited their assistance in the selection of "gentlemen of honor & discretion qualified to execute a trust of such interest & delicacy." [2] Thus the groundwork was laid for a smooth assumption of authority in West Florida by the United States while Claiborne was closeted with senior administration officials in Washington.

The revolutionary movement began in Feliciana and Baton Rouge parishes in the western part of West Florida, but it spread immediately to St. Helena and St. Tammany (Tangipahoa) parishes. Feliciana was the wealthiest and most densely populated of the parishes, and Americans who had arrived recently from the Mississippi Territory were clearly in the majority. The Feliciana residents called a meeting and selected Fulwar Skipwith to write a constitution, and similar meetings were held shortly afterward in the other three parishes. Fourteen representatives then met in a convention at St. John's Plains, fifteen miles from Baton Rouge, on July 25. The delegates chose John Rhea of Feliciana Parish as president of the convention whose objective at the moment was to share authority with Delassus. Most of the residents who participated in the meetings and convention favored the annexation of West Florida to the United States, but they were not prepared to make the bid overtly because they knew the federal government would be unable to act immediately, if at all. If they made their bid prematurely, Delassus might be able to secure reinforcements from Governor Folch or possibly from the Marquis de Someruelos, captain general of Cuba. After agreeing initially to share his responsibility with the convention leaders, Delassus declined to recognize their authority. One of the convention delegates informed Thomas B. Robertson, secretary of the Orleans Territory, that the convention would probably seek an alliance with England if the United States failed to respond to their overtures,[23] the basic purpose of which probably was to spur national leaders to action.

When the revolutionary leaders learned that Delassus had appealed to Folch and Someruelos for support, they made their bid. On the morning of September 22 John Rhea met with six convention members at St. Francisville. They decided to depose Delassus, seize the fort at Baton Rouge, and apply to Governor David Holmes of the Mississippi Territory for annexation to the United States. Colonel Philemon Thomas and a small force seized the fort without serious resistance and took Delassus captive during the predawn hours on September 23. Rhea and his six associates met at Baton Rouge two days later, drew up a statement explaining their action, and appealed for local support. On the following day they set the stage for annexation to the United States by proclaiming the independence of West Florida and selecting Fulwar Skipwith as president. The convention adjourned on October 11 after the delegates adopted measures to finance the new government and provide for its security. They also appointed a three-man committee of safety to administer the new government and formulate a constitution which would be submitted to the convention in November. An abortive mutiny subsequently occurred at Baton Rouge fort which necessitated another convention meeting from October 24 until October 28, during which time the delegates adopted the constitution formulated by the committee. Popular elections were held on November 10 to ratify the constitution and to elect representatives. The new legislature then convened at St. Francisville on November 26 and the West Florida government was formally inaugurated three days later.[24]

On October 27, the day before the West Florida convention ended its four-day emergency session, President Madison issued a proclamation. He declared that the lands lying south of the Mississippi Territory and extending eastward from the Mississippi River to the Perdido River belonged to the United States under the terms of the Treaty of Paris of April 30, 1803. The acquiescence of the United States in continued Spanish jurisdiction over the region after that date resulted not from uncertainty about the validity of the American claims, Madison declared, but rather was occasioned by a continuing desire to be conciliatory and the hope of obtaining a solution through diplomatic discussions. But continued delays, the development of a crisis, and a fear that the forbearance of the United States might be erroneously "construed into a dereliction of their title or an insensibility to the importance of the stake," caused the president to act. Nonetheless, the patronizing president declared his willingness to negotiate a mutually satisfactory settlement with Spanish leaders. At the same time Madison directed Governor Claiborne to implement the executive order and incorporate the region into the Orleans Territory.[25]

While some of these events were unfolding in Washington and West Florida, the inadequately informed governor impatiently marked time and worried. In late August he wrote to Secretary of State Robert Smith from New York that he had heard nothing further about West Florida since leaving Philadelphia. But if Madison needed him in West Florida he would leave within the hour. This indicated that a precise plan and timetable were not worked out during Claiborne's several days in Washington. Now seriously concerned about internal political developments in West Florida, Claiborne was particularly fearful that his arch-nemesis, Daniel Clark, would use the revolutionary leaders to serve his own selfish purposes. Clark's object, he ventured, was to consolidate his claim to several hundred thousand acres of land in West Florida which he had acquired from Morales.[26] The governor subsequently took passage and returned to New Orleans and awaited further developments.

After receiving instructions from Washington, Governor Claiborne went to Natchez on December 1 and worked out arrangements for the occupation of West Florida with Governor David Holmes. The two agreed that Holmes would go to St. Francisville to explain the government's action and smooth the way for a peaceful occupation of the territory. Claiborne would confer with senior military officers about the occupation, and would then proceed ahead of Colonel Leonard Covington and about four hundred regular troops to Pointe Coupée. The remaining available troops would follow when ready under the command of Colonel Zebulon M. Pike. Holmes arrived in St. Francisville on December 6 and discussed the president's proclamation, which Claiborne had printed upon arrival in Mississippi and had arranged to have distributed in St. Francisville on the previous evening, with interested local citizens. He had an informal and inconclusive conference with Skipwith who spoke of his desire to have West Florida come under American jurisdiction but was extremely disappointed by the president's decision to claim it under the terms of the Franco-American treaty. Holmes was still in St. Francisville when Skipwith and several legislators left for Baton Rouge where the next legislative session was scheduled to be held. Holmes proceeded to nearby Pointe Coupée the next day where he met Governor Claiborne by prearrangement. Claiborne, who was well received locally, proceeded to carry out his occupational task. The two governors conferred again that evening and agreed that Holmes should go on to Baton Rouge and make advance preparations. Claiborne would follow as soon as Covington and his military detachment joined him at Pointe Coupée. Holmes left the following morning and arrived in Baton Rouge the next day. Messengers had preceded Holmes with copies of the president's proclamation for local distribution, as they had at St. Francisville. Holmes learned that the West Florida legislature was again in session. That evening he conferred with Skipwith who told him that he had decided not to resist the American occupation. The next morning Holmes and Skipwith went to the Baton Rouge fort and conferred with Lieutenant Colonel John Ballenger, the commanding officer. Governor Claiborne and the military force arrived shortly afterward. Colonel Covington demanded the surrender of the fort, Colonel Ballenger hesitated for a tense moment before surrendering it, and the newly arrived forces raised the American flag over the place at about two o'clock on the afternoon of December 10. Governor Claiborne took possession of the Baton Rouge district and erected it into a county of the Orleans Territory. Over the next several days Claiborne extended American jurisdiction to the Pearl River and shortly afterward to the Pascagoula River. Mobile remained under Spanish jurisdiction because instructions from Washington explicitly forbade an attack on the Spanish garrison. The city was threatened for a time by Colonel Reuben Kemper and a hastily organized militia force organized under the standard of West Florida, a small force of regulars under Colonel Thomas Cushing, and a militia force under Colonel Richard Sparks, then in command at Fort Stoddert. However, the planned assault on Mobile was called off at the last moment upon learning of the federal prohibition.[27]

Fulwar Skipwith grudgingly reconciled himself to the American authority. On the day that Claiborne claimed Baton Rouge in the name of the United States, Skipwith growled that the transfer came about "under circumstances which I cannot at this moment reconcile with my ideas of honor, justice, and sound policy on the part of the Government under whose orders you act." About two weeks later and still smarting from Claiborne's forceful action, Skipwith wrote to John Graham, former secretary of the Orleans Territory and now chief clerk in the State Department, about the "hostile means & manner" by which Claiborne took possession of West Florida. Nonetheless, Skipwith expressed relief that he had been "redeemed" from "that high but perilous & painful situation, in which the People of Florida" had placed him. He expressed his gratitude for the magnanimity with which he and his followers had been treated by Claiborne after their surrender to his "victorious & all conquering arms." Finally, he conceded that Claiborne, after dividing West Florida into parishes, had acted commendably in the appointment of "Patriot Americans" to fill the new offices.[28]

While Skipwith expressed mixed emotions about the course of events, Claiborne communicated with his superiors in Washington about the acquisition. On December 24, 1810, he wrote to Secretary of the Treasury Gallatin from Baton Rouge and informed him that the occupation of West Florida was almost complete. The president's action had been well received in the Mississippi and Orleans territories and the western country generally. Aware of Federalist sentiment, particularly in New England, however, he was dubious about the reaction of the Atlantic states. No doubt remembering vividly the earlier criticism to which he and Wilkinson had been subjected for the expenses incurred in the Louisiana transfer, he boasted about his record of "prudent oeconomy" in West Florida. He estimated his expenses to be $1,800 or less in taking possession of the district. "Not a 'segar' has been smoked at public expence; and no 'capers' can be had here."[29]

The expansionist and expansive governor wrote to Jefferson on the same day and informed him that the occupation was almost complete. The Spaniards were still in possession of Mobile, the mouth of the Pascagoula River, and Christian Pass. He expected, however, to receive orders from Washington at any moment to expel them. Indeed, Claiborne saw no reason why the United States should not seize Cuba, reported to be in a state of revolution at the time and viewed by Claiborne as the real mouth of the Mississippi River. He exclaimed that he would love to see the American flag flying over Morro Castle. The nation that possessed Cuba, he prophesied, "may possibly at a future day command the Western country. But let that Island be ours, and the American Union is beyond the reach of change."[30]

It appeared for a time that some of Governor Claiborne's expansionist dreams would be realized, especially after the Madison administration was nudged along by a British protest over the American occupation of Baton Rouge. On January 3, 1811, Madison asked for and received authorization from Congress to occupy temporarily any part or parts of East Florida threatened by any foreign power or voluntarily relinquished by Spanish colonial authorities. Congress approved the use of the military and naval forces and appropriated $100,000 for this purpose, but on the condition that any occupied territory was to remain subject to negotiation. Continuing overtures were also made to Governor Vicente Folch to relinquish the province of Florida but he stubbornly refused and vowed to defend it at all costs in the absence of orders from a higher authority.[31] Having failed to secure its objective by negotiations and unwilling to settle the issue by military force, the Madison administration reconciled itself to modest territorial gains at the expense of the haughty but hapless and impotent dons. The waiting game would persist a few years longer; there was no doubt in Washington about the ultimate outcome.

Governor Claiborne had been restrained from erasing the Spanish enclaves and from continuing an eastern sweep by firm instructions from national leaders to avoid conflict with the Spaniards. Disappointed and frustrated by the Madison administration's failure to press its advantages over the Spaniards, he marked time in West Florida and then sullenly withdrew to New Orleans and turned his attention to less viscerally stimulating but nonetheless important territorial matters. Public interest had again turned to the territory's admission to statehood, but it was overshadowed for a time by the West Florida eruption in 1810.

The territorial legislature drew up a formal petition for statehood and presented it to Congress on March 12, 1810. Earlier claims to statehood, including the petition to Washington in 1804, had been argued as a right provided under the Franco-American treaty of 1803. The memorialists now solicited incorporation into the Union as a privilege. Whatever reasons had prompted rejection earlier, the petitioners now believed, had vanished. The loyalty of the Louisianians had remained steadfast during plots, conspiracies, and possible war with Spain. They protested against the "inconveniences" to which they had been subjected: the governor's veto, a judiciary that transcended the authority of the legislature, and a complex system of jurisprudence. The petitioners were also displeased because they were denied a voice in the selection of some public officers, and they resented the ignorance of municipal laws displayed by a number of public officials. The situation would have been even more intolerable, the memorialists declared, if Governor Claiborne had not been sympathetic to their situation and worked with them to improve it. They requested a waiver of the provision requiring a population of 60,000 people for statehood, contending that the Ordinance of 1787 should not be obligatory upon the Louisianians since they "stipulated, approved, accepted nothing; and the Ordinance with regard to us is a law like the others, emanating solely from your will." If the federal government waited until the Orleans Territory had 60,000 citizens, the memorialists feared the territory would never qualify. Although the territory was immense in size, the petitioners doubted that it would ever sustain appreciable population increases. The memorialists ended by proclaiming that acceptance by the United States would insure the friendship and devotion of the Louisianians.[12]

On April 9, almost a month after Senator William B. Giles of Virginia presented the petition, a bill providing for the admission of the Orleans Territory to statehood was introduced and accepted by the Senate. The House of Representatives, however, did not act on the measure. When Congress convened in December, George Poindexter, delegate from the Mississippi Territory, offered a bill for the admission of the Orleans Territory, enlarged by the addition of West Florida, to statehood. The lawmakers amended the bill to exclude West Florida as a part of the new state since West Florida remained subject to negotiation. If incorporated into the state, national leaders could no longer negotiate its status. Mainly from New England, the Federalists opposed the statehood bill because they feared an alliance between the southern and western states which would achieve national political domination. Addressing the House on January 14, 1811, Congressman Josiah Quincy of Massachusetts warned that passage of the measure might result in the dissolution of the Union. Nonetheless, the House passed the Enabling Act on the following day by a vote of 77 to 36. Some delay resulted when the Senate added the word "white" before "male citizens" as a qualification for electors to the constitutional convention. The House and Senate finally approved the amended bill and President Madison signed it on February 20, 1811. [33]

Territorial leaders made provisions over the succeeding months for the constitutional convention provided for in the Enabling Act. The legislature apportioned representation among the counties for a total of forty-five delegates. Governor Claiborne, falsely accused by some of his political opponents of being against statehood, issued a proclamation calling for the election of delegates on the third Monday in September. He directed the elected delegates to convene in New Orleans on the first Monday in November. The convention, however, got off to a slow and uncertain start because of widespread illness, resulting from what appeared to be a massive outbreak of yellow fever. John Watkins, who had resigned his position as judge four years earlier because of General Wilkinson's arbitrary arrests and who had savagely criticized Governor Claiborne for having allowed the general to trample civil authority, called the meeting to order on November 4. First observing that a number of delegates were absent, Watkins launched a harsh attack against Claiborne for being absent and for not having submitted the election returns to the legislature. Upon Watkin's motion the convention adjourned until November 18.[34]

A newspaper writer rebuked Watkins for his unprovoked attack on the governor. Watkins was well aware that Claiborne had been ill, the writer contended, and he challenged the ex-judge's accusation that Claiborne had neglected his duties. Indeed, asserted the governor's defender, Claiborne had made every effort to continue working despite his feverish condition and, having left the city for a time because of the delicate state of his health, had tried to return to New Orleans in time to prevent a delay in the convention proceedings. The governor arrived on November 5 and, according to the usual procedure, awaited notification that a quorum had been formed. Only then, the writer pointed out, were the election results to be submitted to the convention. The governor's apologist claimed that an attack on Claiborne by any other delegate could have been excused on the basis of excessive zeal, but from Watkins the criticism was the "first indices of a preconcerted attack meditated with all the reflexion of the most egregious uncandidness." [35]

When the convention resumed after the two-week hiatus, the delegates elected Julien Poydras as president over Claiborne's tormentor, Watkins, by a vote of 24 to 10.[36] Poydras, opening a lengthy address, spoke of the American government as being "the most perfect that the human mind has hitherto framed" and enumerated the many benefits it had provided. But, concluding the laudatory introduction, Poydras then lashed out at "that execrable Territorial Government, that monstrosity in the annals of free people." Having worked closely with the Claiborne administration despite strong personal reservations about the territorial government imposed on Louisianians by Congress, Poydras continued: "Let us hail our emancipation from that odious servitude which has cost us so dear; let us hail it, I say, with transports of gratitude, with that sensibility of soul, those emotions, those throbbings of the heart felt by a navigator when after, having been the sport of adverse winds, tempest tossed, fatigued, harassed, and on the point of perishing from want, he enters the port which is the object of his wishes and the hope of his fortune."[37]

Using the United States and the South Carolina constitutions as models, the delegates drafted a constitution which bore the imprint of both archetypes. The charter provided for the usual separation of powers. There was to be a state supreme court consisting of from three to five justices. The tribunal was to hold its sessions in the eastern district at New Orleans and in the western district at Opelousas. Seven district courts were to be established and the regular parish courts were to be continued. The legislative powers were to be vested in a general assembly consisting of a senate and house of representatives. To be eligible to serve in the lower house, one had to possess property worth $500, a requirement that was doubled for service in the senate. Further, those who participated in elections to the general assembly had to own at least fifty acres of land or pay taxes on equivalent property. Gubernatorial candidates had to be at least thirty-five years of age, have been residents of the state at least six years prior to filing, and possess property worth $5,000 or more, as shown on the tax list. Qualified voters were to cast votes for gubernatorial candidates at the same time they elected members of the legislature. After the legislature was convened, the two houses would meet jointly and select the governor from the two candidates getting the greatest number of votes. The selection by the lawmakers was to be strictly by preference since the constitution did not require them to choose the candidate who had received the greatest number of popular votes. The governor would serve a four-year term and would be ineligible to succeed himself.[38]

While formulating the constitutional draft and meeting the conditions for statehood, Governor Claiborne and the delegates acted to include West Florida in the new state. When he learned that the West Florida inhabitants had met about a month earlier to ask Congress for inclusion, Claiborne directed them to present their petition and assured them that the president and Congress wanted to include them in the "American family."[39] Then, on January 23, 1812, the day after the convention adopted the constitution, the territorial delegates drew up a memorial calling for the inclusion of West Florida in the state of Louisiana, rather than incorporate it into the Mississippi Territory. The memorialists declared explicitly that the inclusion of West Florida was not to be regarded as a condition for the admission of the Orleans Territory to statehood. Rather, while the inclusion of West Florida as a part of the state was desirable, they were prepared to accept statehood without it if necessary.[40]

Governor Claiborne also exerted as much influence as possible upon the Madison administration to act favorably on the petition for statehood. He told Gallatin that a delay would result in great local disappointment, and would "Augment the embarrassments which already attend the administration of the Temporary Government." After eight years the territorial government, he declared, was "viewed in the light of a Merchant on the eve of bankruptcy—distrusted by its former friends—abused by Enemies, and slighted by all."[41] In short, the national government's failure to support the bid would disappoint the Louisianians and embarrass him personally. But Claiborne's worries were without foundation. President Madison notified Congress in early March that Louisiana had fulfilled the requirements for admission to statehood. The House approved the measure on March 20 and the Senate took similar action eleven days later. President Madison signed the bill on April 8, 1812. The protracted and sometimes acrimonious battle for statehood had finally been concluded successfully. Six days after the new state came into existence Madison signed a bill extending the boundaries of Louisiana to include those lands lying south of the Mississippi Territory and east of the Mississippi River to the Pearl River. The addition was contingent upon approval by the Louisiana legislature and representation for the former West Florida inhabitants in that body. The state lawmakers fulfilled both conditions in August.[42]

Competition between the Orleans and Mississippi territories for West Florida ultimately resulted in a compromise settlement. When Governor Claiborne had written to Gallatin on February 18, 1811, during which time he expectantly awaited orders from the president to seize Mobile, he had expressed the hope that the Madison administration would permit him to extend American control to the Perdido River. He was inclined to think at the time that Congress would probably annex the area to the Mississippi Territory or give it territorial status. If the latter occurred, he recommended that Colonel Zebulon Pike, then in command at Baton Rouge, be appointed territorial governor.[43] Less than a week after the Orleans Territory was admitted to statehood, Congress extended the state's eastern boundaries to the Pearl River, but the Spanish presence east of the Pearl River was not removed until General Wilkinson captured Fort Charlotte just below Mobile in the spring of 1813. The national lawmakers later incorporated those lands lying between the Pearl and Perdido rivers into the Mississippi Territory.[44]

From the time he had met with national leaders in Washington in mid-1810 until the achievement of statehood two years later, Governor Claiborne had maintained a hectic and often almost frantic pace. During those two years he had survived another yellow-fever attack but each recurring illness after his initial seizure in 1804 had further eroded his general physical condition. He had suppressed a short-lived but violent slave insurrection in early 1811 and easily demonstrated that he could provide adequate internal security. But his primary preoccupation had been with the West Florida revolution and the opportunities it provided for territorial gain. As the West Florida furor receded, he worked with legislative leaders to formulate a constitutional draft acceptable to the president and Congress and to fulfill the other conditions required for statehood. Throughout the eight-year territorial period, he had engaged in an ongoing political thrust and parry with "Clark, Livingston, & Company" and their coterie who worked unceasingly to effect his political demise. He had not achieved full acceptance by the haughty Creole elite despite his position and marriage into the prominent Duralde family. As statehood became a reality and fully cognizant of the political liabilities he had accumulated over the preceding eight years, Governor Claiborne quite naturally pondered his uncertain political future.

XI

LOUISIANA: POLITICS, REDMEN, AND THE BARATARIANS

From the moment he entered the gubernatorial race, Governor Claiborne knew he would have to contend with the exclusive Creoles who would field their own candidates and with the partisan machinations of "Clark, Livingston, & Company."

As the election campaign heated up, Claiborne bled freely from the political lacerations inflicted by both opposition camps. An "ancient inhabitant" expressed concern and dismay because Claiborne's political prospects were improved by the emergence of three Creole candidates. Asserting stoutly that a *sine qua non* should be that any candidate aspiring to the governorship should be a native, he implored: "Reflect upon it, O my countrymen, our honor, and our interest claim a Creole."[1] Six days afterward "A Louisianian" called upon the people to awaken from a century of slumber. The happiness and prosperity of the people would be assured, he declared, if they elected Jacques Villeré, a Creole.[2]

Three weeks later a committee of local leaders encouraged the Creoles to close ranks and attacked Claiborne's record as chief executive. They inquired rhetorically if the person elected as governor should be a Creole or a newcomer, and whether he should be one who knew their language. The committee members contended that the question should be determined by feelings rather than by logic and reason. It naturally followed then that the new chief executive should be a Creole who could converse easily and freely in the native language. Moreover, the committee charged that Governor Claiborne was ineligible and unfit for the office. He had held the posts of governor and Indian commissioner simultaneously when the federal Constitution forbade the holding of more than one federal post. Claiborne was also attempting to violate the spirit of the state constitution, the committee charged, which prohibited a governor from succeeding himself. Claiborne was unfit because he had approved laws "subversive of every principle of free government." Furthermore, he had neglected the militia except in his annual addresses, and had been unable to cope with the abortive slave insurrection of the previous year.[3]

A more visceral critic who identified himself as "Phocion" asserted flatly that circumstances had allowed Claiborne a position not intended by nature. "Scarcely capable of turning a wheel in the movement of government, you have, by some odd disposition of affairs, had the direction of the machine." Predicting that Claiborne would be turned out naked and forlorn, the critic declared that the people would look back and wonder that "so Pigmy an agent could occasion so Giant a mischief." He dutifully reminded the electorate that the governor had made a ballroom incident a national affair. "Phocion" castigated Claiborne for his efforts to cast the judiciary into disrepute and for his partisan appointments. He vowed to expose the chief executive in all of his mediocrity, to point out his vain boastings, and added scornfully: "the funeral pomp and soberness of your manners (so interestingly copied by some of your satellites) are the assumptions of a child of obscurity without one single qualification to support them." The voters, he predicted, "will sweep you (together with the lacqueys of your power, the beings you have engendered to encumber our soil, like vermin on the lion's crest) into an insignificance something worse than mere oblivion." Since Claiborne had calumniated and traduced the Louisianians, it was inconceivable to "Phocion" that he should then appeal for popular support. Although "Phocion" advised Claiborne to withdraw from the race because it would result in shame and defeat for him, he hardly thought Claiborne would accept his advice, saying: "I am sufficiently acquainted with you to know that any appeal to the rectitude of your head, or to the humanity of your heart, would be ineffective and absurd."[4] "Phocion" returned to the attack two days later, proclaiming that he had not met a person who would suggest that Claiborne was a man of talent. Rather, even those who were kindly disposed toward Claiborne could say only that the governor was not as great a fool as he was generally represented.

One did not have to look beyond Washington's valedictory address to determine his greatness, Claiborne's detractor wrote, and added caustically: "If Mr. Claiborne's reputation could only be put, however sophistically, on a similar basis, I could almost have the courtesy to give up the point." Even Solomon would be unable to comprehend why Claiborne was assigned to a post requiring wisdom and virtue. A few days later "Phocion" remarked that a partisan had spoken of Claiborne as being a countryman of Washington, to which he retorted that Titus Oates was also a countryman of Alfred the Great.⁵

Another critic rebuked the governor for his aloofness. He had not mingled among the masses except as "HIS EXCELLENCY." The people were subjects; their problems went unnoticed in the palace. He also criticized Claiborne for seeking a ninth year in office because it was a flagrant violation of the precedent set by Washington and Jefferson. Yet Claiborne was unwilling "to let go the *sceptre* until the killing letter of your constitution wrests it from him."⁶

A week before the voters were scheduled to go to the polls "An Elector" proclaimed that he was writing to obtain a hearing. He charged that Claiborne had filled posts with his own "creatures," many of whom were "phantoms of public officers." Although the governor actually knew very little about the militia, he displayed much ridiculous zeal. The governor consulted almost every person he met, according to the "Elector," and armed the people indiscriminately. Having been condemned earlier by the Creoles for introducing the English common-law system into Louisiana, Governor Claiborne was now accused by the "Elector," apparently a newcomer to the state himself, of blocking its introduction.⁷

Although Claiborne had several vocal opponents, he also had a number of ardent supporters. Indeed, with the governorship at stake and in view of his sensitivity to criticism, Claiborne probably inspired, either directly or indirectly, some of the newspaper paeans. Moreover, Claiborne had been carefully but unobtrusively laying the groundwork for his political bid long before such Creole leaders as Jacques Villeré and Jean-Noël Destréhan mounted campaigns to replace him. Following Claiborne's trip to Washington and his assignment in West Florida, a partisan wrote in early 1811 that Claiborne's return was like that of a father to his family. Intimating that there were those who had sought to undermine Claiborne during his absence, the defender spoke of profligate and ungrateful children "who may blush to see the parent who has made sacrifices for their welfare." The federal government had given every proof of its faith and confidence in Claiborne. Consequently, every personal consideration should be swept aside and full support pledged to him if they, both Creoles and native Americans, approved and supported the general government. Justice to Claiborne, to property rights, and to the government required that a deaf ear be turned to those base calumniators whose machinations had "torn asunder the social compact by which society ought to be bound together."[8] Another supporter offered a strong defense of the Claiborne administration in mid-July. After attacking critics who refused to identify themselves, the partisan ended by declaring: "Let any man lay his hand upon his heart and say, whether it is possible, humanly speaking, for any man to have done more than Governor Claiborne has done during the course of his whole administration."[9]

Claiborne's adherents strove mightily to sell their candidate to the electorate as the campaign accelerated. "Quintus Curius" taunted "Phocion" and the opposition by saying they could print against Claiborne until doomsday, which he identified as election day, but "you might as well try to batter down the walls of Quebec with snowballs as to try to injure his election by your Philippics." As for his candidate's natural abilities, "Quintus Curius" declared expansively that Claiborne's "intuitive mind took no middle flight, but soaring far above youths of his age, he was filling the first offices at an age when others of more limited talents were poring over mouldy pages, seeking for what heaven had by inspiration bestowed upon him." In a methodical refutation of charges made by "Phocion," "Quintus Curius" contended that Claiborne possessed superior military talent, had faced dangers dauntlessly, had given the people security, and had made sound appointments. To those who favored a Creole for the governorship, "Quintus Curius" quipped that such action by the "unlearned natives" would simply mean that the blind would be leading the blind.[10]

Other more restrained Claiborne supporters entered the verbal fray while lamenting the volume of invective being heaped upon their candidate. "An American" pointed out that abuse merely excited sympathy for the abused. When the whole alpha and omega of accusation and scurrility were without supporting facts, the accusers themselves became suspect.[11] Another defender remarked that it was unnecessary to "descend into the infernal regions and there to stir up the bitter waters of the Acheron" in the selection of a governor. To those who accused Claiborne of weakness, the defender cautioned the people not to confuse affability with weakness. Responding to the charge that the governor had favored Americans over the Louisianians, the writer supplied a list of Creoles who had received appointments in the territorial and municipal governments but had refused to serve. Finally, in view of Claiborne's record, the writer asserted that even the governor's enemies could not seriously accuse him of being incompetent and unfit.[12]

A week before the election another Claiborne partisan meticulously identified a number of people who opposed the governor and explained why. The people knew that Edward Livingston was fighting Claiborne, he declared, because the governor had consistently opposed his claim to the Batture. John Watkins opposed him, the writer accused, because Claiborne had replaced him as mayor of New Orleans. He admitted that he was not aware of the reasons why certain other local leaders supported the opposition candidates. Nonetheless, he concluded obliquely that the stakes must have been sufficiently attractive for them to join Livingston in his effort to unseat Claiborne.[13]

At about the same time "A Louisianian" pointed out that some local critics of the Claiborne administration were intimating that not to have been born in Louisiana constituted a crime. Claiborne's opponents had accused him of evincing "frigid apathy, supineness and an egregious want of military skill, at the time of the insurrection of the slaves." Others contended that Claiborne's conduct was above reproach. It was inconceivable, the "Louisianian" proclaimed, that anyone could be the object of such contradictory assertions. But even as he defended the governor's ability and record, the "Louisianian" readily conceded that the opposition had fielded some worthy candidates. Therefore, the voters should make their choices on the basis of objectivity, not because of emotional issues and subjective reasoning.[14]

Aside from his own personal preference, the "Louisianian" put the campaign and the candidates in proper perspective. Moreover, with the exception of the newcomer versus native feature, the political campaign could just as easily have transpired in almost any state in the Union. As expected, charges made by Claiborne's opponents ranged from outright incompetence, personal aloofness, and inability to speak French, to favoritism toward American newcomers in filling appointive offices, the imposition of American institutions on the natives, and actual or intended constitutional violations. To Claiborne's partisan adherents, on the other hand, their candidate possessed outstanding native abilities and had provided unexampled leadership. Although Claiborne had served as chief executive for almost nine years and had engaged in some stormy encounters with his opponents, no unusual or sensational disclosures surfaced or were even hinted at during the campaign. Some personal invective was injected, but at no time was Claiborne or his administration accused of corruption, dishonesty, or malfeasance. If there had been a substantive basis for such charges, they certainly would not have gone unnoticed by either the Creoles or "Clark, Livingston, & Company." The closest critics had come to making a serious charge of irregularity was the "Elector's" oblique assertion that some of Claiborne's appointees were "phantoms of public officers."

Governor Claiborne himself was usually ambivalent about his political prospects. When assailed by his critics and in doubt about the ultimate outcome, he frequently assumed a posture of moral self-righteousness and indignation that a people could be so ungrateful and fickle. Almost eleven months before the election he had told Gallatin that the outcome would be in extreme doubt if the election were held then. Several enemies were working incessantly to end his political career, he lamented, in an indirect allusion to "Clark, Livingston, & Company." Nonetheless, he was exempt from self-reproach, he declared defensively, because his motives were pure and he had always acted on the basis of sound judgment.[15] On February 1, 1812, he complained to Secretary of Navy Paul Hamilton that the newspapers were groaning with abuse and attempting to convert the most meritorious acts into crimes. Although he had survived strong political buffeting for over eight years, Claiborne expressed uncertainty about his ability to surmount the calumnious shafts and political intrigue. Yet he vowed to fight it out, asserting dramatically: "Clouds are now arising & a Tempest [is] near at hand;—Its rage may drive me into port—But never from my duty." To Robert R. Livingston, who was seeking navigation rights on the Mississippi River, Claiborne lamented that people often looked askance upon those who had long served in a public capacity and sometimes cast them aside "with as little Ceremony, as they would an old Coat."[16] At other times Claiborne ventured cautious predictions that he would win, especially if he carried the interior counties. On June 25, 1812, four days before the election, he appeared resigned to the outcome declaring that his mind was in that state which was regarded in the scriptures as being desirable: "Happy is the man who expects nothing, for if he gets nothing he will not be disappointed."[17] In facing up to the exactions of the political campaign, Claiborne displayed contrasting emotions. Forcefulness clashed head on with timidity, determination with resignation, and confidence with uncertainty. Although he infrequently appeared to be casually indifferent to the sharp political volleys of his opponents, he usually reacted privately with hurt self-pity.

Engrossed by the sound and fury of the campaign and beset by harsh criticisms from rival political camps, Governor Claiborne had no real perception of his basic political strength either among the people generally or among the elected leaders. As a result probably no one was more surprised than the innately modest Claiborne as the election returns trickled in and it became increasingly obvious that his victory had assumed landslide proportions. Even in New Orleans, which the governor fully expected to lose to a native candidate, he won decisively. Although he carried every county in the state, he achieved an almost complete sweep in some. He received a total of 3,757 popular votes compared to 1,947 for Jacques Villeré, and a mere 268 votes for Jean-Noël Destréhan who had been one of his most persistent political opponents. According to the state constitution, the general assembly would then choose the governor from the two candidates who received the greatest number of votes. The Creoles easily dominated the new legislature; if they closed ranks, Claiborne would still lose. Nevertheless, the general assembly met on July 28 and selected Claiborne over Villeré by an astounding vote of 35 to 6.[18]

Governor Claiborne was obviously the overwhelming choice of the Louisianians and he had every reason to take personal pride in his political triumph. The people had been disappointed by the national government's refusal to grant statehood to Louisiana for several years and they resented the territorial government, but they obviously had not held Claiborne personally responsible. In their view, Claiborne had made the best of an unfortunate situation. He had been sympathetic to their plight and to their wishes and aspirations unless they too clearly contravened the policies of the Jefferson and Madison administrations and national interests. The people had been disappointed by Claiborne's meek submissiveness when Wilkinson had trampled on the civil authority five years earlier, but they had approved his handling of the border crises, the Burr conspiracy, and the West Florida "revolution." He had stamped out the slave insurrection in early 1811, further reinforcing popular feelings that the territorial government could provide the necessary protection and security. He had won much popular goodwill by opposing Livingston's claim to the Batture, and his marriage into the Duralde family probably enhanced his political stature among Louisianians. Although war with England had already erupted before the popular election was held, news of the American declaration of war did not reach Louisiana until over a week later and therefore did not appreciably influence its outsome. The war, however, probably explains Claiborne's lopsided victory in the general assembly on July 28. In the broader sense, Claiborne's triumph could be interpreted as a victory for the United States. The governor's patience, perseverance, and generally sound judgement had contributed greatly to the assimilation of Louisianians. The native people not only had voted to be admitted to the Union, but their assimilation was further confirmed by the fact that they chose an American as their first elected governor over a highly respected Creole.

Although Governor Claiborne easily won the election, his efforts as governor continued to be impeded and frustrated by his enterprising opponents as they had done during the territorial period. They lost the governorship to him but they elected a number of their candidates to Congress which enabled them to control much of the federal patronage in Louisiana. Edward Livingston made unsuccessful bids for the Senate and House of Representatives, but Jean-Noël Destréhan was elected to the Senate by the general assembly and Thomas B. Robertson, territorial secretary and another political antagonist, easily won election to the House of Representatives.[19] Destréhan, however, resigned before taking his seat in the Senate, and Governor Claiborne appointed Thomas Posey to replace him. Allan B. Magruder, whom Claiborne viewed as a man of ability but apparently was not closely identified with any political faction, was chosen as Louisiana's other senator. The governor did display some slight concern because of Magruder's "former unfortunate attachment . . . to drink." Claiborne's opponents also elected several representatives to the state legislature and then, to embarrass and hamper his administration, a number of those who were elected refused to serve.[20] Claiborne largely controlled the house of representatives but the senate stubbornly opposed his policies and blocked a number of his appointments.[21]

In an address to the legislature on July 30, 1812, Governor Claiborne informed the lawmakers that one of their first duties should be to establish a supreme court and to improve the organization of the inferior courts. In the discharge of these responsibilities, vested in the legislature by the state constitution, Claiborne admonished the legislators to utilize their knowledge of the prevailing situation in the counties and "the habits & sentiments of your Constitution." In making his recommendations he requested that they not act too hastily or to mistake innovation for reform. A month later he asked that the judges be relieved of the responsibility of collecting taxes, pointing out that this burden had caused a number of judges to resign and that he was having difficulty finding qualified personnel to fill the vacancies.[22]

The lawmakers cooperated by passing the legislation necessary to organize the judiciary. A supreme court consisting of three justices was to be established with two justices constituting a quorum. They provided for seven circuit courts, and they retained the parish courts but with diminished authority, as Claiborne had recommended.[23] Although the judiciary had remained a source of continuing controversy, the implementation of the act appeared generally routine since the judicial system had been functioning with limited success for several years. The organization of the parish and circuit courts proceeded smoothly, but differences between the executive and legislative branches of government delayed the organization of the state supreme court until early 1813. Governor Claiborne nominated Pierre Derbigny and George Mathews, Jr. to positions on the state supreme court and the senate routinely confirmed them. That body, however, refused to confirm his third appointment and attempted instead to select its own candidate for the post. A critic lashed out at the obduracy of both the governor and senate since they were aware that the supreme court could not be organized and proceed constitutionally until the appointment was confirmed.[24] Judge Dominic A. Hall of the Federal District Court ultimately accepted the appointment to the state bench and the problem appeared to be resolved since Claiborne was at last able to organize the court. But when Hall returned to the federal court in 1814 and Claiborne appointed a successor the battle was renewed. A newspaper critic blamed the governor for the resulting impasse, charging that he deliberately delayed the nomination until the legislature was ready to adjourn. By doing this, the critic accused, Claiborne was attempting to force the senate to accept his nomination or be accused of obstructing justice. The senate had its own nominee for the vacated post, in fact, having resolved by a vote of 14 to 3 that James Brown, a critic of the Claiborne administration, be appointed. Again rising to the legislative challenge, Claiborne curtly reminded the senate that it was his responsibility to make appointments and added bluntly that he had no intention of taking "shelter under the Senate." If the senate considered an appointment unwise it could withhold confirmation, but he would not give up his appointive power.[25] As a result the governor made a number of appointments to fill the vacancy and the senate proceeded just as methodically to reject them.

As a backlog of cases developed, and Claiborne finally became convinced that a mutually acceptable replacement for Judge Hall could not be found at the time, the governor requested a number of advisory opinions from Attorney General François-Xavier Martin who had served earlier as a superior court judge. Although the state constitution stipulated that two justices constituted a quorum, Claiborne asked specifically if two judges could legally conduct judicial sessions. Second, he asked about the possibility of making a recess appointment as a possible solution to the dilemma. Third, Claiborne wanted to know whether he should exercise his power of appointment independently of senatorial pressures. The attorney general agreed that two justices could conduct the business of the court. He ruled against recess appointments, but supported the governor's position on regular appointments, declaring that he should rebuff all efforts by the senate to influence nominations.[26] Although Martin's ruling enabled the supreme court to resume its normal judicial functions, repeated clashes between the chief executive and legislature continued to impede governmental effectiveness throughout Claiborne's elective term.

Peace had prevailed throughout the territorial period despite recurring threats of war between the United States and Great Britain. Governor Claiborne therefore had benefited from American neutrality by focusing his energies and resources on territorial problems and introducing American institutions in

Louisiana. War with England, however, had preceded Claiborne's inauguration as the state's first elective governor by several weeks and added to the complexity and delicacy of his tasks. After the United States and Great Britain stumbled into war, the British encouraged the Indian tribes to join them in the conflict and avenge Indian losses and humiliations at the hands of the Americans. Moreover, this came at a time when the Indians had an excellent leader in the person of the politically astute Tecumseh, thought to have been of Shawnee and Creek ancestry. Tecumseh was convinced that Indian survival was contingent upon the unification of the tribes through the establishment of a great Indian confederacy. Apprehensive and nervous about the intentions of the Indian tribes, Governor Claiborne employed his usual stratagems to insure Indian neutrality in the Anglo-American conflict.

The governor was particularly concerned about the Choctaws since the Creeks were exerting pressures on neighboring tribes to align themselves with the British. In addition to sending an agent among them to secure information and keep them pacified, Governor Claiborne addressed the Choctaw leaders personally. Having earlier appealed to the Indians not to become involved in white controversies, he implored the Choctaws to maintain neutrality. He reminded them of the earlier fate of the Creeks, Cherokees, and others who allied themselves with the British during the American Revolutionary War. The "big knife Men" burned their homes and fields and forced the Indian women and children to seek refuge elsewhere. For their efforts on behalf of the English, they had received only a few "shirt Blankets, some kegs of Rum, & two or three dozen Medals made of bad Mettle." He asked the Choctaw leaders if they had been approached by either Tecumseh or the Prophet and warned them not to be influenced by them. At the same time he asked them to use their influence against the more precipitate Creeks. The war had been provoked by the English who had seized American property, impressed American citizens into the English navy, and shed American blood. Thirty years earlier, Claiborne reminded the Choctaws, the English had fought the Americans and had been forced to accept peace on American terms. Having attained greater maturity and strength, the United States was much more formidable. If the Indians remained neutral in this conflict between whites, Claiborne assured them: "Your squaws & little

Children will rest undisturbed in their Cabbins, Your old Men will discourse & smoke without fear, under the shade of the Tree, & your Warriors may hunt & dance & be merry until they have an enemy of their own to strike."[27] Despite the activities of British agents and the efforts of the Creeks, the Choctaws heeded the governor's appeal and remained neutral throughout the war. This was probably due in part to the personal influence of Claiborne, who in preceding years in both the Orleans and Mississippi territories had dealt fairly and honorably with the Choctaws and other Indian tribes and had consistently appealed to Indian leaders to remain aloof from conflict which did not concern them and which would work only to their disadvantage.

Governor Claiborne also made special efforts to keep the Caddo Indians, whom he considered to be the most influential Indian tribe in the Red River country, from joining the Creeks against the United States. On October 18, 1813, he sent them a "talk" from Natchitoches. The Caddoes were at war with the Osage Indians at the time which Claiborne shrewdly seized upon in his personal appeal. The governor declared that the Great Spirit had placed an abundance of game at the disposal of the Indians but the Osages had robbed other tribes. The Osages among the whites, Claiborne cunningly observed, were the English. The "big water" was great enough for all, but the English had plundered and committed outrages against the others. They had seized American vessels and property, they had pressed American citizens into service aboard their "war canoes," and they had forced them to fight their native countrymen. The English were also attempting to enlist Indian support, the governor continued, but they would be unable to shield those Indians from American vengeance who bowed to British pressures and spilled innocent American blood. Having eloquently presented a case for Caddo neutrality, Claiborne ended his "talk" by promising their chieftain a sword as a gift.[28] The small Caddo tribe, traditionally close to the United States, remained at peace.

American successes with the Choctaws, Caddoes, and other Indian tribes did not extend to the Creek Nation. On June 20, 1813, Creek braves slaughtered a number of fellow tribesmen who were sympathetic to the United States, which convinced Claiborne that they would soon seek American scalps. A few weeks later Governor Claiborne reported that the Creeks had failed to secure arms from the Spaniards at Pensacola, but he assumed nonetheless that the English would be able to enlist their support. On August 1, 1813, he informed James Monroe that seven hundred Creek warriors presumably had crossed the Perdido River to make war on the United States.[29] In late August he told Andrew Jackson that the British, having moved into Pensacola, were training the Creek warriors and providing them with arms, clothing, and provisions. The governor's apprehensions were increased further by rumors that some of the leading subordinates of Big Warrior, the Creek chieftain, were conferring at Pensacola with Captain George Woodbine, a British officer who later led the Indians in an attack against Fort Bowyer at Mobile.[30] Within hours after Claiborne's warning to Jackson, some Creek hotbloods struck Fort Mims on the lower Alabama River above Mobile and slaughtered 350 men, women, and children who had concentrated there for protection. Upon learning of the massacre the governor directed his militia colonels to maintain strict vigilance, and he asked Louisiana's Senator Eligius Fromentin to use his influence to expedite an arms shipment then being filled by the quartermaster general in Pittsburgh and consigned to Louisiana.[31] Claiborne also visited Attakapas, Baton Rouge, Lafourche, Natchitoches, Opelousas, and St. Tammany to check on local militia capabilities and prevent a possible Indian massacre in Louisiana. While in Natchitoches he also met with the Caddo Indian chieftain.[32] But the Creeks were never able to repeat the Fort Mims triumph. Instead, Andrew Jackson and his militia forces pressed them relentlessly and destroyed their war-making capabilities at Horseshoe Bend (Tohopeka) on March 27, 1814. Jackson then compelled the thoroughly chastened Creeks to sign a treaty at Fort Jackson, located near the confluence of the Coosa and Tallapoosa rivers, on August 9, 1814.[33] Although the militia forces maintained some vigilance, the Indian threat on the southwestern frontier was largely eradicated by the wholesale Creek slaughter.

During the same period in which the Fort Mims massacre sent tremors throughout much of the southwest, Governor Claiborne finally acted to remove a problem which had plagued him increasingly since 1803. Using the island of Barataria (Grande Terre) as a base of operations, a notorious band of freebooters engaged in piracy and smuggling in defiance of the local and federal authorities. Jean Laffite, reported to have been born in Bordeaux, France, was the leader of the "hellish banditti," as Andrew

Jackson once called them. He was ably assisted by his brother Pierre, an experienced seaman, and several lieutenants in the Baratarian Association. The Baratarians had become an institution in Louisiana and enjoyed considerable support from the people who were able to avail themselves of their plunder at bargain prices. Jean Laffite contended that Governor Claiborne sanctioned their "mercantile" activities for some time, and that he had personally examined their silks and quality fabrics in 1805 and had even accepted some as a gift. As the Baratarians continued to expand their activities Claiborne became increasingly uncomfortable but was restrained for some time, according to Jean, by John Grymes, who resigned as a United States Attorney to serve as a lawyer for the Laffites. Finally, Claiborne openly declared his opposition to the Baratarians in 1812, but popular support mounted for the freebooters when he seriously attempted to stamp out the illicit traffic. [34]

On March 15, 1813, the exasperated governor issued a proclamation in which he charged that the Baratarians, who preferred to regard themselves as privateers sailing under commissions from Cartagena and France, were committing depredations and preying upon ships belonging to nations which were at peace with the United States. Goods and merchandise taken from the captured ships were then sold to the local inhabitants. Claiborne ordered the buccaneers to cease their activities and break up. Further, he warned the inhabitants of the state to have nothing to do with the Baratarians and asked them to assist the civil and military authorities in their efforts to halt the flow of contraband. In his ringing appeal Claiborne, who apparently thought mistakenly that local sentiment toward the Baratarians had changed enough to enable him to move aggressively against the pirates, beseeched the people to "rescue Louisiana from the foul reproach" resulting from the asylum afforded the Baratarians in the state and local toleration of their activities. No person could avail himself of their "ill begotten treasure," he exclaimed indignantly, "without being forever dishonored, and exposing himself to the severest punishment."[35]

The proclamation had no substantive effect on the illegal traffic. Following this initial action against the Baratarians, a lively personal rivalry blossomed between Jean Laffite, who regarded himself as "an errant liberator of the suffering masses," and Claiborne, who viewed himself as the protector of the people. The authorities initiated litigation against Jean and Pierre Laffite in the United States District Court on April 7, 1813. They charged them with violations of the revenue and neutrality laws of the United States but they did not formally accuse them of piracy. The Laffites and some of their assoicates were captured and held in custody for a time, but no convictions were forthcoming.[36] When the Laffites recaptured some goods taken from them earlier by Walker Gilbert, a revenue officer, Governor Claiborne again appealed to the people in a second proclamation issued on November 24, 1813. He rebuked the Louisianians for their apathy, implored them to assist the enforcement officers, and urged the apprehension of the Baratarians. As an incentive he offered a reward of $500 for the capture of Jean Laffite.[37] Not to be outdone, the bold Laffite reciprocated with a reward of $15,000 for the apprehension of the governor which he had posted publicly on November 27.[38]

Neither reward was collected and the tug-of-war continued, as did the traffic in illicit goods. Following a skirmish between the Baratarians and revenue officers in early 1814, Governor Claiborne made two appeals to the legislature for assistance in coping with the arrogant freebooters. In his second appeal to the legislature on March 2, 1814, Claiborne, aware that the Baratarians had several artillery pieces on the island for defense, asked the lawmakers to provide the means to "disperse these desperate men on Lake Barataria, whose piracies have rendered our shores a terror to neutral flags, and diverted from New Orleans that lucrative intercourse with Vera Cruz and other neutral ports which formerly filled our banks with the richest deposits."[39] But again his appeal fell on deaf ears.

Aside from the arrest and imprisonment of Pierre Laffite for a short time, the Baratarians continued to defy Claiborne with impunity. On August 21, 1814, Claiborne told Andrew Jackson that the Baratarians were continuing to violate "all laws human and divine." He spoke of having tried unsuccessfully to persuade the legislature to provide for a militia force to destroy the pirate stronghold. Since the legislature had steadfastly refused to support his appeals, he said, the responsibility devolved upon the United States. Therefore, the governor had consulted with Colonel G. T. Ross of the Forty-Fourth Regiment and Commodore Daniel L. Patterson, who had succeeded Captain John Shaw of the New Orleans naval command. The two men at the time were drawing up plans for a joint land and sea assault against the pirate stronghold.[40] At the last minute, however, Claiborne sought to block the move because of the imminent invasion of Louisiana by British forces, thinking he might be able to enlist the support of the Baratarians against the invaders. Nonetheless, using the schooner *Carolina* and available gunboats, Patterson and Ross proceeded with the attack and overran Barataria.[41]

Following the successful assault, Claiborne reported to Jackson that the pirate ships and booty had been seized but that the Laffites and a number of their accomplices had managed to elude the invasion force and escape. In fact, some had found refuge among contacts and sympathizers in New Orleans itself. Jackson responded shortly afterward, warning the governor to take every possible precaution against the "wretches." He was particularly fearful that the pirates might attempt to burn New Orleans in retaliation for the destruction of their operational base.[42]

Several weeks afterward Governor Claiborne reported the dispersal of the Baratarians and the seizure of their cruisers and contraband to United States Attorney General Richard Rush. He readily conceded that his efforts to educate and convince the native inhabitants that smuggling was a moral offense had been only partially successful at best. After all, he pointed out, smuggling had become a tradition in Louisiana. Moreover, a number of Louisianians or their ancestors had been freebooters and smugglers at an earlier time and this constituted a source of family pride. Indeed, Claiborne suggested that some of the state's most exemplary leaders actively or tacitly sanctioned smuggling for these reasons and because of the competitive prices offered by the smugglers. Having explicated the primary reasons why smuggling had achieved widespread popular acceptance in Louisiana, Claiborne discussed the fate of the apprehended Baratarians. The Federal District Court was ready to begin legal proceedings against the smugglers and the governor wished to intercede in behalf of all but the most blatant offenders. "Justice demands that the more Culpable be punished with severity—but I see no good end to be attained by making the penalties of the law to fall extensively and heavily. The example is not the less imposing by circumscribing the number of victims, and the mercy which should dictate it, seldom fails to make a salutary and lasting impression." The governor ended his appeal by saying that while some of his fellow countrymen heartily disagreed, he was convinced that "as much may be done with the Louisianians by a mild policy, and the act of persuasion, as any People I ever knew. Such impression has always influenced my public conduct."[43]

The governor's plea for leniency for the Baratarians derived chiefly from his personal philosophy toward the punishment of crime and the government of the Louisianians, as expressed in his communication to Rush. Also as he explained to the attorney general, smuggling was indeed firmly entrenched in Louisiana and had become a way of life with its exciting and romantic implications. Moreover, Claiborne was clearly influenced in his plea for leniency by the support provided by the Baratarians in the repulse of the British invasion force. As a result of this support, President Madison issued a proclamation in which he pardoned the Baratarians for offenses committed prior to January 8, 1815.[44]

The Laffite band received the presidential pardon, but Governor Claiborne remained understandably cautious despite his expressed sympathy. Having painfully observed their illicit operations in open defiance of his administration for twelve years, he was not so naive as to think that the free-wheeling ex-Baratarians had undergone a spiritual regeneration. On April 5, 1815, as New Orleans was again settling into a state of normality, he alerted Commodore Patterson and the naval command in New Orleans when he detected some suspicious activities. He had reason to believe that a ship which had sailed a few days earlier from New Orleans had captured two craft in the Gulf of Mexico. He identified the captain of the pirate ship as Vincent Gambier, formerly one of the chieftains of the "Baratarian Association." No expense should be spared, he exhorted the New Orleans naval command, to stamp out such nefarious activities and prevent the resumption of the piratical and smuggling activities of the earlier period.[45]

As the governor anticipated, the Laffites and many of their followers did not avail themselves of the presidential pardon to begin life anew as law-abiding citizens of Louisiana. Instead, they continued to prowl the Gulf of Mexico from such bases as Galveston and Port-au-Prince following the brief hiatus. They preyed upon gulf shipping generally, but Spanish commerce in particular suffered heavily as a result of their exploits. They apparently made no serious attempt, however, to reestablish themselves in Barataria or to resume an illicit trade with the Louisianians as they had done earlier. The American expedition against the pirate stronghold and the presidential pardon had convinced the colorful and romantic freebooters that the privileges and opportunities they had known previously no longer existed. Furthermore, the growing enforcement capabilities of the state and federal authorities in the coastal areas made the risks increasingly prohibitive even if popular attitudes toward the smugglers had not changed appreciably. And having achieved major success at long last, Governor Claiborne had absolutely no intention of allowing the problem to resurface.

XII

LOUISIANA: THE WAR OF 1812 AND ITS AFTERMATH

The Bartarian buccaneers cast their lot with the United States in the critical battle of New Orleans, but they and the options available to them were exceptional to say the least. The position of the Louisianians generally was a completely different matter. Throughout the territorial period Governor Claiborne had noted carefully the political and diplomatic pyrotechnics between London and Washington from his distant post in New Orleans. When recriminations between the two countries threatened to produce a recourse to arms, he had naturally pondered the probable reaction of his native constituency. In view of their Gallic origins, the Creoles were hardly likely to rush headlong into a Britannic embrace to escape what they sometimes regarded in moments of exasperation and pique as a crude, odious, and oppressive American overlordship. Barring such an untoward development, Louisianians would probably react in one of three ways. First, they might adopt a "pox on both houses" demeanor and "sit out" the war. Second, they might view the United States as the lesser of two evils and offer detached support. Third, they might commit their loyalties and resources generally to the United States, while allowing themselves sufficient latitude in which to assert their French prerogatives and thereby maintain an element of exhilarating uncertainty. Meanwhile, Governor Claiborne, a perceptive judge of native character and disposition, conveyed his tentative impressions to his superiors in Washington and nervously awaited tests of their validity. But at the same time the governor pondered the loyalties and attachments of Louisianians and eagerly followed the course of international developments, he was also alert to any opportunities that might accrue to the United States as a result of the continuing European war.

When the *Leopard* forced the unprepared and unsuspecting *Chesapeake* to strike its colors during the summer of 1807 and American indignation and wrath threatened to produce war, Claiborne had assured the president that Louisianians would uphold the nation's honor. If war erupted, the governor felt they would "cheerfully meet their share of its dangers & Burthens." The government made intensive preparations for possible war, including congressional authorization to raise 100,000 militiamen, but emotions subsided somewhat and a brief period of relative quiescence followed. Relations again took a turn for the worse, however, when Great Britain insisted upon adherence to its Orders in Council and the American minister in London returned to the United States in 1811. As war fever again mounted in the United States, whetted by further naval clashes, Claiborne confided to Madison his belief that a confrontation with Great Britain was inevitable despite the peaceful disposition of American leaders. "At such a Crisis, our Nation will unquestionably be united," he assured the president, "& the Government firmly & bravely supported."[1] Yet as war became increasingly imminent, Claiborne laboriously attempted to reassure himself even more than the president of local loyalties. Louisianians had provided hesitant support during the tense boundary crisis in 1806 and the ensuing Burr fiasco, but doubts persisted.

Local newspaper appeals for unity increased as tensions mounted. On July 5, 1811, a writer implored Louisianians to compose their political differences in the face of threats from both Britain and France, and he castigated those who promoted discord at such a critical time. Shortly afterward another writer stated that England had always been a piratical country, and called upon Louisianians to unite solidly in opposition to that "despicable cabal, whose patriotism is a mere bale of foreign goods."[2] Others made similar appeals to the populace but their increasing frequency merely added to the prevailing air of uncertainty about native dispositions.

If doubts existed about the loyalty of Louisianians, there were also uncertainties about the extent to which the country at large would be united in the event of war. Governor Claiborne was

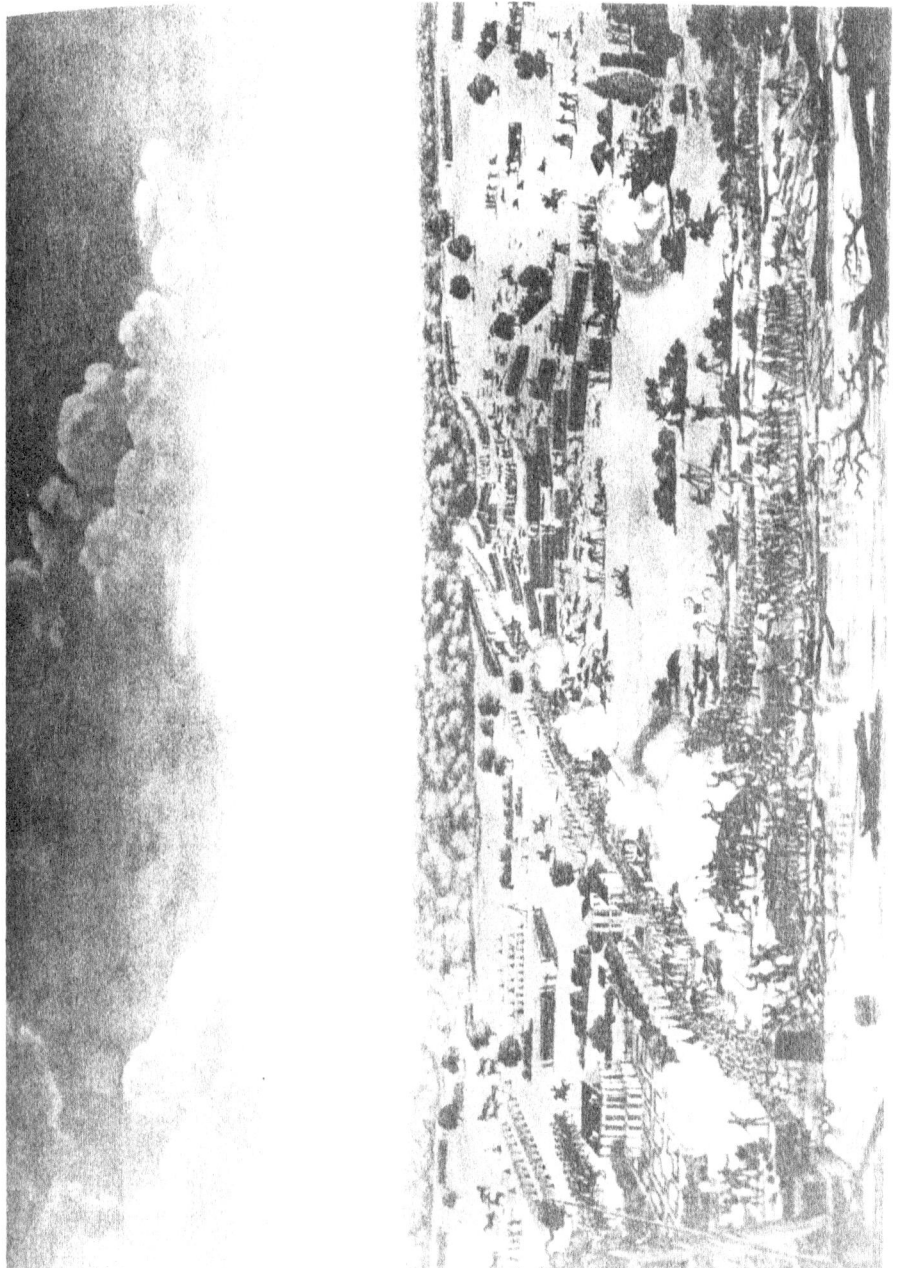

Battle of New Orleans

General Andrew Jackson

disturbed by news in late 1811 that the British had offered reparations for the *Chesapeake* outrage since he viewed the English overture as a temporizing action intended to divide the American people. He told Secretary of Navy Paul Hamilton that the United States should demand that England cease the abusive Orders in Council. If England persisted, Claiborne advocated "an open, avowed & relentless War." [3]

The governor, accelerating his correspondence with national leaders, encouraged them not to compromise upon hearing that England was willing to make concessions to avert war. Moreover, he was concerned about Britain's growing interest in Central and South America as the Spanish Empire tottered and colonial appendages ceased to look to Madrid for guidance and direction. In a letter to Hamilton on December 26, 1811, Claiborne asserted that the British were striving to gain in the Western Hemisphere the ascendancy they had lost in Europe, and he charged further that Great Britain hoped to secure a trade monopoly with the Spanish holdings in the New World. He was particularly concerned about the fate of Cuba at the time. Fearful that England planned to establish political and economic hegemony over the island, he assured Hamilton that this could be easily thwarted. Cuban leaders were contemplating a proclamation of independence, he reported, and they anticipated an "intimate Connection" with the United States. These Cuban leaders should be given encouragement, arms, and financial support to achieve their aspirations. By doing this, he added, the United States could either acquire the island or make it an economic dependency. The governor's letter to Albert Gallatin eight days later was even more bellicose and expansionist in tone. If England threatened our seaports, we could do likewise with England. Canada to the north and the Spanish possessions to the south of the United States, including Cuba, should be removed entirely from European authority and influence. According to Claiborne's perspective, American security demanded it. If Cuba came under English domination, England would have a chain of bases extending in a vast arc from Halifax to Jamaica. Britain could then effectively blockade the American coastline, endanger lower Louisiana, and destroy the Mississippi trade. But if Cuba came under American control, its resources could be developed, its ports could be used by American merchant ships and war vessels, and British trade in the region could be disrupted. [4]

Although he insisted that the United States acquire Cuba by the most expedient means, Governor Claiborne's panoramic vision encompassed the Western Hemisphere. He told Albert Gallatin that Spain would risk the loss of its American holdings if it, as England's ally, supported Britain's aggressive policies. The time was opportune, he suggested, to acquire Canada and "New Spain." In late January 1812, he wrote to Senator Joseph B. Varnum of Massachusetts and proposed a regional delineation of responsibilities. The people of the Southwest would seize the Spanish Floridas while "our Northern Brethren" conquered Canada. "Cuba, Mexico, and the Spanish American possessions generally deserve our particular attention," he continued. "The occasion is favorable to free them of all European Influence either Commercial or Political, & to effect *whatever else* the Interests of the United States may suggest." Exasperated and impatient with the Madison administration for its caution and reluctance, Claiborne insisted that the United States should seize Mobile and East Florida, at the very least.

Governor Claiborne's disappointment with national leaders derived only in part from their refusal to seize British and Spanish holdings in the Western Hemisphere. His fundamental objective was active American involvement in the continuing war. But as an ardent Jeffersonian disciple and republican standard-bearer, Claiborne was inclined to overlook or forgive French outrages against the United States while insisting that England was fledgling America's implacable foe. Always in close touch with the national leadership, the governor sought to influence their policies upon learning of incidents and developments which might be exploited to plunge the two nations into war. Indeed, the volume of correspondence from New Orleans to Washington in the years following Claiborne's appointment in Louisiana at the end of 1803 provided a generally reliable indicator of the state of Anglo-American relations at any given time.

Claiborne finally concluded that the United States and Great Britain would never exchange anything more violent than verbal salvos. After all, American leaders had managed to remain aloof from the European conflict for two decades. Claiborne was therefore taken by surprise when the Madison administration suddenly rushed into war with England and considered the inclusion of imperial France in its declaration of hostilities. On June 4, 1812, the House approved the war resolution by a vote of 79 to 49. The Senate adopted the measure thirteen days later by the uneasy margin of 19 to 13 and the vote to include France was defeated 18 to 14.

The Americans had cause for sober second thoughts once the war erupted and England made its second and final bid to restore the former American appendage to the fold and establish itself as the political and economic hegemon in the Western Hemisphere. The Americans were well on the way toward the establishment of two outstanding traditions, the first of which was unpreparedness for war. President James Madison and his cabinet, with the notable exception of James Monroe, provided very little effective leadership; financing the war effort was difficult because of an inadequate system of taxation and the expiration of the Bank of the United States; and the regular armed forces consisted of seven thousand men led by "decayed gentlemen," according to Winfield Scott, who were "utterly unfit for any military purpose whatsoever." The other emerging tradition was that of divisiveness of American public opinion. Popular attitudes during the American Revolutionary War had ranged from a complete commitment to independence, to concerned neutrality, to steadfast loyalty to the crown. Then, when the French Revolution sparked a quarter century of European warfare, Federalists generally supported England while Republicans supported France, but there were many Americans who adhered to President Washington's admonition against any involvement in European affairs.

With war a reality, Americans made their bid. Ill-prepared and inadequately led offensive lunges in both the Northwest and Northeast produced almost unrelieved embarrassment. Even the American successes at sea in the initial stages of the war were ephemeral and of no substantive military consequence. They served, however, to arrest sagging American spirits while embarrassing British naval officers who earlier had been inclined to dismiss with supreme disdain the American *"fir-built frigates*, manned by a handful of bastards and outlaws."[6] The British blockade of the American coastline was extended and tightened after the winter of 1812-13. Following the defeat of Napoleon at Leipzig in the autumn of 1813, British leaders were in the position at last to concentrate their substantial military resources on the nettling American nuisance. Fortunately for the hard-pressed American defenders, the Duke of Wellington declined the assignment and advised against such an effort because the British had been unable to establish naval supremacy on the Great Lakes, and this was essential to the defeat of their American adversaries. Even so, American pride was dealt an excruciating blow when British troops marched smartly into Washington on August 24, 1814, and some of their officers enjoyed a dinner prepared for the Madisons. Earlier in the day President Madison had invited some cabinet members to accompany him as he casually strolled out to see his numerically superior militiamen—his mentor, Thomas Jefferson, had always insisted that "citizen soldiers" were superior to professional troops—give the approaching Redcoats a savage thrust of the bayonet. Instead, the faint-hearted warriors broke ranks and took ignominious flight. British troops then methodically put the torch to most of the capital's public buildings, including the White House, and thereby savored revenge for a similar American action at York, the capital of Upper Canada, in April of the preceding year.

To add to the American plight, New England's Federalist leaders began to intensify their threats of secession. Congressman Josiah Quincy of Massachusetts had trumpeted such a threat as early as 1811 during discussion of a bill to admit the Orleans Territory to statehood. Fearing that adoption of the bill would presage an alliance between the southern and western states which would dominate national politics, Quincy had exclaimed with oracular acuity that the enactment of the bill would free the states from their original obligations to the federal compact. If Congress approved the measure, he had persisted with the moral certitude of an Increase Mather, "as it will be the right of all, so it will be the duty of some, definitely to prepare for separation—amicably if they can, violently if they must."[7] Flagrantly conducting a flourishing trade with the British following the outbreak of war, some New England leaders came to view secession as a logical and even desirable development. The Hartford Convention, convoked almost three months after the British bonfire at Washington, was therefore a logical culmination of secessionist sentiments in the rapidly diminishing Federalist citadel.

In remote Louisiana, finally admitted to statehood about the time the "Second War of Independence" erupted, the situation appeared similarly distressing. When he finally learned of the congressional declaration of war on July 9, three weeks after the fact, Claiborne was highly elated. But when the harsh realities of the nation's precarious position intruded jarringly and came into sharper focus, he fretted and pondered the probable reaction of his native constituency to the fateful development. The loyalty and commitment of the "ancient" Louisianians still remained in doubt after nine trying and not infrequently tedious years of American administration.

Thus, at his inauguration as Louisiana's first elective governor on July 30, 1812, Claiborne devoted most of his address to the conflict and the security of the state. The United States had managed for years to avoid a conflict which was "filling the world with widows and orphans," but finally had been drawn into it by British aggressions. Continued American submission to British outrages, he asserted, would have reflected cowardice, invited national dishonor, and led ultimately to slavery. Although Louisiana appeared to lie safely beyond the field of direct martial encounter—Louisianians were fully convinced it was—he pleaded for unity and commitment: *"In such a contest the issue cannot be doubtful. In such a cause every American should make bare his bosom.* 'Where justice is the standard, Heaven is the warrior's shield.' " [8] Despite the governor's pleas and exhortations for an effective militia law and a state of readiness in the event of an enemy attack, local ennui stubbornly persisted. In the absence of an immediate and direct threat to their persons and property, the local inhabitants continued to question the need of a militia force at all. Although the United States was now at war, the governor's urgent warning that the state militia remained woefully unprepared still fell on deaf or unsympathetic ears, as it had regularly for nine years.

A number of factors contributed to the "deranged and feeble state" of the state militia. This included an acute arms shortage, the inadequacies of the state militia laws, the distance militiamen had to travel in rural Louisiana for musters and training exercises, language problems resulting from the heterogeneity of the people, and the nonchalant attitude of the public, influenced in particular by the planter and merchant classes toward militia service. Moreover, the continued refusal of the state lawmakers to display any significant commitment toward the development of a viable militia had not gone unnoticed among the masses. Nevertheless, ultimate responsibility for the plight of the militia must be assigned chiefly to Governor Claiborne, as commander of the militia, and to his officer corps. Although the governor appealed repeatedly to the lawmakers to amend the existing militia laws, there is absolutely no evidence to indicate that he made any meaningful effort to infuse discipline and order in the militia ranks.

Much to the consternation and embarrassment of the chief executive, the state militia remained unprepared and unwilling to cooperate throughout most of the war. Following erroneous reports in the late summer of 1812 that British troops had appeared at the Balize on the gulf coast below New Orleans, Governor Claiborne called out eight companies of the municipal militia and requested volunteers to assist the regular military forces stationed in Louisiana. A sixty-man company flatly refused to serve under a regular army officer. Even as they did so, the members of the company insisted that they would be available "in case of danger," the implication of which was that they would themselves decide whether a danger existed.[9] Claiborne's problem was compounded by his inability to secure badly needed arms and materiel from the federal government. The national arms deficiency was too pervasive, and the Southwest had the lowest priority of any region in the United States. This sober fact was underscored by the small trickle of arms and equipment allocated to Louisiana, but even more explicitly by the transfer of the Louisiana-based Third Regiment of the regular army to Ohio.[10] In view of these developments, there was even less likelihood that the chief executive would be able to convince either the militiamen or the Creole-dominated legislature that Louisiana's security was precarious enough to command more than casual attention.

Governor Claiborne was reluctant to force a showdown, rationalizing lamely that the existing laws did not give him the authority to activate the recalcitrant militia. As long as General Wilkinson commanded the Seventh Military District, which included Louisiana, the Mississippi Territory, and Tennessee, Claiborne continued to avoid a clash although the two men discussed possible means of arousing the people and securing their active support. General Thomas Flournoy, who arrived in New Orleans to replace Wilkinson in the spring of 1813, pointed out, however, that the governor was empowered to call the militia into active service when the public safety was threatened or an insurrection or invasion was imminent. A few weeks afterward, Claiborne activated one militia brigade and informed President Madison that other units would be placed on active duty when they reached an acceptable state of preparedness. As anticipated, a howl of strident protest followed in New Orleans which the governor attributed to a few chronic opponents of his administration and to "many well disposed citizens." [11]

The first substantive test developed when General Flournoy formally requisitioned one thousand militiamen as Louisiana's quota under the national requisition. Anticipating the requisition, Claiborne visited a number of the American-dominated interior counties to inspect their militia units during the autumn of 1813. By the time he returned to New Orleans, he was fully convinced that the safety of the city itself was dependent upon the Americans from those areas and the few regular forces remaining in Louisiana. On Christmas day he issued a general order for one thousand militiamen to be placed on active duty up to six months, depending upon the need. About four hundred militiamen from the Second Dvision in the interior moved into barracks in New Orleans shortly afterward; however, opposition to the requisition within the city itself was almost universal. The state senate flatly declared the general order illegal, and the house of representatives rejected by one vote a resolution of support for it. Despite the clamor, Claiborne repeated the requisition on February 18, 1814. The municipal militia again refused to be activated, and a clash appeared imminent when officers of the Second Division volunteered to enforce compliance. If the chief executive accepted the offer, an effusion of blood and further division among the people would surely result, and no person was more acutely aware of this probability than Claiborne. Yet to decline the proffered assistance would have a demoralizing influence on the activated militia while encouraging further local opposition. He quietly declined to press the issue. Shortly afterward he discharged the Second Division militiamen altogether as desertion rates soared. Considering the options open to him and the charged atmosphere of the moment, the governor's decision was highly defensible. In fact, it confirmed the judgment of the national leaders and the Louisiana electorate in their choice of leadership. But even as he relented and accepted the concomitant personal humiliation, he tenaciously insisted that the municipal militia would respond with "promptitude and firmness" to an enemy threat. Again he attributed the opposition in part to the devious influence of determined political opponents, but he readily admitted that some of his friends opposed the general order because they felt it was oppressive, illegal, and unnecessary. [12]

When newspaper critics roundly condemned the governor for having issued the militia order at all, he responded with hurt indignation and injected a rare note of humor. Asserting that he had been subjected to such criticisms from the time he first arrived in New Orleans, he added: "I do not find that against the integrity of my private and public life they have made the smallest breach." He conceded wryly that during his first two or three years his "blood was occasionally up to fever heat" because of the criticisms and climate but he was now "happily acclimated to both." He readily admitted that freedom of the press was a vital necessity in a democracy despite its not uncommon excesses, and then added philosophically: "Perhaps it is an inseparable evil from the good with which it is allied; perhaps it is a shoot which cannot be stripped from the stalk without injuring the plant itself."[13]

The newspapers continued to snipe at Claiborne throughout much of the summer of 1814, especially since it was a political year and the governor was a natural target. The emerging threat of a British invasion of Louisiana by late summer, however, again focused attention on the state's vulnerabilities. Having subdued the Napoleonic forces, British leaders turned their attention to their American adversaries. As the British threat became increasingly apparent, the attitude of the local press in New Orleans underwent an almost instantaneous change. When Governor Claiborne, acting under presidential orders, issued a call for one thousand militiamen on August 6, the newspapers responded with a clarion call for unity behind the governor. Those Louisianians who appeared unarmed and supplicating before the British forces, the newspapers warned, would be ruthlessly crushed by the foe.[14]

Encouraged by the newfound press support, Governor Claiborne intensified his efforts. Upon receipt of a dispatch from General Andrew Jackson, who had succeeded General Flournoy as commander of the Seventh Military District in May 1814, the governor issued a general militia order on September 5. He asserted that Jackson had instructed him "to lose no time in preparing for the defense of the State. This gallant commander is now at or near Mobile watching the movements of the enemy, and making necessary preparations to cover and defend this section of the Union. He will in due time receive reinforcements from the other States on the Mississippi; he calculates also on the zealous support of the Louisianians, and must not be disappointed." The governor ordered Major General Jacques Villeré to organize the militia companies immediately in New Orleans, and he instructed Major General Philemon Thomas to do likewise in the Baton Rouge area by the first of October. In further general orders, Governor Claiborne directed the militia companies in metropolitan New Orleans to muster twice weekly for inspection and exercise, and for those militia units in the interior counties to muster weekly for the same purpose. At the same time, he appealed to fathers and other male citizens exempted from active militia service to organize auxiliary associations. Carefully disclaiming any intent to excite alarm, a charge levelled several months earlier, Claiborne warned the men that they might be called upon at any moment to defend their homes and families. Although he had hoped that the Anglo-American peace negotiations then in progress at Ghent would be successful, there was "too much reason to apprehend that the enemy feeling power may forget right." A British invasion force was being assembled, he reported, and enemy naval units were hovering off the coast of Louisiana. Appealing for "one opinion, one sentiment," he called upon Louisianians to dispute every inch of ground. If any person believed that his individual rights would be respected by the enemy, "the weakness of his head should excite pity."[15] Unlike the Burr crisis eight years earlier when feverish defensive preparations were made while ignoring the masses, Claiborne made a special effort to keep the local inhabitants fully informed about the extent and scope of the danger. Moreover, he sedulously cultivated popular support during the developing crisis.

Despite his fighting appeals and confident public demeanor, Governor Claiborne was privately beset with grave doubts about local loyalties. In mid-August he had observed to Jackson: "On the native American and a vast majority of the Creoles of the country I place much confidence, nor do I doubt the fidelity of many Europeans who have long resided in the country. But there are others much devoted to the interest of Spain, and their partiality to the English is no less observable than their dislike for the American government."[16] Almost two weeks later he informed Jackson that the state's defense would be primarily contingent upon the regular military forces and the militia of the western states and territories. The Louisianians themselves would offer only feeble resistance because of their heterogeneity and internal differences. This was quickly followed by yet another gloomy report in which he professed that a greater spirit of popular disaffection actually existed than he had anticipated. Even among loyal Louisianians, he continued darkly, "there is a Despondency which palsies all my preparations." Furthermore, he was apprehensive about internal enemies and disaffected elements within the city. Two days afterward the dejected chief executive appealed to Jackson to make a "flying visit" to New Orleans to spur on defensive preparations.[17] The governor had lapsed momentarily into the luxury of self-pity and despair at a time when neither he nor Louisianians could afford such an extravagance. He fortunately conveyed no public hint of his private doubts about the loyalties and intentions of his temperamental constituency in New Orleans.

General Jackson was too occupied at the time to heed the governor's frantic appeal to visit New Orleans since the British were already beginning to make their final bid. Earlier, British hopes of cutting off New England from the rest of the country had vanished when Sir George Prevost and an 11,000-man force retreated to Canda following a spectular American naval victory on Lake Champlain. The British created some consternation by burning Washington and marching on nearby Baltimore; however, they abandoned this offensive when General Robert Ross was killed during a futile attack on Fort McHenry in early September 1814. The only remaining British hope of territorial conquest in support of their diplomatic initiatives at Ghent now lay in the conquest of New Orleans. Albert Gallatin warned Secretary of State James Monroe from Ghent that England's "true and immediate object is New Orleans," despite enemy offensive operations in the ares of Lakes Erie and Ontario. Whether this was the result of Gallatin's own shrewd deduction or of intelligence he had received from sources in London is not known. At any rate, as British forces began to make their moves as a preliminary to the invasion of New Orleans, General Jackson was already rushing ahead with bold measures of his own to thwart the hated enemy.[18]

British plans called for support from Spanish forces stationed in the Floridas and elsewhere, and from the Indians and dissident local elements. While in Havana, British Colonel Edward Nicholls specifically requested assistance from the Spanish governor general, and for permission to establish his headquarters in Pensacola. Both requests were denied. Nonetheless, Nicholls and his small staff proceeded to Pensacola, established their headquarters, and issued a proclamation on August 29, in which they called upon Louisianians and Kentuckians for support against the American government. Five days later, British naval Captain Nicholas Lockyer and Captain John McWilliams of the marines made unsuccessful overtures to Jean Laffite and his Baratarian buccaneers. These initial efforts to mobilize local support were followed by a probing attack on Fort Bowyer, located on Mobile Point at the entrance to Mobile Bay. Jackson, however, had dispatched a 160-man contingent of regulars to the fort several days earlier, and the defenders were ready when the attackers appeared. The small British assault force was led by two frigates, the *Hermes* and *Sophie*. Almost two hundred marines and Indians, led by Colonel Nicholls, moved against the fort from the east. The attack was called off following the loss of the *Hermes* in a cannonade on September 15. Fearing an American offensive in the wake of the British failure at Fort Bowyer, the Spanish governor in Pensacola appealed to the British for help. Colonel Nicholls and his small force returned to Pensacola aboard the *Sophie* on October 31.[19]

The Spanish governor had good reason to be concerned. Even before the attack on Fort Bowyer, General Jackson had issued urgent orders for all available forces to rendezvous at Fort Jackson, located at the confluence of the Coosa and Tallapoosa rivers, preparatory to an assault on Pensacola. In early October General John Coffee began riding southward at the head of a two thousand-man force of Tennesseeans and several hundred others joined them along the way. As the Tennesseeans poured into the staging area, Jackson informed Monroe of his decision to launch an attack on Pensacola. The safety of the Southwest hinged on it, he contended, and Pensacola had assumed the "character of British Territory." If the government failed to approve, Jackson said he would have the satisfaction of having "done the only thing in my opinion which could give security to the country." Although it appeared that the general was running some risk of rebuke from national leaders, including the possible loss of his commission, he actually had private assurances that Monroe personally approved the expedition.[20]

Leading a force of three thousand militiamen and regulars, Jackson arrived at the outskirts of Pensacola on November 6. He demanded that Fort Barrancas and other fortifications in the city be relinquished to the American force as a guarantee of Spanish neutrality. When the Spanish defenders refused to negotiate and fired on the American flag of truce, Jackson's forces moved into the city and occupied it after a sharp skirmish on November 7. By this time, however, Colonel Nicholls and his force had destroyed Fort Barrancas and escaped. Jackson then evacuated Pensacola on November 9 and sped back to Mobile.[21]

Jackson's bold move against Pensacola created some consternation in Washington, mainly because of the resultant vulnerability of Mobile and New Orleans while it was in progress, but the general's tactics had a significance of outstanding magnitude. Jackson's action had a tremendous impact on the people of the Southwest, boosting their morale, making them more certain of their abilities, and, at the same time, increasing their confidence in him as a military leader. At the same time, Jackson's tactics threw the British off balance as they continued their offensive buildup. The Spaniards, Cherokees, and Choctaws thus became less confident of British intentions and capabilities. Finally, the general's Pensacola incursion, with his earlier successes against the British and Indians, influenced the attitude and conduct of Louisianians when the British finally made their move against New Orleans.

General Jackson had been too busy to accept Claiborne's invitation to visit New Orleans for the purpose of allaying mounting popular concern and breathing life into local defensive preparations. Nonetheless, he took the time to issue a proclamation to Louisianians from his Mobile headquarters on September 21, some six days after the British withdrew from Fort Bowyer. The fiery exhortation to the Creoles reflected at once a clever insight and a surprising imperception. Jackson first informed them of the attack on Fort Bowyer by the "perfidious Britons" and their "incongruous horde of Indian and negro assassins." He called upon the native inhabitants to reject the appeal made three weeks earlier by British Colonel Nicholls for local assistance in the liberation of Louisiana. The British proposed, with native support, "to prostrate the holy temple of our liberty. Can Louisianians, can Frenchmen, can Americans, ever stoop to be the slaves or allies of Britons?" The general expressed the hope that every Louisianian was prepared to "rally around the Eagle of Columbia, secure it from impending danger, or nobly die in the last ditch in its defense." The effectiveness of Jackson's appeal to the Creoles was unfortunately diminished by the emphasis he placed upon British overtures to the "Hellish Banditti" of Barataria. Although supremely confident of his capacity to repulse the British, he declared flatly that he had no intention of enlisting the support of pirates and robbers in the "glorious cause."[22] Jackson was obviously unaware that the Laffites and their Baratarian associates were folk heroes and a source of local pride and support. Moreover, he had publicly rejected a source of materiel, technical, intelligence, and advisory assistance at a time when he could ill afford to do so.

Realizing that time was of the essence and that Jackson would be unable to come to New Orleans for some time, Governor Claiborne became more assertive and appeared more assured of his own ability to lead the people as the crisis heightened. Vowing never to relent to the enemy, he exhorted the young men to look to their weapons, and he expressed appreciation to those who were enrolled in voluntary associations formed to support the war effort. In late October and again in early November he sent Jackson a comprehensive report on the local deployment of available forces, offered specific explanations for the deployments, and included a report on available naval units. He paused long enough to write a lengthy letter to Secretary of State Monroe in which he requested that the government authorize Jackson's attack on Pensacola. This was an indication, at least, that Claiborne had some awareness of Jackson's plans. Not only was Pensacola being used as a British base and as a haven for Creek braves who had survived the Indian disaster at Horseshoe Bend (Tohopeka), but it would be a logical base from which to launch an invasion of Louisiana. Then on November 5 he reported to Jackson that the one-thousand-man requisition was virtually completed and that he had a twelve-hundred-man auxiliary force. He convoked a special legislative session five days later. Although somewhat wary of the lawmakers, he expressed confidence that they would sanction his militia requisition and support his defensive measures.[23] Moreover, while the governor's attitude about local loyalties had fluctuated with facility, he now appeared more genuinely convinced of active public support.

When the legislature convened, Claiborne spoke at length upon the impending crisis. The lawmakers had been called into special session primarily, he pointed out, to provide necessary funds for the state's defense. He asked them to approve a loan of $20,000 which he had arranged, and then return to their respective parishes to assist with defensive preparations. Although the legislators quickly approved the loan, they insisted upon remaining in session in order to provide needed leadership. Governor Claiborne's confidence was buoyed further upon learning from Jackson that five thousand militiamen from Kentucky and Tennessee were rushing to New Orleans, and that the Mississippi Territory's entire militia force was being held in readiness to march southward immediately.[24] Order was at last beginning to emerge from the confusion and uncertainty of the preceding months.

As the security situation in New Orleans began to assume respectable dimensions, British preparations at Negril Bay in western Jamaica were approaching completion. A full-dress review of the naval and military forces was held on November 24. Two days later the invasion force, equipped at a cost of one million pounds sterling, left the bay and sailed northwestward. Aboard the *Tonnant*, captured from the French at Aboukir, Admiral Sir Alexander Cochrane proudly surveyed the majestic scene as his naval units moved ponderously but confidently toward the Louisiana coast. The fifty-vessel, six-thousand-man armada finally cast anchor in the channel between Cat and Ship islands in the Mississippi Sound on December 10, some two weeks later.[25] The long-awaited attack on New Orleans was about to begin.

General Jackson briskly prepared to accommodate the invaders. Regular troops and militiamen from Kentucky, Tennessee, and Georgia were already converging on Mobile and New Orleans in response to James Monroe's appeals and Jackson's orders. Earlier, Jackson had dispatched Lieutenant Colonel William McRae and Colonel Arthur P. Hayne to New Orleans to deploy available troops and strengthen the city's forts, most of which were in disrepair. Leaving a substantial force under General James Winchester to protect the Mobile area, General Jackson himself set out for New Orleans on November 22. Displaying no sign of undue anxiety, Jackson carefully studied the topography and possible landing points by enemy forces during the measured ten-day trip. Arriving in the city on the morning of December 1, he rushed ahead with defensive preparations. The tall, slender, and ailing military commander was a study in motion as he introduced to the uncertain city a prodigious vitality and consuming determination which enabled him to impress, to inspire, and to command the local inhabitants. Governor Claiborne simply did not possess such an enviable quality of leadership. Responding to Jackson's request, Claiborne appeared before the state lawmakers on December 14 and asked them to suspend the writ of habeas corpus. This would enable the authorities to move decisively against internal enemies and disaffected elements within the city. The legislators peremptorily refused. Spurred by recurring reports of sedition while denying rumors that England would return Louisiana to Spain, a rumor which obviously appealed to some "ancient" Louisianians, the general issued a bristling proclamation the next day. Branding Britain as the "common enemy of mankind, the highway robber of the world," he told the people that he expected them to close ranks and "dispute every inch of ground." Should they disappoint him, he would be compelled to "separate our enemies from our friends—those who are not for us are against us, and will be dealt with accordingly." Secret correspondence with the enemy, he warned, was punishable by death.[26] The man on horseback had finally arrived. Furthermore, he swiftly prepared a warm reception for his expected but uninvited guests, some of whom had already begun to appear.

Encouraged and stimulated by the presence of the peripatetic Jackson, Governor Claiborne intensified his efforts to mobilize local forces while making a determined effort to form a close working relationship with the general. Following initial exchanges between the invaders and defenders, he called out the militia *en masse*. His growing confidence in Louisianians was heightened by the emergence of a number of new volunteer units and the expansion of established ones through recruitment as American "newcomers" joined with "ancient" Louisianians in a common effort to surmount the developing crisis. Most of the local militia forces were unfortunately under strength, inadequately armed, and poorly trained. The resplendent Battalion of New Orleans Volunteers consisted predominantly of young men from prominent Creole families and a number of Napoleonic veterans, but it also boasted a number of Irishmen. Thomas Beale's newly formed company of Volunteer Rifles was composed of middle-aged and older business and professional leaders who ostensibly were proficient marksmen. Pierre Jugeat organized a battalion of Choctaws. Major Jean Daquin commanded a newly created battalion of free blacks, organized by Jean-Baptiste Savary from among refugees from Santo Domingo. When the assistant paymaster challenged Jackson's authority to do this, the general answered impatiently: "It is enough for you to receive my orders for the payment of the troops with the necessary muster rolls without inquiring whether the troops are white, black, or tea." This was the second of two battalions of free blacks which participated in the defense of New Orleans. Governor Claiborne himself had been primarily responsible for the recommissioning of the battalion of Free Men of Color after finally receiving authorization from Congress in 1811. The Spanish authorities had engaged black soldiers, but Claiborne had been forced to discontinue the practice following the Louisiana transfer because of opposition from the planter class. At the time of the British invasion in late 1814, the battalion of Free Men of Color was one of the few state militia units which was largely ready for combat, having mustered fairly regularly for training exercises. Although the two black battalions included Negro officers who had been commissioned by Governor Claiborne, they were under the command of Colonel Michael Fortier, who had armed and equipped them at his personal expense.[27] A substantial number of Baratarian buccaneers were also enlisted in the now almost frenzied defensive buildup. The Creole society of New Orleans was as startled as the enemy invaders by the colorful disparities among the Louisiana forces, the neighboring Mississippi dragoons, the "dirty shirts" from Tennessee and Kentucky, and regular troops.

Several sharp skirmishes ensued between the time of the unequal naval contest on Lake Borgne on December 14 and the decisive engagement on January 8 some twenty-five days later. Informed of the loss of the American flotilla of five gunboats to superior British naval units on December 15, Jackson issued urgent pleas for his commanders to rush their forces to New Orleans. To reliable John Coffee at Baton Rouge he appealed: "You must not sleep until you reach me." Coffee and eight hundred of his hardy Tennesseeans poured into New Orleans on December 20—450 arrived later but some seven hundred remained in Baton Rouge because of illness—having completed the 135-mile trip in slightly over three days. General William Carroll and another three thousand Tennesseeans arrived on the same day, having embarked from Nashville a month earlier. Before the day was over, Thomas Hinds and his Mississippi Dragoons also rode into town, adding about 150 men to Jackson's burgeoning forces.

On December 23—the day before American and British commissioners signed the peace treaty at Ghent—Jackson was surprised to learn that British forces were in the vicinity of Bayou Bienvenu and Jacques Villeré's plantation between Lake Borgne and the Mississippi River, about ten miles south of New Orleans. Informed by young Major Gabriel Villeré, who had escaped his British captors, Jackson launched a brisk night attack and created some consternation in the British camp. Having accomplished his purpose, Jackson then pulled back his forces to his primary defense line at the Rodriguez Canal. Fairly heavy fighting erupted again on December 28 when Lieutenant General Edward M. Pakenham's infantrymen, supported by field guns and rockets, launched an indecisive attack. Jackson's forces hurled them back, assisted by five field pieces and decimating fire from the damaged American ship *Louisiana*, strategically anchored in the Mississippi River. Over the next several days action was largely limited to artillery duels, light skirmishes, and exploratory probes. Both sides received reinforcements and additional guns over the next few days to force the issue and determine the fate of Louisiana. General John Thomas arrived with 2,268 Kentucky militiamen on January 3. Over two-thirds of the total force were without guns, which prompted the astonished Jackson to exclaim in utter disbelief: "I have never seen a Kentuckian without a gun and a pack of cards and a bottle of whiskey in my life." Major General John Lambert arrived with two regiments on the same day to strengthen enemy ranks. British commanders committed in excess of six thousand men to the endeavor; General Jackson massed almost fifty-two hundred defenders behind protective earthen parapets to repulse the Redcoats.[28]

At six o'clock on Sunday morning, January 8, Pakenham sent his troops forward under cover of screaming congreve rockets and thunderous artillery fire. Although fascines made of bundles of sugarcane stalks and ladders had been prepared for the attacking troops to cross the ditch and climb the parapet erected by the defenders, the advance units rushed forward only to discover that they had forgotten them in the excitement and turmoil. By the time the mistake was discovered and they were able to rush the fascines and ladders forward, too much confusion had developed in British ranks. Moreover, the defenders were alerted to British intentions, and Jackson and his colorful collection of regular troops, backwoodsmen, blacks, buccaneers, Creoles, and Choctaw Indians were not disposed to excuse such an egregious lapse of memory. The confused and milling troops were cut down by withering fire from defending artillery and musketry as Jackson moved along the line exhorting his warriors. Pakenham himself died heroically, performing the last ritual function of a defeated general, and Sir Samuel Gibbs and Sir John Keane, the second and third generals in line of command, were mortally wounded. General John Lambert, the only surviving general officer, quickly surveyed the carnage and shattered ranks of the broken British forces and ordered a retreat. English Captain John Henry Cooke observed sorrowfully that British troops had fallen "like blades of grass beneath the scythe of the mower; brigades dispersed like dust before the whirlwind."[29] George R. Gleig, another British officer, was stunned by the unmitigated disaster, painfully noting: "Within the narrow compass of a few hundred yards were gathered together nearly a thousand bodies, all of them arrayed in British uniforms. Not a single American was among them; all were English."[30] The only serious threat occurred when Colonel William Thornton's brigade crossed the Mississippi River, drove back General David B. Morgan's inadequate militia force, and threatened momentarily to outflank Jackson's line. The thoroughly chastened but stubborn British forces evacuated Louisiana ten days afterward, having taken in excess of two thousand casualties in the disastrous assault from dawn until the defending musketry ceased firing at 8:30. A mere thirteen Americans were killed and fifty-eight were wounded during the same fateful two and a half hours. Jackson's triumph over the Creeks at Horseshoe Bend the preceding march paled by comparison with his incredible performance against the proud British foe; at the same time it confirmed the Jackson legend.

 The native Louisianians contributed substantially to Jackson's stunning victory although their efforts went largely unnoticed at the time as the brilliant spotlight played upon the craggy features of the Hero of New Orleans. The number of persons who volunteered for militia service was well in excess of the thousand-man militia requisition, and local leaders provided work forces to assist with defensive fortifications and the construction of gun emplacements and earthen parapets. The state lawmakers imposed an embargo and authorized bounties to secure experienced seamen for Commodore David Patterson's small naval force until the imposition of martial law made impressment possible. The legislators also authorized funds for the purchase of needed supplies. Males not subject to active militia service joined auxiliary organizations, and women provided blankets and clothing for the tattered and largely unarmed militiamen from Kentucky, in particular, who poured into New Orleans to help repulse the invaders. Louisianians, whose loyalties had never been subjected to a real test during the preceding twelve years, clearly committed themselves in the crucible of war and snuffed out all doubts and uncertainties. In fact, their conduct generally reflected a commitment equal to that of the citizenry of a number of the more established states and even transcended that of others at the time. Governor Claiborne had expressed repeatedly the conviction that the local inhabitants would rise to the occasion, provided a clear and present danger developed. Admiral Cochrane's ill-fated expedition had offered proof positive of a clear and present danger.

The most spectacular local support was provided by the Baratarian buccaneers, led by the colorful Jean Laffite who ostensibly was offered a captain's commission in the British navy and 30,000 pounds sterling. Although federal and local authorities had overrun the pirate lair as the invasion was shaping up, the governor promised to recommend that the Baratarians be granted amnesty in return for their assistance against the British invasion force, provided they acquitted themselves honorably. The American defenders badly needed these experienced craftsmen, artillerists, and sailors, and the buccaneers possessed a thorough knowledge of the terrain with its intricate network of canals, passages, and cypress swamps. The Baratarians accepted, and Jean personally recommended a critical extension of Jackson's eastern defense line to prevent enemy forces from outflanking the general's main position. According to the pirate chieftain, he also supplied eleven hundred men and 362 cannons as well as substantial quantities of rifles and ammunition.[31] Moreover, according to Jean, his brother Alexander (also known as Dominique You) swept General Pakenham from his saddle with artillery fire. The Baratarian artillerists assigned to some of the batteries were so devastating that General Jackson ostensibly exclaimed: "I wish I had fifty of such guns on this line with five hundred of such devils as those fellows at their butts."[32] Once the battle ended, Jackson praised the "brothers Lafitte," mentioning Captains Dominique You and "Oncle" Renato Beluche specifically. The "hellish banditti" and "wretches" of the preceding September emerged as "privateers and gentlemen" in January. President Madison, acting on the recommendations of Claiborne and Jackson, granted the freebooters amnesty for their exemplary services. The proclamation read, in part: "Offenders, who have refused to become the associates of the enemy in war, upon the most seducing terms of invitation, and who have aided to repel his hostile invasion of the territory of the United States, can no longer be considered as objects of punishment, but as objects of generous forgiveness." [33]

Governor Claiborne had hoped almost desperately to provide distinguished leadership during the crisis, but Jackson thwarted his aspirations repeatedly and thrust him into a thoroughly pedestrian role. A number of factors contributed to the almost immediate estrangement which developed between the two leaders following Jackson's arrival in New Orleans. One of the more obvious was a basic personality conflict. Although stubbornly persistent, Claiborne was not a leader in the brash and boastful frontier mold. He suffered from a certain vanity and exaggerated sense of dignity, and he was sometimes unduly preoccupied with the trappings and prerogatives of his office. These personal qualities put him at a distinct disadvantage in his relationship with such frontier personalities as Jackson. On the other hand, Jackson possessed some decided personality flaws, including a sometimes ungovernable temper which "would glow at the slightest blowing." The general was a formidable antagonist who "never saw both sides of a subject," and "the frontiersman's habits of braggadocio and bluster were very deeply fixed in his nature." [34] In view of these qualities, it should have occasioned no particular surprise when he became immersed in a number of controversies during his five months in New Orleans. It is altogether too convenient and tempting to defend Jackson's weaknesses by smugly asserting that the general "was too busy to play politics or attend to wounded feelings."[35] Considering the magnitude of the task before him, Jackson had a special responsibility to mobilize political, as well as military, support. The situation in New Orleans was admittedly abnormal; yet conditions were not so exceptional that they invited bitter confrontations with the executive, legislative, and judicial authorities.

Jackson's arrival in New Orleans also awakened in both leaders a certain sense of jealousy and competition despite their occasional professions of friendship. As ambitious young men, both Claiborne and Jackson had migrated to the "Old Southwest" to launch their professional careers. They had served as representatives to the

Tennessee constitutional convention in 1796. Following the admission of Tennessee to statehood, Jackson was elected to the United States House of Representatives while Claiborne was appointed to the state supreme court. When Jackson was elevated to the Senate in 1797, Claiborne, then only twenty-two years old, made a bid for his vacated seat and won it. After serving two terms, Claiborne was appointed by President Jefferson to receive Louisiana from France and then to serve as governor of the Orleans Territory when Louisiana was divided in 1804. Giving up his seat in the Senate after a few months to accept a judgeship on the Tennessee supreme court, Jackson had expressed some interest in the Louisiana post. Jackson relinquished the judicial post after six years, immersed himself in private business affairs, and advanced to the rank of major general in the Tennessee militia. Although Jackson and Claiborne were not close personal friends, they exchanged some correspondence when regional problems developed. Jackson invoked their friendship during the period of the Burr threat in 1806-07, and Claiborne did likewise seven years later when he invited Jackson to visit New Orleans as the British invasion loomed ahead.

About a week after Jackson's dramatic appearance in New Orleans, Claiborne had made his own bid for military appointment. Declaring that he did not intend to remain a silent spectator, he asked James Monroe to persuade President Madison to give him command authority as Jackson's immediate subordinate. He would obey Jackson's orders, he declared bluntly, but he would not accept any other regular or militia officer as his military superior.[36] Although unsuccessful in his appeal, the governor nonetheless took to the field and attempted to provide meaningful military leadership. Jackson methodically parried each bid and forced Claiborne to remain inactive and unnoticed on the periphery. These leadership tensions naturally produced a spate of rumors about the growing "war" between the two men. The Creole community was amused by unlikely whispers that Claiborne had slapped Jackson during a stormy personal encounter. On another occasion, a bystander ostensibly overheard Jackson warn the insistent Claiborne: "Governor if you are not more cautious in [the] future, I shall have to shoot you."[37]

Jackson's choice of local aides also contributed significantly to his frictions with Claiborne. In fact, the aides were either opposition leaders or were closely identified with Claiborne's acknowledged political enemies. Jackson chose Edward Livingston, the most prominent and vocal Claiborne critic at the time, as his military secretary. Livingston, whom John Randolph of Virginia later described as an utterly corrupt man of splendid abilities who "shines and stinks like a rotten mackerel by moonlight," had been absolutely unrelenting in his personal warfare against Claiborne from the time of his own arrival in New Orleans from New York a short time after the transfer of Louisiana to the United States. Despite the acute crisis and possible loss of Louisiana to invaders, Edward Livingston remained "Claiborne's enemy before he was Jackson's counseller."[38]

Always capable of strong feelings and partisan conduct, Jackson began to circumscribe Claiborne's leadership options almost immediately. His task was greatly simplified, of course, following his proclamation of martial law on December 16. The first concrete evidence that a strained relationship between the two men had developed, however, was reflected in Claiborne's appeal for a private interview on December 22. *"The times require our union,"* he implored, "nor is there anything I more desire than to maintain with you, the most friendly understanding, and a cooperation zealous and cordial."[39] No evidence exists of a response by Jackson.

The next day when Claiborne sought to participate in the fighting which erupted around Bayou Bienvenu and the Villeré plantation, Jackson ordered him to move back with the First, Second, and Fourth Louisiana militia regiments to guard the Gentilly Road to the east of New Orleans between Lakes Borgne and Pontchartrain. This effectively removed Claiborne from the field of action and precluded further active participation in the combat. Over the next few days Jackson transferred most of the men under Claiborne's command to other units, leaving only a skeletal force encamped on the Gentilly Road. Governor Claiborne then returned to New Orleans to check on security conditions, a logical precaution in view of uncertain local loyalties and his responsibility as the chief civil authority. When the decisive battle of January 8 erupted, Claiborne once more appeared on the scene to provide assistance as the battle raged. But as Jackson mauled the confused and milling enemy, a Creole-Kentuckian force under General David B. Morgan on the west bank of the Mississippi River fell back before an enemy assault. If Colonel William Thornton's brigade had exploited its advantage, it would have posed a serious threat to Jackson's defense line. Jackson dispatched French General

Jean J. A. Humbert, who had served earlier under Napoleon, to replace Morgan. Morgan challenged the order, creating further confusion and adding to the threat. Jackson subsequently informed Claiborne that he could not afford any more men, but he emphasized that Thornton's brigade would have to be destroyed. Interpreting this as an order, Claiborne crossed the river the same day and added to the confusion since he regarded himself as the senior officer, outranking both Morgan and Humbert.[40] Jackson's failure to be more explicit at this critical juncture could have had disastrous consequences because of the momentary command confusion, as well as by his failure to devote more direct attention to defensive preparations on the west bank. Fortunately for the Americans, Jackson's bloody repulse of Pakenham's offensive thrust forced the British to withdraw and the threat was removed. Claiborne retained command of the state militia forces on the west bank and "maintained a semblance of order in that quarter until the disappearance of danger."[41]

The British invasion force evacuated Louisiana on January 18. When General Jackson prepared to break camp below New Orleans three days later, he issued a general order in which he offered his thanks to those who had contributed to the American victory. This included expressions of appreciation to the regular troops, the numerous state militia units and their commanders, the Baratarians, and his aides-de-camp. In late January he wrote to Nicholas Girod, mayor of New Orleans, to thank him and the local inhabitants, including the "softer sex," for their support during the crisis.[42] The general, however, conspicuously refrained from extending an expression of appreciation to Governor Claiborne, either for his defensive preparations when the invasion threat began to assume tangible form or for the supportive role he played during the course of the invasion itself. This could hardly be viewed as an innocent oversight; the general clearly intended to exclude Claiborne. While the deliberate omission did not detract from Jackson's authenticity as a battlefield hero, it nonetheless revealed a pronounced character flaw.

Jackson's slight of the governor provided tacit encouragement to local political enemies who never relented in their efforts to discredit Claiborne. They made a number of oblique accusations against the chief executive, one of which was a charge of personal cowardice on January 8. One of the accusers was Major Auguste Davezac, a Jackson aide and brother of Mrs. Edward Livingston.

The other was Surgeon General David C. Ker, who contended that he saw Claiborne sitting on his horse behind the field hospital where he was protected from enemy fire. General Jackson readily lent credence to the malicious whispers, although his own personal contacts with Claiborne on December 23 and again on January 8 were clearly sufficient to refute them. Stung by the vicious rumors and charges of inadequate leadership, Claiborne drew up a long list of questions and sent them to several leaders who had been active in the defense of the city, including David B. Morgan, John Thomas, Commodore David Patterson, Baptiste Labatut, and Michael Fortier, Jr. Their responses confirmed the governor's contention that he had made every effort to place New Orleans in readiness and had been vigilant. According to the evidence, Claiborne had bowed to Jackson's order on December 23 and marched to Chef Menteur at the head of his three militia regiments and remained there until virtually all of the units under his command had been transferred. While defending Chef Menteur, Claiborne also made visits to New Orleans to consult with General Labatut, whom Claiborne left in command of the city's security forces when he made his bid for a field assignment. Also, the replies proved that the governor visited Jackson in the lines at the height of the battle on January 8. Colonel Bartholomew Shaumburgh, the governor's aide, declared that he and Claiborne were actively engaged in defensive preparations in anticipation of an enemy assault on Jackson's right flank when Jackson arrived and ordered Claiborne to cross the Mississippi and destroy the enemy force there. The governor ceased his activities immediately to carry out the order and joined General Morgan on the right bank the same day.[43] Governor Claiborne's conduct hardly merited the reproaches to which it was subjected but he, in characteristic form, methodically refuted the charges made by his chronic critics. Nonetheless, the accusations and criticisms made by these long-standing opponents and supported by Jackson cast shadows on Claiborne's reputation which were never entirely removed.

Much of the criticism to which Governor Claiborne had been subjected before and during the crisis was transferred to General Jackson for a time when he continued to enforce martial law following the British evacuation. Strained relations had developed between the general and state lawmakers in mid-December when they refused to adjourn, and Jackson responded with a proclamation of martial law. Then the legislators heard that

Jackson ostensibly had threatened to put the torch to New Orleans before he would allow enemy forces to occupy it. In turn, Jackson reacted sharply to a rumor that the lawmakers planned to surrender the city to the invaders, and he directed Claiborne to "blow them up" if they attempted such a move.[44] As the British threat receded, an open quarrel ensued. Jackson maintained martial law for an unduly long period of time because of the temporary loss of a dispatch from the War Department announcing the ratification of the peace treaty on February 17, and because of personal obduracy when the civil authorities challenged the general's unbridled authoritarianism.

On January 31—ten days after the British evacuation—and again on February 24, Governor Claiborne pressed Jackson to release conscripted local militiamen not actually needed for security purposes. He also inquired apologetically about some Negro slaves taken by the British forces when they evacuated Louisiana, and asked permission to send a dispatch to the English commander about the slaves which would be delivered by "three distinguished citizens, if you should not already have effected the restoration of their property." Jackson responded stridently by first accusing two Louisiana regiments of insubordination during the crisis and lecturing Claiborne on the militia offense. The general proclaimed imperiously that he would not permit the "Laurels of Louisiana to be Tarnished by the Lurking Demon of discord that attempts to insinuate itself into her ranks," and charged Claiborne with responsibility for the destruction of the "hidra." Moreover, Jackson warned bluntly that neither the governor nor the legislative leaders had permission to negotiate with the British or to interfere with the existing authority. Interference, the volatile general threatened, would force him to order the arrest of offenders.[45] The governor had no intention of rising to the fiery general's bristling challenge. He issued a circular in which he alluded to Jackson's "misunderstanding" with himself and the legislators and disclaimed any intent to engage in a contest with a "Victorious Chief whose gallantry and exploits have attracted so much *admiration*." After duly praising the general, Claiborne moved on to the basic purpose of the circular. Jackson's violence had cast shadows on his reputation, he asserted, and added that the general's conduct while in New Orleans could not be excused, "much less justified by those who feel a proper regard for the rights of others."[46]

In view of his conciliatory disposition, Governor Claiborne's closing missive constituted an unusually trenchant indictment of Jackson's intolerable conduct following the British evacuation. That he was contemplating possible action was evidenced in an oblique remark that "serious difficulties" would ensue shortly in New Orleans. Moreover, on February 24 when Claiborne again implored Jackson to release unneeded state militiamen, he exclaimed to the state's attorney general that New Orleans remained a "theatre of Military Dominion" even though the enemy had withdrawn. Martial law should not be endured in the absence of an actual invasion, and in New Orleans the plea of necessity was without validity. The governor declared that, in view of Jackson's insistence upon such a policy, he personally could not "remain a Silent Spectator of the prostration of the Laws." He sternly instructed the attorney general to resume his duties, aid the civil magistrates, avenge the "Injured Laws of this State," and protect private citizens threatened with arrest by military authorities.[47]

Even though a showdown with the civil authorities appeared almost certain, Jackson angrily brushed aside their protestations for several weeks. The release of French subjects from the state militia service touched off a series of events which threatened to engulf New Orleans in an explosive civil-military confrontation. The French consul, Louis Chevalier de Toussard, interceded to have French citizens serving in the militia register their nationality with his office in order to be discharged immediately. A number of American citizens of French extraction immediately seized upon the opportunity to register with the consulate since Toussard made no serious effort to screen the registrants. Quickly sensing the ploy the irate Jackson halted the practice and ordered the French consul and those who had received discharge papers to leave New Orleans immediately under threat of seizure and imprisonment and remain in Baton Rouge throughout the emergency. A state legislator, Louis Louailler, published an article highly critical of Jackson's order in the *Louisiana Courier* on March 3. Two days later Jackson ordered Louailler's arrest as a spy. On the same day Federal District Judge Dominic Hall issued a writ of habeas corpus for Louailler. In turn, Jackson ordered Hall arrested for "aiding, abetting and exciting mutiny," and the judge was escorted several miles north of the city by a cavalry unit after having been confined briefly in the barracks with Louailler. Federal District Attorney John Dick applied to Judge Seth Lewis of the First Judicial District of Louisiana for a writ of habeas corpus for Judge Hall. The application was approved, but it led to Dick's arrest. An order was even issued for the apprehension of Judge Lewis, but Jackson recalled it. Governor Claiborne reported these developments to Secretary of State Monroe and requested that President Madison be informed. Jackson had prostrated the laws and the civil authority, he added, while converting New Orleans and its environs into a military camp.[48] But on March 8, four days before he received official notification of the Anglo-American peace pact, Jackson finally released the militia although he had vowed earlier not to do so until he received official confirmation of the treaty. Nonetheless, Jackson had succeeded by his harsh policies in halting mass desertions by local militia forces and maintaining a state of readiness in the event the enemy threat reemerged. While all of these turbulent events were transpiring, the disciplined militiamen from Tennessee and Kentucky had held fast without serious protest, although their ranks were decimated by yellow fever during the three-month interval between the decisive battle of January 8 and their release.

Jackson savored his weeks of whimsical tyranny, and then the judiciary exacted retribution. District Attorney Dick wanted to press charges immediately against Jackson, but Judge Hall benevolently permitted a few days in which to celebrate the war's end and the restoration of the civil authority. The judicial leaders afterward cited Jackson for contempt of court, for the seizure of court records, for the obstruction of justice, and for "going beyond martial law." The accused protested against the illegality and unconstitutionality of the proceedings, but his personal demeanor in court was exemplary. When declared guilty and fined $1,000 and court costs, Jackson accepted the penalty and refused a proffered refund by supporters. The judicial decision sparked a partisan demonstration in Jackson's behalf, but Jackson intervened and counseled obedience to the laws. A few days later, after having detracted from his dignified deportment in court by offering an unsubstantiated criticism of Judge Hall, the redoubtable general left the city.[49]

The usual partisan atmosphere reemerged following the abortive British invasion and the restoration of the civil authority. Any immunity Governor Claiborne may have had during the emergency was swept aside precipitately. General Jackson had stridden manfully into New Orleans as its savior, and he later assumed the appearance of a fascist tyrant in the popular view because of his exceptional conduct following the repulse of the British forces. In fact, the lawmakers deliberately omitted Jackson's name from the long list of individuals whom the solons thanked, on behalf of Louisianians, for their contributions to the defense of the state. But after the general's departure, the lustre of his reputation was restored and quickly soared to legendary dimensions. Governor Claiborne remained among the Louisianians and he, not Jackson, bore the brunt of popular criticism. As he had been castigated for permitting General James Wilkinson to assume command of the militia during the Burr crisis in the winter of 1806-07, Claiborne was also criticized for relinquishing the militia to General Jackson. Claiborne attempted to defend himself, but in doing so he necessarily was critical of the Hero of New Orleans. While Jackson had justified his conduct in terms of necessity, Claiborne told the state legislature that the end did not justify the means. He roundly condemned Jackson's prostration of the laws and civil authority in New Orleans. The lawmakers, having earlier displayed intense hostility toward the general, now stoutly defended him and rapped the governor's wrists by asserting that "where there is so much to admire, we are not disposed to dwell upon some deed which we cannot approve."[50] The loyal opposition was again making its influence felt, a clear signal that the situation in New Orleans was indeed normal at last.

On balance, Governor Claiborne acquitted himself ably, honorably, and unselfishly during the hectic months of the emergency. In view of the narrow confines in which he was compelled by perceptive judgment to function, he served with statesmanlike distinction, even if his leadership was not particularly appreciated by those who generally supported him or by chronic opponents whose consuming passion was to embarrass and discredit the Claiborne administration. He painfully accepted the humiliations and embarrassments of 1813 and much of the following year while gambling on the conviction that Louisianians would close ranks and support his leadership when they became convinced in their minds that an unmistakable emergency confronted them. By the time Jackson marched into New Orleans to assume personal command on December 1, Governor Claiborne had made as many defensive preparations and had mobilized the populace as fully as anyone could have done under the particular circumstances which prevailed at the time in the Creole-dominated society. From the moment of his initial appearance in the city until he departed five months later, Jackson was in full and complete command, and he made abundantly clear that his imperial prerogatives were not subject to challenge by the executive, legislative, and judicial authorities. During the period in which enemy forces occupied native soil, the emergency was simply too critical and pervasive for Governor Claiborne to challenge General Jackson and risk the greater divisions and torn loyalties that would have ensued. Anything less than full local support for Jackson's heroic defense would have invited defeat and the occupation of New Orleans by enemy forces. Fully cognizant of this overriding fact, Claiborne accepted the personal indignities and disappointments inflicted by the volatile general. And while adhering relentlessly to his subjective policies toward the governor, Jackson was abetted and encouraged unceasingly by "Clark, Livingston, and Company" and their clique of Claiborne detractors.

During the weeks following the British evacuation of Louisiana in which Jackson maintained martial law, Governor Claiborne again acted in the greater interests of Louisiana and Louisianians. He simply could do no more than maintain cautious but persistent pressures upon Jackson and gingerly prod him to relax his policies while keeping national leaders informed of the general's contempt for the civil authority. Since the state militia remained on active duty during this delicate period, the governor lacked any meaningful enforcement authority. And even if he had had the services of the state militia, a challenge would have resulted in an unnecessary and prohibitive effusion of blood. Thus, Governor Claiborne quietly protested against the general's policies and waited him out, knowing that Jackson could not maintain martial law indefinitely. In view of the unacceptable alternatives, the governor's conduct during the critical months from December until the following March was exemplary. Indeed, the real measure of the man emerged in the crucible of war and its delicate aftermath, although it was easily overlooked as the battle raged and afterward when taut emotions threatened internecine violence and bloodshed.

Aside from specific political-military developments during the course of the crisis itself, the Battle of New Orleans provided an acid test of Governor Claiborne's twelve years of leadership in Louisiana. He had been charged by President Jefferson with responsibility for the introduction of republican institutions, and the assimilation of Louisiana's Gallic and Iberian inhabitants. Governor Claiborne himself was painfully and laboriously ambivalent about the degree to which these objectives had been achieved as enemy forces landed on the Louisiana coast. That the republican institutions he had carefully introduced and nurtured had taken firm root was clearly demonstrated both by the British invasion itself and by Jackson's assault upon them following the enemy withdrawal. The British threat also produced a popular unity and cohesion among the continental Creoles heretofore unrealized under American administration. In essence, the assimilation of Louisianians into the mainstream of the American nation was completed and verified under the influence of British guns. Governor Claiborne's patient and sensitive attention to the particular needs of his constituency largely assured these results. The military heroics of the brilliant Jackson during the Battle of New Orleans unfortunately made it virtually impossible for the Louisianians to comprehend or to appreciate the scope and magnitude of Governor Claiborne's substantial contributions to the overall American success. The dashing Jackson fully deserved the accolades and plaudits of the Louisianians as the Hero of New Orleans. At the same time, Governor Claiborne's unheralded but nonetheless vital longer term achievements made him the unsung hero of Louisiana.

XIII

LOUISIANA: ANTICLIMAX AND EPILOGUE

By the time Louisianians finished the last *Te Deum* and concluded their celebrations of Jackson's triumph, another political campaign had begun to take form. Once more Governor Claiborne donned his political armor and awaited the inevitable onslaught. He had been active in behalf of candidates favorable to his administration two years earlier and had been the target of some sharp political missives as a result. As a consequence, he fully expected to draw intense political fire in 1816. According to the state constitution, the governor could not succeed himself; however, Louisianians expected Governor Claiborne to campaign in support of his candidate for the post since he was the state's foremost political leader. The basic political appeal in the campaign again centered around the native inhabitant-newcomer dichotomy. The Claiborne, or American, faction selected Judge Joshua Lewis as its standard-bearer. Lewis, a Kentuckian appointed initially as land commissioner of the Eastern District of the Orleans Territory in 1805 and then as judge of the superior court to succeed Judge John B. Prevost in 1807,[1] had served quietly and without distinction and therefore was not a particularly strong candidate. The Creoles, or Ancients, selected Jacques Villeré, a major general in the state militia and Claiborne's gubernatorial opponent four years earlier. Lewis drew his support largely from the old West Florida, central, and northern sections of Louisiana, while Villeré relied generally on the city of New Orleans and the southern section of the state.[2]

The newspapers were active as usual in the campaign. One writer felt that Claiborne's selection as governor in 1812 had been both logical and just because of his long service to the territory and state. After all, he was the one who "first learned us to appreciate and cherish liberty," and his selection was only natural as an expression of respect for the government he represented. But the "debt of gratitude" was fulfilled; the time had now come for Louisianians to elect someone from their own ranks. At about the same time a Lewis partisan noted that Villeré's English was as deficient as Claiborne's French. Another newspaper writer noted that Villeré should be the legislature's choice if he obtained a majority of the popular vote despite constitutional provisions to the contrary. The Villeré partisan was obviously fearful that the general assembly would choose Lewis because of American intimidation even if Villeré was the overwhelming choice of the people. The final returns dispelled the Creole partisan's worries. Villeré received a total of 2,314 votes to 2,145 for his opponent, less than a two hundred-vote margin. In the general assembly, however, Villeré completely routed Lewis and even surpassed Claiborne's triumph four years earlier, winning by a vote of 44 to 3 with 1 abstention.[3] In the Creole view, the government had become genuinely representative; after thirteen years the native inhabitants had succeeded at last in electing one of their leaders as governor.

The changing of the political guard followed shortly. On November 20, 1816, Governor Claiborne delivered a farewell address before the general assembly. He stressed education as a bulwark of liberty, adding his annual refrain that the state's youth should be reared "in the paths of virtue, science, and patriotism." As he had also done annually, he appealed for an effective militia system as the "safest defence of a free people." The militia lacked discipline and tactical competency and should be reformed completely. He appealed for municipal laws and regulations to enhance the appeal and services of New Orleans to its diverse community, and called for an improved drainage system and reinforced levees to contain the "Nile of America." The retiring governor then reminisced about his thirteen years as chief executive. When he first accepted the post, he had agreed to discharge his duties zealously, faithfully, and to the best of his judgment. This he had done to his personal satisfaction, conceding modestly and realistically that "I am far from supposing it has not been my misfortune to commit many errors." He expressed gratitude that Louisiana had achieved statehood and its people received "into the bosom of the American Union, with equal privileges. Let, then, no improper jealousies be fostered, no injurious distinctions be made. We are members of one family, and all have the same common interest." On Tuesday, December 17, 1816, Jacques Villeré was sworn in as governor and William Claiborne again became a private citizen.[4]

Although his candidate lost the gubernatorial contest, Governor Claiborne's own political career appeared to take on new life. The general assembly was to choose a United States senator, and the two candidates for the post were Claiborne and incumbent Senator James Brown whose political rivalry dated back to Brown's brief tenure as territorial secretary in late 1804. On January 13, 1817, the fifty members present cast their ballots. Claiborne received 27 votes, Brown received 22, and 1 blank ballot was returned.[5] Claiborne's victory was not as decisive as it had been earlier, but it proved once again that his influence among the people was yet substantial despite his deteriorating health and the usual vulnerabilities produced by long public service.

Twelve days after the general assembly made its selection, local leaders arranged a public dinner in Claiborne's honor. Governor Villeré and most of the state's leading citizens were in attendance. The first toast offered was to Claiborne, "the happy man who after having faithfully served his country for many years has an opportunity of serving it again." Eighteen toasts followed and then Governor Claiborne offered a toast to the government of Louisiana, "and the highest reward to those who administer it—The approbation of a brave and generous people."[6] A grateful public servant stood ready once more to serve the nation and the people of Louisiana; however, he was to be denied the opportunity and the honor. He had almost died himself when his family succumbed to "yellow jack" in 1804 and recurring attacks continued to impair his health. Finally, on November 23, 1817, after a protracted and painful illness and not having taken his seat in the Senate, Governor Claiborne died of a "liver ailment." The municipal council of New Orleans proclaimed a week of mourning and agreed to erect a monument in his memory.[7]

At the time of his death, Governor Claiborne had devoted over half of his life to public service. Death cut short a return to Congress where he had begun as an enrolling clerk a quarter of a century earlier. He was only forty-two and his political star was still soaring when he died. Aside from an early death, Claiborne was handicapped by his occupancy of a lonely outpost on the periphery rather than in the mainstream of American life. A potent political force in the Southwest throughout most of his active life, Claiborne did not possess the erudition, intellectual capacity, or political acumen of his Montecello mentor. Nor did he display the martial prowess, fierce determination, or visceral appeal of the Southwest's most celebrated Indian fighter and spoiler of British dreams of a continent reconquered. Of moderate innate abilities, Claiborne nonetheless excelled because he was a masterful practitioner of the "soft sell" who relied heavily upon tact, diplomacy, and patient persuasion to achieve his aspirations and goals. Although he did not emerge fully as a national figure, Claiborne hovered on the fringes and achieved a broader prominence than such regional leaders as William Blount, John Sevier, or even Andrew Jackson until his electrifying emergence during the last few months of the War of 1812. Indeed, circumstances, time, place, and personality had ultimately lent a certain credence to Blount's prediction about the young enrolling clerk's future.

Unlike a number of frontier contemporaries, including Andrew Jackson, who sought to amass great private fortunes through land speculation and other convenient enterprises, Claiborne's abiding interest was public service. When he rejected the advice of personal friends and accepted the Tennessee judgeship in late 1796, he asserted that material accumulations were not his consuming interest. Rather, if he could be of assistance to his friend John Sevier by serving in his administration, he would do so without hesitation. Although this was patently altruistic, it was nonetheless typical of Claiborne who practiced what he preached as a public figure. At no time during the course of his years in public service did Claiborne's most uncompromising critics accuse him of using his influence as a public servant for private gain. Moreover, born into modest circumstances and in the emerging Jeffersonian tradition, Claiborne became a man of the people and champion of common causes. As a congressman from frontier Tennessee, he sometimes reminded his colleagues that the constituency he represented enjoyed few of the "conveniences which flow from wealth." He fought repeatedly for preemption rights for settlers in the Old Southwest, Mississippi, and Orleans territories and assisted actual settlers in the registration of their land claims while at the same time attempting to curb the exploitive land speculators. This was particularly noteworthy in view of his earlier association with the land barons. He acted in the interest of the "have nots" by supporting minimal taxes and the regulation of legal fees. As governor of the Orleans Territory he vetoed a measure which would have permitted exorbitant interest rates for borrowers, and he insisted that honest and well-intentioned debtors be protected from arbitrary imprisonment, hitherto a common punitive practice. By the same token, Claiborne's shrill response to the Spanish denial of the right of deposit at New Orleans in late 1802 and early 1803 was prompted in good measure by its adverse effect upon the economic well-being of the western farmers.

Also in the tradition of the Jeffersonian Republicans, Claiborne committed himself fully to the transcendent virtues of democracy and individual rights. When he served as a delegate to the Tennessee constitutional convention in 1796, he demanded that a bill of rights be included. He also favored voting by ballot in preference to the more common but inhibited practice of voting *viva voce*. While in Congress he roundly denounced the Federalist-sponsored Alien and Sedition Acts because they were intended, he charged, to subvert individual rights and constituted an insidious threat to the freedom and happiness of the people. Furthermore, as chief executive in the Mississippi and Orleans territories and as governor of Louisiana he steadfastly safeguarded individual liberties and promoted democratic processes. He insisted upon this because it was essential to his greater aspirations and goals, although it frequently required the shorter-term sacrifice of smooth and orderly government to achieve it. He vowed never to circumscribe the freedom of the press, for example, despite frequent newspaper attacks upon his administration and upon him personally.

As a committed Jeffersonian Republican, Claiborne himself never succumbed to the Nietzschean "will to power." During his first year in New Orleans, he possessed almost full and complete authority as governor and intendant, but he exercised his powers sparingly and judiciously. The combined titles and concomitant authority grated harshly on his republican conscience, embarrassed him personally, and made him squirm uncomfortably, always fearful that he would be accused of arrogating to himself a "plenitude of power which the haughtiest of my predecessors had never employed." The Creoles sometimes accused him of exercising his powers arrogantly and irresponsibly, particularly since they were defensive about their culture and traditions and resented his "Americanization" efforts. "Clark, Livingston, & Company" also made the charge repeatedly in an effort to mobilize local opposition against the Claiborne administration. Nonetheless, at no time during his fourteen years in Louisiana did he take a substantive action which served to corroborate the charge. In fact, Claiborne was disposed to lean heavily in precisely the opposite direction. Although personally distressed, he gave opposition forces free rein and sometimes tolerated defiance of legitimate governmental authority and occasional license.

Claiborne advocated and practiced "oeconomy," another salient virtue sedulously cultivated by the Republicans, throughout his public life. Governmental leaders should always take into full account the "situation and resources of the country." Economy, he regularly observed, was "an amiable trait in any government." His adherence to this principle in determining reimbursement rates for the Tennessee convention delegates underscored his affinity for economic prudence just as clearly as his proud assertion to national leaders following the acquisition of a part of West Florida in 1810 that not a cigar had been smoked at public expense. Despite his admiration and reverence for George Washington, he advocated an equestrian statue not only on the ground that it would be more commensurate with his achievements but also because it would be more economical. Indeed, Governor Claiborne felt an acute personal embarrassment when General Wilkinson insisted upon an extended and expensive celebration of Louisiana's transfer to the United States which completely overshadowed the diplomatic and social observances arranged by the French and Spanish colonial officials.

As a two-term congressman from frontier Tennessee, Claiborne reflected a national point of view without losing sight of the regional constituency he represented. During that time he also emerged fully as a Jeffersonian Republican in his commitment to Thomas Jefferson personally and to the virtues with which the brilliant Virginian was associated. When partisan controversies flared, Claiborne almost invariably supported the stand taken by his party. He looked with suspicion upon the Senate and president during the Federalist period, and believed with Jefferson that that government was best which governed least. When France and the United States almost went to war in 1798 Claiborne not only hewed to the prevailing policies of the Republican party but emerged as one of his party's most energetic spokesmen in the House despite a lack of experience, status, and influence even within his own party.

Like other Republicans, he was a Gallic partisan, defending or passively tolerating real and alleged French aggressions and railing against Britannic outrages. Also as a Republican, Claiborne stubbornly insisted that the nation's security would be guaranteed by citizen-soldiers or militiamen rather than by professional soldiers. Finally, he argued strongly for isolation from the affairs of Europe, maintaining that representatives should be assigned only in the major European capitals. These became trademarks of the Jefferson and Madison administration. Furthermore, he steadfastly supported Thomas Jefferson in the famous Jefferson-Burr presidential contest in 1800. In view of the fact that he was only twenty-two years old when he entered Congress—three years under the minimum stipulated in the Constitution—Claiborne's congressional career assumed an even more significant dimension.

Following his four years in the House of Representatives, William Claiborne spent the rest of his life in the Southwest. His decision to accept the governorship of the isolated and primitive Mississippi Territory was obviously a political gamble. In making this decision, Claiborne relinquished what appeared to be a promising congressional career and an emerging prominence within the ranks of the Jeffersonian Republicans. The two years he spent in Mississippi, however, provided excellent political and administrative experience and contributed immensely to his professional development and maturity. Events, time, and place again conspired to advance the career of the young Virginian and to assign an added measure of respectability to his political judgment.

When the Spanish intendant, acting on secret orders from his home government, foolishly closed the port of New Orleans to American commerce in late 1802, the intemperate act alerted national leaders in Washington to the necessity of acquiring all of the lower Mississippi Valley to insure American control of the vital Mississippi River. Failure to do so would hamper and stifle the growth and development of the western states and territories and possibly lend encouragement to a separatist movement. From his station in Natchez, Governor Claiborne independently exerted pressures on the Spanish colonial authorities in New Orleans to rescind the action while encouraging the Jefferson administration to explore the possibility of acquiring the territory. At the same time, he informed national leaders of Spain's inability to defend New Orleans and pointedly exclaimed that he could seize and hold the city with a few hundred Mississippi militiamen. Jefferson, concerned and apprehensive about the retrocession of Louisiana to France in the autumn of 1800 and its possible implications for the United States, sent James Monroe to Paris to assist Robert Livingston with the negotiations. The president also supplied the two American representatives with Claiborne's reports to keep them abreast of Spanish-American developments in the lower Mississippi region. The American and French officials then consummated the Franco-American treaty of 1803 and the Louisiana Territory was relinquished to the United States.

The proximity of the Mississippi Territory to Louisiana explained in part Claiborne's initial appointment as governor and intendant of the sprawling Louisiana Territory. Although not the preferred choice of President Jefferson initially or of the people over whom he was appointed to preside in Louisiana, he ultimately became the choice of both. Both Presidents Jefferson and Madison kept their options open and made periodic overtures to such experienced and eminent leaders as James Monroe and the Marquis de Lafayette, but this was not necessarily a reflection on the less eminent, less prominent Claiborne and certainly was not intended by either president as an expression of personal disappointment or disapproval. When Claiborne completed each of his three-year terms in the post, the president methodically reappointed him and the Senate confirmed the appointment as a matter of course. Although Claiborne's position as governor of the Orleans Territory was never fully secure at any time throughout the territorial period, it did not appear to impair his overall effectiveness. Nonetheless, public knowledge that Jefferson and Madison were considering other possible candidates for the Louisiana post undoubtedly added to the difficulties of the Claiborne administration since it contributed to Claiborne's personal uncertainties and his political opponents were able to exploit it to some degree against his administration. That he continued to serve both presidents throughout Louisiana's territorial period and then became the elective choice of Louisianians in 1812 were solid tributes to Claiborne and the leadership he provided.

Because of the Gallic-Iberian culture and temperament of Louisianians, the governorship required a personality who was capable of exercising patience and understanding without having such qualities misinterpreted as uncertainty and weakness by the local inhabitants. Claiborne charted and steered a course which allowed for a minimum of instability and disruption in view of the potential for turmoil and upheaval in that unique environment. To have been less firm and determined would have engendered great political dissidence and possible anarchy. To have acted with irresponsible forcefulness or the imperiousness of an Andrew Jackson would have invited outright revolution and bloodshed. Thus, the establishment of a delicate balance between the two extremes was essential to the achievement of national objectives. Governor Claiborne's basic formula for success in the Orleans Territory was expressed succinctly to Attorney General Richard Rush when he interceded in behalf of Jean Laffite and the Baratarian buccaneers in 1814. In his capacity as a public servant, he declared simply, he had always followed a policy of sympathetic persuasion and moderation. He employed it in Louisiana much as he had earlier in the Mississippi Territory but, despite fundamental differences between the inhabitants of the two territories, it was similarly successful. That his administration in Louisiana, based on this simple philosophy, was successful and was appreciated by Louisianians was borne out in the state elections of 1812 and again in 1816. Governor Claiborne carried every parish in Louisiana, including New Orleans which was the focal point of his political opposition, in handily winning the race for the governorship in 1812. Moreover, he triumphed over Jacques Villeré, one of the most respected of the "ancient inhabitants" who succeeded him as governor four years later. The modest Claiborne was surprised by his easy victory, but he wisely declined to take advantage of his political sweep to accelerate the "Americanization" of the Louisianians. Unable to succeed himself as governor because of a constitutional restriction, Claiborne won a post in the United States Senate over incumbent James Brown. That Claiborne was unable to utilize his political influence to support candidates endorsed by him in 1812 and 1816 while emerging triumphant himself was actually a tribute to Claiborne personally and was a testimonial to the respect and esteem in which he was held by Louisianians.

Governor Claiborne was only partially successful in his efforts to establish a smoothly functioning government while at the same time executing the policy directives of the Jefferson and Madison administrations. The judicial system introduced by Claiborne staggered along throughout the territorial period and functioned unevenly at best. Nonetheless, its very establishment was no mean accomplishment, especially since it constituted such a radical departure from the native experience and was the single greatest source of controversy among the local inhabitants. The governor succeeded in this delicate endeavor chiefly because of his broader tactical policy of gradualism, his patient efforts to educate the people, his willingness to incorporate traditional legal precepts and practices, and finally his flexible application of the newly introduced system. The legislative branch of government functioned more effectively generally than the judiciary, but initially it too existed largely in name only. After the turbulent and largely sterile sessions of 1805 and 1806, however, the lawmakers became more responsible and responsive. Very seldom after the climactic encounter with the executive authority in the early summer of 1806 did the members of the legislature pursue a policy of deliberate obstructionism. This certainly was not the basic intent of the legislators in 1813 when they refused to support the militia requisition or again in late 1814 when Claiborne and Jackson asked them to adjourn and return to their respective parishes. Indeed, their stubborn refusal to accede to the request in 1814 was prompted primarily by a sense of responsibility to protect the civil liberties of Louisianians while at the same time assuming some meaningful responsibility for the defense of New Orleans against the British invasion force. The executive branch of government itself was not demonstrably superior to the other two branches of government. Governor Claiborne provided experienced leadership and continuity, but frequent resignations and personnel changes at subordinate levels impeded the efforts of the executive branch of government and imposed an undue burden on the governor himself.

Governor Claiborne consistently stressed the necessity of education in Louisiana, as he had earlier in Mississippi, regarding it as an indispensable vehicle in the longer-term "Americanization" of Louisianians. It was essential to the development of republican institutions, he insisted, and was a bulwark against threats to the fundamental liberties of the people. Yet formal achievements in the field of public education were modest at best. No meaningful progress was realized in the Orleans Territory, in fact, until the territorial legislature finally appropriated funds for a college and parish schools in 1811. In his last address to the state legislature in late 1816, Governor Claiborne's appeal for legislative support for education bore more than a superficial similarity to his appeals when he first went to New Orleans. In short, the governor implicitly conceded that he had merely provided an educational foundation. His successors hopefully would add to it.

Although trained personnel, facilities, and resources were limited in the southwestern frontier regions, the governor strove diligently to maintain law and order. He tried to mobilize popular support while attempting with varying degrees of success to curb the excesses of organized banditti, whether they were the Mason gang in Mississippi, outlaws operating from the no-man's land of the Sabine-Arroyo Hondo strip, or Jean Laffite and the Baratarians. In doing this, he often cooperated with the Spanish authorities and other state and territorial officials. Moreover, he consistently advocated a policy of moderation toward criminals, stressing both preventive and rehabilitative measures. In this particular respect, Claiborne manifested a more progressive and enlightened policy than most frontier contemporaries.

Governor Claiborne, assisted by regular forces, quickly suppressed a slave insurrection in the Orleans Territory in 1811, and pursued a generally progressive Indian policy in both Mississippi and Louisiana. When the long anticipated slave revolt was stamped out, the governor requested that only the leaders of the insurrection be dealt with harshly. Moreover, he applied himself assiduously to the task of maintaining a peaceful relationship with the Indian tribes in Mississippi and Louisiana. He promoted husbandry among the Indians in compliance with national Indian policies, and directed his agents to prevent unprincipled white traders from taking advantage of the Indians. While incidents among the white settlers and Indians were not uncommon, Claiborne prevented them from assuming serious proportions and intervened to mollify the offended and to offer assurances. In dealing with Indian grievances against the white settlers, however, Claiborne relied too heavily on "dollar diplomacy." Like his contemporaries, Claiborne too offered beads and trinkets to smooth over injuries and ruffled feelings. Nonetheless, he proved to be an abiding friend of the Indians, a fact which was brought into focus when relations between Spain and the United States were strained almost to the breaking point in 1806 and again when war erupted between England and the United States in 1812. Unlike both the English and Spanish, Claiborne at no time attempted to enlist Indian support, even when American defensive capabilities were limited and uncertain. Rather, in his addresses to the Indian leaders, he emphasized that the frictions and conflicts were among white men and did not concern the Indian tribes.

One of the most frustrating problems with which Governor Claiborne had to contend in Mississippi and Louisiana was the organization of an effective militia. In his initial address to the Mississippi legislature, he stressed the necessity of getting the militia properly organized, and he emphasized this point repeatedly in subsequent messages over the following two years. But shortly before he left Natchez in 1803 he admitted that the militia had shown no substantive improvement, and his attempts to organize an effective militia force in Louisiana likewise failed to fulfill his expectations. When war almost erupted with Spain over the Sabine boundary in 1806 the territorial militia dragged its feet momentarily and some of the New Orleans militiamen refused to leave the city. Then, in the winter of 1813-1814, some municipal militia units refused to honor Governor Claiborne's orders in a time of imminent danger and possible invasion. Claiborne must have been tempted to take punitive action against them, but precipitate punishment might well have driven the temperamental Louisianaians into the arms of the enemy despite their loathing of the English and have produced a greater cleavage between the American newcomers and native inhabitants. As it was, Claiborne accepted the personal humiliation and embarrassment and pursued a tediously patient course, assuring both himself and national leaders that Louisianians would rally to the defense when fully convinced of the gravity of the situation. So it turned out. The militia and private citizens rendered generally disciplined and exemplary service and contributed substantially to the successful defense of New Orleans. Thus the Louisiana militia at no time displayed blind obedience to authority but it performed creditably in the field when needed most.

In the aftermath of both the Sabine crisis and the Battle of New Orleans, Claiborne was subjected to stringent criticism and he deserved it in part. The governor's critics castigated him for turning over the militia to General James Wilkinson following the return to New Orleans from the Sabine region and in the midst of a flurry of rumors that Aaron Burr and an invasion force were poised to descend on the city. The governor was also criticized for his refusal to intervene when General Wilkinson exercised dictatorial powers for several weeks. Claiborne's relinquishment of the territorial militia to Wilkinson, who commanded the Seventh Military District and which included the Orleans Territory, was understandable. Although he personally disliked and distrusted the free-wheeling and devious Wilkinson and had received a number of direct and oblique warnings from Jackson and others to the effect that Wilkinson was a traitor, Claiborne weighed the options open to him and gambled on Wilkinson's loyalty. The threat failed to materialize, but Claiborne's decision was correct. His acquiescence when Wilkinson rode rough-shod over the civil authority, however, was indefensible and inexcusable. Governor Claiborne should have asserted himself resolutely when it became obvious that no real danger existed, but timidity stifled any inclination he may have had to act in defense of the republican principles he had so feelingly espoused throughout life. Claiborne not only allowed himself to be swaddled and "laid . . . to bed like a great baby," as President Jefferson exclaimed reproachfully, but he compounded the error by defending Wilkinson's reprehensible conduct to the Jefferson administration.

History largely repeated itself following the Battle of New Orleans eight years later, although a real threat to the security of New Orleans had indeed developed. Local critics lashed out at the weary and frustrated governor for turning over the militia to General Andrew Jackson. But to have done otherwise would have been foolhardy both because of the British threat and Jackson's certain reaction since he would have used the forces under his command to enforce his will. Jackson, too, trampled on the civil authority and maintained martial law for an unnecessarily extended period of time after the British evacuation of Louisiana. Claiborne first protested almost inaudibly, then with some hint of resoluteness, but at no time did he offer a forthright challenge to the redoubtable Jackson. Yet Jackson's decision to release the militia a few days before he actually received official notification of the peace treaty, which he had earlier insisted upon as a condition for the release of the local militia, relieved the tense situation. Some members of the legislature brought pressures to bear on the governor to call Jackson's hand, even to the point of using the militia if necessary. The more detached and reasonable judgment of Claiborne fortunately prevailed and headed off a resort to arms between Louisianians and the Jackson forces. And in the event of a clash, the resultant effusion of blood would have been preponderantly Creole blood. Jackson and others later charged that Claiborne had done nothing to prepare New Orleans for the British invasion and that the city was virtually defenseless. Although Jackson's arrival in the city had the effect of lifting morale and accelerating defensive preparations, the criticisms of Claiborne were unfounded and unmerited. Indeed, Governor Claiborne received the necessary cooperation from the legislature and citizenry and defensive preparations proceeded smoothly during the autumn and early winter of 1814. Claiborne also provided Jackson with detailed information about defense plans and troop deployments in New Orleans and its environs. Moreover, after Jackson's arrival in the city, Claiborne displayed a transparent eagerness to cooperate but was relegated to a meaningless role by Jackson. Thus, a rift developed almost immediately between the two men at a critical time but Jackson, not Claiborne, was responsible for it. Further, any possible hope of a rapprochement between the imperious general and republican governor vanished when Jackson chose to surround himself with local aides who were inveterate enemies of the Claiborne administration and were fully prepared to avail themselves of the unexpected opportunity to embarrass and humiliate Claiborne. Jackson later joined with these same elements to cast unwarranted aspersions on Governor Claiborne's conduct during the course of the emergency. After the British evacuation, Claiborne methodically and patiently accumulated evidence to exonerate himself of the calumnious charges of personal cowardice and dereliction of duty.

   Although he displayed a tedious patience and philosophical benevolence at the local level, the governor proved to be one of the nation's most ardent war hawks and exponents of manifest destiny. Time and again during the uneasy months before the outbreak of the Anglo-American war, Claiborne pressed the Madison administration to become more aggressive. The national honor had been compromised repeatedly by British outrages, he continued to remind national leaders, and the only way to restore it was on the battlefield. He was grievously disappointed when he thought for a time that the United States and England would do no more than exchange vocal charges and recriminations as they had done for years. When Congress finally declared war he received the delayed news with confidence and enthusiasm but it waned perceptibly as the war progressed. Nonetheless, his determination to continue the struggle remained steadfast despite repeated disappointments and uncertainties. Finally, when he learned about the peace treaty, he reassured national leaders that the country could not have sheathed its sword under more favorable circumstances.

Claiborne's zeal as a war hawk was easily matched by his expansionist commitment. He had proposed the American seizure of New Orleans when the city's harbor facilities were denied to the United States in 1802. When the United States acquired the Louisiana Territory, he became one of the foremost proponents of a "greater Louisiana" by insisting upon an interpretation of the ambiguous boundary stipulations in the Franco-American treaty which would clearly benefit the United States. When boundary disputes erupted with Spain, as Napoleon had anticipated with a certain amusement, Claiborne invariably sought to use the occasions to extend the national domain. When the United States and Spain almost went to war over the contested ownership of those lands lying immediately east of the Sabine River, the governor viewed it as an opportunity to send American troops into Mexico City. Moreover, Claiborne's desire for added territory was only whetted by his personal role in the West Florida Revolution of 1810 and the American absorption of a part of West Florida. When the War of 1812 broke out, he envisaged an extension of American authority over the Spanish holdings in the Caribbean, Central, and South America and the British possessions extending from the Caribbean to Canada. Yet he was able to smother his disappointments when the defending American forces failed to achieve a decisive victory over the enemy forces and this lack of martial achievement precluded any territorial gains for the United States. But even so, he readily recognized that time was an enviable ally of the United States if not for himself personally.

Governor Claiborne was never able to shrug off criticisms of himself and his administration either easily or gracefully during his years in Mississippi and Louisiana. Instead, an undue sensitivity to partisan criticisms lingered with him, caused him to fret unduly, and hampered his effectiveness at times. He had sometimes expressed the hope that political factionalism would not develop, but to engage in such idle dreams betrayed an unbecoming political naïvete for a man who had known and experienced partisan political warfare from the time he began his career as a fifteen-year-old enrolling clerk. He encountered pungent opposition in both Mississippi and Louisiana. He was very much aware of the existing political dichotomy before he replaced Winthrop Sargent in Natchez; to have entertained for an instant the thought that the removal of the austere New Englander would also moderate and compose political passions was sheer fantasy. The heterogeneity of the Louisianians should have led Claiborne to expect far less in the way of unanimity and much more criticism than he had encountered in Mississippi. In New Orleans, in particular, the sensitive governor had been compelled to come to grips almost immediately with a pervasive native resentment and with powerful political forces spearheaded by "Clark, Livingston, & Company." To add to the governor's woes, the political opposition which crystallized almost from the time of Claiborne's arrival in New Orleans largely controlled the press. The newspapers hurled journalistic broadsides at "His Excellency" much to his almost unrelieved discomfiture.

Governor Claiborne's chronic sensitivity to criticism was occasionally accompanied by lapses into uncertainty and indecision, not infrequently aggravated by brief but pronounced pangs of self-pity. These handicaps were induced in part by a consuming desire to excel. This would enable him to win the enthusiastic approval of the Jefferson and Madison administrations while enjoying the accolades of the regional constituency he served and represented. But at no time in his professional career were his achievements or opportunities for achievement so spectacular that he became the instantaneous object of great adulation and honor nationally or regionally. He never emerged fully or was received by national leaders or by Louisianians as a *bona fide* man on horseback. In view of his driving ambitions and compulsions, this denial surely must have been a source of egregious personal frustration and disappointment.

Governor Claiborne nonetheless was infinitely more successful and influential than he realized privately because of his innately modest disposition and temperament. He had a legitimate claim to national prominence even if it was unrecognized by himself, by his contemporaries, or by posterity. He was a dedicated and enthusiastic spokesman, interpreter, and exemplar of early nineteenth-century Jeffersonian Republicanism which made such an indelible imprint upon American institutions and thought. Moreover, he exerted an influence upon the national and foreign policies of the Jefferson and Madison administrations, especially as they focused on Spain and its crumbling colonial empire, and he helped to lay the groundwork for national initiatives under the aegis of manifest destiny.

Yet Governor Claiborne's greatest and most concrete contribution undeniably lay in his fourteen years in Louisiana. He provided the unique leadership required to pull, push, coax, and convince the temperamental Louisianians that their greater interests would be best served and assured by their assimilation into the "American family." When the twenty-eight-year-old Claiborne descended the Mississippi River to receive Louisiana in the name of the United States and remained as governor, he had been charged with the introduction of republican institutions and the assimilation of the native inhabitants. These would have been formidable or even forbidding tasks for the most experienced, skillful, and resourceful national leaders in view of the predominantly Gallic and Iberian culture of Louisiana and the precarious geopolitical realities of the period. Nonetheless, committing himself to an essential stratagem of flexibility and gradualism, Claiborne proceeded methodically and confidently to the two-fold task at hand. The eminent but unspectacular success of this endeavor provided proof that diverse cultures could be brought into harmony and may have influenced, either consciously or unconsciously, similar efforts by national leaders in succeeding years as the United States extended its boundaries and influence. Although he was often criticized by a people who were sometimes unable to comprehend or appreciate the intricacies of the emerging Americanism, His Excellency proved himself worthy of the trust with which he was vested by national leaders and Louisianians.

On November 25, 1817, two days after William Claiborne's death, an encomium appeared in the *Louisiana Courier*. It stated, in part: "He exerted his influence in propagating that inviolable attachment which he bore to republican institutions; and if we now hold a rank among the most patriotic States of the Union, it is, in great measure, owing to the example and precepts of Mr. Claiborne." He had brought Louisianians into the American fold while enunciating, extending, and popularizing the commandments and ideals of Jeffersonian Republicanism. And at the same time the paternalistic Claiborne had jealously protected his native Creole charges "from the wolves prowling around to devour them," as Jefferson had encouraged him to do in the spring of 1810 when personal bereavement had left the governor momentarily shaken and uncertain. His was a job well done.

NOTES

Chapter I

ROAD TO PREFERMENT

1. Thomas Perkins Abernethy, *From Frontier to Plantation in Tennessee: A Study in Frontier Democracy* (Chapel Hill, 1932), p. 161. Hereafter cited as Abernethy, *Tennessee*.

2. Merrill D. Peterson, *Thomas Jefferson and the New Nation: A Biography* (New York, 1970), p. 785. Hereafter cited as Peterson, *Jefferson*.

3. Wilburt S. Brown, *The Amphibious Campaign for West Florida and Louisiana, 1814-1815: A Critical Review of Strategy and Tactics at New Orleans* (University Alabama, 1969), p. 11. Hereafter cited as Brown, *Amphibious Campaign*.

4. John D. Winters, "William C. C. Claiborne: Profile of a Democrat," *Louisiana History*, X, no. 3 (Summer, 1969), 190. Hereafter cited as Winters, "Claiborne."

5. Dunbar Rowland, comp. and ed., *This Mississippi Territorial Archives, 1798-1803; Executive Journals of Governor Winthrop Sargent and Governor William Charles Cole Claiborne* (Nashville, 1905), I, 337-8. Hereafter cited as Rowland, *Mississippi Territorial Archives*.

6. Winters, "Claiborne," 190.

7. James Street, *The Revolutionary War: Being a De-Mythed Account of How the Thirteen Colonies Turned a World Upside Down* (New York, 1954), pp. 6, 18.

8. Nathaniel H. Claiborne, *Notes on the War in the South; with Biographical Sketches of the Lives of Montgomery, Jackson, Sevier, the Late Gov. Claiborne, and Others* (Richmond, 1819), pp. 92-5. Hereafter cited as N. H. Claiborne, *Notes on the War in the South*. See also Allen Johnson and Dumas Malone, eds., *Dictionary of American Biography* (New York, 1930), IV, 115-6. Of the several biographical sketches of Claiborne's life, most writers have borrowed heavily from Nathaniel H. Claiborne, who, unfortunately, is the only real source of information about William's early years. The reader should keep in mind that Nathaniel Claiborne, William's brother, was understandably prejudiced.

9. N. H. Claiborne, *Notes on the War in the South*, pp. 92-5.

10. *Ibid.* See Dunbar Rowland, ed., *Official Letter Books of W. C. C. Claiborne, 1801-1816* (Jackson, Mississippi, 1917), I, 2 (footnote). Hereafter cited as Rowland, *Letter Books*.

11. James B. Longacre and James Herring, *The National Portrait Gallery of Distinguished Americans* (New York, 1834-1839), IV, 2-3. Hereafter cited as Longacre and Herring, *Distinguished Americans*.

12. N. H. Claiborne, *Notes on the War in the South*, pp. 96-7, 111; Longacre and Herring, *Distinguished Americans*, IV, 3-4.

13. N. H. Claiborne, *Notes on the War in the South*, pp. 96-7.

14. *Ibid.*, p. 97.

15. *Ibid.*, pp. 97-8; Longacre and Herring, *Distinguished Americans*, IV, 3-4.

16. N. H. Claiborne, *Notes on the War in the South*, pp. 99-100.

17. Rowland, *Mississippi Territorial Archives*, I, 250-1.

18. N. H. Claiborne, *Notes on the War in the South*, pp. 100-1.

19. Clarence E. Carter, comp. and ed., *The Territorial Papers of the United States* (Washington, 1937), IV, 60. Hereafter cited as Carter, *Territorial Papers*.

20. Abernethy, *Tennessee*, pp. 55, 116. Abernethy provides an excellent account of the Southwest Territory and its leading personalities. See in particular chapters VIII-X.

21. Abernethy, *Tennessee*, p. 87.

22. *Ibid.*, pp. 52-3, 121-6, 128-9.

23. Rowland, *Letter Books*, I, 2 (footnote); N. H. Claiborne, *Notes on the War in the South*, pp. 100-2.

24. Jack D. L. Holmes, "William C. C. Claiborne Predicts the Future of Tennessee," *Tennessee Historical Quarterly*, XXIV, no. 2 (Summer, 1965), 181-3.

25. *Ibid.*, 183-4.

26. N. H. Claiborne, *Notes on the War in the South*, p. 102.

27. Abernethy, *Tennessee*, pp. 134-6.

28. James G. M. Ramsey, *The Annals of Tennessee to the End of the Eighteenth Century* (Kingsport, Tennessee, 1926), p. 651. Hereafter cited as Ramsey, *Annals of Tennessee*. Dr. J. G. M. Ramsey (1797-1884) was a "distinguished physician, historian, and civic leader of Knowxville." See M. Thomas Inge, "G. W. Harris's 'The Doctor's Bill': A Tale About Dr. J. G. M. Ramsey," *Tennessee Historical Quarterly*, XXIV, no. 2 (Summer, 1965), 185-94.

29. "Journal of the Proceedings of a Convention, Began and Held at Knoxville, on the Eleventh Day of January, One Thousand Seven Hundred and Ninety-Six, for the Purpose of Forming a Constitution, or Form of Government, for the Permanent Government of the People," *Journals of the Territorial Councils Senate and House Tenn. 1794-1796* (Knoxville, 1852), pp. 3-4. Hereafter cited as *Journals of the Territorial Councils*. Apparently no records exist of the actual debates of the Tennessee constitutional convention.

30. *Journals of the Territorial Councils*, p. 5.

31. *Ibid.*

32. *Ibid.*, pp. 5-6.

33. *Ibid.*, pp. 8-10, 12, 22.

34. *Ibid.*, pp. 14, 17.

35. *Ibid.*, p. 23. Some of the state constitutions imposed similar restrictions on the clergy, although they did not derive from antireligious motives. Instead, they stemmed mainly from the philosophy that there should be a separation between spiritual and temporal affairs and that clergymen should restrict themselves to the former.

36. *Journals of the Territorial Councils*, pp. 18, 23-4, 28.

37. *Ibid.*, pp. 18, 27-8.

38. John F. H. Claiborne, *Mississippi, as a Province, Territory and State, with Biographical Notices of Eminent Citizens* (Jackson, Mississippi, 1880), I, 250. Hereafter cited as J. F. H. Claiborne, *Mississippi*.

39. Ramsey, *Annals of Tennessee*, pp. 622-5.

40. Abernethy, *Tennessee*, p. 136.

41. Ramsey, *Annals of Tennessee*, pp. 652-4, 657.

42. N. H. Claiborne, *Notes on the War in the South*, p. 103; Henry E. Chambers, "William Charles Cole Claiborne: Governor of Mississippi Territory and First Governor of Louisiana; How He Solved America's First Problem of Expansion," *Publications of the Mississippi Historical Society*, III (1900), 249.

43. Abernethy, *Tennessee*, pp. 137-138.

44. Ramsey, *Annals of Tennessee*, pp. 657-8, 662.

45. Longacre and Herring, *Distinguished Americans*, IV, 6; N. H. Claiborne, *Notes on the War in the South*, pp. 103-4. According to Judge Samuel C. Williams, Claiborne was twenty-four years old when he was appointed to the Superior Court of Law and Equity, but was still the youngest person to take a seat on this tribunal. See Samuel C. Williams, *Phases of the History of the Supreme Court of Tennessee* (Johnson City, Tennessee, 1944), p. 60.

46. Joshua W. Caldwell, *Sketches of the Bench and Bar of Tennessee* (Knoxville, 1898), 60.

Chapter 2

Republican Congressman

1. Thomas P. Abernethy, *The South in the New Nation, 1789-1819* (Baton Rouge, 1961), pp. 169-191. Hereafter cited as Abernethy, *The New Nation*. See also Abernethy, *Tennessee*, pp. 167-68.

2. Abernethy, *Tennessee*, pp. 166-69.

3. Carter, *Territorial Papers*, IV, 470.

4. Abernethy, *The New Nation*, p. 183.

5. N. H. Claiborne, *Notes on the War in the South*, pp. 103-04.

6. *Annals of the Congress of the United States*, 5th Congress, 2nd Session, p. 630. Hereafter cited as *Annals of Congress*. The author published an article on Claiborne's Congressional career in 1965. See Joseph Tennis Hatfield, "William C. C. Claiborne, Congress, and Republicanism, 1797-1801," *Tennessee Historical Quarterly*, XXIV, no. 2 (Summer, 1965), 156-80.

7. *Annals of Congress*, 5th Cong., 2nd Sess., pp. 777-78.

8. *Ibid.*, pp. 814-17.

9. *Ibid.*, pp. 919, 1058-60.

10. *Ibid.*, pp. 1895-96, 1918, 1922.

11. *Ibid.*, 5th Cong., 3rd Sess., pp. 2456-65.

12. *Ibid.*, 5th Cong., 2 Sess., pp. 1050, 1063-68.

13. N. H. Claiborne, *Notes on the War in the South*, pp. 103-04.

14. *Annals of Congress*, 6th Cong., 2nd Sess., pp. 900-15.

15. *Ibid.*, 6th Cong., 1st Sess., pp. 314-16.

16. *Ibid.*, 6th Cong., 2nd Sess., pp. 709, 749, 799-804, 817-20.

17. *Ibid.*, 5th Cong., 2nd Sess., pp. 1211, 1653.

18. *Ibid.*, pp. 848-49, 852, 917.

19. *Ibid.*, pp. 916-17, 1207-11.

20. *Ibid.*, pp. 1651-54, 1771-72, 2131.

21. William C. C. Claiborne to Colonel David Henley, February 5 and March 14, 1800. Both letters are in the Tennessee State Library and Archives, Nasvhille, Tennessee. Shortly after Claiborne wrote to Colonel Henley, the House approved the establishment of a military academy by a vote of 64-23, with Claiborne voting affirmatively. See *Annals of Congress*, 6th Cong., 1st Sess., p. 690.

22. *Annals of Congress*, 5th Cong., 2nd Sess., pp. 1783, 1801-03, 1812.

23. *Ibid.*, pp. 1882-83, 1892.

24. *Ibid.*, pp. 2073-78, 2181.

25. *Ibid.*, pp. 2116, 2127-28.

26. *Ibid.*, pp. 1775-83.

27. *Ibid.*, pp. 1786-96, 1973-97, 2028, 2049-50.

28. *Ibid.*, pp. 2135-37; *Journal of the House of Representatives*, 5th Cong., 2nd Sess., pp. 379-380.

29. *Annals of Congress*, 5th Cong., 3rd Sess., pp. 2445, 2449-51.

30. *Ibid.*, pp. 2897-99.

31. *Ibid.*, pp. 2583-91, 2678-79.

32. *Ibid.*, pp. 2959-73.

33. *Ibid.*, 6th Cong., 1st Sess., pp. 404, 419.

34. *Ibid.*, 6th Cong., 2nd Sess., pp. 751-52, 928-30.

35. N. H. Claiborne, *Notes on the War in the South, pp. 106-08.*

36. John S. Bassett, *The Federalist System, 1789-1801* (New York, 1906), pp. 292-93.

37. Vincent O. Nolte, *The Memoirs of Vincent Nolte: Reminiscences in the Period of Anthony Adverse: or Fifty Years in Both Hemispheres* (New York, 1934), p. 86.

Chapter 3

Mississippi: Politics, Indians, and Frontier Justice

1. Richard A. McLemore, ed., *A History of Mississippi* (Jackson, 1973), I, 174. Hereafter cited as McLemore, *Mississippi.* Chapter 8 and 9 of the first volume, which deal with Mississippi's territorial period, were written by Robert V. Haynes.

2. *Ibid.*, I, 178-82.

3. Dumas Malone, *Jefferson the President: First Term, 1801-1805* (Boston, 1970), pp. 245-56. Hereafter cited as Malone, *Jeffeson.* See also Carter, *Territorial Papers*, V, 126.

4. Carter, *Territorial Papers*, V, 78-85, 99-100; *Annals of Congress*, 6th Cong., 1st Sess., pp. 625-26.

5. *Annals of Congress*, 6th Cong., 2nd Sess., pp. 837-54, 1074-75; Carter, *Territorial Papers*, V, 95-8.

6. Carter, *Territorial Papers*, V, pp. 105-06, 121.

7. Robert Lowry and William H. McCardle, *A History of Mississippi: From the Discovery of the Great River by Hernando De Soto, Including the Earliest Settlement Made by the French under Iberville, to the Death of Jefferson Davis* (Jackson, 1891), pp. 179-80. Hereafter cited as Lowry and McCardle, *History of Mississippi*.

8. MSS Territorial Archives (1798-1817), Series A. Governors' Records, Executive Journal, Gov. W. C. C. Claiborne, 1803-04. Hereafter cited as MSS Executive Journal, W. C. C. Claiborne. These manuscripts are located in the Department of Archives and History, Jackson, Mississippi.

9. Rowland, *Mississippi Territorial Archives*, I, 345-47; Rowland, *Letter Books*, I, 9-10.

10. Dunbar Rowland, *History of Mississippi: The Heart of the South* (Jackson, 1925), I, 376-80. Hereafter cited as Rowland, *History of Mississippi*.

11. McLemore, *Mississippi*, I, 178, 197.

12. Rowland, *Mississippi Territorial Archives*, I, 334, 344-45.

13. Robert V. Haynes, "A Political History of the Mississippi Territory" (Master's thesis, The Rice Institute, Houston, Texas, 1958), p. 87. Hereafter cited as Haynes, "Mississippi Territory."

14. Rowland, *Mississippi Territorial Archives*, I, 373-74.

15. *Ibid.*, I, 388.

16. Haynes, "Mississippi Territory," pp. 91-6. See also Haynes' comprehensive treatment of the complex subject in McLemore, *Mississippi*, I, 178-99.

17. Haynes, "Mississippi Territory," pp. 104-05.

18. Rowland, *Mississippi Territorial Archives*, I, 350, 417-18.

19. MSS The Proceedings of the Governor of the Mississippi Territory as Superintendant (*sic*) of Indian Affairs, pp. 40-41. Hereafter cited as MSS Superintendant of Indian Affairs. This journal is found in the Department of Archives and History, Jackson, Misissippi.

20. Rowland, *Mississippi Territorial Archives*, I, 485-86.

21. MSS Superintendant of Indian Affairs, pp. 15-16, 19-22, 37-38

22. Rowland, *Mississippi Territorial Archives*, I, 350, 417-18.

23. MSS Executive Journal, W. C. C. Claiborne.

24. MSS Territorial Papers, Mississippi, 1797-1810, General Records of the United States Government, Record Group I, 25. Hereafter cited as MSS General Records.

25. Rowland, *Mississippi Territorial Archives*, I, 393-94, 400-02, 405-06.

26. *Ibid.*, I, 527-29.

27. MSS Superintendant of Indian Affairs, pp. 27-28.

28. *Ibid.*, pp. 29-31, 41-42, 51.

29. *Ibid.*, pp. 39-42.

30. *Ibid.*, pp. 29-33.

31. *Ibid.*, pp. 33-35.

32. *Ibid.*, 53-55.

33. *Ibid.*, pp. 49-50, 52, 55-56.

34. *Ibid.*, pp. 31-33; Towland, *Mississippi Territorial Archives*, I, 476-77, 480, 547-50.

35. MSS Superintendant of Indian Affairs, p. 15; Rowland, *Mississippi Territorial Archives*, I, 520-21.

36. MSS Superintendant of Indian Affairs, pp. 31, 37-38.

37. *Ibid.*, pp. 2-9.

38. *Ibid.*, pp. 46-48, 53.

39. Rowland, *Mississippi Territorial Archives*, I, 563-64, 599.

40. *Ibid.*, I, 379-81, 394-97.

41. Rowland, *Letter Books*, I, 46, 91-94. For a more complete narrative of the Harpes and Mason gang, see Robert M. Coates, *The Outlaw Years, The History of the Land Pirates of the Natchez Trace* (New York, 1930), pp. 21-73, 109-69. Hereafter cited as Coates, *The Outlaw Years*.

42. MSS Executive Journal, W. C. C. Claiborne.

43. Coates, *The Outlaw Years*, pp. 153-61.

44. MSS Superintendant of Indian Affairs, p. 35.

45. Rowland, *History of Mississippi*, I, 383-84. Three years after he left Mississippi, Claiborne was asked by Seth Caston to pay a reward of $100 for the latter's capture of John Sutton and James May of the Mason gang. Claiborne denied any individual responsibility for the payment of the reward, but he asked Governor Robert Williams of the Mississippi Territory to pay it from the territorial treasury, if Caston was entitled to it. See Rowland, *Letter Books*, III, 244-45.

Chapter 4

Mississippi: Problems on Both Sides of the River

1. Rowland, *Mississippi Territorial Archives*, I, 353-54; Rowland, *Letter Books*, I, 16-17.

2. Rowland, *Mississippi Territorial Archives*, I, 365-66.

3. *Ibid.*, I, 375-78.

4. *Ibid.*, I, 478, 582-83, 589-90, 596.

5. *Ibid.*, I, 402, 411-12, 428, 434-37, 478-79, 508-09.

6. McLemore, *Mississippi*, I, 190.

7. Rowland, *Mississippi Territorial Archives*, I, 402, 433-34, 478-81; Rowland, *Letter Books*, I, 51-52.

8. MSS Legislative Records, Series D, Territorial Archives, 1798-1817. Hereafter cited as MSS Legislative Records, Series D. These records are located in the Department of Archives and History, Jackson, Mississippi.

9. MSS Journal of the House of Representatives of the Mississippi Territory, 1803, pp. 4-5, 12-17.

10. Carter, *Territorial Papers*, IX, 96-98.

11. Rowland, *Mississippi Territorial Archives*, I, 363-66. When he wrote Madison, Claiborne stated erroneously that the judiciary was the only substantive source of "political disquietude."

12. Towland, *Mississippi Territorial Archives*, I, 367, 487.

13. Carter, *Territorial Papers*, V, 129. Judge Tilton did not resign officially until October 10, 1802. See *ibid.*, V, 178. Judge Bruin resigned in 1808 to avoid impeachment for drunkenness and neglect of duty. See McLemore, *Mississippi*, I, 214.

14. MSS Executive Journal, W.C.C. Claiborne.

15. MSS Journal of the House of Representatives of the Mississippi Territory, 1803, n.p.

16. Carter, *Territorial Papers*, V, 215.

17. McLemore, *Mississippi*, I, 181-82.

18. Rowland, *Mississippi Territorial Archives*, I, 374.

19. *Ibid.*, I, 429-30.

20. MSS Journal of the House of Representatives of the Mississippi Territory, 1803, pp. 6-7, 22-24.

21. MSS Legislative Records, Series D. Sheriffs' fees, for example, included the folowing: for every arrest, $1.25; for every bail-bond, fifty cents; for serving a writ, twenty-five cents, and for serving a subpoena for each person named in the same, fifty cents; for "hanging a person in conformity to a judgment of a Superior Court, ten dollars"; for pillorying a convicted person, $1; for each commitment and for "every releasement," fifty cents; and "for imprisoning of felons or debtors, or any other person, for each prisoner per day, for finding one pound of wholesome bread, one pound of good roasted or boiled flesh, and a sufficient quantity of fresh water, and every other necessary attendance, keeping the prison clean, etc., fortycents." The territory was not liable for any fees except those of constables and corners.

22. Ramsay, *Annals of Tennessee*, p. 642.

23. Rowland, *Mississippi Territorial Archives*, I, 431-32.

24. Haynes, "Mississippi Territory," p. 94.

25. Rowland, *Mississippi Territorial Archives*, I, 438-39. A collection of offers for land sites for Jefferson College, lottery

receipts, the names of financial contributors, and plans for the building itself are found in MSS A Journal of the Proceedings of the Board of Trustees of Jefferson College, pp. 1-33. Hereafter cited as MSS Board of Trustees of Jefferson College. This collection is in the Jefferson College Papers, Box 1, Vols. I-II, Department of Archives and History Jackson, Mississippi. See also McLemore, *Mississippi*, I, 358.

26. MSS Executive Journal, W. C. C. Claiborne.

27. MSS Board of Trustees of Jefferson College, pp. 1-4; Carter, *Territorial Papers*, V, 181-82.

28. Carter, *Territorial Papers*, V, 203.

29. MSS Executive Journal, W. C. C. Claiborne.

30. Carter, *Territorial Papers*, VI, 735—36.

31. MSS Journal of the House of Representatives of the Mississippi Territory, 1803, pp. 21-22, 65. The Mississippi inhabitants petitioned Congress on several occasions for the support of public education. One of the earliest petitions was made to Governor Winthrop Sargent who was asked to lay the petition before Congress. The petition, dated November 26, 1798, first noted congressional support for the "spiritual concerns" and education of the inhabitants of the Northwest Territory, and declared: "We most respectfully look up to you, Sir, to lay our case before them we standing in the greatest need of having the regular Ministry of the Gospel among us, and Schools for the education of our youth. But being as yet, in an infant state, and our population not yet equivalent to the extensiveness of our Country, renders it difficult to raise salaries adequate to induce a sufficient number of persons properly qualified for these offices to come among us, whose moral conduct and conversation, as well as doctrinal precepts, might be conducive to the maintaining of good order in the Government, and rendering our Offspring not only useful but ornamental to society by spreading among us a taste for polite literature." See Carter, *Territorial Papers*, V, 50-51.

32. Rowland, *Mississippi Territorial Archives*, I, 363-66, 369-70.

33. Carter, *Territorial Papers*, V, 142-45. A protracted quarrel developed over the fraudulent Yazoo land grants, but the Yazoo companies were supported by the United States Supreme Court in the case of *Fletcher* v. *Peck* (1810). See Charles H. Haskins, "The Yazoo Land Companies," *Papers of the American Historical Association* (New York, 1891), V, 395-437.

34. Carter, *Territorial Papers*, V, 156-58.

35. *American State Papers: Documents, Legislative and Executive, of the Congress of the United States, in Relation to the Public Lands, from the First Session of the Twenty-Third Congress: March 4, 1789 to June 15, 1834* (Washington, 1834), I, 123-25. Herafter cited as *American State Papers: Public Lands*.

36. Rowland, *Mississippi Territorial Archives*, I, 536-45.

37. *American State Papers: Public Lands*, I, 123-25.

38. Rowland, *Mississippi Territorial Archives*, I, 584-85.

39. Carter, *Territorial Papers*, V, 192-205.

40. *Ibid.*, V, 272-75.

41. Rowland, *Mississippi Territorial Archives*, I, 340.42. *Ibid.*, I, 415-16.

43. *Ibid.*, I, 449; Rowland, *Letter Books*, I, 95, 99-100.

44. Rowland, *Letter Books*, I, 198-201.

45. MSS Superintendant of Indian Affairs, 38-39.

46. "Documents: Dispatches from the United States Consulate in New Orleans, 1801-1803," Part I, *The American Historical Review*, XXXII, 803-15. Hereafter cited as "Despatches from the

United States Consulate in New Orleans," *American Historical Review.*

47. Arthur P. Whitaker, *The Mississippi Question, 1795-1803, A Study in Trade, Politics, and Diplomacy* (New York, 1934), 189-92. Hereafter cited as Whitaker, *Mississippi Question.*

48. Rowland, *Mississippi Territorial Archives*, I, 534-35.

49. James D. Richardson, comp., *A Compilation of the Messages and Papers of the Presidents, 1789-1897* (Washington, 1896), I, 349-50. Hereafter cited as Richardson, *Messages and Papers of the Presidents.*

50. Whitaker, *Mississippi Question*, pp. 189-93, 197-98. For the Claiborne-Hulings correspondence about the intendant's proclamation, see Rowland, *Mississippi Territorial Archives*, I, 532-35.

51. Rowland, *Letter Books*, I, 239-40, 243-47.

54. *Ibid.*, I, 211, 250-251.

55. Charles E. A. Gayarré, *History of Louisiana: The Spanish Domination* (New York, 1854), III, 457. Hereafter cited as Gayarré, *Louisiana.*

56. James A. Robertson, *Louisiana under the Rule of Spain, France, and the United States, 1785-1807* (Cleveland, 1911), II, 15-16. Hereafter cited as Robertson, *Louisiana.*

57. J. F. H. Claiborne, *Mississippi*, I, 239.

58. Rowland, *Letter Books*, I, 253.

59. "Despatches from the United States Consulate in New Orleans," Part I, *American Historical Review*, XXXII, 823.

60. *Ibid.*, Part II, XXXIII, 332, 351-52.

61. Rowland, *Letter Books*, I, 273-75.

62. *Ibid.*, I, 255-56, 267.

63. *Ibid.*, I, 283-85.

64. *Ibid.*, I, 274, 277.

65. *Ibid.*, I, 275.

66. Whitaker, *Mississippi Question*, pp. 231-32.

Chapter 5

Louisiana: Acquisition, Appointment, and an American Introduction

1. Whitaker, *Mississippi Question*, 180.

2. Rowland, *Mississippi Territorial Archives*, I, 346.

3. Ronald D. Smith, "Napoleon and Louisiana: Failure of the Proposed Expedition to Occupy and Defend Louisiana, 1801-1803," *Louisiana History*, XII (1971), 23-32. Hereafter cited as Smith, "Napoleon and Louisiana."

4. Abernethy, *The South in the New Nation*, pp. 246-249; Smith, "Napoleon and Louisiana," 32-35.

5. Smith, "Napoleon and Louisiana," 40.

6. Abernethy, *The South in the New Nation*, p. 249.

7. Smith, "Napoleon and Louisiana," 34-35.

8. Rowland, *Mississippi Territorial Archives*, I, 549, 553.

9. MSS Executive Journal, W. C. C. Claiborne.

10. Whitaker, *Mississippi Question*, pp. 250, 256.

11. Robertson, *Louisiana*, II, 50-51.

12. *The Union; or, New Orleans Advertiser*, December 27, 1803.

13. Carter, *Territorial Papers*, IX, 3-5.

14. *Ibid.*, IX, 11.

15. MSS Executive Journal, W. C. C. Claiborne.

16. MSS Superintendant of Indian Affairs, pp. 4-5, 19-20, 46-47.

17. Carter, *Territorial Papers*, IX, 14, 89-90, 94; Robertson, *Louisiana*, II, 77-78, 81-82, 121, 124-125.

18. Isaac J. Cox, *The West Florida Controversy, 1798-1813: A Study in American Diplomacy* (Baltimore, 1918), p. 145. Hereafter cited as Cox, *West Florida Controversy*.

19. John S. Bassett, ed., *Correspondence of Andrew Jackson* (Washington, D. C., 1926), I, 90. Hereafter cited as Bassett, *Correspondence of Andrew Jackson*.

20. Carter, *Territorial Papers*, IX, 136, 233.

21. *Ibid.*, IX, 91-94.

22. *Ibid.*, IX, 96-98.

23. *Ibid.*, IX, 95-96.

24. MSS Executive Journal, W. C. C. Claiborne.

25. Carter, *Territorial Papers*, IX, 59, 101-106, 108, 114-119.

26. *Ibid.*, IX, 119-121.

27. Robertson, *Louisiana*, II, 217-219.

28. Carter, *Territorial Papers*, IX, 137.

29. Albert E. Bergh, ed., *The Writings of Thomas Jefferson* (Washington, D. C., 1907), XVIII, 244. Hereafter cited as Bergh, *Thomas Jefferson*.

30. Marietta Marie Lebreton, "A History of the Territory of Orleans, 1803-1812" (Ph.D. dissertation, Louisiana State University, Baton Rouge, Louisiana, 1969), 28. Hereafter cited as LeBreton, "Territory of Orleans."

31. MSS Executive Journal, W. C. C. Claiborne.

32. *Ibid.*; LeBreton, "Territory of Orleans," pp. 31, 33.

33. LeBreton, "Territory of Orleans," pp. 33-35.

34. MSS Executive Journal, W. C. C. C.aiborne; Carter, *Territorial Papers*, IX, 136.

35. *The Union; or, New Orleans Advertiser*, December 27, 1803; Carter, *Territorial Papers*, IX, 138; LeBreton, "Territory of Orleans," pp. 34-35.

36. E. Wilson Lyon, *Louisiana in French Diplomacy, 1759-1804* (Norman, Oklahoma, 1934), pp. 245-246.

37. LeBreton, "Territory of Orleans," p. 36.

38. Charles P. Dimitry, "The Story of the Ancient Cabildo," *Louisiana Historical Quarterly*, III (1920), 57-67.

39. Robertson, *Louisiana*, II, 225-226.

40. Rowland, *Letter Books*, I, 307; MSS Executive Journal, W. C. C. Claiborne.

41. *American State Papers: Foreign Relations*, II, 582-583.

42. LeBreton, "Territory of Orleans," pp. 43-45; Carter, *Territorial Papers*, IX, 138-139.

43. Abernethy, *The South in the New Nation*, pp. 259-260; Carter, *Territorial Papers*, IX, 92, 105-106, 847; *The Louisiana Gazette*, April 11, 1809.

44. Bergh, *Thomas Jefferson*, X, 432-433.

45. William E. Foley, *A History of Missouri, 1763-1820* (Columbia, Missouri, 1971), pp. 70-72. Hereafter cited as Foley, *Missouri*. See also Henry E. Chambers, *Mississippi Valley Beginnings: An Outline of the Early History of the Earlier West* (New York, 1922), p. 212. Hereafter cited as Chambers, *Mississippi Valley Beginnings*.

46. Cox, *West Florida Controversy*, pp. 81-82.

47. Carter, *Territorial Papers*, IX, 16-17, 25.

48. Robertson *Louisiana*, II, 290-291.

49. Amos Stoddard, *Sketches, Historical and Descriptive, of Louisiana* (Philadelphia, 1811), pp. 148-149. Hereafter cited as Stoddard, *Sketches*.

50. LeBreton, "Territory of Orleans," pp. 14-20.

51. *Ibid.*, p. 6.

52. Carter, *Territorial Papers*, IX, 702.

53. Henry E. Chambers, "William Charles Cole Claiborne: Governor of Mississippi Territory and First Governor of Louisiana; How he Solved America's First Problem of Expansion,"

Mississippi Society, III (1900), 253-257. For good description of the native inhabitants of Louisiana, see *Niles' Weekly Register*, I (December 7, 1811), 243-48.

54. Carter, *Territorial Papers*, IX, 202.

55. Walter Prichard, "Selecting a Governor for the Territory of Orleans," *Louisiana Historical Quarterly*, XXXI (1948), 289-353. Hereafter cited as Prichard, "Selecting a Governor for the Territory of Orleans."

56. Cox, *West Florida Controversy*, p. 188; *The Louisiana Gazette*, June 11, 1805; June 4, 1806.

57. Bergh, *Thomas Jefferson*, XI, 47.

58. Bassett, *Correspondence of Andrew Jackson*, I, 90-91.

59. MSS Executive Journal, W. C. C. Claiborne.

60. Carter, *Territorial Papers, IX, 146-148, 197-198.*

61. *Ibid.*, IX, 190-191.

62. *Ibid.*, IX, 281-282.

63. Charles F. Adams, ed., *Memoirs of John Quincy Adams, Comprising Portions of His Diary from 1795 to 1848* (Philadelphia, 1874), I, 315, 321.

64. Carter, *Territorial Papers*, IX, 291.

65. Malone, *Jefferson*, IV, 348.

66. LeBreton, "Territory of Orleans," pp. 48-58.

67. Carter, *Territorial Papers*, IX, 162-163, 191.

68. James E. Scanlon, "A Sudden Conceit: Jefferson and the Louisiana Government Bill of 1804," *Louisiana History*, IX, no. 2 (Spring, 1968), 139-162

69. Carter, *Territorial Papers*, IX, 202-213.

70. LeBreton, "Territory of Orleans," pp. 116-117.

71. *The Louisiana Gazette*, August 7, 1804.

72. Carter, *Territorial Papers*, IX, 241-242, 245-246, 260-261, 265-266, 304-305, 310, 312, 314-315, 343-344; Everett S. Brown, *The Constitutional History of the Louisiana Purchase, 1803-1812* (Berkeley, California, 1920), pp. 147-148.

73. Chambers, *Mississippi Valley Beginnings*, p. 223.

74. *The Louisiana Gazette*, October 5, 1804.

75. LeBreton, "Territory of Orleans," 127-128.

76. Carter, *Territorial Papers*, IX, 282-85, 307-308, 310, 317-318, 320, 334-345, 347-348, 426-427.

77. *The Louisiana Gazette*, December 7, 14, 1804; April 18, 26, 1805; LeBreton, "Territory of Orleans," pp. 135-136. For a summary of the accomplishments of the legislative council, see also François-Xavier Martin, *The History of Louisiana from the Earliest Period* (New Orleans, 1882), pp. 325-326. Hereafter cited as Martin, *Louisiana*.

78. LeBreton, "Territory of Orleans," pp. 152-154.

79. *The Louisiana Gazette*, January 22, June 28, July 26, 1805.

80. *Ibid.*, July 9, 1805.

81. Carter, *Territorial Papers*, IX, 405-407.

348 Notes

Chapter 6

Orleans Territory: The Dynamics of Politics

1. Carter, *Territorial Papers*, IX, 281-284, 478-481, 520-532, 544; *The Louisiana Gazette*, November 8, 11-12, 1805.

2. *The Louisiana Gazette*, March 28, 1806.

3. LeBreton, "Territory of Orleans," pp. 173-174.

4. *The Louisiana Gazette*, March 18, 1808.

5. *Ibid.*, December 7, 1804; April 19, 26, 1805; August 6, 20, 1805.

6. *Ibid.*, April 7, 10, 1807.

7. *Ibid.*, January 19, 1808.

8. *Ibid.*, January 17, 1809.

9. Henry P. Dart, "The History of the Supreme Court of Louisiana," *Louisiana Historical Quarterly*, IV (1921), 23-32. Hereafter cited as Dart, "Supreme Court of Louisiana."

10. *The Union; or, The New Orleans Advertiser*, December 27, 1803.

11. Rowland, *Letter Books*, I, 323-325.

12. Robertson, *Louisiana*, II, 250; Everett S. Brown, *The Constitutional History of the Louisiana Purchase, 1803-1812* (Berkeley, California, 1920), pp. 147-148.

13. LeBreton, "Territory of Orleans," pp. 49-52.

14. Perre Derbigny (supposed author), *Esquisse de la situation politique et civile de la Louisiane, depuis de 30 Novembre 1803,*

jusqu'au Octobre 1804, par un Louisianais (New Orleans, 1804). Hereafter cited as Derbigny, *Esquisse de la situation*. This pamphlet is in the Rare Book Room, Library of Congress.

15. *The Louisiana Gazette*, January 15, 1804.

16. Martin, *Louisiana*, pp. 344-345.

17. *The Louisiana Gazette*, December 7, 1804. Governor Claiborne continued to support a system of justice characterized by concern and compassion for the criminal. When he addressed the territorial legislature in early 1809 and requested revisions of the territory's system of criminal jurisprudence, he lamented that offenders were sometimes given terms of life imprisonment "whose reformation might probably be effected by less rigorous suffering." See *ibid.*, January 14, 1809.

18. *The Louisiana Gazette*, January 29, 1805. The governor had issued an ordinance several months earlier in which he decreed that no one would be imprisoned without cause, as determined by a justice of the court of pleas. The ordinance also guaranteed both a trial for the accused and a specific sentence, if found guilty. See *ibid.*, July 31, August 7, 1804.

19. *The Louisiana Gazette*, June 28, 1805.

20. *Ibid.*, February 1, 1805.

21. *Ibid.*, May 28, 31, June 4, 1805. Punishments included death for willful murder and life imprisonment at hard labor for serious arson cases and rape. Convicted robbers were to be whipped publicly and imprisoned at hard labor from seven to fourteen years. Accessories to murder, rape, arson, robbery, and burglary were to be fined up to $500 or receive 39 lashes on the bare back. Persons found guilty of stealing horses, mules, or slaves were to be whipped publicly and sentenced to imprisonment at hard labor for seven to fourteen years.

22. Carter, *Territorial Papers*, IX, 356-357, 378-380.

23. *The Louisiana Gazette*, March 28, 1806.

24. *Ibid.*, June 6, 1806.

25. *Ibid.*, June 6, 1806; Carter, *Territorial Papers*, IX, 642-657.

26. *The Louisiana Gazette*, June 10, 1806; Carter, *Territorial Papers*, IX, 641, 659-660, 668.

27. Carter, *Territorial Papers*, IX, 657-658.

28. *The Louisiana Gazette*, January 16, 1807.

29. Martin, *Louisiana*, p. 344.

30. Carter, *Territorial Papers*, IX, 780-781.

31. Henry L. Favrot, "The First Governor of the First Code," *Report of the Louisiana Bar Association for 1909* (New Orleans, 1909), pp. 127-131 (Appendix).

32. Carter, *Territorial Papers*, IX, 317, 673-674, 753-754.

33. *The Louisiana Gazette*, January 22, 1805.

34. *Ibid.*, May 3, 1805.

35. *Ibid.*, February 23, 1808.

36. *Ibid.*, January 22, 28, 1808.

37. *Ibid.*, January 22, 1805; Carter, *Territorial Papers*, IX, 225.

38. *The Balance and Columbian Repository*, IV (1805), 139. Taken from the *Evening Post*, February 22, 1805.

39. Carter, *Territorial Papers*, IX, 340; Robertson, *Louisiana*, II, 268-271.

40. *The Louisiana Gazette*, January 22, 25, 1805; James R. Jacobs, *Tarnished Warrior: Major-General James Wilkinson* (New York, 1938), pp. 204-205. Hereafter cited as Jacobs, *Tarnished Warrior*. See also Carter, *Territorial Papers*, IX, 177-182.

41. *The Union: New Orleans Advertiser*, August 11, 1804.

42. Carter, *Territorial Papers*, IX, 376-377.

43. *The Louisiana Gazette*, November 9, 1804.

44. Robertson, *Louisiana*, II, 277-278.

45. Carter, *Territorial Papers*, IX, 506-513.

46. *The Louisiana Gazette*, February 8, 15, 1805.

47. *The Union: New Orleans Advertiser*, October 15, 20, 1804.

48. Carter, *Territorial Papers*, IX, 242, 245-246, 348-349, 386, 736-737, 765-766, 806-807, 843-844, 907. See also the *Louisiana Courier*, April 25, 1808; November 21, 1810; May 8, 1812.

49. *The Louisiana Gazette*, September 18, 1807.

50. Whitaker, *Mississippi Question*, pp. 92-93, 245.

51. Carter, *Territorial Papers*, IX, 255.

52. James Wilkinson, *Memoirs of General Wilkinson: Burr's Conspiracy Exposed, and General Wilkinson Vindicated Against the Slanders of His Enemies on the Important Occasion* (Washington, 1811), II, 81-82. Hereafter cited as Wilkinson, *Memoirs*.

53. Carter, *Territorial Papers*, IX, 242-243, 310, 320, 344-345, 374-375, 660-661, 670, 685.

54. *Annals of Congress*, 9th Cong., 1st Sess., 570.

55. *Ibid.*, 9th Cong., 2nd Sess., 215.

56. *The Times-Picayune*, December 20, 1936, section 2, p. 11; *The Louisiana Gazette*, June 12, 1807. See also John Kendall, "According to the Corde," *Louisiana Historical Quarterly*, XXIII (1940), 141-146.

57. Carter, *Territorial Papers*, IX, 743, 745-746. The general assembly of the Mississippi Territory passed and Governor Claiborne approved a law against duelling on November 11, 1803. According to the law, any person engaging in a duel, either as a principal or second, was subject to a fine of $1,000 and a year in jail, and was excluded from holding territorial office of honor, profit, or trust for five years. See MSS Executive Journal, W. C. C. Claiborne.

58. Bergh, *Thomas Jefferson*, XI, 288; Carter, *Territorial Papers*, IX, 761-762.

59. Carter, *Territorial Papers*, IX, 907.

Chapter 7

Orleans Territory: Militiamen, Indians, and Slaves

1. Le Breton, "Territory of Orleans," 351-352.

2. Robertson, *Louisiana*, II, 225.

3. Rowland, *Letter Books*, I, 325.

4. Derbigny, *Esquisse de la situation*, 24.

5. *The Louisiana Gazette*, November 9, 1804.

6. Robertson, *Louisiana*, II, 228-229.

7. LeBreton, "Territory of Orleans," 68-73.

8. *The Louisiana Gazette*, January 29, 1805.

9. Carter, *Territorial Papers*, IX, 610-611, 738.

10. *The Louisiana Gazette*, December 7, 1804.

11. *Ibid.*, June 7, 11, 14, August 30, 1805.

12. Rowland, *Letter Books*, III, 235-237, 279-281, 357-358. Carter, *Territorial Papers*, IX, 432, 550-551, 584-586, 592, 620-622, 675, 713-718, 784.

13. *The Louisiana Gazette*, January 16, 30, 1807.

14. *Ibid.*, February 19, 1808.

15. *Ibid.*, December 27, 1808. Carter, *Territorial Papers*, IX, 739-741, 813-815.

16. *Louisiana Courier*, December 26, 1807.

17. Rowland, *Letter Books*, IV, 268, 298, 310-311.

18. *The Louisiana Gazette*, January 17, 1809.

19. *Ibid.*, August 11, 1809.

20. Carter, *Territorial Papers*, IX, 738-739, 854-855, 857.

21. *The Louisiana Gazette*, January 12, 1810.

22. Carter, *Territorial Papers*, IX, 854, 886.

23. *The Louisiana Gazette*, February 9, 1811.

24. LeBreton, "Territory of Orleans," 347.

25. Rowland, *Letter Books*, V, 252-253, 259-260, 336-337.

26. Carter, *Territorial Papers*, IX, 318-319. Rowland, *Letter Books*, II, 220-222, 390.

27. Carter, *Territorial Papers*, IX, 384-385, 387.

28. *Ibid.*, IX, 292-293. Rowland, *Letter Books*, III, 81-82.

29. *Mississippi Messenger*, September 30, 1806.

30. Carter, *Territorial Papers*, IX, 745, 757-758, 760. Rowland, *Letter Books*, IV, 21-22, 223-224.

31. MS Claiborne to Jefferson, November 15, 1808, National Archives.

32. *The Louisiana Gazette*, July 31, 1807.

33. Carter, *Territorial Papers*, IX, 754-760.

34. Rowland, *Letter Books*, IV, 223.

35. MSS Claiborne to Jefferson, November 5, 1808, National Archives.

36. Carter, *Territorial Papers*, IX, 754.

37. LeBreton, "Territory of Orleans," 80.

38. Carter, *Territorial Papers*, IX, 209-210.

39. *Ibid.*, IX, 222, 340.

40. *Ibid.*, IX 340.

41. Gayarre, *Louisiana*, IV, 62. *The Louisiana Gazette*, January 15, 1805.

42. Carter, *Territorial Papers*, IX, 503-504.

43. Rowland, *Letter Books*, V, 267, 269, 273.

44. LeBreton, "Territory of Orleans," 81-82.

45. Carter, *Territorial Papers*, IX, 414-415, 424-425. Rowland, *Letter Books*, V, 273-275.

46. Alice D. Nelson, "People of Color in Louisiana," *Journal of Negro History*, II (1917), 52.

47. Carter, *Territorial Papers*, IX, 840-843, 847-848.

48. Robertson, *Louisiana*, II, 276-277.

49. *The Louisiana Gazette*, January 29, 1805.

50. *Ibid.*, May 8, 1807.

51. Rowland, *Letter Books*, I, 379-381, 386-388; II, 319-320; III, 8-9, 385-386; IV, 166-167, 244, 254-255, 288, 299, 319. Carter, *Territorial Papers*, IX, 14, 273-274, 331-332, 335, 683. *The Louisiana Gazette*, January 24, 1809.

52. *The Louisiana Gazette*, May 24, 1805.

53. Carter, *Territorial Papers*, IX, 385 (Footnote), 621.

54. LeBreton, "Territory of Orleans," 281-283.

55. *The Louisiana Gazette*, May 8, 1807.

56. *Ibid.*, May 12, 1807.

57. Carter, *Territorial Papers*, IX, 139, 702.

58. Albert Phelps, *Louisiana: A Record of Expansion* (New York, 1905), 171-172.

59. Robertson, *Louisiana*, II, 317-319.

60. Carter, *Territorial Papers*, IX, 297-298, 326.

61. Rowland, *Letter Books*, III, 5-7.

62. Carter, *Territorial Papers*, IX, 575-576.

63. *Ibid.*, IX, 915—917. Gayarre, *Louisiana*, IV, 266-267.

64. Carter, *Territorial Papers*, IX, 917-918. See also the *Louisiana Courier*, January 11, 14, 1811.

65. Rowland, *Letter Books*, V. 123, 127, 136.

66. *Ibid.*, V, 107-108, 112.

67. *Ibid.*, V, 218-219.

68. *Ibid.*, VI, 16, 20.

69. LeBreton, "Territory of Orleans," 287-288. *Courier de la Louisiane*, January 19, 1811.

70. *The Louisiana Gazette*, January 30, 1811.

Chapter 8

Orleans Territory: The Routine of Administration

1. Stuart G. Noble, "Governor Claiborne and the Public School System of the Territorial Government in Louisiana," *Louisiana Historical Quarterly*, XI (1928), 535-536. Hereafter cited as Noble, "Public School System."

2. John Watkins, mayor of New Orleans, was indignant when the city's only school buiding was taken over by Colonel Constant Freemen following the transfer, and he enquired of Claiborne: "What has Minerva done in this part of the American dominions, that she should be compeled to cede her place to Mars?" See Carter, *Territorial Papers*, IX, 21, 487-488.

3. Robertson, *Louisiana* II, 229-230.

4. Carter, *Territorial Papers*, IX, 21-22.

5. Rowland, *Letter Books*, I, 326-327, 346; II, 74-75.

6. *Ibid.*, II, 73-74, 83, 101-103.

7. *The Louisiana Gazette*, December 27, 1804; January 29, June 19, 25, August 13, 1805. Raleigh A. Suarez, "Chronicle of a Failure: Public Education in Antebellum Louisiana," *Louisiana History* Spring, 1971), XII, 109-110. Hereafter cited as Suarez, "Public Education in Antebellum Louisiana."

8. *The Louisiana Gazette*, March 28, 1806.

9. Suarez, "Public Education in Antebellum Louisiana," 110-111.

10. *The Louisiana Gazette*, January 19, 1808.

11. Suarez, "Public Education in Antebellum Louisiana," 110-111.

12. *The Louisiana Gazette*, January 17, 1809.

13. Suarez, "Public Education in Antebellum Louisiana," 111.

14. *The Louisiana Gazette*, January 30, 1811.

15. Suarez, "Public Education in Antebellum Louisiana," 111-112. Noble, "Public School System," 532-552. Carter, *Territorial Papers*, IX, 543-544, 621. Rowland, *Letter Books*, III, 111, 126, 277-278; IV, 143-144, 293; V, 126, 128, 131.

16. Rowland, *Letter Books*, V, 224.

17. Carter, *Territorial Papers*, IX, 1014-1016.

18. *Louisiana Courier*, June 5, 1811.

19. Carter, *Territorial Papers*, IX, 17-18.

20. *Ibid.*, IX, 545-547, 550, 580.

21. *Ibid.*, IX, 26-27, 56, 66.

22. *Ibid.*, IX, 408-414. *The Louisiana Gazette*, August 7, 1804.

23. Carter, *Territorial Papers*, IX, 496-498, 545-547.

24. *Ibid.*, IX, 476-478.

25. Rowland, *Letter Books*, III, 125, 180-181, 238, 331-332, 334; IV, 214-215, 349.

26. *The Planter*, August 11, 1811.

27. Carter, *Territorial Papers*, IX, 956-960.

28. Rowland, *Letter Books*, III, 150-151, 158, 161, 167-168, 170-175, 178-179.

29. Carter, *Territorial Papers*, IX, 492.

30. Rowland, *Letter Books*, V, 68-70, 140; VI, 44-45.

31. *Ibid.*, III, 83, 115, 131, 156. Carter, *Territorial Papers*, IX, 57, 110, 168, 219, 363-364, 417-419, 439-440, 444-445.

32. Carter, *Territorial Papers*, IX, 611-612, 672.

33. Rowland, *Letter Books*, II, 206, 212-213; V, 354-355, 381, 383-384, 393-394.

34. *Ibid.*, II, 328; III, 202-203; IV, 132, 168-169; VI, 103.

35. Martin, *Louisiana*, 323.

36. Rowland, *Letter Books*, II, 22-34, 41-42.

37. Carter, *Territorial Papers*, IX, 226, 232-233.

38. Rowland, *Letter Books*, II, 160-164, 180-182, 187-190, 204-205, 213-214.

39. Carter, *Territorial Papers*, IX, 284-285, 361-362.

40. Rowland, *Letter Books*, V, 124-125. *The Louisiana Gazette*, January 11, 1805. Julian Poydras was chosen president of the board of directors of the first bank.

41. Carter, *Territorial Papers*, IX, 163, 286, 294, 298, 309.

42. *Ibid.*, IX, 163, 294.

43. LeBreton, "Territory of Orleans," 351-352.

44. *Ibid.*, 389-399.

45. Carter, *Territorial Papers*, IX, 294, 298, 948-950.

46. *Ibid.*, IX, 247, 276, 286, 288-289, 306-307, 310, 335, 361-362, 377, 386, 395, 672, 675, 677-678, 944, 961.

47. *Ibid.*, IX, 221, 241, 243, 276, 279-280, 286-287, 294, 299, 303-304, 306-307. On October 1, *The Union: New Orleans Advertiser* printed a warm eulogy to Mrs. Claiborne. "This person of dignified deportment and masculine understanding," the eulogy read, devoted every day "to the encrease [*sic*] of human happiness and the diminution of human misery, and was the object of universal admiration." On September 28, *The Louisiana Gazette* eulogy described the late Mrs. Claiborne as "an elegant person, with every qualification that would render her dear to society, her conciliating manners, and unaffected modesty, added to the most benevolent disposition, made her the admiration of all who had the honor of her acquaintance. Regret could not be more strongly manifested than by the conduct of the citizens of every description on this occasion. Many thousands attended her interment and that of her infant daughter who died tha same day--business of almost every kind was suspended."

48. *The Louisiana Gazette*, October 5, 1804.

49. Carter, *Territorial Papers*, IX, 686-687, 736, 859-860. About three years after the death of his second wife, Claiborne married Sophronia Bosque of New Orleans. She survived his death and later married John Randolph Grymes. The governor's marriages into prominent Creole families added to his political strength among the native inhabitants.

50. Bergh, *Thomas Jefferson*, IX, 385.

51. *The Louisiana Gazette*, January 12, 1810.

52. Carter, *Territorial Papers*, IX, 286-287.

53. *The Union: New Orleans Advertiser*, August 11, 1804. The article spoke of the city being wet incessantly, of vapors rising and making the air humid mornings and evenings, "for the moisture evaporates while the sun is up, condenses after it is set, and the descending vapor falls upon the town in the form of a thick fog, this mingling with the putrid matter, with which our streets are strewed, exhales an odour, not merely unpleasant to the olfactory organs but in its consequences too often fatal."

54. Carter, *Territorial Papers*, IX, 286-287, 482-483, 806-807, 864, 955-956.

Chapter 9

The Sabine Frontier and the Burr Conspiracy

1. Jared W. Bradley, "W.C.C. Claiborne and Spain: Foreign Affairs Under Jefferson and Madison, 1801-1811," *Louisiana History*, XII (Fall, 1971), 297-303. Hereafter cited as Bradley, "Claiborne and Spain."

2. Robertson, *Louisiana*, II, 290.

3. Carter, *Territorial Papers*, IX, 155-157, 221-222, 391-392.

4. *Ibid.*, IX, 201-202, 484-487, 564-566, 576-579, 664-665.

5. *Ibid.*, IX 484-487, 533, 534, 536, 556-558, 561-565, 581-582, 603.

6. Robertson, *Louisiana, II, 184-185, 291, 331*.

7. Carter, *Territorial Papers*, IX, 312-315, 425, 435, 436, 504-505, 560-561.

8. *Ibid.*, IX, 76-77, 271-272, 336.

9. Thomas P. Abernethy, *The Burr Conspiracy* (New York, 1954), 47-51. Hereafter cited as Abernethy, *Burr Conspiracy.*

10. LeBreton, "Territory of Orleans," 369-370.

11. Carter, Territorial Papers, IX, 451-452, 616.

12. MSS Executive Journal, W.C.C. Claiborne.

13. *American State Papers: Foreign Relation*, II, 801-803.

14. Richardson, *Messages and Papers of the Presidents*, I, 400.

15. Bradley, "Claiborne and Spain," 313.

16. Wilkinson, *Memoirs* (Appendix), II, 37.

17. Jacobs, *Tarnished Warrior*, 229.

18. *American State Papers: Foreign Relations*, II, 801-802.

19. Carter, *Territorial Papers*, IX, 696-697.

20. Abernethy, *Burr Conspiracy*, 52.

21. "A Faithful Picture of the Political Situation in New Orleans at the Close of the Last and the Beginning of the Present Year, 1807," *Louisiana Historical Quarterly*, XI, (1928), 375. Hereafter cited as "A Faithful Picture of the Political Situation in New Orleans." This criticism of the Claiborne administration was probably written by Edward Livingston or Judge James Workman.

22. MSS Executive Journal, W.C.C. Claiborne.

23. Abernethy, *The South in the New Nation*, 278.

24. Wilkinson, *Memoirs. [Appendix]*, *46-48.*

25. LeBreton, "Territory of Orleans," 376—377.

26. Wilkinson, *Memoirs* [*Appendix*], II, 49-52, 55, 59-63, 74-75. The Sabine agreement proved to be generally satisfactory, although some concern was expressed a few years afterward when the Arroyo Hondo-Sabine area became an outlaw refuge. See Rowland, *Letter Books*, VI, 34-39, 57, 80, 104. Carter, *Territorial Papers*, IX, 975-978, 989-990, 999.

27. Abernethy, *Burr Conspiracy*, 154-155. On August 11, 1807, in the wake of the Burr conspiracy and Wilkinson's arbitrary actions, General Winkinson was accused in the *Mississippi messenger* of having received $120,000 from the Spaniards for a guarantee not to attack.

28. Wilkinson, *Memoirs* (Appendix), II, 28.

29. Rowland, *Letter Books*, IV, 9-10, 15-16. Although Governor Claiborne was unable during the territorial period to instill in the territorial militia the discipline and effectiveness he desired, his record nonetheless in securing miliamen during times of emergency was generally satisfactory. In 1809 Adjutant General Henry Hopkins spoke of the hundreds of citizens who volunteered in 1806. Moreover, Claiborne easily met the national quota established for the territory in 1808 by calling for voluntary enlistments.

30. *The Louisiana Gazette*, January 6, 1807.

31. Abernethy, *Burr Conspiracy*, 148—149. Abernethy, *The South in the New Nation*, 279-280.

32. Wilkinson, *Memoirs* (Appendix), II, 74-81.

33. Abbernethy, *Burr Conspiracy*, 159-160, 174.

34. Bassett, *Correspondence of Andrew Jackson*, I, 152-153.

35. *Ibid.*, I, 163-166.

36. Abernethy, *Burr Conspiracy*, 203-204.

37. *Ibid.*, 158-159, 174-176.

38. *The Louisiana Gazette*, December 9, 12, 1806.

39. Wilkinson, *Memoirs* (Appendix), II, 85.

40. Carter, *Territorial Papers*, IX, 694-695. *The Louisiana Gazette*, December 16, 23, 1806; January 2, 1807.

41. LeBreton, "Territory of Orleans," 417.

42. Abernethy, *Burr Conspiracy*, 178-181. Abernethy, *The South in the New Nation*, 267, 279—280. Wilkinson, *Memoirs* (Appendix), II, 89-91.

43. Wilkinson, *Memoirs* (Appendix), II, 89-91.

44. *The Louisiana Gazette*, January, 30, 1807.

45. Abernethy, *The South in the New Nation*, 291-296. Abernethy, *Burr Conspiracy*, 201-202, 204-205, 209, 215-222.

46. LeBreton, "Territory of Orleans," 431-432, 435-436. *The Louisiana Gazette*, January 16, 1807.

47. *The Louisiana Gazette*, April 10, 14, 1807.

48. *Ibid.*, April 14, 1807.

49. *Ibid.*, May 8, 1807. Captain George T. Ross of the Orleans Rangers resigned his commission in protest against the use of the militia. Some of the officers and men in the unit held a dinner in his honor at Madame Fourage's and commended him for his "nobleness and firmness of mind." See *ibid.*, May 12, 1807.

50. *Mississippi Messenger*, March 31, 1807. When Wilkinson learned that the legislature was considering the memorial to Congress, he asked Governor Vicente Folch of Pensacola, who was visiting Baton Rouge at the time, to use his influence with the lawmakers to block the move. See Abernethy, *Burr Conspiracy*, 214.

51. *The Louisiana Gazette*, December 20, 1806.

52. Bassett, *Correspondence of Andrew Jackson*, VI, 426-427.

53. Wilkinson, *Memoirs*, II, 24-25. *Ibid.* (Appendix), II, 96, 102-103.

54. *Mississippi Messenger*, June 30, 1807.

55. Carter, *Territorial Papers*, IX, 712, 729-731.

56. *Ibid.*, IX, 723.

57. Bassett, *Correspondence of Andrew Jackson*, I, 179.

58. Jacobs, *Tarnished Warrior*, 234-235.

Chapter 10

The West Florida Controversy and Statehood

1. Rowland, *Mississippi Territorial Archives*, I, 467.

2. Carter, *Territorial Papers,*, IX, 58-59.

3. Robertson, *Louisiana*, II, 172, 290.

4. Carter, *Territorial Papers*, IX, 200, 216-217.

5. Robertson, *Louisiana*, II, 236-237, 291.

6. Carter, *Territorial Papers*, IX, 333-334.

7. Robertson, *Louisiana*, II, 332-347.

8. Abernethy, *The South in the New Nation*, 330-331.

9. *Ibid.*, 338-340.

10. *Ibid.*, 341.

12. Bradley, "Claiborne and Spain," 304-305.

13. Abernethy, *The South in the New Nation*, 342. Cox, *West Florida Controversy*, 168-169.

14. Carter, *Territorial Papers*, IX, 267, 437-438, 505, 542-543, 616-617, 727-728.

15. Bradley, "Claiborne and Spain," 313.

16. Abernethy, *The South in the New Nation*, 333-334.

17. *Ibid.*, 334-335. Cox, *West Florida Controversy*, 151-167.

18. Carter, *Territorial Papers*, IX, 315, 320, 332-333, 438. Bradley, "Claiborne and Spain," 305-306.

19. MSS Executive Journal, W.C.C. C.laiborne.

20. Bradley, "Claiborne and Spain," 307-311.

21. Carter, *Territorial Papers*, IX, 535-536, 604, 675-676. "A Faithful Picture of the Political Situation in New Orleans," 368-369.

22. Abernethy, *The South in the New Nation*, 343. Cox, *West Florida Controversy*, 329-330. Irving Brant, *James Madison, The President, 1809-1812* (New York, 1956), V, 175-176. Hereafter cited as Brant, *James Madison*.

23. Abernethy, *The South in the New Nation*, 344-348.

24. *Ibid.*, 350-354. Cox, *West Florida Controversy*, 333-436.

25. Richardson, *Messages and Papers of the Presidents*, I, 480-481. For Congressional approval of Madison's action, see *Annals of Congress*, 11th Cong. 3rd Sess., 11-17, 25-28, 37-66, 84, 369-380, 387-388, 1116-1148.

26. Carter, *Territorial Papers*, IX, 898.

27. *Ibid.*, IX, 905-913. Abernethy, *The South in the New Nation*, 356-363. Cox, *West Florida Controversy*, 489-506. According to newspaper accounts, the American flag was torn down

momentarily when Colonel Covington occupied the fort at Baton Rouge before Colonel Ballenger and the West Florida contingent at the fort bowed to the new American authority. See the *Louisiana Courier*, February 22, 1811.

28. James A. Padgett, ed., "The West Florida Revolution of 1810, as Told in the Letters of John Rhea, Fulwar Skipwith, Reuben Kemper, and Others," *Louisiana Historical Quarterly*, XXI (1938), 76-79, 149-150, 156-158. Although a few of the West Florida inhabitants opposed the transfer, much of the opposition subsided when the United States adhered to a liberal land policy and made no attempt to punish army deserters who had found refuge in West Florida. Also, the expenses incurred by the West Florida government, amounting to $40,000, were paid back a few years later by the Federal government.

29. Carter, *Territorial Papers*, IX, 903-905.

30. *Ibid.*, IX, 905-907.

31. Abernethy, *The South in the New Nation*, 363.

32. Carter, *Territorial Papers*, IX, 873-877.

33. Abernethy, *The South in the New Nation*, 364-365.

34. *Louisiana Courier*, May 3, November 6, 1811. *The Louisiana Gazette*, June 4, 1811.

35. *Louisiana Courier*, November 8, 1811.

36. *Ibid.*, November 20, 1811.

37. Gayarre, *Louisiana*, IV, 269-270.

38. Martin, *Louisiana*, 352-355.

39. Rowland, *Letter Books*, VI, 10-11.

40. Carter, *Territorial Papers*, IX, 991-992.

41. *Ibid.*, IX, 1000, 1019.

42. Martin, *Louisiana*, 354-355.

43. Carter, *Territorial Papers*, IX, 927-928.

44. Rowland, *Letter Books*, VI, 31-32.

Chapter 11

Louisiana: Politics, Redmen, and the Baratarians

1. *Louisiana Courier*, May 29, 1812.

2. *The Louisiana Gazette*, June 4, 1812.

3. *Louisiana Courier*, June 24, 1812.

4. *The Louisiana Gazette*, June 1, 1812.

5. *Ibid.*, June 3, 13, 1812.

6. *Ibid.*, June 17, 1812.

7. *Louisiana Courier*, June 22, 1812.

8. *Ibid.*, January 9, 1811.

9. *Ibid.*, July 17, 1811.

10. *The Louisiana Gazette*, June 5, 1812.

11. *Ibid.*, June 16, 1812.

12. *Louisiana Courier*, June 17, 1812.

13. *Ibid.*, June 22, 1812.

14. *The Louisiana Gazette*, June 19, 1812.

15. Carter, *Territorial Papers*, IX, 944-945.

16. Rowland, *Letter Books*, VI, 2, 46.

17. *Ibid*, VI, 116.

18. J.F.H. Claiborne, *Mississippi*, 256. See also *The Louisiana Gazette*, July 2, 3, 11, 1812.

19. *The Louisiana Gazette*, September 5, October 22, 1812.

20. Hatcher, *Edward Livingston*, 197. Carter, *Territorial Papers*, IX, 997.

21. Gayarre, *Louisiana*, IV, 317.

22. *Ibid.*, VI, 143, 169. For the numerous resignations, see *ibid.*, VI, 176-178, 185, 187-189, 194-198.

23. Dart, "The Supreme Court of Louisiana," 23-32. Rowland, *Letter Books*, VI, 143, 208-209.

24. *The Louisiana Gazette*, March 6, 1813.

25. *Louisiana Courier*, March 18, 25, 1814.

26. Gayarre, *Louisiana*, IV, 316-319.

27. Rowland, *Letter Books*, VI, 153-155. *Louisiana Courier*, August 12, 1812.

28. Gayarre, *Louisiana*, IV, 299-301. Rowland, *Letter Books*, VI, 275-278, 293-294.

29. Rowland, *Letter Books*, VI, 246, 248-250.

30. Bassett, *Correspondence of Andrew Jackson*, II, 35-36.

31. Rowland, *Letter Books*, VI, 265, 270.

32. Gayarre, *Louisiana*, IV, 298-299.

33. Abernethy, *The South in the New Nation*, 370.

34. Jean Lafitte, *Journal of Jean Lafitte: The Pioneer-Patriot's Story* (New York, 1958), 38-39. Hereafter cited as Lafitte, *Journal*.

Jean Lafitte, who spelled his name "Laffite," wrote an account of his experiences for his grandchildren.

35. Rowland, *Letter Books*, VI, 232-233.

36. Alcee Fortier, *A History of Louisiana* (New York, 1904), III, 87. Hereafter cited as Fortier, *Louisiana*.

37. Rowland, *Letter Books*, VI, 279-280.

38. Lafitte, *Journal*, 39-41. Jean Lafitte said his intention was to capture Claiborne, take him to the Lafitte "comune," and then deport him to Virginia and replace him with a military governor.

39. Fortier, *Louisiana*, III, 88.

40. Bassett, *Correspondence of Andrew Jackson*, VI, 437.

41. Gayarre, *Louisiana*, IV, 357-364. Fortier, *Louisiana*, III, 90-94.

42. Bassett, *Correspondence of Andrew Jackson*, II, 54-56; VI, 439-440.

43. MSS Executive Journal, Governor W.C.C. Claiborne. Rowland, *Letter Books*, VI, 300-302.

44. Gayarre, *Louisiana* IV, 504, 628.

45. MSS Executive Journal, Governor W.C.C. Claiborne.

Chapter 12

Louisiana: War With Great Britain
and the New Orleans Campaign

1. Carter *Territorial Papers*, IX, 763-764, 947-948.

2. *Louisiana Courier*, July 5, October 18, 1811.

3. Rowland, *Letter Books*, VI, 4-5, 13.

4. *Ibid.*, VI, 21-22, 27-28, 37-38.

5. *Ibid.*, VI, 37-38, 40, 57-58.

6. Thomas Bailey, *A Diplomatic History of the American People* (New York, 1969), 8th edition, 156.

7.. Abernethy, *The South in the New Nation*, 364-365.

8. *Louisiana Gazette*, August 1, 1812.

9. *Ibid.*, September 12, 17, 1812.

10. Rowland, *Letter Books*, VI, 220-221, 241, 282. Gayarre, *Louisiana*, IV, 294-295.

11. Rowland, *Letter Books*, VI, 146-147, 166-167, 180-181, 204-205, 225, 225-227, 237, 250-251, 269.

12. Gayarre, *Louisiana*, IV, 327-328. Hatcher, *Edward Livingston*, 199-200.

13. Gayarre, *Louisiana*, IV, 327-328.

14. *Louisiana Courier*, August 8, 24, 1814.

15. Fortier, *Louisiana*, III, 95-96. See also the *Mississippi Republican*, September 21, 1814.

16. Fortier, *Louisiana*, III, 89.

17. Bassett, *Correspondence of Andrew Jackson*, II, 27, 29-30, 40-41; VI, 433-436, 438-440.

18. Robin Reilly, *The British at the Gates: The New Orleans Campaign in the War of 1812* (New York, 1974), 167-170. Hereafter cited as Reilly, *The British at the Gates*.

19. *Ibid.*, 174, 206.

20. Marquis James, *The Life of Andrew Jackson* (New York, 1938), 196. Hereafter cited as James, *Andrew Jackson*.

21. Abernethy, *The South in the New Nation*, 376-382.

22. *Louisiana Gazette*, October 18, 1814.

23. Rowland, *Letter Books*, VI, 285—287. 297-298, 305-308, 310-311, 314-315.

24. Bassett, *Correspondence of Andrew Jackson*, II, 87. Gayarre, *Louisiana*, IV, 375—378, 396-397.

25. Fortier, *Louisiana* III, 101-103.

26. Gayarre, *Louisiana*, IV, 402-404. Reilly, *The British at the Gates*, 230.

27. Reilly, *The British at the Gates*, 210-213, 234-235.

28. Abernethy, *The South in the New Nation*, 382-394.

29. *Ibid.*, 393. See also Reilly, *The British at the Gates*, 340-341.

30. Fortier, *Louisiana*, III, 141.

31. Laffite, *Journal of Jean Lafitte*, 39-41, 47, 50, 55-56, 61-62.

32. Chamber, *Mississippi Valley Beginnings*, 296-297.

33. Fortier, *Louisiana*, III, 137-138.

34. Bassett, *The Life of Andrew Jackson*, I, 66, 141, 215.

35. Reilly, *The British at the Gates*, 324.

36. MSS Executive Journal, Governor W.C.C. Claiborne. See also Rowland, *Letter Books*, Vi, 321-323.

37. MSS Bartholomew Shaumburgh to General James B. Wilkinson, January 25, 1815, Box 1, Battle of New Orleans, Historic New Orleans Collection.

38. Wilburt S. Brown, *The Amphibious Campaign for West Florida and Louisiana, 1814-1815: A Critical Review of Strategy and Tactics at New Orleans* (University, Alabama, 1969), 12.

39. Bassett, *The Life of Andrew Jackson*, II, 220-221.

40. Gayarre, *Louisiana*, IV, 478-496.

41. Bassett, *The Life of Andrew Jackson*, I, 221.

42. Fortier, *Louisiana*, III, 135-141, 147-148.

43. Rowland, *Letter Books*, VI, 366-390.

44. Hatcher, *Edward Livingston*, 215-216. Bassett, *The Life of Andrew Jackson*, I, 217-218.

45. MSS Executive Journal, Governor W.C.C. Claiborne. Bassett, *Correspondence of Andrew Jackson*, II, 155-157, 180.

46. Rowland, *Letter Books*, VI, 346-347.

47. *Ibid.*, VI, 338-339.).

48. MSS Executive Journal, Governor W.C.C. Claiborne. Martin, *Louisiana, 373-374*.

49. Bassett, *The Life of Andrew Jackson*, I, 228-230.

50. Gayarre, *Louisiana*, IV, 630-631.

Chapter 13

Louisiana: Climax and Epilogue

1. Carter, *Territorial Papers*, IX, 490, 703, 812.

2. Hatcher, *Edward Livingston*, 228.

3. *Louisiana Courier*, June 24, July 1, September 9, November 20, 1816.

4. *Journal of the Senate, During the First Session of the Third Legislature of the State of Louisiana* (1816-1831), 5-7, 18-19.

5. *Louisiana State Journal*, 3rd, leg., 1st sess.(1816-1824), 27-28.

6. *Louisiana Courier*, January 27, 1817.

7. *Ibid.*, November 26, 1817. Governor Claiborne was buried in the old St. Louis Cemetery. However, it aroused some controversy because it was a Catholic cemetery and Claiborne was a Protestant. Consequently, his remains were removed many years afterward to the Metarie Cemetery, also in New Orleans.

BIBLIOGRAPHICAL ESSAY

The Claiborne bibliography includes most of the basic sources on the subject while at the same time listing works of some considerable significance for those who wish to explore more exhaustively further aspects of the subject's life and times. The author's chief reliance was upon primary source materials, supported by appropriate secondary works. While the sources generally were adequate and provided a rather comprehensive study of the subject, Nathaniel H. Claiborne, a younger brother, was the only real source of information about William's formative years. This was one of the more obvious problems, of course, since Nathaniel's recollections and impressions were predictably subjective. Also, another significant weakness derived from the virtual absence of personal papers and correspondence. Consequently, insights into the Claiborne personality are gleaned only from his public acts and utterances. Nonetheless, the study was much more stimulating and rewarding personally because of the absence of a published biography, general history, or reference work which offered more than fragmentary insights into the historical milieu in which Claiborne functioned and performed.

Manuscripts

The manuscripts collection of the Department of Archives and History in Jackson, Mississippi, contains invaluable information about Claiborne's two-year term as governor of the Mississippi Territory. These include, in particular, the Territorial Archives (1798-1817), Series A, Governors' Records, Executive Journal, Gov. W. C. C. Claiborne, 1803-04; the Proceedings of the Governor of the Mississippi Territory as Superintendant [sic] of Indian Affairs; Legislative Records, Series D, Territorial Archives, 1798-1817; and Journal of the House of Representatives of the Mississippi Territory, 1803. Claiborne's activities in the promotion of higher education are contained in the manuscript journal of the Board of Trustees of Jefferson College, also located in the Mississippi Department of Archives and History. Additional documents relating to Claiborne's leadership in the Mississippi Territory are included in the Territorial Papers, Mississippi, 1797-1810, General Records of the United States Government, Record Groups I and II, in the National Archives in Washington, D. C.

The Historic New Orleans Collection in New Orleans possesses three cases of manuscripts which focus on the emergency created by the British invasion of Louisiana in late 1814. See in particular Box 1, Battle of New Orleans, the Villeré Papers, excerpts from the *Autobiography of Admiral R. Aitchison*, and manuscript accounts of British efforts to enlist the support of Jean Lafitte and the Baratarians while also appealing to the local inhabitants. Tensions between Governor Claiborne and General Andrew Jackson are discussed in some detail in a lengthy letter to General James B. Wilkinson from Bartholomew Shaumburgh, Claiborne's military aide, on January 25, 1815, in the Battle of New Orleans Papers.

Published Documents and Works

The Claiborne study was heavily dependent upon published manuscripts and documents, especially those relating to the territorial periods in Tennessee, Mississippi, and Orleans. Claiborne's active role in the Tennessee constitutional convention of 1796 is found in the *Journals of the Territorial Councils Senate & House Tenn. 1794-1796* Knoxville, 1852, reprinted). Unfortunately, the *Journals of the Territorial Councils* do not include the constitutional debates. *The Territorial Papers of the United States*, 26 vols. (Washington, D. C., 1934--), ably compiled and edited by Clarence E. Carter, constitutes by far the most comprehensive single collection of documents relating to the territorial periods in Tennessee, Mississippi, and Orleans. The volume cited specifically in the series relating to Tennessee is *The Territory South of the River Ohio, 1790-1796* (Washington, D. C., 1936), IV.

Volumes I-III of *The Annals of the Congress of the United States, 1789-1824*, 42 vols. (Washington, D. C., 1834-1866) are critically important sources of information about Claiborne's service in the national House of Representatives from 1797 until 1801. The *Foreign Relations* volume of *The American States Papers: Documents, Legislative and Executive, of the Congress of the United States*, 38 vols. (Washington, D. C., 1832-1861) reflect some of the foreign policy issues and concerns of the period.

The basic sources covering Claiborne's tenure as governor of the Mississippi Territory from 1801 until 1803 are Carter, *Territorial Papers, The Territory of Mississippi, 1798-1817* (Washington, D. C., 1937, 1938), V and VI; *The Mississippi Territorial Archives*,

1798-1817 (Nashville, 1905), compiled and edited by Dunbar Rowland; and Volume I of the *Official Letter Books of W. C. C. Claiborne, 1801-1816*, 6 vols. (Jackson, 1917), likewise compiled and edited by Dunbar Rowland. The *Public Lands* volume of the *American States Papers: Documents, Legislative and Executive, of the Congress of the United States*, 38 vols. (Washington, D. C., 1832-1861) was helpful as a source of information about contested land titles in Mississippi.

The single most valuable official work dealing with the acquisition of Louisiana and Claiborne's activities as governor of the Territory of Orleans is Carter, *Territorial Papers, The Territory of Orleans, 1803-1812* (Washington, D. C., 1940), IX. Several items found in Rowland's *Official Letter Books* and in *Louisiana Under the Rule of Spain, France and the United States, 1785-1807*, 2 vols. (Cleveland, 1911), translated and edited by James A. Robertson, are also helpful. Concern about Spain's sudden denial of the American right of deposit at New Orleans shortly before the United States acquired Louisiana and the reactions of American consular officials in New Orleans are reflected in "Despatches from the United States Consulate in New Orleans, 1801-1803," printed in two installments in *The American Historical Review*, XXXII, 801-824, and XXXIII, 331-359. Some of the intense local confusion resulting from the introduction of the American judicial and legal system into Gallic Louisiana is reflected in a pamphlet supposedly written by Pierre Derbigny and entitled *Esquisse de la situation politique et civile de la Louisiane, depuis le 30 novembre 1803, jusqu'au octobre 1804, par un Louisianais* (New Orleans, 1804), Rare Book Room, Library of Congress. Works that were particularly useful in the coverage of Spanish-American boundary tensions along the Sabine River in 1806 and the so-called Burr conspiracy immediately afterward include the following: John S. Bassett, ed., *Correspondence of Andrew Jackson*, 7 vols. (Washington, D. C., 1926); James D. Richardson, ed., *A Compilation of the Messages and Papers of the Presidents, 1789-1902*, 10 vols. (New York, 1903); James Wilkinson, *Memoirs of General Wilkinson* (Washington, D. C., 1811); and the *Foreign Relations* volume of *The American States Papers*. Useful documents dealing with Spanish Florida and the West Florida controversy between Spain and the United States are found in James A. Padgett, "The West Florida Revolution of 1810, as Told in the Letters of John Rhea, Fulwar Skipwith, Reuben Kemper, and Others," *Louisiana Historical Quarterly*, XXI (1938), 76-202; and James A. Padgett, "official Records of the West Florida Revolution and Republic," *ibid.*, XXI (1938), 685-805.

Rowland's *Official Letter Books* provide good coverage of the Claiborne administration following the admission of Louisiana to statehood. Bassett's *Correspondence of Andrew Jackson* is particularly helpful in dealing with the Battle of New Orleans and American civil-military tensions during the emergency. British efforts to enlist the support of Jean Lafitte and the Baratarian buccaneers as the British proceeded with their invasion plans are interestingly recounted in Jean Laffite, *Journal of Jean Laffite: The Pioneer-Patriot's Own Story* (New York, 1958). Finally, Governor Claiborne's farewell address to the state legislature in late 1816 and his election to the United States Senate by the general assembly several months before his death in 1817 are printed in the *Journal of the Senate* (New Orleans, 1817) and the *Louisiana State Journal* (New Orleans, 1816-1824).

Official and published works consulted but incidental to the finished Claiborne study include the following: Charles F. Adams, ed., *Memoirs of John Quincy Adams Comprising Portions of His Diary from 1795-1848*, 12 vols. (Philadelphia, 1874); Albert E. Bergh, ed., *The Writings of Thomas Jefferson*, 20 vols. (Washington, D. C., 1907); Vincent O. Nolte, *The Memoirs of Vincent Nolte* (New York, 1934); H. P. Nugent, "A Letter to His Excellency William C. C. Claiborne, Governor of the Territory of Orleans," *Political Pamphlets*, CV (New Orleans, 1808); and *Letters of Louis Tousard, French Consul at New Orleans, to Governor William C. C. Claiborne Pertaining to French Citizens Who Claimed They Should Be Exempt from U. S. Millitary Service*, W. P. A. Project (Baton Rouge, 1938).

Theses and Dissertations

A number of theses and dissertations relating to Claiborne's public career have been written, including the author's earlier study. See Joseph Tennis Hatfield, "The Public Career of William C. C. Claiborne," doctoral dissertation, Emory University, 1962. Claiborne's earlier political activities and accomplishments are traced by Elvina M. Echezabal in "The Public Career of W. C. C. Claiborne from 1795-1804," master's thesis, Tulane University, 1935. Robert V. Haynes provided a more comprehensive account of the subject's term as governor of the Mississippi Territory in "A Political History of the Mississippi Territory," doctoral disertation, The Rice Institute, 1958. Much of this study was published in the first volume of *A History of Mississippi*, 2 vols. (Jackson, 1973), edited by Richard A. McLemore. Marietta LeBreton's interesting and well-written narrative about the complex problems confronting Claiborne as governor of the Orleans Territory are related in "A History of the Territory of Orleans, 1803-1812," doctoral dissertation, Louisiana State University, 1969. Finally, a less comprehensive study spanning Claiborne's years as territorial and state governor of Louisiana is provided by Aussie L. Porter in "W. C. C. Claiborne's Administrations in Louisiana, Provincial, Territorial, and State," master's thesis, Tulane University, 1932.

Newspapers

Newspapers were introduced into the Mississippi Territory a short time before Claiborne's appointment as governor, but local files for the 1801-1803 period are not available. Incomplete files of the later *Mississippi Messenger* and *Mississippi Republican*, both of which are cited in the Claiborne study, are located in the Mississippi Department of Archives and History. Newspaper coverage of Claiborne's fourteen years in Louisiana is much more extensive, but again no complete files exist. The two newspapers cited most frequently are the *Louisiana Courier* (*Courrier de la Louisiane*), printed triweekly in English and French, and *Louisiana Gazette*. Other specific numbers of period newspapers reviewed and infrequently cited are *The Union: New Orleans Advertiser*, *Le Telegraphe*, and *The Planter*. Later feature articles dealing with the Claiborne administrations in Louisiana are printed in *The New Orleans Times*, May 1, 1864, and *The Times-Picayune: New Orleans States*, December 20, 1936. Broken files of the newspapers cited are located in the New Orleans Municipal Library and Archives and the Louisiana State Museum and Library in New Orleans.

Books and Articles

The books and articles consulted far exceeds the selected number cited specifically in the Claiborne study. Several were particularly helpful as sources of knowledge about particular aspects of the subject's life and times, while others provided general background information. Since Claiborne lived during one of the most stimulating and dynamic eras in American history and experienced a varied political career, the number of books and articles having direct or indirect application are quite extensive.

Although a number of biographical sketches of Claiborne's formative years are available, most are based on information provided by Claiborne's younger brother. See in particular Nathaniel H. Claiborne, *Notes on the War in the South; with Biographical Sketches of the Lives of Montgomery, Jackson, Sevier, the Late Gov. Claiborne, and Others* (Richmond, 1819); Allen Johnson and Dumas Malone, eds., *Dictionary of American Biography* (New York, 1930), IV; James B. Longacre and James Herring, *The National Portrait Gallery of Distinguished Americans*, 4 vols. (New York, 1934-1939), IV; and John D. Winters, "William C. C. Claiborne: Profile of a Democrat," *Louisiana History*, X, No. 3 (Summer, 1969).

Sources providing valuable information about Claiborne's brief career as a lawyer, delegate to the Tennessee constitutional convention, and as a Tennessee supreme court justice are Thomas P. Abernethy, *From Frontier to Plantation in Tennessee* (Chapel Hill, 1932); Joshua W. Caldwell, *Sketches of the Bench and Bar of Tennessee* (Knoxville, Mo., 1898); James G. M. Ramsey, *The Annals of Tennessee to the End of the Eighteenth Century* (Kingsport, 1926); and Samuel C. Williams, *Phases of the History of the Supreme Court of Tennessee* [*Johnson City, 1944*].

Very few secondary sources provide substantive information about Claiborne's two terms in the House of Representatives from 1797 until 1801. The following works are helpful: Thomas P. Abernethy, *The South in the New Nation, 1789-1819* (Baton Rouge, 1961), which is Volume IV in *A History of the South*, Wendell H. Stephenson and E. Merton Coulter, eds., 10 vols. (Baton Rouge, 1949-1967); John S. Bassett, *The Federalist System, 1789-1801* (New York, 1906); and Joseph Tennis Hatfield, "William C. C. Claiborne, Congress, and Republicanism, 1797-1801," *Tennessee Historical Quarterly*, XXIV, No. 2 (Summer, 1965). For a good account of the controversial Alien and Sedition Acts, see James M. Smith, *Freedom's Fetters: The Alien and Sedition Laws and American Civil Liberties* (Ithaca, 1956).

Several works on Mississippi specifically or on the Southwest more generally as a region provide useful information about Claiborne's two-year term as governor of the Mississippi Territory. The most comprehensive and important work published recently is Richard A. Mclemore, ed., *A History of Mississippi*, 2 vols. (Jackson, 1973). See in particular chapters 8 and 9 of Volume I of this bicentennial history, written by Robert V. Haynes. Much of the information provided in the two chapters is taken from Haynes' doctoral dissertation, "A Political History of the

Mississippi Territory," The Rice Institute (Houston, 1958). Other general works frequently cited include the following: Henry E. Chambers, *Mississippi Valley Beginnings: An Outline of the Early History of the Earlier West* (New York, 1922); John F. H. Claiborne, *Mississippi, as a Province, Territory and State, with Biographical Notices of Eminent Citizens* (Jackson, 1880); Robert Lowry and William H. McCardle, *A History of Mississippi* (Jackson, 1891); and Dunbar Rowland, *History of Mississippi: The Heart of the South*, 2 vols. (Jackson, 1925).

INDEX

Abbe Roland's Academy, 190
Aboukir, 292
Acheron, 263
Adair, John, 2, 12, 229, 233
Adais, 216, 218
Adams County, Miss., 61, 70. 82, 83
Adams, John, 7, 45, 51, 112; appoints boundary commission, 22; appoints territorial supreme court, 73; election of 1800, 39; estimates number of neutralists, 4; Matthew Lyon's defamation, 37
Adams, Samuel, 3
Africa, 178
Aish Indians, 171
Alabama, 48, 53
Alabama Indians, 175, 176
Alabama River, 59
Alexander, James, 229
Alexandria, Egypt, 102
Alfred the Great, 261
Alien Act, 35, 36, 38
Alien and Sedition Acts, 35, 36, 313
America, 28, 30, 31, 98, 173, 176, 180, 190
"An American," 262
American Revolution, 1, 16, 45, 48, 115, 157, 172, 269, 281
Amite River, 118
Anderson, Joseph, 14
Andes Mountains, 117
Andry, Manuel, 185, 186
Arkansas River, 62
Armisto, Andre de, 196
Arroyo Hondo, 216, 217, 329
Assembly of Notables, 127
Atlantic Coast, 202
Atlantic Ocean, 19, 92
Attakapas District, 127, 163, 208, 214, 220, 221, 271

Baldwin, Abraham, 21
Balize, 178, 284
Balize River, 118
Ballenger, John, 250, 251
Baltimore, Md., 93, 288

Bank of the United States, 203, 204, 281
Banking, 202-204
Barataria (Grande Terre), 271, 274
Baratarian Association, 272, 275
Barbe-Marbois, Francois, 97
Basset, 63
Baton Rouge, La., 161, 178, 201, 202, 215, 243-252, 257, 271, 287, 294, 304
Battalion of Free People of Color, 164, 165
Battalion of Orleans Volunteers, 164, 165, 168, 293
Bayard, James, 21, 36
Bayou Bienvenu, 295, 300
Bayou Funda, 220
Bayou Manchac, 118
Bayou Pierre, 64, 216-218, 220, 230
Bayou St. John, 214
Bayou Tunica, 111
Beale, Thomas, 293
Bear Creek, 63
Beckley, John, 5-7, 231
Bellechasse, Joseph Deville D., 137
Bellemont Plantation, 45
Beluche, Renato, 297
Berlin, Prussia, 30, 31
Bermoudi, Francis, 185, 186
Berry, David, 56
Bible, New Testament, 6
Big Pigeon River, 15
Big Warrior, 271
Bilboa, 109, 111
Bissel, Daniel, 115
Black Code, 181
Blackstone, William, 8
Blanchardville, La., 202
Blount, William, 2, 3, 7, 9, 15, 16, 312; conspiracy against the Floridas, 19; expelled from the Senate, 20; governor of Southwest Territory, 11-13; land baron, 200; praise for Claiborne, 17; statehood for Tennessee, 17; supports Claiborne for House, 20; Treaty of

Holston, 22; Willie Blount, 18
Blount, Willie, 18
Bollman, Justus Eric, 229
Bonaparte, Joseph, 242, 246
Bonaparte, Napoleon, 31, 95, 129, 169, 301, 323; ambiguities re: La. territory, 116, 237; decision not to occupy La., 100; defeat at Leipzig, 281; expeditionary force to La, 100; Joseph Bonaparte as Spanish king, 242, 246; negotiations to sell La., 99; overthrow of the Directory, 37; proposed sale of Florida, 241
Bordeaux, France, 154, 271
Bore, J. Etienne de, 129
Boston, Mass., 2
Boston Tea Party, 3
Boundaries, 22, 116-118, 214-223, 238-241, 246, 247-249
Bourbon County, 81
Bourbon County Act, 81
Bradford, James M., 229
Breckenridge, John C., 83, 127
Breed's Hill, Mass., 3
Brewster, 217
Briggs, Isaac, 122, 123
Briggs, Joseph, 206
Brown, James, abstractor of land claims, 196, 197; defeat for re-election to Senate, 311, 317; efforts to formulate a legal code for La., 147; nominated for Senate, 268; territorial secretary, 130, 142
Bruin, Peter B., 42, 73, 230
Burnet, Daniel, 63
Burr, Aaron, 2, 41, 120, 138, 142, 152, 210, 218, 223, 226, 231, 232, 234-236; apprehension, 230; conspiracy activities in La., 222-230; involvement of Gen. Wilkinson in conspiracy, 224, 225; Republican nominee for vice president, 38; tie to Jefferson, 39
Burr conspiracy, 150, 166, 218, 222-236, 266, 287, 299, 315, 321

Cabildo, 101, 112, 113, 163
Cadoquia, see Caddo Indians

Caddo Indian Nation, 172, 173, 176, 217, 270, 271
Callender, James C., 38
"Camillus," 198
Canada, 3, 117, 279, 280, 282, 288, 323
Canton, China, 54
Carey, James, 19, 20
Caribbean Islands, 178, 183
Caribbean Sea, 323
Carolina, 274
Carroll, William, 294
Cartagena, 272
Casa Calvo, Marquis de, 102, 155, 211, 243; assistance to runaway slaves, 180; "Boundary commissioner," 215; Clark's opinion of, 107; Creole plot in New Orleans, 184; efforts to undermine American authority, 171, 172; expulsion from Orleans Territory, 246; gives a ball in Laussat's honor, 113; invited to participate in the Red River expedition, 217; land sales in West Florida, 199; protection of mail carriers to West Florida, 201; reluctance to leave La., 213-215; represents Spain at transfer of La., 101; "Revolts" in West Florida, 243-246
Casa Irujo, Marquis de, 88, 94
Casada Indian Nation, 171
Cat Island, 292
Central America, 279, 323
"Centurio," 231
Chambers, Joseph, 59, 103; agent in eastern land office, 83; reports arrival of Laussat in La., 100; trade with the Indians, 60; trouble with Spanish customs policies, 242, 243
Charity Hospital, 207
Chase, Samuel, 72
Chattahoochee River, 42
Chef Menteur, 302
Cherokee Indians, 9, 19, 22, 48, 54, 60, 269, 290
Chesapeake Affair, 242, 278, 279
Chickasaw Bluffs, 48, 60, 64
Chickasaw Indians, 10, 53, 54, 57-61, 64

383

Choctaw Indians, 52-61, 64, 100, 173, 174, 269, 270, 290, 293, 295
Christian Pass, 252
City of Brotherly Love, 96
Claiborne, Cornelia Tennessee, 207
Claiborne County, 63, 82
Claiborne, Ferdinand Leigh, 4, 83, 230
Claiborne, Mary Leigh, 3
Claiborne, Nathaniel Herbert, comments on Eldridge Harris, 4; description of W. C. C. Claiborne, 6; notes on political career of W. C. C. Claiborne, 17; opinion of W. C. C. Claiborne's education and ability, 8, 9; William as a Republican, 27
Claiborne, William, 3, 4
Claiborne, William Charles Cole, Baton Rouge annexation, 238-252; battle of New Orleans, 295-301; boundary disputes with Spain, 214-223; Burr conspiracy, 223-230; criticisms, 230-236; duel with Clark, 159-161; establishment of educational institutions, 77-80, 189-195; early employment and training in politics, 5-8; education, 4, 5; efforts to establish banks, 202-204; family background, 3, 4; gubernatorial race and election, 257-263; Indian affairs, 51-61, 65, 66, 170-176, 270-271; influence on judiciary, 71-77; judicial system in the state, 267-268; land grants and titles, 80-83, 195-200; law and order, 62-66; law practice, 8-10; mail service in the state, 200-202; militia, 67-71; national politics, 20-43; penal reforms, 61, 62; pirates, 271-276; public health measures, 83-85, 204-209; right of deposit, 85-95; slave trade, 176-187; Southwest Territory, 253-257; Tennessee Constitutional Convention, 1796, 13-17; Tennessee politics, 18; Tennessee State Supreme Court, 18; transfer of Louisiana, 103-106, 111-116; West Forida annexation, 238-252
Clark, Daniel, 86, 102, 106, 109, 116, 125, 137, 157, 189, 204, 227, 244, 249, 250; anti-Claiborne moves, 159; Burr conspiracy, 229; charges against Claiborne, 160; description of, 159; duel with Claiborne, 161; elected to Congress, 160; his opinion of Laussat, 101; his opinion of Spanish intendant, 89; land grants west of the Mississippi, 195, 196; mentioned as nominee for territorial governor, 120; organized volunteer troops, 115; preparations for transfer of Louisiana, 107, 108
Clark, Livingston & Company, 159, 258, 259, 264, 307, 314, 324
Cochrane, Alexander, 292, 297
Cocke, William, 19
Coffee, John, 289, 294
College of Orleans, 193, 194
Collins, 63
Collot, Victor, 98
Colorado River, 241
Commentaries on the Laws of England, 8
Committee of Revisal and Unfinished Business, 38
Committee on Indian Relations, 21
Concord, Mass., 3
Concordia, 126
Concordia County, 140
Congress, 17, 22, 29, 30, 33, 34, 36, 37, 40, 41-44, 47, 48, 53, 54, 71, 79, 82, 83, 91, 99, 103, 104, 114, 117, 120, 121, 123-126, 128, 129, 132, 134-136, 140, 142, 145, 148, 158, 160, 167, 176, 177, 179, 190, 192, 194, 196-198, 203, 207, 209, 218, 232, 240, 241, 252-255, 257, 266, 282, 294, 311, 313, 315, 323
Connecticut, 22
Conseil de Ville, 113
Cooke, John Henry, 296
Cooper, Thomas, 38
Coosa, River, 271, 289

Cordero, Antonio, 180, 216, 219, 221-223
Coushatta Indians, 174-176
Covington, Leonard, 250, 251
Crawford, William H., 247
Creek Indians, 10, 48, 54, 58, 269-271, 296
Cuba, 88, 178, 242, 247-249, 279, 280
Cumberland River, 47, 226
Cumberland Settlement, 10
Cushing, Thomas H., 219, 222, 223, 251

Dallas, Alexander J., 8
Daquin, Jean, 293
Davezac, Auguste, 301
Davidson County, Tenn., 12, 14
Davis, Thomas T., 44, 45
Dearborn, Henry, 57, 58, 60, 68, 70, 85, 100, 109, 123, 174; advises acceptance of free Negroes in militia, 164; Indian affairs, 51-53; military organization in Mississippi Territory, 69; orders to Claiborne to act against Burr conspiracy, 231; orders Wilkinson and Claiborne to New Orleans, 106; preparations to defend New Orleans against Spaniards, 218-221
Decres, Denis, 98, 99, 100
Dehahuit, 172, 173
Delassus, Carlos Dehault, 115, 213, 247, 248
Delaware, 30, 36
Derbigny, Pierre, 129, 177, 179, 267
Destrehan, Jean-Noel, efforts to replace Claiborne, 261; election to Senate, 266; legislative council, 137; loss in gubernatorial race, 265; present memorial to Congress, 129, 177; speaker of territorial house of representatives, 136
Dick, John, 304, 305
Dinsmoor, Silas, Choctaw indebtedness to Panton, Leslie & Co., 52, 53; effort to control Indian visits to white settlements, 55, 56; efforts to teach Indians useful arts, 60, 61; Indian trouble along Wilderness Road, 57, 58; reports Laussat's arrival to Claiborne, 100
Disease, 83-85, 130-156, 204-209, 254, 305
Doherty, George, 14
Donaldsonville, La., 201
Duane, William, 38
Duck River, 54
Dunkirk, France, 98
Du Pont de Nemours, Pierre, 99, 194
Duralde, Clarissa, 208
Duralde, Marie Josephe Perrault, 208
Duralde, Martin Milony, 208

East Florida, 97, 238-241, 248, 252, 280, 288
East Texas, 215
Eaton, William 224
Education (Miss.), 77-80; (La.) 189-194
Eighth Militia Regiment, 174
"An Elector," 261, 264
Electoral College, 39
Ellicott, Andrew, 43
Embargo Act, 169
England, 19, 28, 32, 35, 100, 139, 166, 205, 241, 242, 248, 266, 267, 269, 278-281, 288, 293, 320, 322
Europe, 19, 29, 30-33, 71, 87, 89, 94, 99, 166, 190, 205, 242, 246, 279, 315
Eustis, William, 205
Ewing, George, 245

Federalist Party, 17, 19, 25, 26, 28, 29-32, 37-42, 45, 47, 49-51, 70, 74, 85, 86, 100, 128, 153, 224, 241, 252, 254, 281, 282, 313, 314
Feliciana Parish, 244, 247, 248
"Fidelis," 156
"Flagellus," 157
Florida, 12, 19, 43, 52, 118
Flournoy, Thomas, 284-286
Folch, Vicente, 211, 248; accuses French of encouraging Spanish-American hostility, 201; attempts to quell Kemper "revolt," 254; governor of West Florida, 201;

objects to Mobile customs district, 242, 243; postal routes, 202, 246; refuses to relinquish Florida to U. S., 252; treatise on exchange of West Florida for U. S. trans-Mississippi claims, 239, 240
Fort Adams, 68, 106, 109-111, 115, 201, 205, 212, 218, 227, 244
Fort Barrancas, 289, 290
Fort Bowyer, 271, 289, 290
Fort Charlotte, 257
Fort Claiborne, 216
Fort Dearborn, 69
Fort Jackson, 271, 289
Fort McHenry, 48, 287
Fort Manchac, 161, 165
Fort Massac, 226
Fort Mims, 271
Fort Nogales, 48
Fort Pickering, 48, 63
Fort St. Stephens, 59, 60, 103, 110, 242
Fort Stoddert, 201, 230, 240, 243, 251
Fortier, Michael, Jr., 164, 185, 294, 302
France, 19, 27, 28, 32-34, 36, 38, 39, 86, 93, 95, 97, 99, 101, 102, 104, 108, 111, 115, 116, 139, 164, 173, 176, 212, 238, 239, 241, 242, 272, 278, 280, 281, 299, 315, 316
Franco-American Agreements of 1778, 33, 128, 129, 132
Franklin, State of, 9
Franklin veterans, 8, 12
Free Men of Color, 294
Freeman, Constant, 163, 178, 217
French Broad River, 15
French Directory, 32, 36, 38
French Revolution, 178, 281
Fromentin, Eligius, 271

Gaines, Edmund P., 230
Gallatin, Albert, 21, 114, 120, 178, 195-197, 200, 204, 251, 257, 264, 279, 280; Alien Acts, 35, 36; warns Monroe of England's aims for New Orleans, 288
Galveston 275
Gambier, Vincent 275
Genet, Edmond, 101

Gentilly Road, 300
George III, 3
Georgia, 42, 48, 80, 81, 247, 292
German Coast, 185, 186
Gibbs, Samuel, 296
Gilbert, Walker, 273
Giles, William B., 253
Girod, Nicholas, 301
Glass, 63
Gleig, George R., 296
Godoy, Manuel de, 97
Goodrich, Chauncey, 22
Goths, 239
Grafton, Daniel, 56
Graham, John, 130, 161, 177, 243, 251
Graham, William, 171
Grand Pre, Carlos de, 244, 247
Granger, Gideon, 200
Gravier, John, 158
Great Britain, see England
Great Lakes, 282
Greeley, Horace, 1
Green, Thomas M., 43, 51, 70, 83
Greene, Richard R., 160
Greenville, 65, 78
Griswold-Lyon Confrontation, 26, 38
Griswold, Roger, 26
Grymes, John 272
Gulf of Mexico, 90, 117, 118, 212, 275
Gurley, John W., 137, 160, 196, 197

Halifax, 279
Hall, Dominic A., 229, 268; arrested by Andrew Jackson, 304; cites Jackson, fines him, 305; judge, 143; state supreme court, 267
Hamilton, Alexander 25, 29, 39
Hamilton, Paul, 264, 279
Hampton, Wade, 185, 206
Hannibal, 31
Harpe, Wiley (Little), 63, 64
Harper, Robert Goodloe, 21, 30, 35, 37
Harris, Eldridge, 4, 6
Hartford Convention, 282
Havana, Cuba, 89, 124, 288
Hayne, Arthur, P., 292

Helvoet Sluys, 98, 100
Hermes, 289
Herrera, Simon de, 216-221, 223
Hinds, Thomas 294
Hinson, John 230
Hispanola, 180
Holmes, David, 248, 250
Holston River, 15
Hooshee Hoomah, 57
Hopkins, Henry, 168
Horseshoe Bend (Tohopeka), 271, 291, 296
Hulings, William E., 86-88, 92-94
Humbert, Jean J. A., 301
Hunter, Narsworthy, 43, 44

Ibanez, Ferdinand, 196
Iberville, River, 118, 238
Independence Hall, 96
Indian Relations (Miss), 51-61, 66, 67; (La.) 170-176, 269
Irujo, see also Casa Irujo, Marquis de
Irujo (Yrujo), Carlos Martinez de, 104, 245
Irvin, 217
Isle of Orleans, 117, 118, 238

Jackson, Andrew, 2, 3, 15, 21, 41, 66, 143, 211, 272, 309, 312, 317, 318; appointed to Senate, 20; characterization, 9; committee to draft Tennessee constitution, 13; conflict with Clairborn, 298-304, 321, 322; elected to House of Representatives, 20; Indian war, 271, 273; investigates chances of being governor of Louisiana Territory, 121; martial law in New Orleans, 304-308; pirates support Americans in Battle of New Orleans, 297, 298; preparations for and war against the British, 286-296; representative to Tennessee statehood convention, 12; supports actions of Claiborne and Wilkinson re: Burr conspiracy in New Orleans, 234, 235; suspects dispute between Claiborne and Wilkinson, 233; warns Claiborne against the Laffites, 274; warns Claiborne re: Burr conspiracy in Louisiana, 226
Jamaica, 177, 279, 292
Jamestown, Va., 3
Jay-Gardoqui Negotiations of 1785, 15, 90
Jefferson College, 77, 78
Jefferson County, Tenn., 14, 70, 82, 195
Jefferson, Thomas, 7, 16, 27, 29, 33, 34, 36, 38, 41, 50, 54, 60, 65, 69, 71, 76, 77, 83, 86, 92, 95, 105, 110, 115, 117, 137, 151, 152, 158, 160, 161, 170, 171, 176, 188-190, 194, 197, 205-208, 210, 212, 213, 222, 228, 232, 233, 236, 239, 242, 244, 246, 247, 252, 261, 266, 282, 299, 307, 314, 316, 318, 321, 324, 325; appoints Claiborne, 46, 47; appoints David Ker, 74; appoints Monroe minister to France, 93; approves fort at Washington, Miss., 68; attempts to purchase Florida, 241; bank established in New Orleans, 203, 204; begins negotiations for the purchase of New Orleans and West Florida, 99; Burr conspiracy, 224; complainst against Wilkinson, 234; election as president, 38-39; exploratory expedition up the Red River, 217; fear of Federalist courts, 72; government for Louisiana, 127, 128; guidelines for appointments to legislative council, 131; judiciary in Louisiana, 140, 141-144; Mobile customs district established, 240; orders to restrain expeditions against Spanish territory, 246; postal service in Louisiana, 200, 201; preparations for the transfer, 102-104; proclaims conspiracy, 227; requests information on Louisiana, 116, 125; satisfaction over purchase, 120-123; seeks governor for Louisiana, 120-123; Spanish-American tensions, 218; vice president of the U. S., 252; Wilkinson warns of Burr, 225
Jones, Evan, 86, 137, 147, 157-159

Judiciary (Miss.), 50, 51, 71-77; (La.) 140-152
Judiciary Act of 1801, 27, 72
Jugeat, Pierre, 293

Keane, John 296
Kemper, Nathan, 244, 246
Kemper, Reuben, 244, 245, 251
Kemper, Samuel, 244, 245
Kentucky, 27, 44, 57, 64, 65, 83, 84, 91, 106, 127, 130, 217, 226, 272, 294, 295, 297, 305
Kentucky Resolution, 38
Ker, David C., 74, 78, 302
Kerr, Lewis, 165
Kerr, James, 229
Kidder, Joseph, 154, 155
King, George, 175
Knox County, Tenn., 12
Knoxville, Tenn., 12, 13, 15, 17, 18, 21, 47, 49, 60

La Rochelle, France, 98
Labatut, Baptiste, 302
Labigarre, 159
"Laelius," 154, 155, 164
Lafayette, Marquis de, 120, 121, 123, 316
Laffite, Alexander, 297
Laffite, Jean, 291, 317, 319; aided Americans at New Orleans, 297; background, 271, 272; British overtures to, 289, Claiborne's oppositions, 272; Laffite and Claiborne offer rewards for each other, 273; litigation instituted against, 273
Laffite, Pierre, 272, 273
Lafon, Bartholomew, 196
Lafourche Parish, 271
Lake Barataria, 273
Lake Borgne, 117, 293-295, 300
Lake Borne, 177
Lake Champlain, 288
Lake Maurepas, 118, 178, 238
Lake Ontario, 288
Lake Pontchartrain, 118, 178, 238, 300
Lambert, John, 294-296
Land titles, 15, 16, 21-23, (Miss.) 80-83; (La.) 194-200
Lattimore, David, 84

Lattimore, William, 84
Laussat, Pierre Clement, 100, 106-109, 115, 117, 153, 155, 157, 239; celebrations after transfer, 113; encouraged statehood for Louisiana, 128; left France for Louisiana, 98; outlines eastern boundary, 238; represents France at transfer, 101, 104, 105, 112; suggests Rio Grande as western boundary of Louisiana, 215
LeGendre, Mme, 154
Legislatures (Miss.), 50, 51; (La.) 131-133, 136-140, 147-149, 187, 190-193, 256, 267, 268, 291
Leipzig, 281
Leopard, 278
Lewis and Clark expedition, 100
Lewis, Elizabeth (Eliza) W., 40, 47, 207
Lewis, Joel, 14
Lewis, Jushua, 309, 310
Lewis, Meriwether, 115
Lewis, Micajah G., 156
Lewis, Seth, 50, 73, 74, 304, 305
Lewis, William Terrell, 40, 207
Lexington, Mass., 3
Lisbon, Portugal, 30, 32
Lislet, Moreau, 147
Liverpool, England, 74
Livingston, Edward, 137, 209, 229, 244, 258, 259, 263, 266, 307, 314; batture controversy, 158, 159; Jackson's military secretary, 300; organizes territorial bank, 204
Livingston, Mrs. Edward, 301
Livingston, Robert R., 95, 99, 120, 264, 316
Lockyer, Nicholas, 289
Logan Act of 1799, 36
Logan, George, 36
London, England, 2, 19, 30, 31, 99, 121, 277, 278, 288
Looney, David, 18
Louailler, Louis, 304
Louisiana, 295
Louisiana Courier, 304, 325
Louisiana, District of, 117, 119, 128, 196
Louisiana Purchase, 96, 158
Louisiana, Territory of, 19, 61, 62, 70, 71, 82, 85-87, 92, 93, 96, 104,

108, 111-122, 124-130, 132, 134, 135, 155, 157-160, 162, 164, 172, 176, 179, 180, 183, 189, 194, 195, 197, 207, 211, 213, 215, 216, 237, 238, 316, 319, 320, 323, 324
Louisiana, State of, 256, 257, 261, 263, 265, 269, 271-274, 279, 280, 282-287, 289-293, 299-301, 303, 307-309, 311, 313, 314, 315-318, 320, 321, 323-325
"Louisianian," 145, 154, 164, 179, 259, 263
L'Ouverture, Toussaint, 99, 183
Lyman, William, 120
Lyon, Matthew, 26, 37, 38

Macarty, Jean (John) B., 137
McGuire, William, 42, 50, 73
McHenry, James, 20
McKee, John 52, 56
McNary, John 18
McRae, William, 293
McWilliam, John, 289
Madison, James, 49-51, 68, 69, 88-91, 94, 97, 103, 104, 109, 110, 117, 120, 123, 124, 129, 143, 151, 155, 164, 171, 179, 190, 199, 202, 203 213-215, 234, 238, 242, 243, 253, 254, 256, 266, 278, 284, 299, 305, 315, 316, 318, 322, 324; asks Clark's help with peacekeeping in New Orleans, 106, 107; attempts to insure American rights to the Mississippi River, 93; authorizes governors to use force to prevent expeditions against Spanish territory, 245; authorizes Claiborne to draw money for administrative purposes, 113; criticizes land boards, 198; expells Morales and Calvo, 246; guidelines to Claiborne re: the transfer, 105; institutes negotiations for purchase of Florida, 240; instructs Claiborne re: land claims, 81; Kentucky Resolution, 38; Marbury v. Madison, 72; objects to Spanish military road through Floridas, 201; pardons Baratarians, 275, 297, 298; proclaimes acquisition of West Florida, 249; receives authorization from Congress to use military force against East Florida, 252; Secretary of State, 45, 47; starts activities toward acquisition of West Florida, 247; statehood for Louisiana, 257; war with England, 280, 281; warns Claiborne that Spaniards might remove records from New Orleans, 195; White House burned, 282
Madrid, Spain, 2, 30, 31, 88, 89, 93, 94, 96, 101, 121, 125, 172, 199, 201, 211-215, 245, 279
Magruder, Allan B., 266
Maine, 115
Marbury v. Madison, 72
Marshall, John, 230
Martin, Francois Xavier, 268
Martinique, 177
Massachusetts, 24, 35, 42, 50, 120, 254, 280, 282
Mason gang, 63-65, 319
Mason, John, 63
Mason, Magno, 63
Mason, Samuel, 63, 65
Mason, Thomas, 63
Mather, Increase, 282
Mather, James, 193, 207
Mathews, George, Jr., 229, 267
Maximilian, 97
Mead, Cowles, 219-221, 223, 227, 230
Memphis, Tenn., 64
Mexican Association, 217, 229, 231, 235
Mexico, 118, 180, 217, 224-226, 228-230, 239, 242, 280
Mexico City, 323
Militia, 31, (Miss.) 67-71; (La.) 164-170, 220-222, 283-288, 291, 293, 294
"Misnomus," 152
Mississippi, State of, 294
Mississippi Dragoons, 294
Mississippi militia, 220, 227
Mississippi Valley, 98
Mississippi River, 11, 12, 15, 17, 19, 42, 47-49, 54, 55, 62, 63, 81, 82, 85-87, 90-94, 100, 101, 106, 116-118, 133, 158, 171, 174, 176, 184, 195, 197, 200, 212, 218, 225, 227, 229, 230, 232, 234, 237, 239, 243, 249,

252, 257, 264, 286, 295, 296, 300, 302, 315, 325
Mississippi Society for the Acquirement and Dissemination of Useful Knowledge, 80
Mississippi Sound, 118, 292
Mississippi Territory, 29, 30, 42-49, 51, 54, 55, 59, 64, 65, 67, 71-73, 77, 79, 80, 82-85, 95, 97, 121-123, 134, 151, 170, 173, 176, 194, 195, 197, 199, 200, 204, 207, 210, 219, 227, 230, 241, 244, 245, 248, 249, 250, 252, 254, 256, 257, 270, 284, 292, 312, 313, 315-317, 319, 320, 323, 324
Mitchell, Samuel, 53-55, 57-61, 85
Mobile, Ala., 45, 59, 110, 178, 215, 240, 242, 243, 246, 251, 252, 257, 271, 280, 286, 289, 292
Mobile Bay, 289
Mobile Point, 289
Mobile River, 59, 81, 82, 201, 243, 244
Monroe, James, 38, 120, 123, 178, 201, 207, 214, 271, 281, 288, 289, 291, 299, 305; appoints special envoy to assist Livingston in Parish, 99, 316; appointed minister to France, 93, 95; Claiborne's reports to, 211; negotiates Perdido River boundary, 240; offered post as governor of Louisiana, 121
Monroe Doctrine, 242
Morales, Juan Ventura, 92-95, 160, 211, 212, 214, 238, 246, 250; land titles and grants, 196, 197, 199, 200; refuses to leave Louisiana, 213; reprecussions of suspension, 91; suspends American right of deposit, 85-89
Morgan, Benjamin, 161
Morgan, David, B., 296, 300-302
Morocco, 154
Morro Castle, 252
Mount Vernon, Va., 36

Nacogdoches, Texas, 180, 216, 222, 223
Napoleonic Code, 150
Napoleonic Wars, 178

Nashville, Tenn., 9, 12, 40, 47, 55, 57, 59, 202, 207, 226, 294
Natchez Artillery Company, 109
Natchez Landing, 57, 109
Natchez Miss., 41, 42, 45, 47-51, 55-57, 59, 63, 64, 67, 68, 70, 77-79, 82, 84, 90, 92, 94, 95, 100, 106, 108, 110, 113, 170, 195, 200, 202, 205, 207, 219-221, 224, 228, 230, 250 315, 320, 324
Natchez Rifle Company, 109
Natchez Trace, 57
Natchitoches, La., 116, 117, 126, 163, 170-174, 180, 184, 214, 216-224, 227, 229, 270, 271
Naturalization Act, 38
Negril Bay, 292
New England, 252, 254, 282, 288
New Hampshire, 42
New Madrid, Mo., 48, 64, 115
New Orleans, La., 2, 64, 74, 84-95, 99-103, 105-111, 113-116, 118-120, 126, 129-133, 135-137, 141-144, 151, 153-161, 163, 165, 167, 170, 177-180, 183-186, 189-191, 195, 199-205, 207, 209, 212-214, 217, 218, 220, 222, 224-229, 232, 233, 235, 236, 238, 240, 242-244, 246, 250, 253-256, 263, 265, 273-276, 280, 284-288, 290-292, 294, 295, 297-307, 309, 313, 315, 316, 318-321, 322-324
New Orleans, Battle of, 277, 307, 308, 320, 321
New York, 5-7, 21, 142, 232, 249, 300
Nicholls, Edward, 288, 289, 290
Nile of America, 101
Nolte, Vincent O., 39
North America, 97, 100, 212
North Carolina, 9, 22, 23, 48, 81
Northwest Ordinance of 1787, 11, 12, 42, 43, 74, 79, 127, 128, 136, 253
Northwest Territory, 42, 75

Oates, Titus, 261
Ogden, Peter V., 229
Ohio, 106, 124, 244, 284
Ohio River, 47, 48, 224-226, 228
Olmutz, 121
Opelousas District, 126, 163, 174, 175, 208, 220, 221, 256, 271

Orleans County, 136, 140, 141, 191
Orleans Gazette, 160, 229
Orleans militia, 220
Orleans Territory, 7, 29, 83, 117, 119, 121-123, 128, 132, 135, 138, 140, 148, 149-151, 160, 163, 167, 173, 175, 176, 178, 196, 199-202, 204, 205, 210-213, 218, 224, 226, 228-230, 234, 251-254, 256, 257, 270, 282, 299, 309, 312, 313, 316-319, 321
Orleans Troop of Horse, 168
Orleans Volunteers, 227, 231, 232
Orleans, Wester District of, 196, 198
Osage Indians, 270
Ouachita County, 126, 140, 163

Pakenham, Edward M., 295, 296, 301
Panton, Leslie & Co., 52, 53, 60
Paris, France, 2, 30-33, 94-96, 98-100, 120, 211, 241, 316
Parker, Joshua, 63
Parker, Josiah, 36
Pascagoula River, 243, 251, 252
Patterson, David, 273-275, 296, 302
Peace of Paris, 81
Pearl River, 4, 251, 257
Pennsylvania, 28, 33, 34
Pensacola, Florida, 52, 59, 109, 110, 157, 177, 195, 201, 213-215, 243, 270, 271, 288, 289, 291
Perdido River, 117, 178, 199, 200, 238-242, 246, 249, 257, 271
Perkins, Nicholas, 230
Peru, 239
Peterkin, Thomas 60
Peyroux, Henry 64
Philadelphia, Pa., 5, 7, 8, 20, 21, 25, 26, 40, 224, 249
Philips, 63
"Phocion," 260-262
Pichon, Louis Andre, 93
Pickering County, 43
Pickering, Timothy, 20
Pike, Zebulon M., 250, 257
Pinckney, Charles C., 38, 39
Pinckney, Gerry, and Marshall mission, 32
Pinckney's treaty, 12, 41, 42, 85, 86, 91

Pinckneyville, Miss., 201, 244
Pittsburgh, Pa., 271
Place d'Armes, 101, 112
Plaquemines, 163, 178
Poindexter, George, 254
Pointe Coupee County, 64, 110, 118, 133, 140, 184, 192, 247, 250
Port-au-Prince, 275
Porter, Moses, 216, 227
Portugal, 242
Posey, Thomas, 266
Postal Service, 200-202
Poydras, Julien, 137, 179, 190; answers Claiborne's speech to the Council, 131, 132; elected to Congress, 161; president of Louisiana Constitutional Convention, 255; president of the Legislative Council, 131
Prevost, George, 288
Prevost, John B., 142, 143, 146, 147, 309

Quebec, Canada, 262
Quincy, Josiah, 254, 282
"Quintus Curius," 262

Randolph, Edward, 244
Randolph, John, 114, 121, 160, 241, 300
Randolph, Thomas, M., 108
Rapides County, 140, 220-222
Red River, 117, 172, 216, 217, 270
Rennick, Seymore, 63
Republican Party, 25-32, 33, 35-41, 43, 45-47, 49, 51, 70, 72, 85, 124, 153, 224, 230, 281, 313-315, 324, 325
"Revolution of 1800," 25, 46
Rhea, John, 13, 18, 20, 248
Richmond Academy, 4-6, 27
Richmond, Va., 8, 10, 11, 230
Right of Deposit, 15, 85-94
Rio Bravo, 117, 242
Rio Grande River, 215, 216, 221, 241
Roane, Archibald, 18
Robertson, James, 2, 9, 12, 13
Robertson, Thomas B., 161, 248, 266
Rodney, Thomas, 230
Rodrigues Canal, 295

Rome, Italy, 119
Ross, George T., 214, 273, 274
Ross, Robert, 288
Rush, Richard, 274, 275, 317
Rutledge, George, 18
Rotterdam, 98

Sabine River, 116, 117, 171, 173, 174, 201, 210, 215, 216, 218, 221-227, 233, 239, 246, 319, 320, 323
'Sage of Monticello," 116
St. Charles Parish, 169, 185
St. Francis River, 62
St. Francisville, 201, 244, 248-250
St. Helena Parish, 248
St. John the Baptist Parish, 169, 185
St. John's Plains, 201, 248
St. Louis, Mo., 115, 218
St. Stephens, Mo., 42
St Tammany parish, 248, 271
Salcedo, Juan Manuel de, 62-64, 87, 88, 101, 102, 180, 181
Salcedo, Nemesio, 216, 222, 223
San Antonio, Texas, 221
San Bernardo, 118
San Ildefonso, Spain, 97, 101
Santo Domingo, 99, 176-179, 184, 294
Sargent, Winthrop, 49, 51, 67, 68, 72, 73, 324; anti-Claiborne activities, 47, 50; appointed governor of Mississippi Territory, 42; brought up on charges before Congress, 44; judiciary, 74, 75; militia, 70
Sauve, Pierre, 129, 137, 177
Savary, Jean-Baptiste, 293
Scott, Winfield, 281
Second War of Independence, 282
Sedition Act, 35-39
Setton, John, 63, 64
Setton, Thomas, 63
Serpent d'eau, 154
Seven years' War, 96, 97
Sevier, John, 2, 3, 9, 15, 312; aids Claiborne in election to Congress, 20; appointed to Tennessee territorial legislature, 11; Claiborne appointed to Tennessee supreme court, 18; congressman representing Southwest Territory, 7; impression of young Claiborne, 7; "Nolachucky Jack," 8, 66
Sewall, Samuel, 34, 36
Shaumburgh, Bartholomew, 302
Shaw, John, 178, 185, 227, 228, 273
Shawnee Indians, 269
Shelby, John, Jr., 15
Shenandoah Valley, 124
"Shining Mountains," 117
Ship Island, 292
Sibley, John, 174, 216, 217, 236
Sitgreaves, Samuel, 32
Skipworth, Fulwar, 241, 248, 250, 251
Slave Revolts, 169, 183-186
Slavery, 176-187
Smilie, John, 28
Smith, John 244
Smith, Robert, 249
Smuggling, 177, 178, 271-276
Soler, Cayetano, 88, 89
Solomon, 261
Someruelos, Marquis de, 88, 248
Sophie, 289
South America, 279, 323
South Carolina, 30, 48, 81, 255
Southwest Territory, 7, 9-12, 15, 19, 123, 197
Spain, 13, 15, 19, 42, 49, 52, 85, 86, 88, 89, 93, 94, 96, 97, 100, 101, 107, 115-117, 120, 172, 195, 201, 211, 212, 214, 215, 219, 220, 236, 237, 239, 240-242, 246, 287, 292, 316, 320, 323, 324
Sparks, Richard, 63, 251
Steele, John, 42, 45, 49-51
Stephen, 184, 185
Sterry, Mr., 156
Steuben, Baron, 167
Stoddard, Amos, 115, 117, 170
Sullivan County, Tenn., 8, 11-13, 15, 18, 20
Sumner, Thomas, Jr., 120
Sussex County, Va., 3
Swartwout, Samuel, 224, 229
Switzerland, 34

Tallapoosa River, 271, 289
Talleyrand, 95, 100, 116, 237, 240
Tatum, Howell, 18
Taylor, John 63

Tecumseh, 269
Tellico, 60
Tennessee, 8, 9, 11, 15-24, 27, 39, 40, 42, 46, 48, 50, 54, 63, 68, 77, 79-81, 97, 103, 106, 147, 196, 207, 210, 284, 292, 294, 299, 305, 312-314
Tennessee River, 15, 226
Terre aux Boeufs, 118, 205, 206
Texas, 117, 138, 178, 180, 211, 216, 219
Thacher, George, 24
Thomas, 173
Thomas, John 295, 302
Thomas, Philemon, 248, 287
Thompson, John 174
Thornton, William 296, 300, 301
Tilton, Daniel, 42, 73, 74, 78
Tombigbee River, 42, 48, 53, 59, 110, 243
Tonnant, 292
Toussard, Louis de, 304
Treaty of Alliance, 1778, 33
Treaty of Amiens, 87, 99
Treaty of Amity and Commerce, 1778, 33
Treaty of Ghent, 287, 288, 294
Treaty of Holston, 1791, 22, 23, 28, 31
Treat of Parish, 1803, 249
Treaty of San Ildefonso, 116, 117, 238
Treme plantation, 193
Trinity River, 214
Turner, Edward, 83, 109, 170, 171, 184, 216

Ugarte, Joaquin, 180
The Union: New Orleans Advertiser, 154
United States, 12, 14, 17, 22, 23, 25, 31-35, 37, 38, 40, 49, 53-55, 57, 61, 63, 71, 79, 81, 85, 88, 91, 92, 95-97, 99, 101, 102, 104, 105, 111, 112, 115, 117, 123, 124, 132, 135, 139, 143, 152, 155, 157, 159, 162, 171-173, 176, 178, 192, 196, 198, 199-201, 208, 212, 214, 215, 217, 219, 223, 226, 228, 231, 233, 238-242, 245-253, 266, 268-273, 277-280, 283, 284, 298-300, 314-317, 319, 320, 322, 323, 325

United States Army, 2
United States Congress, 5, 7, 9, 10, 17, 20, 21, 22, 24, 28, 29, 31, 34, 35, 37, 38, 41
United States House of Representatives, 5, 11, 17, 18, 20, 21-24, 26-29, 30, 33-35, 37-40
United States Senate, 17, 19, 20, 28, 29, 31, 35
University of North Carolina, 74
University of Orleans, 191
Ursuline Convent, 189

Vandals, 239
Varnum, Joseph B., 280
Venable, Abraham B., 23
Vera Cruz, Mexico, 202, 224, 228, 273
Vermont, 26
Viana, Francisco, 217
Vicksburg, Miss., 64
Victor, Claude, 98, 100
Vidal, Jose, 195, 196
Villiere, Gabriel, 295
Villiere, Jacques, 259, 261, 295, 300, 309, 311, 317; elected governor of Louisiana, 310; loses gubernatorial election to Claiborne, 265; organizes militia to defend New Orleans, 287
Virginia, 3, 8, 10-12, 23, 37, 41, 42, 114, 160, 253, 300
Virginia Resolution, 38
Volunteer Rifles, 293

Walnut Hills, 48, 63, 64
Washington College, 77
Washington County, 76, 82, 83, 121
Washington District, 74
Washington District Court, 76
Washington, D. C., 2, 9, 18, 40, 78, 88, 93, 94, 96, 99, 100, 103, 107, 109, 110, 117, 121, 125, 127, 130, 134, 160, 161, 164, 167, 172, 175, 189, 190, 195, 196, 200-203, 206, 211, 213, 214, 219, 224, 225, 230, 240, 241, 246, 247, 249-253, 277, 280, 282, 288, 290, 315
Washington, George, 11, 25, 28, 30, 36, 39, 261, 281, 314

Washington, Mississippi Territory, 50, 68, 78
Watauga settlement, 9
Watauga veterans, 8, 12
Watkins, John, 137, 177, 184, 254, 255
Waxhaw settlement 9
Weehawken, N. J., 2
Wellington, Duke of, 281
West, Cato, 43, 49, 51, 70, 83
West Florida, 80, 82, 97, 99, 100, 117, 120, 140, 160, 178, 199-201, 211, 213, 215, 216, 237-242, 244, 246-254, 256-258, 261, 266, 288, 309, 323
West Florida Revolution of 1810, 323
West Indies, 34
Westmoreland County, England, 3
White House, 282
Wilderness Road, 57-59, 63, 65, 85, 202
Wilkinson County, 82, 121
Wilkinson, James, 2, 59, 68, 106, 108, 109, 115, 117, 150, 153, 159, 185, 211-213, 215, 219, 220, 231, 232, 236, 238, 252, 266, 284, 306, 320, 321; appointed to receive Louisiana with Claiborne, 104; arrival in new Orleans, 111, 205; arrives to take command of troops against Spaniards, 221; authorizes arms for militia at Fort Dearborn, 69; Burr conspiracy, 223, 224-230, 235; capture of Fort Charlotte, 257; conflict with Claiborne, 105, 233, 234; military preparations for transfer, 110; negotiations with Spaniards, 222, 223; ordered to command of military forces west of the Mississippi River, 218; refuses to leave New Orleans with troops, 206; requests regular troops to guard New Orleans, 113, 183
William and Mary College, 5
Williams, Robert, 218
Winchester, James 292
Wood, 63
Woodbine, George, 271
Wyckoff, William, 150, 151, 247

Xerxes, 31
Ximines, Juan Carlos, 196
XYZ Affair, 32, 39

Yazoo River, 63, 81
You, Dominique, 297

Zeno, 168-170